Selected Excerpts from *Star Wars on Trial*

DAVID BRIN: Your Honor, I am a recognized expert on the politics of Star Wars. I refer you to my infamous Salon.com article published June 15, 1999—

MATTHEW WOODRING STOVER: Recognized by who, the Imperial Sith Show-Trial Fake Certification Committee? Five Kowackian monkey-lizards on a six-day spice-binge? Hey, this reminds me of a joke—a kid, a Jedi and two droids walk into a bar in Mos Eisley—

—

DAVID BRIN: Only demigods need apply . . . and only those demigods Yoda likes. But more about the nasty green oven mitt, anon. . . .

—

MATTHEW WOODRING STOVER: I would like to take this moment to apologize to you personally for not putting some brutal torture of Princess Leia on-screen . . . I'm sure we'd all feel better about her character if we could have watched her screaming in agony.

DAVID BRIN: Objection! That's not a question—he's just abusing the witness.

—

MATTHEW WOODRING STOVER: Shameless padding? "Show, don't tell"? Is that all you've got? No wonder you're an editor instead of a writer. That's the most pathetic excuse for a personal insult I've ever heard. As trash-talk goes, Mr. Hundreds-of-Manuscripts-per-Year, yours barely makes it to the level of a stuck-out tongue.

—

DAVID BRIN: For the record, I never declined a saber duel with Mr. Stover. I'm likely twice his age, yet my rusty skills from the Caltech fencing team should suffice. Bring it on, smart mouth.

STAR WARS
ON TRIAL

OTHER TITLES IN THE SMART POP SERIES

Taking the Red Pill
Science, Philosophy and Religion in The Matrix

Seven Seasons of Buffy
Science Fiction and Fantasy Writers Discuss Their Favorite Television Show

Five Seasons of Angel
Science Fiction and Fantasy Writers Discuss Their Favorite Vampire

What Would Sipowicz Do?
Race, Rights and Redemption in NYPD Blue

Stepping through the Stargate
Science, Archaeology and the Military in Stargate SG-1

The Anthology at the End of the Universe
Leading Science Fiction Authors on Douglas Adams' Hitchhiker's Guide to the Galaxy

Finding Serenity
Anti-heroes, Lost Shepherds and Space Hookers in Joss Whedon's Firefly

The War of the Worlds
Fresh Perspectives on the H. G. Wells Classic

Alias Assumed
Sex, Lies and SD-6

Navigating the Golden Compass
Religion, Science and Dæmonology in Philip Pullman's His Dark Materials

Farscape Forever!
Sex, Drugs and Killer Muppets

Flirting with Pride and Prejudice
Fresh Perspectives on the Original Chick-Lit Masterpiece

Revisiting Narnia
Fantasy, Myth and Religion in C. S. Lewis' Chronicles

Totally Charmed
Demons, Whitelighters and the Power of Three

King Kong Is Back!
An Unauthorized Look at One Humongous Ape

Mapping the World of Harry Potter
Science Fiction and Fantasy Authors Explore the Bestselling Fantasy Series of All Time

The Psychology of The Simpsons
D'oh!

The Unauthorized X-Men
SF and Comic Writers on Mutants, Prejudice and Adamantium

Welcome to Wisteria Lane
On America's Favorite Desperate Housewives

The Man From Krypton
A Closer Look at Superman

Science Fiction and Fantasy Writers
Debate the Most Popular
Science Fiction Films of All Time

STAR WARS

ON TRIAL

THE FORCE AWAKENS EDITION

FOR THE PROSECUTION:
David Brin

FOR THE DEFENSE:
Matthew Woodring Stover

An imprint of BenBella Books, Inc.
DALLAS, TEXAS

The Force Awakens Edition © 2015

"The Madness of King George" Copyright © 2006 by Keith R. A. DeCandido
"May the Midichlorians Be with You" Copyright © 2006 by John C. Wright
"The Son of Skywalker Must Not Become a Jackass, or Finding the Ethical Core of the Star Wars Films by Ignoring the Ghosts and Muppets" Copyright © 2006 by Scott Lynch
"Novels, Novelizations and Tie-ins, Oh My" Copyright © 2006 by Lou Anders
"Are Brain-Dead Chimpanzees Eating My Shelf Space?" Copyright © 2006 by Laura Resnick
"Driving GFFA 1, or How Star Wars Loosened My Corsets" Copyright © 2006 by Karen Traviss
"Barbarian Confessions" Copyright © 2006 by Kristine Kathryn Rusch
"Millions for Special Effects, Not One Cent for Writers" Copyright © 2006 by John G. Hemry
"Good. Bad. I'm the Guy with the Lightsaber." Copyright © 2006 by Bruce Bethke
"It's All in the Numbers" Copyright © 2006 by Tanya Huff
"On Not Flying Solo in Hyperspace" Copyright © 2006 by Richard Garfinkle
"Star Wars: Fantasy, Not Science Fiction" Copyright © 2006 by Ken Wharton
"The Kessel Run" Copyright © 2006 by Robert A. Metzger
"Star Wars as Anime" Copyright © 2006 by Bruce Bethke
"The Joy of Star Wars" Copyright © 2006 by Adam Roberts
"Stop Her, She's Got a Gun! How the Rebel Princess and the Virgin Queen Became Marginalized and Powerless in George Lucas's Fairy Tale" Copyright © 2006 by Jeanne Cavelos
"Fighting Princesses and Other Distressing Damsels" Copyright © 2006 by Bill Spangler
"Laziness Leads to Sloth, Sloth to Incompetence, Incompetence to Stupidity, and Stupidity to the Dark Side of the Force" Copyright © 2006 by Nick Mamatas
"Star Wars Versus Science" Copyright © 2006 by Don DeBrandt
Additional Materials © 2006, 2015 by David Brin
Additional Materials © 2006, 2015 by Matthew Woodring Stover

BenBella Books, Inc.
10300 N. Central Expressway, Suite 530
Dallas, TX 75231
www.benbellabooks.com
Send feedback to feedback@benbellabooks.com

Printed in the United States of America
10 9 8 7 6 5 4 3 2 1

The Library of Congress has cataloged the 2006 edition as follows:

Star Wars on trial : science fiction and fantasy writers debate the most popular science fiction films of all time / for the prosecution, David Brin, for the defense, Matthew Woodring Stover.
    p. cm.
  ISBN 1-932100-89-X
  1. Star Wars films—Moral and ethical aspects. 2. Star Wars films—History and criticism. I. Brin, David. II. Stover, Matthew Woodring.
  PN1995.9.S695S79 2006
  791.43'75—dc22

                                                                    2006005985

Proofreading by Rebecca Green and Stacia Seaman
Supplemental proofreading by Isabella Yeffeth and Erin Files
Cover design by Todd Michael Bushman
Cover illustration by Ralph Voltz
Text design and composition by John Reinhardt Book Design
Printed by Lake Book Manufacturing

Distributed by Perseus Distribution
www.perseusdistribution.com

To place orders through Perseus Distribution:
Tel: (800) 343-4499
Fax: (800) 351-5073
E-mail: orderentry@perseusbooks.com

Significant discounts for bulk sales are available.
Please contact Glenn Yeffeth at glenn@benbellabooks.com or (214) 750-3628.

CONTENTS

FOREWORDS TO THE NEW EDITION
The Mythos Strikes Back by David Brin   xi
The Smartest Thing by Matthew Woodring Stover   xvii

INTRODUCTION
Do Myths Teach Us? by David Brin   1
Star Wars and Truth and Why We Bother
   by Matthew Woodring Stover   7

OPENING STATEMENTS   15
FOR THE PROSECUTION: DAVID BRIN   17
FOR THE DEFENSE: MATTHEW WOODRING STOVER   55

**CHARGE #1: THE POLITICS OF STAR WARS ARE
ANTI-DEMOCRATIC AND ELITIST**   81
FOR THE DEFENSE: KEITH R. A. DeCANDIDO   83

**CHARGE #2: WHILE CLAIMING MYTHIC SIGNIFICANCE,
STAR WARS PORTRAYS NO ADMIRABLE RELIGIOUS
OR ETHICAL BELIEFS**   97
FOR THE PROSECUTION: JOHN C. WRIGHT   99
FOR THE DEFENSE: SCOTT LYNCH   121

**CHARGE #3: STAR WARS NOVELS ARE POOR
SUBSTITUTES FOR REAL SCIENCE FICTION
AND ARE DRIVING REAL SF OFF THE SHELVES**   135
FOR THE PROSECUTION: LOU ANDERS   137
FOR THE DEFENSE: LAURA RESNICK   151
FOR THE DEFENSE: KAREN TRAVISS   159
FOR THE DEFENSE: KRISTINE KATHRYN RUSCH   169

CHARGE #4: SCIENCE FICTION FILMMAKING HAS
BEEN REDUCED BY STAR WARS TO POORLY
WRITTEN SPECIAL EFFECTS EXTRAVAGANZAS 183
FOR THE PROSECUTION: John G. Hemry 185
FOR THE DEFENSE: Bruce Bethke 199

CHARGE #5: STAR WARS HAS DUMBED DOWN
THE PERCEPTION OF SCIENCE FICTION IN
THE POPULAR IMAGINATION 217
FOR THE PROSECUTION: Tanya Huff 219
FOR THE DEFENSE: Richard Garfinkle 233

CHARGE #6: STAR WARS PRETENDS TO BE SCIENCE
FICTION, BUT IS REALLY FANTASY 245
FOR THE PROSECUTION: Ken Wharton 247
FOR THE DEFENSE: Robert A. Metzger 263
FOR THE PROSECUTION: Bruce Bethke 279
FOR THE DEFENSE: Adam Roberts 287

CHARGE #7: WOMEN IN STAR WARS ARE PORTRAYED
AS FUNDAMENTALLY WEAK 303
FOR THE PROSECUTION: Jeanne Cavelos 305
FOR THE DEFENSE: Bill Spangler 329

CHARGE #8: THE PLOT HOLES AND LOGICAL GAPS
IN STAR WARS MAKE IT ILL-SUITED FOR AN
INTELLIGENT VIEWER 341
FOR THE PROSECUTION: Nick Mamatas 343
FOR THE DEFENSE: Don DeBrandt 357

CLOSING STATEMENTS 369
FOR THE PROSECUTION: David Brin 371
FOR THE DEFENSE: Matthew Woodring Stover 379

THE VERDICT 383

FOREWORDS TO THE
NEW EDITION

The Mythos Strikes Back...
or Shall We Awaken the "Force"
of Science Fiction?

David Brin

S I WRITE THIS, flying home from Spain, I cannot help pondering the great character of Cervantes—Don Quixote—who lowered his lance in futile gesture, charging against indomitably indifferent windmills.

So it seemed when first Matt Stover and I presented BenBella Books with a critical examination of Star Wars, the behemoth story-universe of our time. I mean, who takes on a 600 *million* pound gorilla? Only demented sci-fi authors would think to try.

Indeed, shall I count the number of recent messages taunting, *See, Brin? It's baaaack and you couldn't stop it!*?

To which I must reply...who on Earth would want to? Stop it, I mean.

In my original *Salon* article, and in *Star Wars on Trial*, I was always frank in my admiration for many aspects of George Lucas's epic—and so were most of the essayists who served as "prosecution witnesses" in this way-fun volume! There's so much we agree is wonderful—the music and light and color and unabashed verve, for example. Lucas was the Lorenzo di Medici of our time, giving employment to a fair fraction of the finest visual artists of the age.

Even where we (on the prosecution side) have denounced the first three and sixth films of the saga—e.g., for disappointingly puerile characters, insipid dialogue and cartoon-morality—there is this saving grace: That ten million kids swinging light sabers don't give a tonton's patoot for any of Yoda's faux-zen, crackerjack-box "wisdom."

They know Luke Skywalker is a good guy (he is! Though dim). They know you're supposed to be brave and stand up for underdogs. Don't let nasty, abusive bullies become tyrants. Try to stay calm. Those are basic lessons of the first two films (episodes IV and V). All the rest of Mr. Lucas's charm bracelet, fortune cookie claptrap slides past all those boys and girls. They shrug it off and go back to leaping at each other from the couch, making *v-rrrr-m* swordfighting sounds. Envisioning themselves simply being brave.

In other words, the truly nasty messages are mostly shrugged off and ignored.

Sure, it might have been better if, as Richard Dreyfuss suggests, Steven Spielberg's *Close Encounters of a Third Kind* had been released before the original Star Wars. If the archetype seed that crystallized the public's unexpressed need for science fiction (SF) had been something thoughtful and thought provoking, grounded in actual characters. Way fun, but with a grownup side, too. Would that have made a difference?

Or even better, if George Lucas had nurtured his own, early interest in such things—as in the brilliant *Young Indiana Jones Chronicles*.

But no matter. I've been asked by BenBella—whose SmartPop series is the most agile and brilliant niche in all of popular culture criticism—to comment on where things stand, now that control over the Star Wars Universe has shifted from one lone wizard in his tower to the industrial titan of modern myth-spinning.

ENTER THE MOUSE

You'll notice that very few screamed in outrage when Walt Disney Studios purchased the franchise, intending to spin out a third trilogy as soon as possible. Even diehard fans knew that changes were desperately needed at the helm. Indeed, no outcome could have better validated *Star Wars on Trial!*

As of this writing, Disney has kept a very tight lid on information about the plot and character arcs of *The Force Awakens,* so any speculations that you read here may seem off-base, if not hilarious, if, by the time you read this new edition, you have seen Episode VII.

Still, we know a lot from the team that Disney assembled, starting with director J. J. Abrams, whose Star Trek reboot—though controversial in some ways—at least paid close heed to logical consistency and the most-enduring features of a well-loved series. Mr. Abrams is well known for claiming independence of interpretation. At the same time, he is smart enough to know what he has in his hands. He will work hard to learn from the mistakes of Episodes I through III, of that we can be certain.

We do know that *The Force Awakens* will feature the villainous First Order, an offshoot of the Galactic Empire, aligned against the Resistance, sprung from the Rebel Alliance. The story will *not* be based on Star Wars Legends, formerly known as the Expanded Universe.[1] Rather, Episode VII will be an original story set after *Return of the Jedi*.

Moreover, we can assume J. J. Abrams is aware of the most blatant fact about the Star Wars universe—that the best two films out of six had *heart*.

In fact, the first one, *A New Hope,* expressed unadulterated joy!

The best one of all (by near-universal consensus) was much darker, but featured genuinely excellent writing and directing. Indeed, *The Empire Strikes Back* is inarguably one of the most beautiful and inspiring science fiction films ever made.

---

[1] For years I have heard from some Star Wars fans that "all is explained in the novelizations." Indeed, I've watched with wonder as authors of that series of novels and games strove hard to make sense out of chaotic illogic that provoked *Star Wars on Trial*. None of them (that I have seen) could patch up the stunningly vile behavior of that wicked little oven mitt—Yoda—but sincere efforts were made to explain how the Republic operated and to make democracy seem less pathetic than it is in the flicks.

Alas, my response has always been: "Show me when the studios admit that all your efforts are canonical." In other words, let's see one time when a Star Wars novel ever affects events in one of the movies. In his own introduction to this volume, Matt Stover apparently agrees.

Hey, consistency can happen! Paramount Pictures maintains a staff to keep a very close eye on the "factual" galactography and history of Star Trek. A necessity, since there have been more hours of produced material in that universe than any ten others, combined, including Star Wars. And because the caretakers of *Trek* have consistency of storytelling in their blood.

But no. One side effect of the new Disney tenure has been to prove Expanded Universe to be a phantasm. Enjoyable stuff, in many cases! But the novels and games and other rationalizations never affected George Lucas's vision for his cosmos. Those fine creations stand proudly on their own, perhaps. But their contents cannot let mass murderers like Yoda and Darth Vader off the hook.

Hence, a buzz of anticipation when Mr. Abrams hired Lawrence Kasden, who co-wrote *Empire* with the great Leigh Brackett, to work with him on scripting *The Force Awakens* (based on an initial screenplay by Michael Arndt, who also wrote the story treatment). Sure, Kasden's employment is no guarantee. But all by itself it was a declaration of *intent*. And it gave me a new hope.

That hope isn't fizzy or without cavils. Judging from his two Star Trek movies, we know that Mr. Abrams will engage in George Lucas's own self-indulgence of *character coincidence* or allusion. Whether it made sense or not, he just *had* to thrust Kirk, Spock, Scottie, McCoy, Uhura, Sulu, and even Chekov into a blender, without any heed to likelihood or their "actual" ages, while milking recognition *aha!* moments. (Throw in Dr. Carol Marcus and Khaaaaaan? Hey, why not?) Hence, every actor who once played a major Star Wars character will also return in *The Force Awakens*, with many *aha!* bones tossed to fans.

In fact, pre-complaints on the best fan sites prompted Abrams to proclaim that he will limit these, telling *Vanity Fair*, "We used to have more references to things that we pulled out because they almost felt like they were trying too hard to allude to something."

In the same article, Kasden said: "[W]e're getting the band back together, and we know that people are going to want to be reminded of the things they love, but they're going to expect to have a new experience." Well, okay, one can hope they reach a happy medium.

Me? I won't kick a fuss over loving reunions between R2 and Threepio. Nor long, kvelling stares at the Millennium Falcon. Nor even the return of Ewoks! (I never hated them; sorry, but I got other, more important gripes.)

Heck, toss in Jar Jar Binks! I'll only grind my teeth a little.

No, what will irk me is if Episode VII commits many of the same faults of *logic*, *storytelling*, *ethics*, and plain old-fashioned *decency* that we on the prosecution side complained about, here in *Star Wars on Trial*.

Already there are signs that the rampant, awful sexism of the three prequels will be set aside. Well, Mr. Abrams is of a new generation and he knows not to ignore that flame.

But will this new episode diss and disdain democracy, the way George Lucas increasingly did? Never once showing the Old Republic *doing* a single thing? No institution functioning, in any way, at all, ever, but utterly helpless and hapless at the hands of genetic *Chosen Ones?* (Read how we show this, carefully, in the indictment! And how in real life George Lucas openly expressed contempt for democracy, calling for rule by "a benign dictator.")

Will the Force continue to be solely accessible by a few demigods (most of them mutants from one planet—Naboo)? Or will Abrams return the Force to the way it was in *A New Hope?* Mostly a matter of discipline and training, with raw talent serving only as an amplifier? In other words, *not* the exclusive privilege of born-to-power Nietzschean gods?

Will normal people—and aliens—play a bigger role this time? And will the *lesson* be that normal people—citizens of all kinds, along with their institutions—actually matter?

Will Matt Stover be proved right in his introduction to this new edition, following this one, wherein he cops the unusual defense plea that *Yes, all the charges against Star Wars are true! It's drivel, but so what? Fun trumps all other considerations!?*

I leave it to you, the reader, to decide whether it is necessary to lobotomize folks and give nothing to our inner adult in order to satisfy our inner child. I've seen enough exceptions to know that the kid and the grownup within *can* both be entertained at the same time. Try *Close Encounters.* Try *The Empire Strikes Back.*

As I said, we are rushing out this new edition to coincide with *The Force Awakens.* And hence, you'll see no post-mortems here, not this time. No decrypting analyses—

—though each of the essayists in *Star Wars On Trial* will be invited to post their thoughts about Episode VII, after it comes out, at smartpopbooks.com! Postings on which you'll be welcome to comment. In that way, BenBella Books will help to continue the conversation.

After all, there will be at least two more episodes after this one. And who knows? Maybe J. J. Abrams or someone at Disney will be reading this, and your responses, and listening…

...as (according to unscientific and completely unsubstantiated rumors) I am told they paid *some* attention to the earlier edition of *Star Wars on Trial*. Well, we can hope...and we'll find out, soon enough!

Above all, have a good time with this debate. Because we live in a time of bold ideas—and even arguments *about* fun can *be* fun (the way Matt Stover and I, and our Witnesses, had super-fun in *Star Wars on Trial*). Especially when such arguments are taken way "too" (tongue partly in cheek) seriously.

Besides...you'll laugh. Because our Droid Judge is a tough nut! And also because, well, it all boils down to plain...old...fun.

The Smartest Thing

Matthew Woodring Stover

FIRST WE HAVE TO GET some business out of the way, and then we'll play a game.

The Business has to do with discharging the Actual Function of this new introduction, which, according to the Good Folks at BenBella, is supposed to address my thoughts on the upcoming release of *The Force Awakens*, and my thoughts about the Current State of the Star Wars Franchise, and any intuitions I might have about Its Future. The Game, like all proper games, is Just For Fun.

(You'll forgive, I hope, the generous but not indiscriminate use of Untraditional Capitalization. Writing about Star Wars seems to bring out my inner A.A. Milne.)

So, in the spirit of Business, here are the Three Smartest Things the Star Wars franchise has ever done.

Third: It infiltrated Disney.

You think Disney took over Star Wars? Don't be fooled. Anakin Skywalker knew that he and Luke could overthrow the Emperor and rule the galaxy as father and son—he just got the wrong galaxy. The Empire of Mouse is no match for the power of the Force. You heard it here first.

As I write this, *Jurassic World* has broken box-office records for its opening weekend. The record it set won't last past December. I have foreseen it. (Well, I've seen the trailers, anyway.) Sure, always in motion the future is, but this is a safe bet even if *The Force Awakens* stinks. I don't think I'm going out on a limb here to predict that

The Force Awakens will be the highest-grossing film Disney has ever released. I am not alone in this suspicion.

Via Wikipedia:

The [*Force Awakens*] trailer was viewed over 88 million times within the first 24 hours of release, breaking the record of 62 million held by *Furious 7* in November 2014. (from *Forbes*)

[T]he second teaser trailer amassed 30.65 million [views] in 24 hours setting a new world record for the "Most viewed movie trailer on YouTube in 24 hours. (from *Guinness World Records*)

And:

Box office analyst Phil Contrino said the film is in the same spot as *Avatar* (2009) which opened with a $77 million in North America and went on to earn $2.8 billion worldwide. He added saying, "*Force Awakens* will hit $1 billion without blinking. If it's really good, it could cross $2 billion." (from *The Hollywood Reporter*)

Second Smartest Thing: It dumped the Expanded Universe.
Search your feelings. You know it to be true.

This is not an issue of absolute quality. Most of you will be familiar with what is affectionately known as Sturgeon's Law, usually summarized as "90 percent of everything is crap." Star Wars has proven astonishingly resistant to this law; even the franchise's bitterest critics, such as the Distinguished Counsel for the Perse—excuse me, *Prosecution*—freely admit, for example, that at least two of the six films are terrific. With apologies for an extended baseball metaphor, let me point out that batting .333 is Hall of Fame territory, and the Expanded Universe is averaging considerably better than that; at least half of the novels and an easy majority of the comics are base hits, and among those base hits the slugging percentage is pretty damned impressive. There are plenty of readers who count one Star Wars book or another as their single favorite novel.

The problem with the Expanded Universe is those books in the other half—the books nobody loves—and the marketing calculation that assigned the stinkers equal value to the classics. The term of art for this particular marketing calculation is *canon*.

Canon, in this case, was the notion that every novel and comic in the Expanded Universe was part of a single continuity—that the Expanded Universe itself is essentially a chronicle of the actual history of the Galaxy Far, Far Away. In other words, it's all equally true. Fans were forced to accept that the most bloody stupid, not to mention pathetically preposterous, crimes against our most minimal standards of verisimilitude were every bit as valid—as necessary to a deep understanding of the franchise—as the very best of the best. This makes great sense from a marketing standpoint, because it means that if you want to really understand Star Wars—to truly participate in the full story of the franchise you love—you have to read *all* the books and *all* the comics. No matter how awful they might be.

Well, that's over, thank the Force. It's all Legends now, which means even the most die-hard fan has official permission to ignore any story he or she doesn't like. Even—though it pains me to admit the possibility—mine. I don't know what the status of the new generation of Star Wars tie-ins will be, if they'll be considered to establish New Canon or if the Powers That Be have learned a valuable lesson and (wisely, in my view) ditch the idea of canon forever.

Any story with the Force, Jedi Knights, lightsabers, charming rogues, epic villains, and sprawling space battles has plenty of tools in its kit; why add the marketing hammer of *you must read this or you'll never know the whole story*?

To hell with that. Let each and every individual fan (or hater, or member of the vast throng of People Who Don't Actually Give a Crap) make up his or her own mind about what counts and what doesn't. In fact, that's the explicit position of the Defense in the book you're about to read.

And the single smartest thing Star Wars ever did was—

Wait. Stop a minute and think about what you were expecting me to say. Better yet, think about what *you* would say. Hiring an aging carpenter to play Han Solo? Good choice. Giving a lead role to a Muppet? Swell. Inflicting Ewoks on our collective consciousness?

That's okay, too. Hell, there must be somebody out there who is absolutely in love with the comedy stylings of Jar Jar Binks. I'm here to tell you that this is perfectly fine, though it's not exactly my personal pick.

The single smartest thing Star Wars ever did was to decide—well, really, just understand—that Make Believe is too important to be taken seriously.

Instances of this Playful Abandonment of Seriousness are too numerous to catalogue, but I'll hit some of the classics.

- Open a door? Shoot the control pad. Close a door? Shoot the control pad.
- Brand new, untested Super Battle Station has carnivorous monster living in the garbage compactor.
- Four words: Unshielded thermal exhaust port.
- Question: How many shots does a blaster fire? Answer: However many George wants it to, and by the way shut up.
- Question: With antigravity so cheap and plentiful that it is routinely used in consumer vehicles, why does the Empire deploy heavy weapons on slow, clumsy legs? Not to mention make them so fragile that they *blow up when tripped*? Answer: Cuz they look like scary mechanical dinosaurs, and did you not hear me say shut up?
- Question: How long does it actually take to fly across the galaxy in hyperspace? Days? Hours? Seconds? Answer: Shut up shut up shut up.
- The Force has power over weak minds. Except when it doesn't.
- The Force warns you of danger. Except when it doesn't. (I'm looking at you, Darth Maul!)
- The Force lets you see the future. Except when it doesn't.
- The Force has a dark side that if you once give in to, forever will dominate your destiny. Except when it doesn't.
- The Force—oh, hell, everything about the Force. I mean, come on. It's the King of Arbitrary Plot Devices. It exists to do—or not do—whatever best serves plot momentum at the moment.

The point is, all this didn't happen by mistake. It's a feature, not a bug. Mr. Lucas *wanted* it this way. It's his way of inviting all of us to play Let's Pretend with him.

Back in 2004, when I was beginning the novelization for *Revenge of the Sith*, I read a sequence in the source material—the shooting script for the movie—where a ship in the midst of an orbital battle begins to roll...and the characters inside the ship start sliding across the suddenly tilting floors and onto the walls and so forth. I chanced to have dinner with a Very Important Lucas Honcho. I complained to the VILH that this didn't make any goddamn sense. Gravity just doesn't work that way. It *can't*. He grinned at me and said, "Of course it can't. George *loves* that [stuff]."

This is exactly why I, personally, cheered when I heard that J. J. Abrams had signed on to direct *The Force Awakens*—because he's already proven (in his Star Trek reboot, for one) that he won't let details like logical consistency get in the in the way of telling a Ripping Yarn.

So there you have it: My thoughts on the Current State of the Franchise, which concludes the Business of this introduction. On to the Game!

Just for fun, come play Let's Pretend with me.

Let's Pretend that David Brin isn't merely a terrific writer and invaluable public intellectual, because that's *reality*. What fun is that? Let's Pretend that he's secretly a Sith Lord—or in their employ—and that his every objection to Our Sacred Franchise is an Evil Dark Side Plot to undermine all that is good and just in the galaxy...and that Star Wars can be saved only if you—you *personally*—clap your hands because you believe.

Oh, wait, wrong fairy tale.

This is the one with lightsabers instead of cutlasses, Star Destroyers instead of pirate ships, and a villain with a helmet instead of a hook hand.

Ready? Okay...*go!*

Welcome to *Star Wars on Trial*.

INTRODUCTION

Do Myths Teach Us? If So, What Have We All Learned from Star Wars?

David Brin

WELL, IT'S DONE. The sci-fi legend of our generation is now complete. Our parents had *Dr. Strangelove* and *1984*. Their parents were transfixed by H. G. Wells. The generation before that had Jules Verne.

And we got Star Wars, the biggest, most lavish, most popular and by far the most lucrative sci-fi drama ever. George Lucas's grand vision gave us resplendent vistas and a spectacular sense of wonder, while portraying a vivid range of possibilities that science, technology and forward-thinking might eventually bring about—inspiring us and drawing our eyes toward a far horizon.

But *what* horizon?

After all the dazzling explosions and lightsaber duels, all the spaceship chases and cryptic-guru Yoda-isms, all the droids and special effects and obscure political story lines, did we—did anyone—*learn* anything?

George Lucas certainly claims that he's been doing something more important than simply pushing eye candy. More valuable than just diverting the masses with some cash-generating entertainment. In various locales, spanning three decades, the Star Wars creator proclaimed that his epic teaches important lessons. For example, in a famous *New York Times* interview, he said: "Movies have a big voice, and what we filmmakers have to do is to set a good example."

So, after tens of billions of dollars—and human hours—spent watching the films, playing the games, buying the toys, reading the books and buying even more toys, have we come away enlightened, even inspired?

Inspired to do what? To *be*...what?

Science fiction has never been modest about its aim to take on important issues. Beyond just "good versus evil" or "boy meets girl," there has always been a notion that SF is the true descendant and heir of Gilgamesh and Homer, of Virgil and Murasaki, of Dante, Swift and Defoe. Liberated from the constraints of day-to-day existence, it provides a canvas wide enough to portray and discuss real issues. Things that matter over the long run.

Take those stories that Jules Verne created during the latter part of the nineteenth century. In his words, you can hear and feel the spirit of Verne's time—an era of ebullient, *can-do* confidence. Even as the age of earthly *terra incognita* was coming to an end, readers hungered to lift their eyes skyward, seaward—or even *into* the planet itself—certain that new frontiers would soon unfold before a humanity that knew no bounds.

Of course, this surefire naiveté had to crash, or at least grow up a bit. And H. G. Wells was just the man to throw on a little cold water, while taking science fiction to new levels, appealing to the concerns of worried adults. Always the contrarian, Wells told wild-eyed dreamers to grow up and smell the dangers . . . then berated cynics who refused to hope. Technology can *bite back*, he warned, and the universe owes us no favors. On the other hand, he deeply believed that honest men and women might yet pick up tools and make a better world. Wells never stopped using stories to help make that happen.

Indeed, one of civilization's greatest tools has always been mythology. Legends and songs. Stories and dark lore. If George Lucas and I agree on anything, it would be that civilizations turn—they veer or rise and fall—depending upon the inspirations and goals that common people share. In part, this happens through stories, heard and told, then retold, whether around a campfire or a widescreen digital display.

Take the period that followed H. G. Wells. After the calamities of World Wars I and II, we needed something special in our legends. Something potent. We needed *problem solving*. Humanity faced some serious tasks, important maturity issues, like how not to destroy ourselves. And sure enough, science fiction stepped up to do its share.

Rolling up its sleeves, SF gave us the *self-preventing prophecy*…the most serious and frighteningly plausible subgenre of science fiction. Tales about every possible or far-out way that things could go wrong. When they are effective, such stories have the uniquely powerful effect of *ensuring that they do not come true*! They do this by offering up stark and compelling warnings that worry an audience, and make millions think. Warnings that even stir at least a few citizens to take action.

How else can you describe *Dr. Strangelove*, *Fail-Safe* and *On the Beach*, which not only exposed specific failure modes, but also drove home the threat of losing it all to spasmodic nuclear war? Or *Soylent Green*, *Silent Running* and *The China Syndrome*, which prodded millions to join a newborn environmental movement. *The Andromeda Strain* was cited by delegates signing the treaty against biological warfare. *Gattaca* prepared us to wrestle with issues of genetic determinism. Even a spoof like *The President's Analyst* warned, with eerie foresight, about a steady, tech-driven decay of personal privacy.

Or take the greatest self-preventing prophecy of all, the one cited by *every* faction, whenever it perceives some creeping tyranny, *1984*. Millions shuddered at George Orwell's terrifying thoughts, words and images, coming away determined to struggle against Big Brother ever becoming real.

We will never know whether any of these specific warnings—or general morality tales, like *The Day the Earth Stood Still*—actually made a crucial difference. But we *can* say that, unlike those ill-fated Trojans, we do give our Cassandras some attention. Occasionally, we pay them well to scare us into getting a bit better.

Ah but then, at other times, we simply pay them to *scare us*, period, with no other objective beyond a good, thrilling fright! Films like *Alien* point to another side of sci-fi. A side that does not have to justify itself with highfalutin purpose.

And that can be good too! Art is multispectral. There's plenty of room for everything from dark fantasy to heroic sword-'n'-sorcery. From wondrously joyful nonsense like *The Fifth Element* to deeply mystical multiculturalism like *The Last Wave*. From relentlessly serious exploration of a single universe, like Star Trek, to hilarious send-ups like *Galaxy Quest*. Without any doubt, the people have a right to buy the entertainments that most appeal to them. And entrepreneurial storytellers have a right to sell tickets.

So, why did I spend all that time talking about the importance of myths and their role in helping civilization to choose its path? Because storytelling *does* span the entire range. And we have a right, perhaps even a duty when all is said and done, to talk about where a work of art fits along the spectrum, from important to fluff.

Especially a work of art that had the scope of influence, economic power, public exposure and relentless preachiness of the Star Wars epic.

Hence, the first issue to confront the authors and sages participating in this project was to argue *whether the Star Wars saga is worth arguing about*. Throughout this discussion, you will see some people claim—

—that the Star Wars universe and franchise are nothing more than harmless fun. A chance to drop back into childhood and punt your adult cares away for two hours, dwelling in a lavish universe where good and evil are vividly drawn, without all the inconvenient counterpoint distinctions that clutter daily life.

Ever since I first raised the question of Star Wars morality and storytelling flaws, in an infamous article published by *Salon* online, over a thousand people have written to comment, praise, complain, agree, disagree, make additions or offer fresh arguments. It's been lively, democratic and huge fun! Among the many defenses offered by devoted fans, foremost has been: "Chill out, man. It's only a flick. Just relax and enjoy the show."

Indeed, that philosophy has some appeal.

Got a problem? Cleave it with a lightsaber! Wouldn't you love—just once in your life—to dive a fast little ship into your worst enemy's stronghold and set off a chain reaction, blowing up the whole megillah from within its rotten core while you streak away to safety at the speed of light? (Such a nifty notion! Count the number of times it happens in the movies... and the enemy never learns.)

In fact, well, let me admit, that's pretty much how I *did* feel about the first of the Star Wars films to appear, *Episode IV: A New Hope.* What was there not to enjoy? A blatant, Nazi-helmeted mass murderer is bested by a princess, a smuggler and a young knight, avenging his father? Zowee. The movie's very lack of pretension made you take it at face value.

Or, as Yoda would likely put it: fluff and fun, the first movie was! Fluff 'n' fun I was ready for the whole series to be...

...until *The Empire Strikes Back.* Then, wow, did I change my mind. And so did millions of others. Suddenly, thrilled by the deep script of Leigh Brackett and Lawrence Kasdan, and Irvin Kershner's tight direction—and deeply moved by a wondrous John Williams score—many of us simply sat and stared as the final credits rolled by, unable, *unwilling*, to move. This wasn't just fun anymore. It felt... important.

I know I left the theater ebullient after watching *TESB.* Perhaps a little pompously, I told everyone that we had just witnessed the addition of something truly worthy to the Western mythological canon. With any luck, the rest of the saga would be even better.

That wasn't just fannish appreciation. I was at that time in the process of making my own transition from science fiction amateur to professional writer. So I wanted George Lucas to succeed with his grand epic for another reason... to prove, once and for all, that meaning can coexist with adventure, and thought can accompany fun. And in *movies,* even, where there is so little time or room for the kind of extended ponderings that an author may insert in a novel.

What we saw in films like *TESB*—and *Star Trek II: The Wrath of Khan*—was growing confidence in a kind of science fiction that could take on issues (amid spectacular space battles) and ponder human existence (between dramatic laser sword fights).

Moreover, George Lucas clearly agreed. As I intend to repeat, whenever anybody says "they're just movies," Lucas clearly and openly believes in the important effects of storytelling. Touting works of the late Joseph Campbell, he has often spoken of *The Power of Myth.*

Campbell's books, like *Myths to Live By* and *The Hero with a Thousand Faces*, maintain that the biggest legends, those that penetrate the most hearts and fill the most lives, are also powerful in helping to *direct* those lives. Even diverting the path of whole civilizations.

In any event, there is one conclusive answer to "it's only a movie." That answer is: *You've already bought a book whose whole purpose is to discuss meaning and consequence in the Star Wars universe!* Everybody who contributed, from accuser to defender, believes there is something worth arguing about. We'll do it because the topic matters, or because it's fun to argue, or because we're being paid to argue. Most likely, all three.[1]

Indeed, one point that I intend to make later on is that this civilization *likes to argue*. Openly and democratically. Alas, in the Star Wars universe, nobody knows how. At least nobody who matters.

But that's for later. The purpose of this introduction was to set the stage. And now that's done. The participants in our drama—our moot "trial"— were all hand-picked by Benbella Books to participate in something fun. They are standing by, ready to begin yet another entertaining riff on George Lucas's epic masterpiece. A journey into the dark heart of *meaning* that some of us believe must lie beneath, under all the glossy surfaces.

If stories and myths reflect who we are, and where we're headed...what does Star Wars say about us?

Where does it say we should be going?

---

[1] The reader deserves a disclaimer about what this book is not. It is not a well-organized scholarly treatise on the Star Wars universe! Or a thorough analysis of the ideas contained therein. For anyone eager to explore the root sources and inspirations for Star Wars, and many other modern myths, an excellent starting point would be the vivid and detailed Web site at Jitterbug.com that explores a vast range of possible, plausible and utterly blatant borrowings from earlier works. Indeed, George Lucas has never denied making liberal use of earlier storytelling tropes and tricks that range from floating space letters (*Buck Rogers*) and secretive mystic cults (Dune) to glowing swords and whining little golem-trolls (The Lord of the Rings). (See http://www.jitterbug.com/origins/index.html. "Star Wars: Origins" was created by Kristen Brennan in September 1999 and updated sporadically, with many contributors, through 2006.) For the most part, the authors and essayists in this book will be concentrating on something else entirely—the moral, ethical and other lessons being taught by this epic series.

In making their arguments, our writers selected by the folks at BenBella Books will largely cite plot events from the Star Wars films themselves–on-screen moments that any Star Wars aficionado ought to recall or recognize, without needing any deep grounding in, say, the "arcana of Western and Asian mythology."

Star Wars and Truth and Why We Even Bother, and Why It's Worth Your Time to Bother, Too

Matthew Woodring Stover

UNLIKE SOME FOLKS 'round these parts, I'm only going to make one Star Trek reference.

Dammit, Jim, I'm a storyteller, not an essayist.

So:

Saturday afternoon, June 1977, Danville, Illinois. Danville is a little industrial town buried in a tangle of railroad tracks and cornfields three hours south of Chicago; in those days it had a GM foundry and some meatpacking plants, a sheet-aluminum producer and some big grain elevators and a fifteen-year-old me, a week out of ninth grade with five bucks lawn-mowing cash in my pocket and a blue Schwinn English Racer, and some goofy flick called *Star Wars* playing at the old Fischer Theater a mile and change downtown. A kid named Jeff Masters showed up at my front door a little after one o'clock with his own bike (also a Schwinn—an Orange Crate, I think) and asked if I wanted to check out this goofy flick, and I'd seen a grand total of one commercial for it (on late-night TV out of Terre Haute, Indiana), but it had lots of shooting, a guy swinging over a chasm with a girl in his arms, spaceships, Peter Cushing and Alec Guinness, and the temperature was already over ninety and our lone window-unit air conditioner was on the fritz, so I said, "What the hell."

That's an exact quote.

I'm not here to talk about the experience of coming to Star Wars on the big screen entirely by surprise. I'll leave that to your imagination. Suffice it to say that even the memory of putting the words "A novel by Matthew Woodring Stover, based on the screenplay by George Lucas" on the title page of *Revenge of the Sith* is still enough to give me a bit of the shakes.

I'm here to talk about the experience of Truth.

By the time I found myself in that Saturday matinée in 1977, I was already an experienced SF geek, though that term had yet to crest our common horizon. My brother Tom, ten years older, long gone to college and off into his career, had left behind a huge library of paperback SF that I had started reading about the time I learned to read, and so when Star Wars rolled around, I'd been through just about every then-published work by Heinlein, Asimov, Anderson, Williamson, Pohl, Niven, the various Smiths (I could fill my word count just with a list of all the authors)...as well as the Big Old Guys like Verne and Wells. Tom—an engineer by temperament as well as by profession—had a prejudice in favor of the hard SF guys, as well as the space opera types; Leiber and Zelazny, Disch and Moorcock and PKD showed up mostly by accident, in magazines or collections he'd bought for other people's work.

This is relevant because of my experience during one particular scene in what is now known as *A New Hope*—the scene in Obi-Wan's cave, after he has rescued Luke from the Sand People, where he gives Luke what we all now know is Anakin Skywalker's lightsaber, and begins to tell him of the Jedi Knights....

I sat in the dark, in that theater, breathless, blinking, trying to listen harder, to hear more than was being said—

Because I knew, then, that here—not just in this moment, but in this story—was something True.

This was not a literal truth. Not factual truth. This was not a delusional moment that blurred the line between fiction and reality.

I was skimming the surface of a Truth that is not expressible in direct language. There is no way to say it other than the way it was being said: in the metaphor of a fantasy.

For make no mistake: Star Wars is, at its heart, fantasy. Knights with magic swords, talking animals, kindly wizards, evil sorcerers, mystic ships that travel in the blink of an eye beyond the ken of mortal man—

But don't take it too hard.

All science fiction is a subset of fantasy. Star Wars just happens to be honest about it.

In fact, all *literature* is a subset of fantasy. Fantasy is the child of myth; the foundation of fantasy is the heroic epic—which is what Star Wars is—and the heroic epic is the initial form of literature in nearly every human culture. Every succeeding literary form comes into existence by limiting itself: by carving away chunks of the possibility that fantasy represents.

By cutting off, one might argue, pieces of Truth.

I recognized that breathless unfolding of Truth inside my chest, because I had felt it before. I'd come across it once or twice in Leiber (at the bitter end of *Ill Met in Lankhmar*, for one). I'd found it when reading of Aslan's sacrifice in *The Lion, the Witch and the Wardrobe*, and of Théoden's sally at Helm's Deep in *The Two Towers*; I would find it again in later years, as I read of Beowulf's weary stand against the dragon, of the Green Knight picking up his severed head and stalking away from the Round Table, of High Lord Elena speaking the Word of Command in *The Illearth War*....

I would find it in 1980, when a certain someone of our mutual acquaintance said (again, for me, entirely unexpectedly), "No, Luke. *I* am your father."

This is an experience I never got from those hard SF guys. Except for Heinlein. And that was *Glory Road*. If you read it, you'll understand why.

Science fiction is usually, quite properly, about what may be. What we might become. (Heinlein himself, for example, is justly legendary for prophesying in "Solution Unsatisfactory" the development of dirty bombs.)

Fantasy, by contrast—real fantasy, not the mocked-up pseudo-medieval horseshit Some People like to pretend encompasses its whole range—is about what already is. It's not about what we might become; it's a metaphor for who we already are.

Each of us.

Fantasy's landscape is the map of our dreams; it is peopled with our personal monsters, and the struggles of its heroes are metaphors for our own.

Which brings us back to Truth.

Now, I have to tell you something about what I mean by Truth, too. I'm not talking about engineer's truth, here: the kind of truth that is visible by microscope, measurable by laser balance or quantifiable by any contortion of mathematics. That kind of truth is commonly referred to as fact, and as such has no need for the uppercase T. There is another, dicier aspect of reality also commonly referred to as truth, and that is the kind that we turn to courts and juries to decide. These are truths that are still describable in plain language, but about which there may be legitimate disagreement, because they can't be reduced to straightforward observation, or measurement. Guilt or innocence, proportional blame—these are what we call decidable questions. Ones that have more or less final answers. That's what we're pretending we're up to here. But we're just pretending.

Because that's still lowercase truth.

When you get to Truth, in the upper case, you face questions of meaning. Maybe I should say Meaning. Uppercase Truth deals with Who We Are, and What It All Means.

That's when direct language begins to fail. Closing in on that kind of Truth, direct statement falters on asymptotic approach—the closer you get, the less useful it becomes. You need imagery to even get into the atmosphere, and metaphor for landing gear.

Which brings us back to Star Wars.

Because uppercase Truth is the real subject of Star Wars. Not who we *might* be, or what *might* happen someday, or what *ought* to happen or what we should *worry about* happening in the future. Star Wars isn't about the future.

There's a reason why the whole saga takes place "a long time ago, in a galaxy far, far away...."

It's not anchored in time or place. It's not about some other galaxy. It's not about the future, or about 1977, or 1980, or 1983, 1999, 2002 or 2005. It's about wherever is here, and whenever is now.

That's a function of myth, and make no mistake: Star Wars is and always has been exactly that. Not only myth, but arguably (and argue is exactly what we'll be doing here, isn't it?) the most powerful mythic cycle of the twentieth century.

The opening passage of the *Tao Te Ching* is commonly translated "The Name that can be named is not the Eternal Name," but—as with all works that deal with Truth—the *Tao Te Ching* is elliptical, and metaphoric. That particular passage might also be translated, for example, as "The Way that can be weighed is not the Eternal Way."

It's worth noting that Stephen Mitchell, in his seminal translation, noted (as George Lucas seems very likely himself to have been aware) that the passage can also be translated as "The Force that can be forced is not the Eternal Force."

Star Wars is about Big Questions.

That's why we bother.

This is why it's worth your time to bother, too:

Because when you get to Truth, you don't get (*pace* Regis Philbin) any final answers. You can't measure it, and you can't trust a jury of your peers to decide the question.

Only you can decide what it means, because in the end, what it means...is what it means to *you*.

THE COURTROOM

DROID JUDGE: Welcome, ladies, gentlemen, clones, droids and other sentient organisms. You all know why we are here. A series of charges have been made against the multimedia empire known as Star Wars. These charges are as follows:

CHARGE #1: The Politics of Star Wars Are Anti-Democratic and Elitist.

CHARGE #2: While Claiming Mythic Significance, Star Wars Portrays No Admirable Religious or Ethical Beliefs.

CHARGE #3: Star Wars Novels Are Poor Substitutes for Real Science Fiction and Are Driving Real SF off the Shelves.

CHARGE #4: Science Fiction Filmmaking Has Been Reduced by Star Wars to Poorly Written Special Effects Extravaganzas.

CHARGE #5: Star Wars Has Dumbed Down the Perception of Science Fiction in the Popular Imagination.

CHARGE #6: Star Wars Pretends to Be Science Fiction, but Is Really Fantasy.

CHARGE #7: Women in Star Wars Are Portrayed as Fundamentally Weak.

CHARGE #8: The Plot Holes and Logical Gaps in Star Wars Make It Ill-Suited for an Intelligent Viewer.

(Noise in the courtroom grows as the charges are read.)

DROID JUDGE: *(hammering his gavel)* Quiet down, quiet down. I intend to run this courtroom in a fair and disciplined fashion, and that means no outbursts from the gallery. Yes, I'm looking at you, Wookiees. Now, to begin, counselors will make their opening statements.

OPENING STATEMENTS

I Accuse...
...or Zola Meets Yoda...

DAVID BRIN

I T CANNOT BE SAID often enough. We are here to have fun, tossing ideas around, pretending that they matter. Nobody, on either side of the coming argument, contends that the fate of Western civilization will hang upon a literary analysis of the epical and epochal Star Wars series! A series that deserves respect at many levels, if only for the marvelous artists it has employed and the raw pleasure that it has given hundreds of millions.

In fact, though some people may find it surprising, let me make clear that I never interfere when my children request—or demand!—the next Star Wars merchandising gambit. A Lego Death Star or Darth Vader mask? Another Obi-Wan Happy Meal? I only grit my teeth a little over the merchandising cash flow going to an empire that (in my opinion) could have been a lot more meaningful, a lot more helpful in making a better world. Certainly, my protective instincts don't get all fired up, eager to shield vulnerable young minds from inimical memes!

Why not?

Because what youngsters—and millions of others—mostly see in movies like these are the simple surfaces. The top layer of lavish, goofy, earnestly preachy and even somewhat noble-minded fun. Out-

17

numbered heroes bravely taking on the odds. Going with your feelings, tossing logic aside and blasting away! It is the innocent spirit of the first movie (*A New Hope*) that seems to have spread and captured the hearts of millions of people, young and old.

If you ask them about the "moral messages" of Star Wars, most people tend to recall that—

- *Mean people suck.*
- *It's good to be brave.*
- *Mean people get yucky-looking.*
- *Defend your friends.*
- *Watch out for mean people playing tricks and telling lies.*
- *Don't let nasty old mean guys goad you into losing your temper.*

Hmm. Well, there may be some problems at *this* level. In fact, entirely on their own, my kids are starting to glance with skepticism at the details in even these simple lessons (e.g., "If something happens to my looks, will I turn into a bad person?").

Still, for the most part, children can take all this in without much harm to their values, or souls. Anyway, who am I to spoil their fun, by yattering on about deeper meaning and symbolism?

But that's the point. I have no intention of spoiling *their* fun at all.

Yours, on the other hand...well, you have already paid for this book. So don't pretend that you're not interested.

After all, there are many levels other than the superficial, and George Lucas would be the first to say so. Keeping faith with the teachings of famed mythology maven Joseph Campbell, Lucas claims that storytelling is a central ritual that both describes and helps to shape the way that people picture themselves in relation to society. So, shouldn't we take him at his word?

Moreover, many of the trends that we see in the Star Wars universe have also manifested elsewhere in a society that's undergoing change. For example, take the rise of *feudal and magical fantasy*, once considered an offshoot of science fiction, but now pushing its high-tech cousin off the bookstore shelves. Even within sci-fi, stories seem increasingly to feature "chosen ones" or demigod-like heroes, often set in structured, aristocratic cultures.

How often, anymore, do you see tales that portray *society itself* functioning, perhaps helping the protagonist, or suggesting solutions that arise from collaborative effort? Maybe even offering hope that hard work and goodwill might bring better days? Do cops ever come when called? Do institutions ever deliver or perform, even partially, in ways that help a little? Are the hero's *neighbors* ever anything other than hapless sheep? Does scientific advancement ever—ever—come to the rescue, anymore, instead of simply causing more problems and provoking lectures about how "mankind shouldn't meddle" in things we do not understand? Do big projects, or ambitious undertakings, or team efforts ever hold a candle to the boldness of the single, archetype hero, *sticking* it to every authority figure in sight?

Are we being taught, gradually but inexorably, to turn away from the whole *modernist agenda*? The concept that science, society, citizenship and faith are things that go well together, contributing to the good of everybody? Or that there was once a good idea—to replace arbitrary leader-worship with democratic institutions that we can all hope to share? What about the notion that any of us *regular people*—not just mutant chosen ones—can be the hero, if we're ever called upon?

Hey, stories like that *can* be told. Take the films of director Steven Spielberg. From *Saving Private Ryan* to *Schindler's List* to *Close Encounters*, these are often stirring stories about people who are only a bit above average, but who achieve great things nonetheless. Sometimes these characters are deeply flawed. They slip up, or get angry, or even do bad things. Only then, they do the unexpected. They stand up.

Taking responsibility for their mistakes, they set things right. And, sometimes, civilization even helps them a bit. All told, Spielberg's central ongoing theme seems to be unswerving *gratitude* toward a society that—in all honesty—has been pretty good to him.

Oh, sure, not every filmmaker has to follow Steven Spielberg's chosen storytelling mode. Anyway, it's hard to live up to that kind of role model. But must nearly *all* of the others who are making movies today relentlessly preach exactly the *opposite* message? Especially, is there some underlying reason why the opposite message wound up pervading the biggest, most lavish, most expensive and most watched series of modern times—the Star Wars epic?

Some of the writers in this volume will talk about matters like these—plumbing *deeper meanings and messages* that are conveyed by Star Wars and its ilk. Others will poke in different directions—at ways that *plot, story* and *character consistency* gradually fell apart (alas) as the Star Wars series declined into grumpy middle age...and then entered what might be called crotchety senescence.

Then, attorneys for the Defense will have their say! For there are many sides to this story, and many who feel eager to defend a series they have come to love.

This should be loads of fun. So let's begin.

IT STARTS WITH THE LITTLEST THINGS...

My own disenchantment began early in my first viewing of *Return of the Jedi*.

Recall how Luke Skywalker shows up at the palace of Jabba the Hutt, calling himself a *Jedi Knight*? He then offers a bag of gold in exchange for the life of his friend, Han Solo. Without any doubt, it was a thrilling moment. Filled with high hopes after *The Empire Strikes Back*, I leaned forward in confident expectation that great things would follow, combining vividly creative action and effects with solid plotting, plus a little decent thoughtfulness for those grown-up parts of the brain. (Isn't that what happens in the best art? You get something for the adult and something for the child. There is no need to completely eliminate one in order to serve the other.)

All right, anticipation was running high, as Luke approached Jabba's fancy desert hut. My own instant theory? Frankly, I expected Luke's offer to be backed up with a threat!

"As you can see, Jabba, from the circle of X-wing fighters surrounding your residence, I am also a high commander of the second most powerful military force in the galaxy. So if you don't *accept this generous offer....*"

I mean...duh? Isn't that what anybody would try first, if he were in Luke's shoes? Combining the carrot with an implied stick?

Oh, sure, that's no fun, so it can't *work*. But this logical plan is an obvious *opening move*. It doesn't make for great adventure, thrills, spills and escapades, so let it *fail*. Have the Empire arrive and chase away all the

Rebel ships, leaving Luke in the lurch! Jabba grabs Luke and the fun can begin! Ninety extra seconds to make the next half hour make sense.

Look, I'm not saying it had to be that way! I am only posing that scenario as an example of how easy it would be to get every part of the opening act that is already there, while still giving a passing nod to common sense. All the leaping and slashing and narrow escapes that we see in the opening act of *ROTJ* could have been the *backup plan*. Because only complete bozos would have walked into an obvious trap—with escape utterly dependent upon all of the bad guys being lousy shots—without having a better scheme, at least to start with.

Okay, I admit it. That's kind of picky. But the infuriating aspect was how little attention to detail it would have taken to continue the kind of plot consistency and plausibility we saw in the brilliant Brackett-Kasdan script for *The Empire Strikes Back*. A few words inserted here and there. Then, every subsequent vivid laser bolt and explosion might proceed as planned. *Would that have been too much to ask?*

A small hole, true. But through it, more nagging thoughts began to fly. Faster than a little ship can dive inside a big ship, shoot the reactor and then run away just ahead of the blast wave. (Yes, I've mentioned that before. But really. I mean...*really*.)

Which leads us to the first of what will be many comparisons between Star Wars and its chief competitor for the hearts of science fiction fandom—Star Trek. A comparison that illuminates two very different views of fiction, civilization and the meaning of a hero.

Here's one way of looking at the underlying implications of these two sci-fi universes. Consider the choice of which kinds of *ship* are featured in each series. Let me invite you to ponder, for a moment, and contrast the *Air Force* metaphor versus one that hearkens up images of the *Navy*.

In Star Wars, the ships that matter are little fighter planes. Series creator George Lucas made liberal use of filmed dogfight footage, from both world wars, in some cases borrowing maneuvers like banking slipstream turns, down to the last detail. The heroic image in this case is the solitary pilot, perhaps assisted by his loyal gunner—or Wookiee or droid—companion. It is the modern version of knight and squire. Symbols as old as Achilles.

In contrast, the federation starship in Trek is vastly bigger, more complex, a veritable city cruising through space. Its captain hero is not only a warrior-knight, but also part scientist and part diplomat, a plenipotentiary representative of his civilization and father figure to his crew...*any one of whom may suddenly become an essential character*, during the very next adventure. While the captain's brilliance and courage are always key elements, so will be the skill and pluck of one or more crewmen and women. People who are much closer to average—like you or me—yet essential helpers, nonetheless. And possibly even—when it is their turn—heroes themselves.

In any event, the ship—Star Trek's *Enterprise*—stands for something, every time we look at it. This traveling city *is* civilization. The Federation's culture and laws, industry and consensus values—like the Prime Directive—are all carried in this condensed vessel, along with the dramatic diversity of its crew. Every single time there is an adventure, the civilization of the United Federation of Planets is put to the test, through its proxy, the hero-ship. And when the *Enterprise* passes each test, often with flying colors, so too, by implication, does civilization itself.

A civilization that might even be worthy of our grandchildren.

Compare this to the role of the Old Republic in the Lucasian universe. A hapless, hopeless, clueless mélange of bickering futility whose political tiffs are as petty as they are incomprehensible. The Republic may be sweet, but it never perceives, never creates or solves anything. Not once do we see any of its institutions actually function well. How can they? The people, the Republic, decent institutions...these cannot be heroes, or even helpers.

There is no room aboard an X-wing fighter for civilization to ride along.

Only for a knight and squire.

All right, you may call this making too much of yet another superficial thing. It can certainly be argued that ship size doesn't really matter. On the other hand, recall how eager Yoda was, in *Attack of the Clones*, to *destroy* the "Federation Starship"? Interesting choice of words, there! Could it be that the director agrees with me?

In sci-fi, ships carry powerful symbolism. They convey contrary ways of viewing *heroes,* and their relationship to common women and men.

Anyway, I couldn't help it. This difference in the *metaphor of the ship* continued to nag at me as every problem with the Star Wars universe just seemed to grow and compound, with each newly released episode. These *superficial things* mounted up, one after another. Deliberate artistic choices bubbled to the foreground, like Darth Vader's Nazi-style helmet and use of the term "stormtroopers." Or the need to be a genetic "midichlorian" mutant in order to use the Force. Or take the difference in educational styles, between the university-like Starfleet Academy and that imperious, overbearing, secretive guru Yoda. Two very different—and iconic—approaches to acquiring and passing on skill. To acquiring power. And then using it.

As the years—and prequels—passed, a list of growing discomforts grew longer and longer....

So let's cut to the chase.

Enough introduction. Get to the indictment!

All right, then. After watching the whole megillah of six long films, it's time to ask the central question.

"Just what bill of goods are we being sold, between the frames?"

Here's my personal list, jotted down across the years since 1984.

In the Star Wars universe:

- True leaders are born. It's genetic. The right to rule is inherited.
- Elites have an inherent right to *arbitrary* rule; common citizens needn't be consulted. They may only choose which born-to-rule elite to follow.
- Any amount of sin can be forgiven if you repent...and if you are important enough.
- "Good" elites should act on their subjective whims, without evidence, argument or accountability. Secrecy and lies are always a good option. They never need to be explained.
- The chief feature distinguishing "good" from "evil" is how pretty the characters look. Oh, and which music theme plays in the background.
- In order to be a skilled and good and worthy warrior, you must

cut yourself off from the very attachments that make a decent coworker, lover, spouse, parent and citizen.

- Justified human emotions can turn a good person evil, like flicking a switch.

I plan to focus primarily on the accusations made above. In particular, I will show how the politics of Star Wars is transparently elitist and anti-democratic. But there are *more* indictments that will be dealt with by some other members of the Prosecution Team.

- While claiming mythic significance, Star Wars portrays no admirable religious or ethical beliefs. In fact, all the religious or ethical trappings in Star Wars are driven by the sudden veers and impulses of plot, not any higher ethical or religious thinking.
- Star Wars novels are poor substitutes for real science fiction and are driving real SF off the shelves.
- Science fiction filmmaking has been reduced to poorly written special effects extravaganzas, and Star Wars shares the blame.
- Star Wars has dumbed down perception of science fiction in the popular imagination.
- Star Wars pretends to be science fiction, but is really feudal fantasy.
- There are troubling ways, in Star Wars, that women are portrayed.
- The Star Wars universe is rife with plot holes and logical flaws that were never necessary, even in a light adventure story. For this, in an epic that took decades and billions of dollars to create, that portrays itself as important storytelling, there is simply no excuse.
- Tragically, there are a few small things—missed opportunities— that could have eased most of these problems and helped the whole thing to make a lot more sense.

The last eight or so items will be handled by others, though I may weigh in here and there, later in the trial, especially in the matter of plot holes and missed opportunities. (In fact, there are some places where I tend to be *more* forgiving than average! For example, I never much minded Ewoks....) But here is where I'll take the time to plunge into crucial issues. Artistic, ethical and mythological. Those that made my original *Salon* magazine articles so controversial.

Especially my argument that George Lucas's grand mythology is *not* a tale that helps a modern and confident enlightenment civilization. It does not reflect our upstart "rebel" values, or provide recompense for all the kindness and good fortune that civilization has heaped upon him.

Indeed, we are very lucky that most people aren't paying attention, playing with the lightsabers but ignoring the "morality" parts. Because, if citizens actually took their moral cues from Star Wars, we would be in very deep trouble, indeed.

THE CAMPBELLIAN TRADITION

In order to argue the core point about *what Star Wars teaches*, we are going to have to step back a bit and talk about *storytelling*, in a far more general sense. None of this has been happening in a vacuum, after all. And George Lucas would be the first to tell you that his epic nestles comfortably in a standard mythic tradition that is as old as written human language. If Star Wars stands indicted, then so will be a lot of other tales, from Gilgamesh to Lancelot.

So please, bear with me, while I take a little time examining that tradition…and some more recent, upstart alternatives.

In *Star Wars: The Magic of Myth*, author Mary Henderson elaborates how much inspiration George Lucas took from classical mythology. Drawing heavily on the works of Mircea Eliade and Joseph Campbell, she parallels Luke Skywalker's adventure with the classical hero's journey, equating the swamps of Dagoba with the sacred grove, the Ewoks with the archetypal helpful animals populating an enchanted forest, and so on. It's all a deeply felt homage to some of our most ancient archetypes.[1]

All right, we start out with a bone of contention. I have my own quirky complaints that start from all this fawning over "ancient archetypes."

For example, I never much cared for the whole Nietzschian Übermensch thing: the notion—pervading so many myths and legends—

---

[1] Though, as reviewer and critic James Lowder points out, there are also much more recent historical and pop culture sources that Lucas mined in creating the films. Henderson downplays or ignores the influence, for example, of Kurosawa samurai films like *Yojimbo* and *The Hidden Fortress*, from which Lucas patterned characters and even borrowed sequences of dialogue.

that a good yarn has to be about demigods who are bigger, badder and better than normal folk by several orders of magnitude. It's an ancient storytelling tradition, all right. But one based on abiding contempt for the masses. One that I gradually came to find suspect in the works of A. E. van Vogt, E. E. Smith, L. Ron Hubbard and wherever you witness *slanlike* superbeings deciding the fate of billions without ever pausing to consider their wishes. Even Orson Scott Card—who has publicly criticized Star Wars for many of the same reasons that I do—nevertheless returns relentlessly to tales of science fictional Übermensch demigods...though Card's are more complex and interesting than most.

Does anyone else find this obsession, well, just a bit creepy?

I admit and avow that I am *no* acolyte of mythology scholar Joseph Campbell, who was made famous by a series of shows on PBS, in which journalist Bill Moyers interviewed him about legends spanning many cultures. In *The Hero with a Thousand Faces*, Campbell combines the earlier insights of many scholars, pointing out how a particular, rhythmic storytelling technique was used in ancient and premodern cultures, depicting protagonists and antagonists with common motives, character traits and plot twists that seem to transcend boundaries of language and culture. In these classic tales, a hero is beckoned to take on a quest. He begins reluctant, though signs foretell greatness. He receives dire warnings and then sage wisdom from a mentor, acquires quirky-but-faithful companions, faces a series of steepening crises, suffers as he explores the pit of his own fears, and finally emerges triumphant, bringing some boon/talisman/victory home to his admiring tribe/people/nation. Distilling the central message in his books and public statements, Campbell prescribes that *all* myths ought to be about these figures—like Achilles, Hercules, Orpheus, or Genji—larger than life, following a precise plot outline that is as old as it is rigid and changeless.

All right, Campbell's admirers use "changeless." The word "rigid" is mine. Still, I'll be the first to admit it's a superb formula—one that I've used at times in my own stories and novels (though always poking at it, trying variations, or even outright reversals). Moreover, by offering valuable insights into this revered storytelling tradition, Joseph Campbell does, indeed, shed light on common spiritual traits that seem to be shared by all human beings.

Alas, he only highlighted *positive* traits, ignoring the darker side—such as how easily this standard fable template was co-opted by kings, priests and tyrants, by extolling the all-importance of elites who tower over common women and men. King Achilles, slaughtering hundreds of common foot soldiers, while the river weeps. King Odysseus crossing the dire straits while his men all perish. King Arthur ruling benevolently—but with fierce enforcement by mystically anointed knights. *King This and brave Prince That*.... Above all, while an occasional dark lord or wicked giant gets toppled, hardly any of these heroes ever pause to question the very setup that made the quest necessary in the first place. The feudal order. The capricious Fates. Cryptic elves. The gods themselves.

I mean, seriously, can you look across the last 4,000 years of recorded history and call it *good* that society remained changeless for the vast majority of that time?

Or call *good* the implication that we must always adhere to variations on a single theme, the same prescribed plot outline, over and over again? Those who praise Joseph Campbell seem to perceive this uniformity as cause for rejoicing—but it isn't. Playing a large part in the tragic miring of our spirit, these demigod/royalty myths helped reinforce sameness and changelessness for millennia, transfixing people in nearly every culture, from Babylon to modern times.

The Professor claims that this pattern represents our deepest shared *zeitgeist,* ingrained in our very souls. But might there be *another reason* that it kept recurring? Picture yourself as Homer, or some other ancient bard. Where do you want to recite? In some peasant hovel, where you'll be fed gruel and nobody will remember? Or in the chief's lodge, the Sacred Temple, perhaps even the High King's hall, where beer and meat will flow, where the powerful may bestow favors, where acolytes will memorize your poesy...

...and all you have to do is flatter a little? Spin tales about knights and *Übermenschen superguys*. Poets and bards faced the same incentive, everywhere, in every era. By keeping to the program—praising elites—you could stay on the gravy train. For life.

All right, that explanation is a bit cynical. But shouldn't it be mentioned, at least as an alternative?

Not when Bill Moyers tossed Campbell one fawning softball question after another. To romantics, that endlessly repeated mythic structure is the *only human* way to tell a story.

Another example: Aristotle—in his *Poetics*—prescribed extremely rigid plot structures that required absolute acceptance of unalterable fate and the will of the gods. Right. Chain up storytelling. Mortify it in rigid stone. And call it a good thing.

Face it. The fix has been in for thousands of years.

Dr. Stephen Potts, of the UCSD Literature Department, has an interesting take on why so many ancient myths seem to have traits in common:

> None of us ever completely shakes loose the scars of adolescent solipsism—our belief that we are special but misunderstood, that we stand aloof from authority figures and peers alike, that we may even have some mysterious origin or unique destiny. Adolescence is the age of identity crisis and formation, of self-doubt and self importance—all reflected in the hero myths we inherit from our barbaric past. Campbell's "monomyth" is itself loaded with Freudian and Jungian assumptions regarding sexual identity, separation from and reconciliation with the parent, connection with a "goddess" or anima figure that naturally assumes the hero is male and in need of sexual completion. It is not a surprise, therefore, that Star Wars and similar vessels provide adolescent wish fulfillment (as do comic superheroes), and while we can all enjoy swinging with Spiderman or kicking ass with the Bat, God help us when we embrace these primitive paradigms as models for real life.

I can think of two recent Western cultures offhand that bought fully and unreservedly into Campbell-style myths, using those fables to forge a unified sense of purpose. In the antebellum American South, the immensely popular and influential novels of Sir Walter Scott—filled with knights errant and questing princes—served the same purpose that Wagner operas and Aryan tales did in pre-WWII Germany, helping to consolidate righteous belief in a clearly defined destiny and purpose. Both the Confederacy and the Nazis emphasized romantic adolescent drama and the glory of a cause to almost complete exclusion of any thought about long-term consequences. Both also had a predilection for archaic weaponry, like swords and daggers (just like the Jedi), as well as a penchant for pageantry, gran-diloquence and authority-as-birthright.

Another dark trait of romanticism, tragically illustrated by both of those cultures, is the willingness (seen in countless Campbel-lian myths) to reclassify whole swaths of humanity as subpar, not even deserving the minimal rights granted to honorable enemies. Whether they are Orcs or soldier-robots or clones...or black slaves or Jews...there is no need to bother the conscience when they are disposed of. No need to answer to their mothers. (In fact, conve-niently, Orcs and robots and clones *have* no mothers.)

Is it, then, any mystery why so few of the traditional romantic myths cited by Joseph Campbell focus upon women heroes? Or on people achieving what should be the highest human goals? Success-fully raising a family. Building a community. Negotiating peace. En-gaging in civilization.

Alas, these are not the tasks or concerns of bold, young, unmar-ried males. Few Campbellian-style heroes—other than great Odys-seus—ever mention or yearn for them.

Nevertheless, these are the proper focus of would-be leaders. The proper study of grown-up human beings.

Commented the critic Curt Jensen, amid one of the swirling on-line exchanges generated by this topic:

> One thing you never see with the Jedi Knights is any kind of criti-cal glance at their merits as peacetime political leaders. Being able to levitate an X-wing doesn't make you a wise leader. Quite the contrary actually. It would tend toward the default attitude that might makes right. Not only are the Jedi wholly unsuited to the demands of domes-tic politics, they seem unaware of their limits and keep insisting on meddling, eventually leading society down the road to disaster. Yet, according to the strange logic of George Lucas, these people are still automatically qualified for leadership, with the inherent right to make vital decisions in secret, affecting the well-being of billions.

Of course, the Defense will argue that Star Wars was never meant for grown-ups! But should not the grown-ups *within* George Lucas's universe be paying a little heed to such matters, even if only in back-ground? If only to point Luke and Han and Leia and Anakin toward the eventual, proper goal of decent heroes—the role that Odysseus took up when his adventure ended—that of ruling wisely?

Ironically, this notion was not alien to George Lucas at all! Few remember his short-lived but brilliant television series, *The Young Indiana Jones Chronicles* (1992). It was no great commercial success. But to aficionados, it appeared to be Lucas's most sincere personal statement—a truly brave attempt to mix adolescent excitement with real thoughtfulness and content. Indeed, it seemed as if Lucas was expressing the same theme we often see from Spielberg—one of deep and genuine gratitude.

In twenty-two episodes, the younger Jones, played by Sean Patrick Flanery, encountered one after another of the greatest minds of the early part of the twentieth century, learning from them, not only as Campbellian journey mentors or spirit guides, but as archetypes of adult ambition and achievement, nearly always representing some key ingredient in a rambunctiously eager and hopeful civilization—from jazz musicians to saintly jungle doctors, from inventors to master spies, from mothers to fathers. And, yes, in confronting war and oppression, firsthand, Indy (and the viewers) learned about civilization's "dark side." There were dour reflections, amid all the dashing, heroic deeds. Though throughout, young Indy never lost faith in the power of reason, discovery and science.

Picture Huckleberry Finn on a raft escapade with Ben Franklin. Imagine something written for all ages, all the parts of your brain.

Alas, *The Young Indiana Jones Chronicles* sometimes got too lecturey and lost pace. Its relative commercial failure provokes one to wonder: did George Lucas learn a lesson—the wrong lesson—never again to even try blending the adult and the child, offering something to both?

No, there are plenty of counterexamples, some even provided by George Lucas, to the dismal notion that we must enslave ourselves to a single, tedious storytelling pattern, even if it pervaded many cultures of the past. *Especially* because it pervaded so many failed, oppressive societies of our bloody, awful past.

Which is why *science fiction*—the real thing—came as such a radical departure. A new kind of storytelling, it often rebels against the very archetypes that Aristotle and the Campbellians venerate.

Take the occasional upstart belief that progress, egalitarianism and positive-sum games are possible—if very hard. Or hopeful confidence in a slim, but very real, possibility of decent human institutions.

Then there is the upstart habit of compulsively questioning rules! *Even rules of storytelling.* Authors like John Brunner, Alice Sheldon, Cordwainer Smith, Greg Bear, Frederik Pohl and Philip K. Dick always looked on any prescriptive storytelling formula as a direct challenge—a dare. A reason to try something different, for a change.

This explains why science fiction has never been much welcomed at either extreme of the literary spectrum—either in comic books or in the halls of "high literature."

BOTH ENDS AGAINST THE MIDDLE

You'd think that science fiction would be natural for comics. Some of our best living graphic artists have become adept, using this static, two-dimensional medium, at conveying startlingly vivid and evocative effects in sequential panels—the kind of imagery that caters naturally to futuristic or exotic locales. And there are other overlaps between SF and comics. For example, both genres are unafraid to posit the possibility of garish transformation and change.

Nevertheless, for decades, people have wondered why illustrated graphic novels and comics focus so thoroughly on superheroes, hardly ever telling the kinds of vivid space or future-oriented adventures penned by Verne, Wells, Vinge, de Camp, Anderson, Pohl, Heinlein and so on.

Returning to the ongoing theme of this essay, you can find a possible explanation in how the writers and publishers of these marvelous illustrated tales *treat* their superheroes—with reverent awe, as demigods were depicted in *The Iliad*. All of the complaints listed earlier about minimizing the importance of normal people—of civilization—apply as much to comics as they do to Star Wars. Comics appear to have their roots firmly planted in the old archetypes. Far too firmly ever to welcome the spirit of true sci-fi.

Or, at least, that is how comics treated their heroes...until recently. Changes do appear to be afoot at last, however. In one of the great ironies, while literary SF has been turning ever more toward the styles and sensibilities of fantasy, many of the best comic book and graphic novel writers have lately been writing almost as if they were...well...science fiction authors!

What's the crucial distinction?

Imagine, for a moment, how a true science fiction author might write about Superman. Picture earthling scientists asking the handsome Man of Steel for *blood samples* (even if it means scraping with a super fingernail) in order to study his puissant powers. And then...maybe...bottling the trick for everyone?

As for the opposite end of the spectrum—the literary elite—it's easy to see that campus postmodernists despise science fiction in part because of the word "science." Another reason is that many scholars find anathema the underlying assumption behind most high-quality SF: a bold assertion that there are no "*eternal human verities*." Things change. Change can be fascinating. And science fiction is the literature of change.

Moreover, our children might outgrow us! They may become better, or learn from our mistakes and not repeat them. And if they don't learn? *That* could be a riveting tragedy, far exceeding Aristotle's cramped, myopic definition.

On the Beach, *Soylent Green* and *1984* plumbed frightening depths. *Brave New World*, "The Screwfly Solution" and *Fahrenheit 451* posed worrying questions. In contrast, *Oedipus Rex* is about as interesting as watching a hooked fish thrash futilely at the end of a line. A modern person may weep at the right moments, as the playwright intended. Only then, you just want to put the poor doomed King of Thebes out of his misery—and find a way to punish his tormentors.

This truly is a different point of view, in direct opposition to older, elitist creeds that preached passivity and awe in nearly every culture. Where asking too many questions was punishable *hubris*. Where a hero's job was to oppose one set-piece villain...in order to defend the aristocratic rights of another.

Imagine Achilles refusing to accept his ordained destiny, taking up his sword and hunting down the Fates, demanding that they give him both a long life *and* a glorious one! Picture Odysseus telling both Agamemnon and Poseidon to go chase themselves, then heading off to join Daedalus in a garage start-up company, mass-producing both wheeled and winged horses, so mortals could swoop about the land and air, like gods—the way common folk do nowadays, so unaware what they are part of. A marvel of collaborative technological progress.

Even if their start-up fails and jealous Olympians crush Odysseus/DaedalusCorp, what a tale it would be!

Can this attitude work in stories? Consider those lowbrow but way fun television series *Hercules*, *Buffy* and *Xena*. Though they wore all the trappings of fantasy—swords and magical spells—each episode told a morality tale that was fiercely pro-democracy, egalitarian, hubristic and rambunctiously antiaristocratic. (In contrast, Star Wars, for all of its laser furniture, appears to defend every mythological aspect of feudalism.)

This new storytelling style was rarely seen till a few generations ago, when aristocrats lost some of their power to punish irreverence. And even now, the new perspective remains shaky. The older notion of punishable "hubris" still pervades a wide range of literature and film, from highbrow to low. From the works of Michael Crichton to those of Margaret Atwood, how many dramas reflexively depict scientists as "mad"? How few depict change in a positive light, or show public institutions functioning well enough to bother fixing them?

No wonder George Lucas openly yearns for the pomp of mighty kings over the drab accountability of republics. Many share his belief that things might be a whole lot more vivid without all the endless, dreary argument and negotiating that make up such a large part of modern life. Even millions of voters have taken to supporting authoritarians, who seek power free of accountability. Aristocrats who say "trust me."

The old yearning is still strong.

For someone to take command. A leader.

THE SHIFTY NOTION OF REBELLION

Ah, but the Star Wars series didn't begin obsessed with leaders. It started as a story about rebels, bravely taking on an empire!

I cannot repeat enough times that I had no particular trouble with the original Star Wars movie—since relabeled *A New Hope*. Lightweight and a bit silly, it nevertheless oozed charm, adventure and good-hearted egalitarian fun. The villain, with a name like "invader," wore a Nazi-style helmet, commanded "stormtroopers" and torture-interrogated princesses. He throttled brave rebel captains with his bare hands and helped blow up planets. Clearly this film played into the greatest American mythos—in fact, the most stunning propaganda campaign of all time—

—*suspicion of authority*.

No, your eyes do not deceive you. Just pause and think about it.

Arguably, the most persistent and incessant propaganda campaign, appearing in countless American movies, novels, myths and TV shows, preaches a message quite opposite to the one we associate with Joseph Campbell. A singular and unswerving theme, so persistent and ubiquitous that most people hardly notice or mention it. And yet, I defy you to name even half a dozen popular movies that don't utilize its appeal.

Yes, that theme is *suspicion of authority*—often accompanied by its junior sidekick *tolerance*. Indeed, watch the heroes of nearly every modern film. Don't most of them bond with the viewer by sticking it to some authority figure, often in the first few minutes?

Oh, you do hear *some* messages of conformity and intolerance, but these fill the mouths of moustache-twirling villains, clearly inviting us to rebel contrary to everything they say. Submission to gray tribal normality is portrayed as one of the most contemptible things an individual can do—a message quite opposite to what was pushed in most other cultures.[2] Take the wildly popular movie *E.T.* whose central message goes something like this: "Little American children, if you ever meet a strange alien from beyond the pale, by all means *hide* him from your own freely elected tribal elders!" I reiterate, no other society preached such a lesson to its offspring.

---

[2] The chief ideological difference between a good Democrat and a good Republican appears to be *whom* you perceive as being a more ominously oppressive potential oligarchy. A Republican worries about intimidation and undue power accumulation by pushy academics and faceless government bureaucrats. The Democrat sees undue accretions of power and influence by monied aristocrats, ideological fanatics and faceless corporations. Libertarians choose one from column A and one from column B! When you put it that way, it seems we've been guarding each other's backs for years; so why do we get so mad at each other for worrying about *different* authority figures? *Which* authority you choose to fear is largely a matter of experience and personal taste. That doesn't mean the other guy's fear is entirely without basis.

Now let me admit, where this strange suspicion-of-authority propaganda campaign comes from I don't know. Even after talking about it publicly for years, I don't have a good theory! Yet, its effects are inarguably spectacular, underlying most of the accomplishments of modern-enlightenment civilization. Half of our prodigious creativity may arise from a restless need to be different in order to prove a sense of individuality that we absorbed from an early age.

Alas, it also results in an occasional Timothy McVeigh...the kind of malignant obsessive who never *gets* the overarching irony—that his own proud antiauthoritarianism was suckled at an early age from the very society he despised, spoon-fed to him *and* millions of other youths by a civilization that does everything possible to create wave after wave of rambunctious rebels.

Rebels. No wonder *A New Hope* (*ANH*) had such resonance. The Empire's bad, so fight it!

Moreover, nostalgia for the Old Republic wasn't yet tainted with the utter contempt for democracy that would pervade Episodes I–III.

Indeed, this rebel spirit continued in *The Empire Strikes Back* (*TESB*). Even though we met Yoda—an authority figure to whom our hero had to bow—neither the Jedi Master nor the Force were yet the cloying, oppressive things they would later become. According to critic Stefan Jones, "In the first film, the Force was a kind of martial art/Zen archery kind of thing. Rather egalitarian: Obi-Wan even offers to teach scoffer Han Solo the ropes, implying anybody can do it. Goofy comic-book mysticism, but kind of charming and innocent, in a Hong Kong kung-fu movie sort of way." And even though Yoda starts throwing his diminutive weight around, in *TESB*, the lessons are still pretty benign.

Stay calm and focused. Um, sure, sounds good. My kids learn the same thing, at their karate studio.

Anyway, Luke even rebels against *that* authority figure! Yoda warns: "If you go and help your friends, lost everything will be!"

But Luke goes anyway...and *lost* everything is *not*! (Whereupon, faced with awkward questions, Yoda performs a handy escape trick. The old "death" fadeaway!)

Alas, as the Übermensch Effect took over—starting in *Return of the*

Jedi (*ROTJ*) and worsening with every film that followed—the Force grew ever more elitist. You had to be born with it! No, not just born with it, you had to be a mutant. No, make that a fore-ordained by destiny, preselected long ago, out-and-out messiah. A bona fide Chosen One. A demigod.

In a progressive universe, Yoda and his competitor sages would set up Jedi-arts studios in every mini-mall on Coruscant—the way karate saturates suburban America—giving millions of kids exposure to a little discipline and fun, plus a chance to better themselves through hard work. Maybe outperform what cynical grown-ups expect of them. But Yoda thinks he can diagnose at age nine who's got it, who hasn't. And who is destined to fail before they try.

Only demigods need apply... and only those demigods Yoda likes.

But more about the nasty green oven mitt anon.

MORE COMPARISONS

Again, is all of this serious rumination just spoilsport grumbling? Or worse, sour grapes? Why look for deep lessons in harmless, escapist entertainment? While some earnestly hold that the moral health of a civilization can be traced in its popular culture, don't moderns tend to feel that ideas, even unpleasant ones, aren't inherently toxic in their own right?

And yet who can deny that people—especially children—*will* be swayed if a message is repeated often enough? It's when a "lesson" gets reiterated relentlessly that even skeptics should sit up and take notice.

Don't be fooled. The moral messages in Star Wars aren't just window dressing. Speeches and lectures drench every film. They take up the slack time that could have been spent on plotting.

They represent an agenda.

Let's go back to comparing George Lucas's space-adventure epic to its chief competitor—Star Trek. The differences at first seem superficial, but they add up.

We have already see how one saga has an air force motif (tiny fighters) while the other appears naval. In Star Trek, the big ship is heroic and the cooperative effort required to maintain it is depicted as honorable. Indeed, Star Trek sees technology as useful and essentially friendly—if at times also dangerous. Education is a great emancipator of the humble (e.g., Starfleet Academy). Futuristic institutions are basically good-natured (the Federation), though of course one must fight outbreaks of incompetence, secrecy and corruption. Professionalism is respected, lesser characters make a difference, and henchmen often become brave whistle-blowers—as they do in America today.

In Star Trek, when authorities are defied, it is in order to overcome their mistakes or expose particular villains, not to portray all government as inherently hopeless. Good cops sometimes come when you call for help. Ironically, this image *fosters* useful criticism of authority, because it suggests that any of us can gain access to our flawed institutions—if we are determined enough—and perhaps even fix them with fierce tools of citizenship.

Above all, whenever you encounter *Homo superior* in Star Trek— some hyper-evolved, better-than-human fellow with powers beyond our mortal kin—the demigod is subjected to scrutiny and skeptical worry! Such mutant *uber*-types are given a chance to prove they mean no harm. But when they throw their weight around, normal folk rise up and look them in the eye. This happens so often in Trek—as well as shows like *Stargate* and *Babylon 5*—that it has become a true sci-fi tradition.

By contrast, the choices in Star Wars are stark and limited. As in Tolkien's Lord of the Rings, you can join either the Dark Lord or the Chosen Prince (with his pointy-eared elf advisors). Ultimately, the oppressed "rebels" in Star Wars have no recourse in law or markets or science or democracy. They can only pick sides in a civil war between two wings of the same genetically superior royal family.

(The same royal family? Oh, but it's right there, in front of you! The implication that bubbles out of the quirky SW obsession, with heaping coincidence upon coincidence. The Emperor comes from the same narrow aristocracy—on Planet Naboo—as Luke's mother. Probably, they're cousins. As for Anakin's mother, who's to say she didn't come from the same place? A gene pool of midichlorian mutants, engaged in a family spat, and galaxy-wide hell ensues. It's a reach, but thought-provoking. Is it any wonder that, in Star Trek, demigod mutants are always treated with skepticism, not reflex worship?)

Yes, Star Trek had its own problems and faults. The television episodes often devolved into soap operas. Many of the movies were very badly written. Trek at times seemed preachy, or turgidly politically correct, especially in its post-Kirk incarnations. (For example, every species has to mate with every other one, interbreeding with almost compulsive abandon. The only male heroes who are allowed any testosterone—in *The Next Generation*—are Klingons, because cultural diversity outweighs sexual correctness. In other words, it's okay for *them* to be macho 'cause it is "their way.") Nevertheless, Trek tried to grapple with genuine issues, giving complex voices even to its villains and asking hard questions about pitfalls we may face while groping for tomorrow.

Anyway, when it comes to portraying human destiny, where would you rather live, assuming you'll be a normal citizen and no demigod? In Roddenberry's Federation? Or Lucas's Empire?

THE FEUDAL REFLEX

George Lucas defends his elitist view, telling the *New York Times*, "That's sort of why I say a benevolent despot is the ideal ruler. He can actually get things done. The idea that power corrupts is very true and it's a big human who can get past that."[3] He further says we are a sad culture, bereft of the confidence or inspiration that strong leaders can provide.

And yet, aren't we the very same culture that produced George Lucas and gave him so many opportunities? The same society that raised all those brilliant experts for him to hire—boldly creative folks who pour both individual inspiration and cooperative skill into his

---

[3] George Lucas, interview by Orville Schell, "I'm a Cynic Who Has Hope for the Human Race," *New York Times*, March 21, 1999.

Another excerpt: "The United States, especially the media, is eating its own tail. The media has a way of leveling everything in its path, which is not good for a society. There's no respect for the office of the Presidency. Not that we need a king, but there's a reason why kings built large palaces, sat on thrones and wore rubies all over. There's a whole social need for that, not to oppress the masses, but to impress the masses and make them proud and allow them to feel good about their culture, their government and their ruler so that they are left feeling that a ruler has the right to rule over them, so that they feel good rather than disgusted about being ruled. In the past, the media basically worked for the state and was there to build the culture. Now, obviously, in some cases it got used in a wrong way and you ended up with the whole balance of power out of whack. But there's probably no better form of government than a good despot."

Let me add that the reader should carefully take into account context. For example, this was said during the height of Clinton-era "morality" witch-hunts. Nevertheless, there is irreducible meaning to the words themselves.

films, working at a monolithic corporate institution that neverthe-less, functions pretty well?

A culture that defies the old homogenizing impulse by worship-ping eccentricity, with unprecedented hunger for the different, new or strange? In what way can such a civilization be said to lack confi-dence? And just how would a king or despot help?

In historical fact, all of history's despots, combined, never man-aged to "get things done" as well as this rambunctious, self-critical civilization of free and sovereign citizens, who have finally broken free of worshipping a ruling class and begun thinking for themselves. Democracy can seem frustrating and messy at times, but it delivers. So why do few filmmakers—other than Steven Spielberg—own up to that basic fact?

Having said all that, let me again acknowledge that Star Wars harks to an old and very, very deeply human archetype. Those who listened to Homer recite *The Iliad* by a roaring fire knew great drama. Achil-les could slay a thousand with the sweep of a hand—as Darth Vader helps Tarkin murder billions with the press of a button—but none of those casualties matters next to the personal saga of a great one. The slaughtered victims are mere minions, after all. Extras, without families or hopes to worry about shattering. Spear-carriers. Only the demigod's personal drama is important.

Thus, few protest the apotheosis of Darth Vader—nee Anakin Sky-walker—in *Return of the Jedi*. With a single, sudden act—slaying his master at the cost of his own life—he gives in to a fatal attachment and saves his own son...and thus achieves redemption. Entry into Jedi Heaven.

To put it in perspective, let's imagine that the allies managed to capture Adolf Hitler at the end of the Second World War, putting him on trial for war crimes. The prosecution spends months listing all the horrors done at his behest. Then it is the turn of Hitler's defense at-torney, who rises and utters just *one sentence*:

"But, Your Honors...Adolf *did* save the life of his own son!"

Gasp! The prosecutors blanch. "We didn't know that! Of course all charges should be dismissed at once!" The allies then throw a big parade for Hitler down the avenues of Nuremberg.

This may sound silly, but isn't that the lesson taught by *Return of the Jedi*?

Along with the bizarre notion that getting angry at an evil will suddenly cause you to *switch* sides and join that evil....Say what?

Then it only gets worse.

How many of us have argued late at night over the philosophical conundrum— "Would you go back in time and kill Hitler *as a boy*, if given a chance?" It's a genuine moral puzzler, with many possible ethical answers. Still, most people, however they ultimately respond, would admit being at least *tempted* to say yes, if only to save millions of Hitler's victims.

Yet in *The Phantom Menace*, George Lucas asks us to gush with warm feelings toward a cute blond little boy...one who will later grow up to help murder the population of Earth many times over. Hey, while we're at it, why not bring out the Hitler family album, so we may croon over pictures of adorable little Adolf and marvel over his childhood exploits! He, too, was innocent till he turned to the "dark side," so by all means let us adore him.

To his credit, Lucas does not try to excuse this macabre joke by citing the lamest excuse of all, "It's only a movie." Rather, he sticks to his guns, holding up his saga as an agonized Greek tragedy worthy of *Oedipus*—an epic tale of a fallen hero, trapped by hubris and fate.

Alas, if that were true, wouldn't Star Wars by now have given us a better-than-caricature view of the dark side? Don't swallow it. The apotheosis of a mass murderer is exactly what it seems. And we should find it chilling.

Only then it gets worse. Much worse. For you see, there is another Lucasian character that makes the adoration of young Darth seem positively benign.

It's *Yoda*. One of the most horrid creatures ever to snarl at us from the silver screen.

VICIOUS LITTLE OVEN MITT

Remember the final scene in *Return of the Jedi*, when Luke gazes into a fire to see Obi-Wan, Yoda and Vader smiling in the flames? I briefly found myself hoping it was *Jedi Hell*, for the amount of pain those three unleashed on their galaxy, and for all the damned lies they told.

Okay, now Brin has gone completely around the bend. What, in all the galaxy, could he have against little Yoda?

Well, for starters, how about this simple challenge: *can you name a single scene in which Yoda is actually forthcoming, informative or generously helpful?*

This supposedly all-wise figure rejects young Anakin, because he senses "too much fear." (Despite the fact that we spent most of *The Phantom Menace* marveling over a nine-year-old's dauntless courage.)

He foresees danger, if the boy isn't trained properly...then refuses to train him.

When Master Mace wants to inform the Republic that dire conspiracies are afoot, Yoda insists on secrecy, which only worsens the calamity. Just as his lies to Luke almost ruin everything much later. Lies that he conveniently gets out of explaining by pulling the old "death-fade" trick. (Well, Luke was always kind of a dim bulb.)

Then there is all that smarmy lecturing—a withered old prune telling a virile young man that he shouldn't give in to the human yearning for "attachments." Forcing Anakin to fulfill those basic human needs in secret.

Um...all right. One can understand demanding that a young adept avoid undue distraction while focusing hard on his training. But to cut off all thought of loved ones, even when they are suffering? Where is the "wisdom" in that?

Especially when it came to the tragic situation of Anakin's mother. Tell me, which approach is more likely to help the boy focus? Leave Mom to endure slavery on far-off Tatooine? Or maybe dip into the treasury to buy her freedom and get her a nice little house on Naboo, in gratitude for the way Anakin saved Amidala and all her people? Would it be too much "attachment" to get a nice card, once a year, showing her happy in her garden? Call it insurance, to keep such a powerful apprentice from getting...well...angry.

Oh, but it gets worse. Later on, other Prosecution witnesses will discuss the charge that Star Wars is less than "elevated" in its attitudes toward women. Those writers focus (for example) on Princess Leia's decline from rambunctious, gun-toting senator and revolutionary bigwig to chained harem girl. Or upon the small—nay token—presence of females in the Jedi Order. But in fact, I do not consider these to be the most worrisome lapses in sexual subtext. After all, it is possibly legitimate for a space *fantasy* society to replicate the pattern that held in 99% of the *real* societies we know from the human past—in which most of the warriors were male. It's not politically correct—and I am proud of an America in which the skilled soldiery has largely turned away from that criterion—but Star Wars does, after all, promote nostalgia for feudalism. Therefore, it is only natural to expect some sexual distinction in roles.

No, what's far more troubling is another aspect of this issue of "attachments." In a few passing lecture-moments, we are told that Jedi are free to enjoy pleasures of the flesh, but that they must not become attached to—or committed to—other people over the long term. Um. Right. Did anyone else catch how this is, well, the bachelor seducer's perfect answer to the famous *apres* question: "will you call me later?" The perfect male cop-out? Getting to have your cake, eat it, but never having to pay for it?

Uh, sorry, babe. I can't commit. Or call. Master Yoda won't let me. But wasn't that fun?

Yeesh. This is "wisdom"? No wonder Young Skywalker gets married without permission!

All right. Point by individual point, this can be called nitpicking. But the *pattern* adds up, relentlessly, to a clear picture of Yoda that doesn't support all the superficial press he's given, as an archetype of right-living. Rather, if you look closer, he's an imperious little elf-guru, secretive and domineering, judgmental and unkind. Humorless and never, ever informative. Oh, one can see how this might fit somebody's cartoon image of an austere and demanding, quasi-oriental sage. Indeed, there are plenty of real and historical figures that Yoda may be modeled after. But must we take this lying down? Even J. R. R. Tolkien, in his later works, ripped the sweet/wise veil off of his elves, exposing them as selfish creatures who brought Middle-earth to the brink of ruin.

Which brings us to the point of ultimate betrayal, pictured in *Attack of the Clones*. One of the most horrific scenes I ever witnessed. Has anyone else noticed?

The Jedi Knights aren't an army. They are an elite corps of secret agents! The 007 James Bonds of the Old Republic. So why does

Yoda order all but one of them to charge—in the worst frontal assault since the Light Brigade—straight into an obvious death trap, where they will be surrounded and slaughtered by innumerable robots, monsters and flying aliens? Only his peer and equal—Master Mace—refuses to fall for this. Instead, Mace does his job as a secret agent, sneaking in the back way and *almost* capturing the villain, single-handedly. Had even *two or three* of the other Jedi Knights accompanied him as helpers, then all would have been well.

But that wasn't Yoda's plan, you see. Instead—how convenient— he takes delivery of a *new army* at just the same moment that he hurls the older one to its doom. A new army trained to be much more obedient than that rabble of psychic adepts and bickering individual agents. A new army that represents everything worrisome about civilizations and institutions. Sameness, rigidity and amoral, ruthless efficiency.

Oh, it's implied that Yoda merely grabs a clone army that *someone else* ordered. But why assume that incredible coincidence? Take the plainest evidence of all, the actual sequence of events. Isn't the simplest answer that *Yoda* was the one to secretly order the clone army? (There is no evidence to contradict it and the astute clone-makers certainly thought they were doing it for Yoda's Council.) Yes, the situation is ambiguous...but it smells of one of the worst betrayals in cinematic history.

Even if you balk at following me that far, remember how, in *The Phantom Menace*, Qui-Gon spoke of a need to "restore balance to the Force." This—like so much about George Lucas's new-agey religion—stays frustratingly unexplained. But it sure implies that old Yoda had an "unbalanced" agenda. One with its own dark side.

We'll get to that matter in just a second, but first, let me reiterate the challenge. *Is there any tangible reason to believe that anybody in his right mind ought to listen to that vile green demon-muppet?* Always secretive, mysterious, grouchy and unhelpful. Never actually achieving anything useful (except to annihilate his own knightly order). Is this an archetype of wisdom that we should hold higher than, say, Benjamin Franklin? Than George Washington, George Marshall, Albert Einstein, Martin Luther King and all the other hero-teacher-leaders of our democratic enlightenment? Or even the hapless Old Republic?

So, what do we make of the "eternal struggle between *two sides of the Force*? Other than the fact that it sounds a bit like Manicheanism, or the Zoroastrian mythos of light vs. darkness, forever equal and tearing the cosmos apart? (One wonders, why has the fundamentalist community gone after Harry Potter, when *this* old heresy is rearing its head, hmm?)

Does Qui-Gon's call for "balance" make any sense? Does this story-promise ever get resolved?

Oh, I have heard lots of this-that, about the differences between the dark side of the Force and the other side. (Force Light?) Sith lords want "progress" through ferocious Darwinian winnowing, kind of like you see in *Dune*. The light side tends to be overprotective, insisting on an eternal, static order. It sounds very Tolkienish, and that's no coincidence... though without Tolkien's cheerful willingness to reevaluate. In any event, notice how these supposed "opposites" have vastly more in common with each other than differences. For example, their shared, relentless devotion to elitist secrecy.

But notice, we are never offered a third choice. The choice of freedom. Of everybody knowing what's going on. A galaxy of openness and transparency, in which institutions and individuals, governments, companies and private citizens of all races get to innovate and compete fairly, thus avoiding *both* static sameness and the horror—slaughter of open warfare? Progress, without vicious winnowing.

Was this what Qui-Gon hoped for, in his yearning for balance? Is this what Darth/Anakin was supposedly preordained to deliver?

Well, I am going to surprise you now, and tell you what I really think.

He did!

EXCUSES FOR A DARK HENCHMAN

Look, I got entirely too much mail—after the *Salon* article—coming up with *rationalizations and excuses to let old Darth off the hook*. Here are just a few of them:

1. Darth kills the Emperor and saves more than his son. He saves the universe!

2. Vader's redemption is personal. It's about a son's forgiveness.
3. Vader isn't the leader, so it's unfair to call him "Hitler." At worst he's a Himmler.
4. Vader was mind-controlled. He was just following orders.
5. Yes, normal people can get really, really mad, and not suddenly "turn evil," reversing all their morals like a switch. But Anakin isn't normal! He's a demigod. That makes him more vulnerable than normal people.
6. Vader's actions were necessary in order to restore balance to the Force/universe/franchise...

... and so on...

I did not simply reject all of the ideas that people sent in. In fact, half of these points are interesting—and possibly valid at some level. (Care to guess which ones?) The others, I'm afraid, still strike me as rather lame, or even provably wrong. We'll deal with some of them later, in the testimony on "plot holes."

But the core point is that we shouldn't have to go trawling around for meaning like this! The biggest and most lavish sci-fi epic of all time should make sense by now.

Alas, you could fill intergalactic space with row after row of giant floating yellow words, and still, nothing would tie together. For example, the political rationale behind the "secessionists," or why the Republic fell apart.

Or how Darth was able to detect Leia's midichlorian-rich blood from a million miles away...but never sniffed a thing when he was interrogating her by hand, with truth serum. Likewise, he doesn't recognize his own hand-built droids, when he meets them again after so many years.

Or why he conveniently orders all the antiaircraft guns and fighters to stop shooting at Luke, so he can do it himself...and somehow keeps missing till the boy gets his shot.

Then there are all sorts of other coincidences. Like the way Vader conveniently persuades Tarkin to let Luke and Leia and the *Millennium Falcon* go...

...or, the way, twenty years earlier, Obi-Wan took the newborn Luke in order to conceal him from Vader, and chose as a hiding place, from all the worlds of the galaxy... *Vader's home planet and Vader's hometown.*

Or a myriad other hints and clues that really *ought* to have added up to something. If anyone had been at the tiller, paying attention.

Want to hear something pathetic? The most pathetic thing of all?

I actually care about this stuff.

I care about it because of all those high hopes, back in the same year that my own first novel came out. I care because I passionately believe that important stories ought to make sense. Even if they are dark tragedies. Even if I disagree with the lesson that's being taught. Because we learn from things that we can decipher. Even if and when we don't like the point being made. But an illogical mish-mash teaches nothing at all.

More the fool, I care so much that this ongoing Star Wars thing sometimes distracted me from some of my own stories. On occasion I would catch myself mulling it over while driving, or sitting in the tub. . . .

. . . until suddenly one day, it came to me.

A simple solution. A way that it all might have made sense.

THERE'S A SECRET PLAN, AFTER ALL

But I'm not going to tell you here.

Because my time's up. There are enough indictments on our plate, and the Defense is already on the wings, ready to weigh in, eager to tell us about the merits and glories of the Star Wars universe!

Also, there's another reason.

As a professional, I live in a world of critics and reviewers. I am used to being told what's wrong with work I've written, even novels that were tested past my special battery of fierce pre-readers, who generally catch most of the slipups before publication. (My aphorism: CITOKATE. *Criticism is the only known antidote to error.*) I am used to others telling me where I failed, or where my creations have problems. That's fine.

But what really prickles is when some upstart tells me *how* I oughta have fixed a problem. What I shoulda done, instead of what I did.

I don't hanker for that.

Furthermore, I don't have any right to do it to George Lucas. Not formally at least, in print. It just isn't right.

Because, having heaped on criticism, for page after page, I really need to add this: *the world would have been a much poorer place without Star Wars!*

Despite my grouchy grumblings about what could have been, the fact is that George Lucas delivered a mainline feed of fantastic imagery and almost-pure joy, straight through the eyes, ears and optic nerves of about a billion people. That's a lot more than *I* have ever reached. It merits respect. The genuine kind, directed toward somebody who has used his talents to make a difference, and had fun doing it, too.

Besides, hey, the man hired and subsidized maybe 10% of the greatest and most groundbreaking technical artists of our age, pushing forward dozens of wondrous new visualization technologies and opening doors for other creators in this wondrously free and open civilization.

Yes, I have complaints about plot and character and *deeper meaning*. But, as I said at the beginning, fortunately, most people just don't care about any of that! We, here, reading (and writing) this book, are among the few who do. Moreover, if we are all lucky, then the "messages" in Star Wars will never matter anywhere near as much as the pure and simple joy.

And yes, my kids cut in at one point, crystallizing this wisdom.

"Cut him some slack, Dad. The lightsabers are cool."

All right then, I'll hold back on my little plot gimmick—*the Darth Vader twist*—that (in my humble opinion) might make sense of so many unfortunate coincidences...fulfill Qui-Gon's dream...and even give the nasty oven mitt some payback, too. There are enough clues. Readers who like to play mental games can follow where they lead, using their own marvelous imaginations.[4]

---

[4] This isn't just a one-time distinction. It marks the main boundary between real, literate, humanistic science fiction—or speculative fiction—and most of the movie "sci-fi" you see nowadays.

The difference isn't really about complexity, childishness, scientific naïveté or haughty prose stylization. I like a good action scene as well as the next guy, and can forgive technical gaffes if the story is way cool! The films of Robert Zemeckis take joy in everything, from rock 'n' roll to some deep scientific paradox, feeding both the child and the adult within. Meanwhile, *noir* tales like *Gattaca* and *The 13th Floor* relish dark stylization while exploring real ideas. Good SF has range.

In the end, what matters is only this: *be willing to look with a complex eye, even upon simple legends.*

You are many. A child, a teen, a grown-up. Individualist and citizen. A worker and a player. Feel free to enjoy any entertainment in the spirit that it's offered...while another part keeps asking "what bill of goods am I being sold between the frames?"

It is a new millennium. There are choices. So be many. Keep looking forward, courageously, into a world of change.

And demand a universe that makes some sense.

THE COURTROOM

MATTHEW WOODRING STOVER: I object!

DROID JUDGE: What is the problem, Mr. Stover?

MATTHEW WOODRING STOVER: That was a lot more than opening comments. For one thing, it was more than 10,000 words. And for another, he essentially offered testimony on the first charge: the politics of Star Wars are anti-democratic and elitist.

DROID JUDGE: Well, that is a fair point. Mr. Brin?

DAVID BRIN: I'm happy to have my comments considered as expert witness testimony on this charge. I believe I've clearly established the anti-democratic and elitist nature of the Star Wars saga. I won't need any additional witnesses on this charge.

DROID JUDGE: Fine, we'll consider Mr. Brin's opening statement as also serving as expert testimony on the first charge.

MATTHEW WOODRING STOVER: Excuse me? That was expert testimony? Now, hold on—

DAVID BRIN: Your Honor, I am a recognized expert on the politics of Star Wars. I refer you to my infamous Salon.com article published June 15, 1999—

MATTHEW WOODRING STOVER: Recognized by who, the Imperial Sith Show-Trial Fake Certification Committee? Five Kowackian monkey-lizards on a six-day spice-binge? Hey, this reminds me of a joke—a kid, a Jedi and two droids walk into a bar in Mos Eisley—

DROID JUDGE: (*severely*) Mr. Stover, you are out of order. Mr. Brin's expert credentials have been accepted by this Court. Do you have a formal objection to offer?

MATTHEW WOODRING STOVER: Hmp. Well...if he's the only witness he can find on this charge, it'd be more appropriate to offer *sympathy*.

(Reaction in the courtroom)

DROID JUDGE: Order! There will be order! Mr. Stover, behave your-self!

MATTHEW WOODRING STOVER: Can I at least cross-examine? A question or two, Your Honor.

DROID JUDGE: You may proceed.

MATTHEW WOODRING STOVER: *(checking his notes)* Mr. Brin, in what verse of *The Iliad* does Achilles slay thousands with a wave of his hand? When I read it, I seem to recall that he actually only fights Trojan heroes (who are hardly disposable extras)—and that each of the Trojans slain by the Greek heroes (and vice versa) is provided by Homer with a capsule biography, specifically referring to details such as his childhood, his homeland and the family that will weep for him—

DROID JUDGE: Mr. Stover, the subject at hand is the politics of Star Wars.

MATTHEW WOODRING STOVER: Yes, Your Honor. Sorry—it's just that all his drivel about flattering the Power Structure doesn't make sense, when Agamemnon comes off as an indecisive blowhard and Menelaos as a cuckolded weakling, Odysseus reads as a conniving bully, and Achilles is a pouting ambiguously gay whiner who lets his "special friend" get killed borrowing his favorite outfit—

DROID JUDGE: Mr. Stover, you will confine yourself to—

MATTHEW WOODRING STOVER: Yes, sorry, Your Honor, it won't happen again. Very soon.

DROID JUDGE: Do you actually have any questions specifically relating to the politics of Star Wars?

MATTHEW WOODRING STOVER: In a backhanded way, Your Honor; since Mr. Brin's criticism of the politics of Star Wars comes by way of un-flattering comparisons with works and authors he considers to be politically more palatable, I suppose I would ask him if Jules Verne's most famous creation, Captain Nemo, is not precisely the kind of "superhero" he derides? If, in fact, the vast majority of the protagonists of Robert A. Heinlein's novels don't fall into that category? If H. G. Wells's most famous novel, *The War of the Worlds*, does not present the absolute failure of democratic society to respond to a threat, requiring a *deus ex machina* to save the human race? If Mr. Wells's other legendary novel, *The Time Machine*, could not be fairly described as unconscionably racist in a biology-as-destiny sense? If the countless German soldiers disposed of by Mr. Spielberg's heroes in the process of *Saving Private Ryan* are any more than "slaughtered victims...mere minions, after all. Extras, without families or hopes to worry about shattering. Spear-carriers"? If the same cannot be said for the numberless Klingons and Romulans and gods-know-what blasted to atoms by the *Enterprise*?

All these questions boil down to One Big Question: when you try hard enough, you can find elements to attack in just about *anything*, can't you?

As Mr. Brin is a hostile witness, a simple "Yes" or "No" will be sufficient. Please remind him that he is under oath.

DAVID BRIN: If it pleases the Court, may I begin my response by quoting from Homer's great epic poem, *The Iliad*, chapter XXI:

Forthwith the hero left his spear upon the bank, leaning it against a tamarisk bush, and plunged into the river like a god, armed with his sword only. Fell was his purpose as he hewed the Trojans down on every side. Their dying groans rose hideous as the sword smote them and the river ran red with blood...

. . . and when Achilles's arms grew weary with killing them, he drew twelve youths alive out of the water, to sacrifice in revenge for Patroclus. He drew them out like dazed fawns, bound their hands behind them.... Then he sprang into the river, thirsting for more blood.

All right, it wasn't just *one* wave of his hand.

Still, might I ask the Court, especially, to note the words "like a god"?

Moreover, let me make something clear: I never claimed that all Campbellian-style legends portray kings in ways that modern people find admirable! After all, despite recent moves back toward aristocratism, we are still rebels! It will take a *lot* of propaganda to make us turn away from our enlightenment revolution, to re-embrace the bad old ways.

Yes, it is easy to see the flaws of kingship in fellows like Agamemnon and Menelaos, though it can be a bit harder to notice in sweetened and sanitized figures like King Arthur, or Elrond, who had better press agents. Still, what's fundamental is that Homer and his ilk never let their common folk choose any other path. As in Star Wars, they must pick sides between demigods—usually the side that looks prettier. They never get to try a wholly different way.

Since Mr. Stover raised the subject of more recent literature, let's discuss Captain Nemo! Without a doubt, Jules Verne did tug at some of the same emotional strings as in classic tragedy. Nemo rails against the warmongering and oppressive "system" fighting it with great courage, ingenuity and success...till he is brought low by his own arrogance and pride. Hubris, again. But, in this case, at least Nemo's rant against entrenched power gets heard. And note, he may be a genius, but he remains nothing without a skilled crew that shares his dream. (Again, the naval metaphor, leaving us with the best character of the book, the *Nautilus*!) This is a complex, hybrid tragedy, but one with lots of modernist elements, more than enough to call Verne a fellow revolutionary!

Let me also leap to defend Steven Spielberg, who actually strove hard to personalize German soldiers in *Saving Private Ryan*, at least as much as an American G. I. might have had time to do. (Limited point of view.) Especially impressive was the personal fight between two alpha warriors, and the way the winning German granted a nearby coward the chance to opt out...only then, later, that coward gathered the courage to do his job. On a larger scale, can Mr. Stover truly not see this wonderful film as a true archetype of what I'm talking about? Myths that portray citizen soldiers standing up for their civilization, sometimes bickering, sometimes getting too angry, but nevertheless always returning to stand up?

It is not merely the fact that millions die that proves a tale to be anti-democratic. Millions are dying during *Deep Space Nine* and during *Schindler's List*! Yet, these dramas preach a very different lesson than kingly leadership or the authority of demigods. The crux is this: are people fighting and dying for elites, or for the accountable institutions, laws and general decency of a civilization that ought to be *theirs* to share and own? Government by, of and for the sapient?

The difference, in a truly modern tale, is that many of those "spear-carrier" millions get to do what they weren't allowed by Homer...and are allowed to do only by accident in Star Wars. They do what our *dads* did, when a Great Leader roused Nazi romantics to follow him, aiming to end our democracy forever.

They stand up.

Your Synthetic Honor, Learned Opposing Counsel, Ladies, Gentlemen and Otherwise of the Jury...

MATTHEW WOODRING STOVER

WITH A CERTAIN AMOUNT of folksy snapping of suspenders and straightening of bowtie, I suppose I have to get up and talk now, about what Learned Opposing Counsel has told you will be the Merits and Glories of Star Wars.

Well, I'm not gonna do it.

That's what I have witnesses for.

Besides, you're hip to the Merits and Glories already, or you wouldn't be reading this.

I'm here only to introduce myself and the subject, and to talk a little bit about the nature of the arguments you'll be reading. Along the way I'll clear up some minor points, and maybe highlight a few of the rhetorical games the Sith—sorry, the Prosecution—might be playing. Brevity being the soul of et cetera, I'll keep it short.

Short-ish.

Let's start right off with some straight truths.

First: I'm not exactly unbiased, and I'm sure as hell not going to pretend to be. In the interests of full disclosure, I'll tell you right up front that I have personally perpetrated *three* (that's three—count 'em) of those *poor substitutes for real science fiction that are driving real SF off the shelves*, including the novelization for *Revenge of the Sith*. Seeing as how one of the basic premises of this argument is a direct attack against my own work, I see no reason to take a high-minded tone. Since the Prosecution is clearly (and wisely) disinclined to accept a duel with lightsabers, I have reluctantly decided to settle for whipping them in print.

Second: as the author of the novelization of *Revenge of the Sith*, I occupy a privileged position in that I have had the pleasure of spending considerable time in a room with Mr. Lucas himself, discussing in detail certain elements of the Saga, including deeper implications of the destruction of the Jedi Order, the nature of the Force and any number of other things, some of which are still covered by the confidentiality clause in my contract. What this means is that I have access to a great deal of inside information, which I fully intend to use in the most ruthless manner possible without actually getting myself hauled off in binders by Lucasfilm Licensing stormtroopers.

Third: I openly admit that playing Defense gives me a number of advantages (for example, I got to read Learned Opposing Counsel's stuff before I had to write my own). The biggest one is that Our Side doesn't have to prove anything; it's the job of the Prosecution to make their case. All the Good Guys—excuse me, the Defense—have to do is demonstrate that the Prosecution, well, hasn't.

That they, in fact, can't. Ever.

That's my plan. That's the entire Defense Strategy.

Now, this will be an unusual trial for any number of reasons, not the least of which is that it's taking place in a virtual space halfway between these pages and your imagination. I want you to keep that in mind; it's important, and we'll be coming back to it.

Another way in which this will be an unusual trial is that you'll be seeing an inversion of the customary relationship between Prosecution and Defense. In an ideal world, at least, the task of the Prosecution is to set forth an unbiased, unvarnished exhibition of the facts of the case, and it is then the task of the Defense to argue and obfuscate and generally aggressively advocate for the innocence of the defendant.

That's exactly the opposite of what you'll be seeing here.

In the subsequent pages, you will see the Prosecution selectively ignore important elements of the Saga in order to support their pernicious misinterpretations; you will see them twist some facts and pretend others have no significance; and you will see them persistently insist that their interpretation is the only valid one.

It is this last which We of the Defense will be attacking directly.

Why?

Because we're the Good Guys, of course.

Well, okay: that's a biased statement. But it's *honestly* biased. I openly admit that you (or, most particularly, the Sith L—um, Learned Opposing Counsel and his evil minions, er, witnesses) might have a different interpretation.

Which might be equally valid.

Hang on to that idea, too.

Because what we'll be arguing here (with only a very few exceptions) will not be the *facts* of the case; those facts are on public display, in six films, dozens of cartoons, over a hundred novels and countless comic books. What will be argued here is the *interpretation* of those facts.

What the Prosecution will attempt, in fact, is to *control* your interpretation of the facts.

Why?

Not because they're the Bad Guys (well, not *just* because they're the Bad Guys), but because that control is necessary to their case. They have to make you agree with their nasty-minded misinterpretations— I would say *force* you, but I won't sink to cheap puns. Very often.

As soon as you start to think that other, alternate, innocent or even *virtuous* interpretations of the facts are available to you, their case falls to pieces. So their only option is to twist the facts—and when the facts cannot be twisted, there's only one avenue left.

Mind control.

It's an insidious game (in-Sidious, yes, I lied about the cheap puns)—for the need to control is the essence of the dark side—and it has already begun.

Let's just take a quick look at Learned Opposing Counsel's opening statement for evidence of careful editing of reality to suit a dark agenda....

For example, Opposing Counsel begins by insisting that Luke Sky-walker, in his very first action as a Jedi Knight, should have violated the most fundamental principles of the Jedi Order. Opposing Counsel will be satisfied only if Luke *threatens* Jabba the Hutt—*bullies* him into *submission*—rather than entering in peace, and offering even a crime lord a simple, straightforward opportunity to Do the Right Thing. Luke—entirely properly, consistent with his principles and those of the Jedi—offers violence only in response to violence. Opposing Counsel, on the other hand, apparently would prefer Luke to have fallen to the dark side by the very first sequence of Episode VI.

Not that I find this in any way suspicious, you understand.

While we're at it, let's swiftly dispose of Opposing Counsel's fetish for the Other Franchise as well. Is it really necessary for us to remind the Court that these "closer to average" minor character types in the Other Franchise are statistically far more likely to be disposable cannon fodder than "heroes themselves"? Does Opposing Counsel expect us to believe he is unaware of the etymology and meaning of the SFnal expression *redshirt*? Does Opposing Counsel expect the Court to forget that—high-minded rhetoric notwithstanding—again, statistically speaking, this so-called Prime Directive has proven to be an SFnal Wicker Man, honored most when it must be burned down in the name of some "greater good"?

Does Opposing Counsel expect the Court to ignore the plain fact that these Vessels of Civilization he so admires are, in fact, heavily armed *warships*? That for all its supposed role as a carrier of some theoretical democratic principle, the *Enterprise* is in fact an authoritarian state in miniature, a collective under the command of an absolute ruler—more often than not in a de facto condition of war.

This is the truth of the Ideal held before the Court by Opposing Counsel: lip service to principles more honored in the breach than in the observance, to create the illusion of democracy—which is actually supported by the suppression of individual rights, in an authoritarian regime justified by a semipermanent state of armed conflict.

Let me remind the Court that the ship Opposing Counsel fetishizes is "vastly bigger, more complex, a veritable city cruising through space"—a city-ship, one might be forgiven for adding, that carries enough firepower (by *no coincidence whatsoever*) to *vaporize* a *planet*.

This, Opposing Counsel freely admits, is his ideal.

Does this remind the Court of anyone in particular?

Not that I'm saying it should.

And the filmmaker he holds up as the egalitarian opposite to George Lucas? Whose *oeuvre* extols the power of the "barely above average"? (In passing, on the subject of *Saving Private Ryan*—I would sincerely love to watch Opposing Counsel explain to a roomful of Army freakin' *Rangers* where he gets the balls to claim they're only "barely above average" ... but that's just in passing, and we'll let it go.)

This filmmaker would be none other than a certain Steven *cough-IndianaJonescough* Spielberg, whose films are notable mostly for demonizing and dehumanizing the heroes' opponents, to make us all comfortable with cheering along as we watch them being eaten alive by, say, the Wrath of God.

As opposed to George Lucas, who has spent half of his life's work putting a human face on what had been previously regarded as the icon of ultimate evil—who spent an entire trilogy of films reminding us that the potential for destruction rests beneath even the noblest motives, and that we should always turn a suspicious eye upon anyone who preaches that They Know Best.

Even the Jedi Council.

Because sometimes they're just plain wrong. And sometimes they're *up to something. . . .*

What I find so astonishing, in fact, in Opposing Counsel's indictment is that he seems to believe that the Saga endorses rule by a secretive unelected elite—*and then spends much of his argument showing how the Saga itself explicitly rejects that very concept.*

Yes, Yoda is secretive, and often unhelpful. The Jedi themselves— SURPRISE!—aren't exactly good guys. Perhaps Opposing Counsel never noticed. Let me enlighten him, and the Court.

If you take a close look at the Jedi Order, you find that—in Mr. Lucas's own words—they're a cross between the Texas Rangers and the Mafia. They are a vast organization of superheroes—real superheroes, with superpowers right out of Marvel or DC Comics—who wield near-absolute power *in secret*, without accountability to anyone but themselves and the Office of the Supreme Chancellor. They are the Justice League with interplanetary Licenses to Kill.

And guess what?

The Chosen One is *chosen to destroy them.*

Does Opposing Counsel expect the Court to believe this is an *accident*?

Everything Opposing Counsel has to say about Yoda actually *undermines* his own *case*!

If Mr. Lucas were truly advocating rule by a benevolent despot, wouldn't Yoda have turned out to be always *right*? Wouldn't Luke's rebellion against him have become a *disaster*, from which Yoda would have had to rescue him, as a father rescues an errant child?

In fact, at every turn in the Saga, when a Figure of Authority speaks out and gives strict orders...they're *wrong.*

Except when that order is to *trust in the Force.*

In other words: trust the voice of the life within you. Trust yourself. Trust love. Trust faith.

Don't trust people who claim they know what's best for you.

The Opposing Counsel makes an eloquent argument on the virtues of questioning authority, calling its effects "inarguably spectacular, underlying most of the accomplishments of modern-enlightenment civilization."

What Opposing Counsel doesn't seem to understand is that George Lucas shares this belief in questioning authority, and that the entire Star Wars saga is a brilliant lesson in the virtues of questioning authority.

Lucas understands that once we start to question Authority, we might end up questioning all manner of authorities. We might start to wonder if they might have their own agenda, or simply be just plain wrong.

Like, for example, our own Emperor, er, president.

It's a terrible shame that our powerful myth of *suspicion of authority* made our Powerful Liberal Media Elite (another myth) ridicule our vice president's assertions about links between Saddam Hussein and al-Qaeda, and dismiss our national security adviser's stern warnings about mushroom clouds over Detroit. It's a terrible shame we were so distrustful of authority that nobody believed the president when he told us that sanctions and inspections weren't working to restrain Iraq's nuclear weapons program, and that Saddam Hussein was a clear and present danger to world peace in general, and the United States in particular.

If only we had *trusted* them, and let them lead us into that quick, cheap, simple war they were asking for; after all, Defense Secretary Rumsfeld assured the nation—before Congress, under oath—that the whole operation in Iraq would have taken only six weeks, would have been almost bloodless, and cost under ten billion dollars. If only we'd *believed* them, instead of being *suspicious of authority*.

We'd have been so much better off right now.

Having dealt with the major issue, let's take a moment here to clear up a thing or two. One of the Heroes of Real SF that Opposing Counsel cites, Robert A. Heinlein, had his alter ego Lazarus Long advise, in *Time Enough for Love*, that we should "Never ascribe to malice what can adequately be explained by..." —well, let me say *ignorance*. Mr. Heinlein's word is less charitable. In that spirit of charity, let us assume that Opposing Counsel is merely mistaken on the following points—as opposed to intentionally misleading or deceptive—and that he, and the Court, will be grateful for the corrections.

1) The ability to use the Force is not the result of a mutation. Midichlorians are the GFFA (Galaxy Far, Far Away) equivalent of mitochondria. Every living thing so far identified in the GFFA has them. This is what is called a metaphor—relating the Force to the essential energy of life in every cell—and anyone who tries to get technical about it is wasting his time.

That is to say, everyone can touch the Force, and the Force can touch everyone. Everyone is, in fact, *part* of the Force, as is everything ("It surrounds us, and binds us," remember?). What Qui-Gon speaks of, when he measures Anakin's "midichlorian count" is *Force potential*, that's all. Does he have more potential than other people? Yes. Why?

Because that's the way the world works. Like it or not.

Some people are gifted. Some people aren't.

Now, certain ideologues may be uncomfortable with this simple truth. No matter how much self-discipline I have, I will never be a composer the equal of Mozart, nor a basketball player the equal of Michael Jordan; I'll never be as handsome as George Clooney nor as brilliant as Stephen Hawking. Given the current state of cognitive science, it can even be argued that self-discipline is itself a talent, given to us in greater or lesser degrees. Neither Mozart nor Jordan, I might add, became great simply as a result of their great talent; they took great talent and developed it into great ability through years of training. Hawking had to train his intellect; even Clooney has to exert some discipline with diet and exercise to maintain his looks. It is *talent* that Qui-Gon measured, not actual ability, or power.

(Is it really necessary to point out that the Jedi possessing the "highest midichlorian count ever recorded" got his high-midichlorian-count butt smoked—literally, as it happens—by Obi-Wan Kenobi, whose own midichlorian count is never described as anything special?)

This, I need hardly point out, makes a fair hash of Opposing Counsel's preposterous "hereditary mutant elite" accusation.

2) Shmi Skywalker is not from Naboo, nor is she related to Palpatine or Padmé Amidala (except by marriage). She just isn't. Sorry. Nor is Palpatine related by blood to Padmé. Sorry again. It just ain't so. You might as well drop that Family Feud crap right now.

Yes, of course there are family elements to the Saga. But those aren't among them.

I could tell you how I know, but then I'd have to send stormtroopers after *your* family.

3) Neither Joseph Campbell nor Bill Moyers ever seriously claimed that the "Hero's Journey" or the "monomyth" is the "only human way to tell a story." Campbell's work is descriptive, not prescriptive, and to pretend that he is somehow responsible for what some unnamed and possibly entirely invented "romantics" have supposedly said is a shoddy con game.

Joseph Campbell's primary work, *The Masks of God*, is precisely about enumerating the *different* ways in which myth is used in human culture, and the differing implications of the various elements, the differing aspects of human psychology that he believed the specific elements seemed to represent, and—only in the final volume, *Creative*

Mythology—the ways in which mythic tropes continue to penetrate twentieth-century culture, and how they might be deliberately used by artists, and by others. Far from glamorizing feudal power structures or glorifying heroes, he was an acute observer and a voluminous synthesizer (which was all he actually claimed to be), as well as a very fine writer and, in worldview, something of a Hinayana Buddhist.

There are plenty of aspects in Campbell's work that are open to criticism (e.g., if I recall correctly, I found his extensive disquisition on the use of pig symbolism from *The Odyssey* through *Finnegan's Wake* to be a bit suspect), but the ones Opposing Counsel has chosen don't happen to be among them.

Aristotle, however, I will not waste words to defend. Aristotle is the most easily refutable philosopher in history; no other man has been so consistently wrong on so many points, with the possible exception of Samuel Johnson.

And, of course, Opposing Counsel.

4) One can hardly hold the Saga accountable for teaching that the "skilled and worthy warrior must cut off all attachments, etc." because this is explicitly defined in the Saga as the primary error of the Prequel-Era Jedi.

With apologies to Opposing Counsel, he simply missed the boat here. That's all there is to it. Not only is that "cutting off all attachment" business defined as exactly what drives Anakin Skywalker to become Darth Vader, but it's precisely the error that Yoda is determined to correct by allowing Luke and Leia to be raised by real families, rather than trained as Jedi from infancy by him and Obi-Wan: so that they will know a family's love, and be connected to the reality of society in ways that the Prequel-Era Jedi could never be.

Sorry.

In all fairness, though, Opposing Counsel should have known better. After all, one of the most skilled and effective warriors in the Original Trilogy is Han Solo—who becomes *more* effective as he allows himself to become more and more emotionally engaged with his companions.

How much more obvious does it have to be?

5) How good-looking a character is bears no actual relation to whether or not he's a Good Guy.

Three words: Jar Jar Binks.

Not to mention Boss Nass. Admiral Ackbar. Kit Fisto. Saesee Tiin. Eeth Koth. Plo Koon. Dex from the Diner. How much longer do I have to go on?

Not to mention that Vader himself is only nasty-looking *without* the armor. It's worth noting that on my Great Friggin' Gonzo *Revenge of the Sith* Tour, it was not uncommon for women from the crowd to request photographs not with me, but with whatever member of the 501st Stormtrooper Legion (wonderful fans doing volunteer work to help promote the book, and the Saga, along with raising money for various children's charities) happened to be wearing the Vader armor that day. It was also not uncommon for these women to burst into tears because they were *so in love with him*. . . . Hey, diff'rent strokes, it takes all kinds, whatever—but you see what I mean.

6) Jedi Hell? Excuse my bleeding ears?

Far from being the fairy-tale Manichaean silliness Opposing Counsel pretends to believe it should be, the redemption at the end of *Return of the Jedi* is not Vader's, but Luke's—and the Galaxy's. Luke has renounced violence in the name of love; it is this which turns the tide, and produces the final victory to save the Galaxy.

That's the true message of *Return of the Jedi*: renounce violence in the name of love. If Opposing Counsel finds this to be a pernicious theme, he should go argue with Jesus and Buddha, and leave Mr. Lucas out of it.

Anakin Skywalker—Darth Vader—fulfills a distinct mythic role in the Saga: the Scourge of God. When the world (society, whatever) has become so corrupt that only destruction can answer, it is the Scourge of God—customarily a tragic character (q.v. *The Tragedy of Hamlet, Prince of Denmark*)—who must carry out that destruction, and in the end be destroyed by his own violence. It's not good vs. evil or black vs. white; Anakin/Vader is in fact *wiping out* that old Manichaean duality that Opposing Counsel so wistfully pines for. Anakin's (and Vader's) destiny is to *bring balance to the Force*, remember? To do this, he destroys *both* the Jedi and the Sith—and, *necessarily*, himself—and leaves Luke with clean hands and a clear conscience, untainted by the corruption of the past, to be half of, ahem, A New Hope for a better future.

The other half?

His twin sister, just as gifted with Force potential, but not turning toward ascetic contemplation as a Jedi. She's turning instead toward full engagement with the world: marriage, and a family and eventual participation in the government of the New Republic (in later years as its Head of State, in fact. *Elected* Head of State, I might add, and without the need for a Supreme Court to steal the election for her, either).

Yeah, there's a nasty message there, all right.

Opposing Counsel's real complaint seems to be that we don't see Anakin Skywalker burning in Jedi Hell.

Ahem again.

Ain't no such animal as *Jedi Hell*. Sorry again.

Corellians (Han Solo's people) have a tradition of Hell—nine of 'em, if I recall correctly—but they're virtually alone in the GFFA in even having the notion of an afterlife at all. The "Force-spirit" phenomenon is not an afterlife as we use the term.

I guess the death penalty just doesn't satisfy some people.

That fellow Nietzsche—the one Opposing Counsel seems to dislike so much—had a saying that's worth keeping in mind here:

"Distrust men in whom the impulse to punish is overwhelming."

Wise words. Worth remembering in any number of situations, including this one. Because that's what's really going on here, isn't it? The overwhelming impulse to punish.

And who does *that* sound like?

The Prosecution—Opposing Counsel and witnesses alike—doesn't like Star Wars. The reasons may vary, but the reality remains. The Prosecution is here to beat on the Saga.

They'll take any excuse. If they can't find one, they'll make one up. Assuming that all the above errors are, ahem, *honest* mistakes, one can only come to the conclusion that Opposing Counsel's lust for conviction has overwhelmed both his critical insight and his ability to do basic research.

All the Defense will do, here, is try to point out where the Prosecution might be, ah, *accidentally* sliding over the foul lines of truth, as it were. Or where there are other, alternate explanations for what the Prosecution will insist is the Way Things Are. Because there are *always* alternate explanations, no matter what they try to tell you.

They will insist You Must Trust Them. They Know Best. Don't Question. Don't Think For Yourself. Believe What You're Told.

In the end, it comes down to a single word.

Obey.

Put in those terms, it all becomes familiar, doesn't it?

Oh, I would never assert that Opposing Counsel is himself a Sith Lord, and his witnesses Sith agents—not at all. Even if true, being Sith is hardly a crime. And they may be entirely innocent; would a Sith Lord reveal himself by publicly attacking Star Wars? Nor would I claim that this entire trial is a sham, a frame, a massive put-up job orchestrated to shake public confidence in the Saga, in order to cement the Sith grip upon our government....

Doesn't seem likely, does it?

The most logical explanation is that the Prosecution is quite sincere; I believe we can safely assume that they are merely helpless dupes.

Remember: treachery is the way of the Sith.

Our best hope of justice in these proceedings is to remind you what this Court actually is. To remind you that that you are the jury. That the only opinion which matters here is yours. That these arguments take place not merely on these pages, but in your head.

And in your heart.

And so I will give you the only direct order you will ever get from the Defense. Don't place your trust in *any of us.*

Trust in the Force, and only in the Force.

That is, trust the voice of the life within you. Think for yourself.

Trust love.

Trust faith.

May the Force be with this Court, and with us all.

THE COURTROOM

DROID JUDGE: Do you wish to comment or cross-examine, Mr. Prosecutor?

DAVID BRIN: A moment, Your Honor. To recover from the Defense Attorney's personal style, and being told that I hold beliefs opposite to those I clearly stated. For the record, I never declined a saber duel with Mr. Stover. I'm likely twice his age, yet my rusty skills from the Caltech fencing team should suffice. At a sci-fi con? Bring it on, smart mouth.

MATTHEW WOODRING STOVER: Cool! We can sell tickets! You have any idea how much fans'd pay to see *this*? Holy crap! And since being twice my age would have you pushing ninety, you seem remarkably, mm, *well-preserved*...not that I find that in any way *suspicious....*

DAVID BRIN: Well, I thought you were a whippersnapper, given your pushy style. Still. However old you are, you better stay off my lawn....And turn down that damn boom box! Dang kids. Where's my saber....

DROID JUDGE (*sighing*): Humans. The Court fines *both* of you five samoleads for immaturity. Now, do you have comments or questions about Mr. Stover's statement?

DAVID BRIN: Well...I expected the Defense to offer glowing praise for Star Wars. I'm sure my own chapter contains more positive statements about the series than Mr. Stover put in his!

MATTHEW WOODRING STOVER: A measure of your innate fairness and nobility of character, sir.

DAVID BRIN: Hm? Well. (*shuffles papers*) Still...let's see. I'll skim past specific sophistries. Like the way Mr. Stover ignores the importance of moral discussion, diplomacy and restraint in the Star Trek universe, where such issues get hashed over perhaps too much.

MATTHEW WOODRING STOVER: Maybe we can save that for a companion volume, eh?

DAVID BRIN: Gotcha. (*eyes glinting*) In fact, I'll concede a point or two. For example, someone else reading the worthy books of Joseph Campbell may find exceptions to my brief (and therefore superficial) summarization. Also, I'll stipulate that supporting characters in Star Wars may look silly, rather than pretty. Good point. And a minor one. Like others that I'll defer answering till our online discussion, when the jurors (readers and fans) may join in.

MATTHEW WOODRING STOVER: Sure. Let's also skip past minor points like I'm here as an advocate, not a witness, and I'm answering your questions as a courtesy. And for fun. Because I'm just friendly that way. I don't claim to be an expert on anything (not even martial arts, Del Rey Publicity's bio on me notwithstanding).

And while we're at it we can skip past the minor point that in your rush to defend Captain Nemo and Pvt. Ryan (neither of whom I was actually attacking, by the way, but merely enumerating as passing examples of how any work of art might be vulnerable to the Prosecution's style of attack), you never actually answered *my* question. Which, as a witness, you really should have, instead of making another speech (admittedly inspiring— hey, my dad, my mom and three of my uncles served in the Big One, too) about citizen soldiers....

I seem to recall somebody once said something about how "the wicked flee where no man pursueth." And if we read *wicked* as merely an overly judgmental code word for, say, *Sith. . .*?

DAVID BRIN: Code word....for *what?* (*pained expression*) I can see this is going to be a long trial. Okay. Let's focus on Mr. Stover's core point—that Darth Vader is the epic's scary but righteously necessary "Scourge of God" who must cleanse the universe of both nasty groups of force-users, allowing a fresh start.

Am I hearing right? For years, people have written to me defending of the core goodness of Yoda and—yes!—old Darth. Now, the Defense concedes that Yoda is a nasty, secretive, lying and loathsomely destructive little demon? This from an author, who repeatedly (if cryptically) claims inside knowledge—*ex cathedra*—from the ultimate source? It's a shock. Like when J. R. R. Tolkien called his elves selfish reactionaries! We're off guard.

Very agile, clever. Except...have we a right to be confused by the apotheosis scene, when Yoda, Anakin and Obi-Wan smile as pals, from Jedi Heaven? Over all the films, about an hour is devoted to Kung-fooey Yoda-isms. If we're meant to see through this smarmy little wise-guy, shouldn't there be at least thirty seconds devoted to someone—(Luke? Mace? Obi-Wan? A shoeshine boy?)—looking Yoda in the eye, and saying, nertz?

MATTHEW WOODRING STOVER: Did I say "righteously necessary"? Excuse me, I must have misspoken. Maybe we should check the transcript. I'm not a moralist; you will find no blue on my nose whatsoever. (A little brown, maybe, after I get back from Skywalker Ranch—but it usually washes right off.) Moralizing is *your* department; I think we can safely leave righteous condemnation entirely in the hands of the Prosecution. Thunder away, sir.

While we're checking the transcript, can you point out where, exactly, that the Defense conceded "Yoda is a nasty, secretive, lying and loathsomely destructive little demon"? Where, in your (apparently confused) moral universe, does being mistaken equate with being evil? Why, if simply being *wrong* were to be taken as the indicator of diabolical nature, that would make *you* . . .

Hey, wait...we could be *on* to something here....

And then you're back with the Jedi Heaven crap, the flipside of your earlier wishful reference to Jedi Hell. I guess you didn't hear me the first time. Let me say it again: the Force-ghost phenomenon is not an afterlife as we use the word, in the sense of a place of otherworldly reward or punishment. This is not *ex cathedra* inside knowledge (if it were, I couldn't share details—I'm still covered by the confidentiality clause in my contract with LucasFilm Licensing). Nor is it my opinion. Check your source. It's available to everyone, in the published screenplay of *Revenge of the Sith*, as well as the, ahem, Official Novelization....You insist upon the value of questioning premises; I concur, and urge you to question yours. Your use of the word "apotheosis" in this context appears, to the Defense, to be either a cheap con or an expression of your confusion.

As far as looking Yoda (and, for that matter, Obi-Wan) in the eye and saying, ahem, *nertz.* . . ? It appears to the Defense that this is exactly what Luke does. In your favorite Star Wars film. I guess you'd prefer that he be rude about it . . . but I hope you might recover from your disappointment.

DAVID BRIN: One of my favorite SW characters, Qui-Jon, represents everything worthy about the Jedi. He serves the Republic—and a trillion citizens—putting them before Yoda. Generous and honest, he wants a different Jedi path, one worth saving. Like the old Republic sure looks worth saving. (At worst, it is portrayed as a bit.)

Still, Mr. Stover's explication? The chosen one is ordained to help annihilate the Jedi order, every earnest apprentice and billions of bystanders, while paving the way for a despicable tyranny. All so that Luke and Leia can lead a cleansed Galaxy from the rubble, with a clear slate.

Um, what kind of political-moral-ethical lesson is that! "We must burn the village, in order to save it?" Might the people of Alderaan and Coruscant prefer to have a voice in this slate-clearing? Must Qui-Jon's sweeter version of Jedi-ness—and those trillions of citizens—suffer because of Yoda's "imbalance"?

Isn't all this "balance" talk just a rationalization for light-dark demigod archetypes to run amok?

MATTHEW WOODRING STOVER: Hey, everybody, watch this: I'm going to do Opposing Counsel the courtesy he refused to do me. Give him a straight answer to a loaded question.

No.

It's not "just a rationalization." It's the looming shadow of a tragedy. It's the GFFA equivalent of the Delphic oracle prophesying that Oedipus would kill his father and marry his mother.

The operative word here is *tragedy*.

Yes, bad things happen to innocent people. The flaws of folk of good will are struck by the hammer of Fate, and everyone suffers. That's what happens in tragedy.

That, apparently, is what pisses off the Prosecution. I suspect Opposing Counsel would similarly fail to find political-moral-ethical uplift in *Hamlet,* or *King Lear*—and we are all aware, I hope, of

Mr. Brin's intimate concern with Uplift. (See? I'll throw in shameless plugs for *your* stuff, too!)

Let's be clear: I am not placing *Star Wars* on a plane with Shakespeare and Sophocles, but the Prequel Trilogy *is* within their continuum. Part of their arc. Where it fits on that arc is a matter of opinion; that it belongs on that arc is not. Both by intention and by execution.

Must everyone suffer? Maybe not. Things could have turned out differently. If Yoda had been younger and more flexible. If Obi-Wan had been less tolerant of Anakin's flaws. If Anakin had been more honest with himself, and with others. If Qui-Gon Jinn (Opposing Counsel's *favorite character*) had been less arrogantly insistent—against all advice, all reason, and 25,000 years of tradition—that Anakin Skywalker *must* be taken from his mother and trained as a Jedi....

These characters are not paragons of perfection. They are flawed, and their mistakes have devastating consequences.

Everyone suffers.

That's how it went. That's how it goes. That's not interpretation; that's the historical record, as presented by the films.

"Political-moral-ethical lessons" are where you find them. The Defense, as I believe I have stated before, is not here to *dictate* interpretation; anyone looking for a dictator will have to search the *other* side of the aisle—

DROID JUDGE: Mr. Stover, please....

MATTHEW WOODRING STOVER: Hey, I already 'fessed up about the cheap puns, okay?

What do you want from me?

Mr. Brin closed his responses to me with a speech. Here's mine.

All I'm trying to say is that on matters of interpretation, my opinion is exactly that: opinion. So is Opposing Counsel's. I try to correct errors on matters of fact, but on matters of interpretation, everyone is...are you ready for this?

Free.

Even Opposing Counsel. I'm willing to grant that Opposing Counsel's interpretation is exactly as valid as that of any other Star Wars fan. No more—but also no less.

I have a great deal of respect for the personal take—the *individual* take—of every Star Wars fan of every age, species, make or model, and I would never dream of trying to tell them what they *should* think. Not even Opposing Counsel.

Nor would I dream of telling George Lucas what he *should have done* in the Saga. I deal with what *is*; "shoulds" and "oughts" and the rest of it can, I hope, be left to the bluenoses and the tubthumpers and all the rest of the red-in-the-face shouters.

Now, I'm willing to admit the possibility that I might be a little out of my depth here. Opposing Counsel is a legitimate Giant Brain out of Caltech, and—if I'm not mistaken—at least a one-time astrophysics professor in the UCal system, and here I am, having ended my formal education by struggling to complete a BFA in theatre from a Midwest liberal arts college. Yeah, it's true: I was an actor... so all of you can probably imagine the intellectual handicap I might be laboring under, here. Basically, I'm just a lucky Star Wars fan who's still holding down a night job as a bartender. (Yes, I do—and not for fun, either.) So maybe I missed something along the way, and I'm hoping somebody can explain it to me. In small words.

In all his talk of examining premises, and all the things that SF and fantasy and Literature in General Should Do For You, it seems to me that Opposing Counsel has been dragging around an unexamined premise of his own, a somewhat Puritan hand-me-down that needs to be dragged from the closet and shaken out in the sunlight every once in a while, because the mold that grows on it can choke art to death.

It's this notion that art has to be Good For You. That beauty is insufficient, and truth irrelevant, unless there's also some Crunchy Whole-Grain Goodness that's gonna Improve Your Psychic Bowel-Function along the way.

Opposing Counsel's view seems—from my admittedly only semi-educated perspective—to be a more limited case of this notion: that art should somehow serve as a comforting social glue. That it should shore up the values of our culture. Or—as he likes to put it—our civilization. That any work of art which does not do this—which presents any *other* way of living one's life, or which might even, all gods forbid, actually *criticize* one or more of Our Mutual Sacred Values—is...well, somehow *wrong*. Bad. Or, as the Soviets used to say, *decadent*.

Now, I'm not gonna claim he's wrong. There's an argument to be made there. I just think he oughta *make* it, instead of simply assuming everybody agrees with him.

Because I don't. And I'm pretty sure I'm not alone.

Hell, I'm not even gonna claim that he really *believes* that. I'm just saying that this is how it looks from over here, and I really think that he ought to come out and make it clear, one way or the other, so we know where we stand.

Does Opposing Counsel contend that the proper function of art is to be a cheerleader for the culture/civilization/state?

If so, fine. I'm willing to grant validity to his viewpoint. That's the crux of the Defense, after all: the freedom of alternate interpretations. That's what I'm here arguing for. Freedom of the individual to make up his, her or its own mind.

But if that's *not* his position, then I'd like to know—

Just what in the name of Thomas sufferin' *Paine* has he been up on his high horse about?

That's my speech. Let him wave the flag all he wants; I'll wave back with a Caravaggio.

DAVID BRIN: Your Honor, since the Defense Attorney keeps talking about my motives (I don't recall ever doing that to him) I need to interject a quick response. I am being portrayed as a judgmental, sourpuss schoolmarm who insists that everybody eat their broccoli and that every plot twist in a story should be analyzed to death. And then pursued and hectored in the afterlife! This is ad hominem argumentation of the worst order...attacking the man, in order to distract from what he says.

DROID JUDGE: Point taken. But keep it under half a page.

DAVID BRIN: Thanks. In fact, I can relish art at many levels, from nutritious to pure brain candy. I was happy to enjoy the original move (*A New Hope*) in the spirit of innocent fun that it was offered. And it is THAT film that ever since inspired kids and adults to wave flashlights and breadsticks at each other, going *zvhooooom!* (I admit, I do it too! What cool archetypes.) Heck, going even further, I love genuinely goofy, good-natured mindless romps like *The Fifth Element*. I don't schoolmarm them.

But that's the point! Count up the number of *hours*, overall, that are spent in the Star Wars movies *lecturing at us!* About focus and purpose and concentration and attachments and the failures of democracy and Manichean mystical forces and prophecy and *balance* (note how Mr. Stover evaded answering that one) and elites justifying secrecy and lies. As relentless plot bummers mounted, so did the preachiness. What can one conclude?

Either George Lucas was inviting us to *converse* with him about heady matters—in which case this book and trial are simply taking him up on his kind offer—or else we in the Prosecution team have a perfect right to point at Mr. Lucas doing *the very thing Mr. Stover accuses me of!* Taking things way too seriously. Ruining fun with endless prattling lecturey, smarmy, contradictory preachifying that has turned a cool sci-fi romp into a thundering, ponderous pile of Tauntaun....

DROID JUDGE: All right, Mr. Prosecutor. I think you have vented enough, in reply to any ad hominem remarks by the Defense. Do you have a final cross-examination question for the witness?

DAVID BRIN: Just one? I'm tempted to ask Mr. Stover what he means by arm-waving vaguely at Star Wars and calling it "Truth." Huh? Or why political issues from 2006 belong in a book about a timeless moral saga. But this wrangle is frustrating enough for the reader. So let's pose a more direct challenge.

If the core lesson of Star Wars is about rejecting both the vile Sith and the evil Jedi, why is it that nobody out there seems to have noticed?

In the United Kingdom, for example, the fastest-growing religion that people write on census forms is "Jedi"! Yes, a few brash cynics are taunting Yoda on the Web sites. But are you saying George Lucas meant for millions to despise what Yoda has done? And that he succeeded?

We could test it, in a room full of (unwarned) Star Wars fans. If I give a dollar to Mr. Stover for every one who says, "Of course Yoda does evil!" ... will Mr. Stover give me a dollar for every one who calls Yoda "wise and good"?

DROID JUDGE: A challenge, then. Mr. Stover may choose to answer here, or else to take up Mr. Brin's dare online.

MATTHEW WOODRING STOVER: I'll do better than that. If Mr. Brin can point to the spot in the transcript where I contended that "the core lesson of Star Wars is about rejecting both the vile Sith and the evil Jedi" I'll get down on my knees right here in court and kiss his stanky—

DROID JUDGE: Mr Stover! I am programmed to keep this PG!

MATTHEW WOODRING STOVER: Sorry; I'm from Chicago. This is the point, Your Synthetic Honor: Mr. Brin has not-so-gracefully skated back to his earlier con game of trying to conflate being arrogant and mistaken with being evil. I hope I never said Yoda was Eeeevil, nor did I mean to characterize the Jedi as such; perhaps we should once again check the transcript.

I do my best not to use the E-word, except when it's flung around by Opposing Counsel. As I said before, I'm not a moralist; even pointing out that Mr. Brin appears to have Sith tendencies is not a *moral* judgment, it's merely an observation—one I've been reconsidering, in fact, after finding out he likes Qui-Gon so much; I like Qui-Gon, too (though now that I think about it, it *was* Qui-Gon who essentially infiltrated Darth Vader into the Jedi Order. . . !).

Hmm . . . no *wonder* he's Brin's favorite. . . .

Anyway, even if I *had* used the E-word in reference to Yoda, the Jedi, Mr Brin or anyone at all, that would be an expression of interpretation—my opinion—which would deserve no greater weight than the opinion of anyone else. Including Opposing Counsel. I do not claim to be an authority on such matters, nor do I receive supernatural advice on the subject.

I do find it curious, however—and I wonder if some few members of the jury might share my surprise—that Mr. Brin, who spent so much of his Opening Statement explaining to all you Star Wars fans out there that Yoda is nothing more than, in his words, "a vicious little oven mitt," now hopes to make some quick cash by betting that the vast majority of you will *think he's wrong*. . . .

I mean, jeez. Talk about having your weed and smoking it too. . . . How high do you have to be to not see though *that* one?

Is it just me, or does this sound like the Prosecution is conceding defeat?

I avoid stating the "core lessons" of any work of art, for two reasons. The first is that I don't believe the function of art is to teach me a lesson—

DAVID BRIN: Not even when a work of art spends every other minute preaching—

MATTHEW WOODRING STOVER: —the second is that such pursuits always result in gross oversimplification. As I advise young writers (advice I once received from a writer older and far wiser than myself): "If you can state your theme in a sentence, don't write a story. Rent a billboard."

That being said, however, I will offer to the Court my own personal interpretation of what I see as central meanings of the two trilogies.

Original Trilogy: *Salvation* (not in the Biblical sense, so don't even start) *comes through friendship and love, not violence.*

Prequel Trilogy: *Things fall apart, the center cannot hold...Nothing gold can stay—To hold anything beyond its time brings suffering.*

However, as I said above: beyond being gross oversimplifications (an astonishing concept, when applied to Star Wars!) those interpretations represent only what the works in question mean to me. What they mean to you, sir, is clearly different. What they mean to someone else will likely be different from either of our interpretations. Which is okay with me. It saddens me that this doesn't seem to be okay with you.

Now let me satisfy those temptations of yours, Mr. Brin. You don't even have to ask. (Won't be the first time I've played at being a bit devilish—goes with the red hair, y'know.)

(And anyone who's "frustrated" by our "wrangling" is absolutely free to skip ahead to the witness testimony, as they have been since before either one of us started yapping. Hell, I'd be surprised if we haven't lost a few already. Doesn't matter: we'll catch 'em when they read the book again...or maybe the third time...or we'll pick up some in the library. Or the bookstore café.. . .

YOU! Yeah, YOU! Don't just sit there sipping that latte! BUY this book, you cheap bastard—!

—Everyone who actually shelled out cash or credit—their own or somebody else's, we're not picky—please ignore the preceding private-service announcement—)

Anyway.. . .

First: I wasn't "arm-waving in the direction of Star Wars and calling it Truth." I apologize for the confusion. I was arm-waving in the direction of Truth, and attempting to remind the Court that stories—all kinds of stories, from *The Iliad* to *Saving Private Ryan* to, yes, Star Wars—carry different truths than those kinds which can be settled by a jury, figured on a calculator or spotted by a telescope, and that stories using mythic elements tap resonances deeper than surface appearance. Forgive me for the apparently unwarranted assumption that—as a storyteller of justly legendary skill himself—Opposing Counsel might have understood what I was talking about. Perhaps we can take *that* up in the online discussion group, as a more fruitful line of inquiry than whether *Star Wars* fans think Yoda might be Eeeevil. . . ?

Though one might be forgiven for wondering, if Opposing Counsel has no fear that Star Wars might convey Truth of some description, precisely why he's gotten so exercised about the whole thing.. . .

Second: the political issues in question were from long before 2006, my friend; they've just been bleeding over ever since. And they belong here precisely *because* the Saga is, in your word, timeless.

Here's another story: To promote the *Revenge of the Sith* novel, Del Rey Books sent me on a brutally exhausting author tour—twenty-three cities in twenty-seven days, if memory serves, with multiple appearances in most of those cities—and at *every appearance except one*, I was asked some variant of the following question:

"Did George Lucas intend the way the Republic falls and Palpatine becomes Emperor to be a direct critique of the Bush Administration?"

In many of those appearances, the question was not framed in such polite terms—it was more of an accusation. By the time the film actually came out, I could not talk about the book *at all* without fielding that question; I spent an entire half hour on a live national radio call-in show out of Dallas trying to explain that I'm *not telepathic, goddammit, so how the hell should I know what George Lucas intended?*

The one event where I didn't get the question? The first one. Due to release restrictions, nobody there had read the book yet.

Not relevant? Thousands of Star Wars fans (not to mention film and book critics and right-wing talk-show hosts all over the country) would disagree.

Now, I'm no fan of President Bush, and this is no secret. However (unlike Opposing Counsel), I don't pretend to know Mr. Lucas's personal politics; it seems to me that if Mr. Lucas is the feudal reactionary that the Prosecution paints him, he'd be an *admirer* of an hereditary aristocrat, ruling our nation with openly stated imperial ambition. . . .

So the answer I gave—the only honest answer I *could* give—is that to the best of my limited knowledge, Mr Lucas sketched the outline of the fall of the Republic and the rise of the Empire back in the seventies, when the Bush Dynasty was merely a blip on the future political radar, and that he took his inspiration from Rome, not from the United States. But when you create a story using a mythic toolbox, you can touch on truths you do not intend; if the Star Wars Empire reminds people too much of ours, it's not a comment on Mr. Lucas's politics, it's a comment on America's.

Again, this was only my opinion. Was and is. Take it for whatever it is, or isn't, worth.

Here again, I will admit to being possibly under-educated and over-opinionated. I'm not here as an expert on politics, either terrestrial or those of Star Wars (again unlike Opposing Counsel). But it sure looks to me like the Prequel Trilogy, on one level, could be read as a cautionary parable on the dangers of giving people— even good people—too much power with too little accountability, on the vulnerability of democracy to demagoguery (especially in wartime, and in the absence of a free, critical and aggressive press), and on how events can transform even the actions of folk of good will into terrible destruction, when arrogance and too much faith in the Unseen blind these folk to the pitfalls in their paths.

This is an interpretation which the jury is free to decide may, or may not, be relevant to our situation in 2006.

Which brings us back to arm-waving and Truth and all that murky metaphoric stuff, and if you keep poking the buttons on any loaded metaphor, eventually it's gonna go off and blow up in your face. Which is another way of saying that there's no need to go staggering out the airlock under the weight of all this, but still—

Yes, Star Wars is about more than lightsabers and spaceships.

Which, I might add, is also Opposing Counsel's opinion. Or we wouldn't be here.

DROID JUDGE: Now let's hear from the next witness for the Defense.

MATTHEW WOODRING STOVER: I call science fiction writer Keith R. A. DeCandido.

CHARGE 1

The Politics of Star Wars
Are Anti-Democratic and Elitist

The Madness of King George

WITNESS FOR THE DEFENSE:
Keith R. A. DeCandido

S O MATTHEW WOODRING STOVER said to me, "Keith," he said, "BenBella's doing a Smart Pop book called *Star Wars on Trial*. I'm one of the editors. How'd you like to contribute?"

Having already contributed to four previous Smart Pop books, BenBella probably figured it was an easy sell. What the good folks at BenBella don't know, of course, is that I have been using Smart Pop to finagle a way to get paid for preexisting rants. I was carrying on about how "The Train Job" sucked as an intro to *Firefly* and how the last line in *King Kong* was bull and how cool Kitty Pryde is for ages before I wrote about those topics for Smart Pop books, and I can rate actors the way I did for the various Superman folks in my sleep. Ben-Bella never cottoned to the fact that this wasn't work, this was fun—and also didn't require anything like effort on my part.

Having half a dozen rants on Star Wars[1] waiting to go, I said, "Sure, no problem."

"You'll be a witness for the Defense," Matt continued.

---

[1] For the purposes of clarity, Star Wars refers below to the saga as a whole. The individual films are referred to by their chapter titles. Yes, this means I'm referring to the film released in 1977 as *A New Hope*, which makes my teeth hurt, for much the same reason that seeing the 1981 Harrison Ford picture being called *Indiana Jones and the Raiders of the Lost Ark* does likewise, but it works better this way. Damn you, George Lucas, damn you to hell.

"Uh, okay." All of a sudden this sounded like work, thus belying my entire Smart Pop credo.

"You'll be taking on David Brin. He'll be arguing that the politics of Star Wars are elitist and anti-democratic. You probably have seen his *Salon* article."

As a matter of fact I had. When the article first went live in 1999, I would never have considered defending Star Wars on this topic. But the world has changed a bit since then, more's the pity. So I said yes to Matt, and here's why. . . .

In 2005, *Revenge of the Sith*, the much-anticipated third film of the Star Wars prequel trilogy, was released to enormous fanfare. I, personally, was dreading this movie, as I knew how it ended: the good guys lose, the bad guys win, and the cute kid from *The Phantom Menace* and the whiny brat from *Attack of the Clones* turns into the nastiest villain of twentieth-century popular culture.

And what do we see?

Chancellor Palpatine is given more executive powers in order to fuel the war effort, and dissenters are painted as unpatriotic. Attempts to change the status quo are refuted or beaten down. Anakin, a crony of Palpatine, is given an important position on the Jedi Council for which he is woefully unqualified. And when Palpatine is made Emperor, he declares that his ascension will ensure that all who live in the Republic-cum-Empire will live in security.

Any of this sounding familiar?

(Okay, to be fair, Michael Brown's disastrous handling of Hurricane Katrina as unqualified head of FEMA and Harriet Miers's nomination to the Supreme Court despite having nothing like the necessary judicial experience both postdate *Revenge of the Sith*'s release, but the parallels with Anakin's appointment to the Jedi Council still struck me while watching the film on DVD in late 2005.)

When Senator John Kerry took on President George W. Bush during the 2004 presidential election, he used logic and truth and experience to try to defeat him; when Mace Windu took on Chancellor Palpatine, he used the same tools (along with the purple lightsaber of badassness). President Bush's refutation was that the people of the United States were safer with him as president than they would be with Senator Kerry. Palpatine's words upon assuming the title of

Emperor were of keeping the people safe and secure. Both President Bush and Emperor Palpatine used the same buzzword: security.

In their face-to-face confrontations, President Bush looked far worse than Senator Kerry; he squirmed, looked uncomfortable, was snappish. In their face-to-face confrontation, Chancellor Palpatine also looked far worse, as Windu turned his power against him and made him look like a raisin. In the end, Anakin Skywalker chose to send Windu to a fiery end while plummeting from a great height; the American people did the same thing, metaphorically speaking, to Senator Kerry. Neither the people of the Republic nor those of the U.S. deemed the disfigurement of their leader to be enough to get rid of him.

George Lucas, fuzzy-brained liberal that he is (that's not an insult; you won't find a liberal more fuzzy-brained than me), can't have done this by accident. The parallels between the chancellor and the president are just too obvious. Padmé Amidala puts the final exclamation point on the whole thing when Palpatine is granted supreme power and she says sadly (and, I might add, with far more convincing emotion than she ever shows in her scenes with Anakin): "So this is how liberty dies—with thunderous applause."

The parallels don't end there. I think that *Revenge of the Sith* in particular was hugely influenced by the direction the country has taken since the fall of 2001 (*Attack of the Clones* was already mostly in the can by that point).

In the classic Salon.com article on Star Wars—an article that was written in June 1999—David Brin imagined that Episode III would be "a real bummer of a movie: Coruscant and a zillion other planets are gonna have to fry as the emperor takes over, since that would only happen over the dead bodies of every decent citizen with any spirit."[2]

Those words sound almost charmingly naïve now.

Something that is often overlooked is that President Bush's approval ratings were in the dumper on the tenth of September 2001. Wracked by corporate scandal and an economy that was taking a serious nose-

---

[2] Brin, David. "What's wrong (and right) with 'The Phantom Menace.'" Salon, June 15, 1999. http://www.salon.com/ent/movies/feature/1999/06/15/brin_side/index.html.

dive, not to mention lingering questions over the legitimacy of the 2000 election, the president was not having a good time of it.

Then two planes flew into the World Trade Center, another crashed in Pennsylvania, and a fourth hit the Pentagon.

Suddenly, President Bush's approval ratings skyrocketed. The U.S. was at war, America was under siege, and we had to hunker down and support our country or we were the same kind of un-American bastards who fly planes into buildings. The PATRIOT Act, a magnificent trampling of the Constitution in the name of security, was passed. Revoltingly, torture became a legitimate tool of a democracy's military, and the Geneva Convention was described by a U.S. government official as "quaint." Everything from traveling to foreign countries to simply entering an office building became considerably more complicated in the name of security.

Meanwhile, the findings of the commission that examined the 2000 election were brushed under the rug, the corporate scandals that hit Enron and WorldCom were forgotten, the still-plummeting economy was tossed aside in favor of a wartime mentality that the country couldn't actually support. Plenty of "decent citizens" of the United States stayed silent, and those who spoke up were shouted down, even as the president gathered more power and tossed aside so much executive oversight and judicial accountability. Those who supported President Bush were lionized and/or reelected and/or given positions far out of their range of qualification; those who didn't were cast aside.

Throughout all of this, we were reminded of the need to maintain our security, so that the attacks of September 11 wouldn't happen again.

On the face of it, everything went wrong. Dissenters were painted as unpatriotic. Anybody who dared question the Bush Administration was accused of playing into the hands of the terrorists—even when it told an outright lie and said that Saddam Hussein was connected to the terrorists. Invading Iraq became our number-one priority—after being told on September 20, 2001 during the public statement that kicked off the war on terror that capturing Osama bin Laden was our number-one priority, one that, over four years later, has yet to be accomplished.

Any of this sounding familiar?

I don't think there can be any doubt that Palpatine is supposed to be evil. Throughout all six movies, Palpatine is the antagonistic force—the puppeteer behind Darth Vader in *A New Hope* and *The Empire Strikes Back*, brought out from behind the curtain in *Return of the Jedi*, and the master manipulator of every single event that occurs in the prequel trilogy. I don't believe that at any point Lucas is saying that Palpatine *should* be in charge.

And this, as much as anything, is why Star Wars is far from elitist and far from condemning the masses. It's the elitists who are portrayed negatively, and the ordinary folks who save the day, and I think that choice is *quite* deliberate.

In Star Wars, the power does indeed belong to the elite. In *The Phantom Menace*—which establishes that those who wield the Force best are those born with a large number of midichlorians, rather than the more egalitarian all-you-need-is-discipline approach presented by *A New Hope*—that notion is glorified. In his defense of the elitist argument in the opening statement to this volume, Brin specifically says that the lessons of Star Wars are:

- Elites have an inherent right to arbitrary rule; common citizens needn't be consulted. They may only choose which born-to-rule elite to follow.
- Any amount of sin can be forgiven if you repent...and if you are important enough.
- "Good" elites should act on their subjective whims, without evidence, argument or accountability. Secrecy and lies are always a good option. They never need to be explained.

Except, I don't think Star Wars preaches this at all. Yes, Palpatine and the Jedi Council each set themselves up as the final authority—the former over the Republic, eventually coming to rule it, the latter of what is good and noble. Yet, both of them ultimately fail.

(The Emperor also is guilty of a major screwup with Luke in *Return of the Jedi*: if he'd just kept his mouth shut, Luke probably would've given in. Seriously, watch the scenes on Death Star II again. Every time Luke is in danger of giving in to his anger and fury, Palpatine says, "Yeeeeeees, give in to the dark side," at which point Luke shakes his head and backs off. If the Emperor had just *kept his damn mouth shut....*)

What other leaders do we get? Well, there's Yoda. The Jedi Master's rejection of Anakin in *The Phantom Menace* is at least partly responsible for the kid's slide into Vaderdom, he's utterly clueless regarding Palpatine's machinations in the entire prequel trilogy, and he lies to Luke about his parentage, which leads to an almost fatal distraction during *The Empire Strikes Back*. But then, Yoda was never meant to be the hero. At best, he was always a plot device.

But let's look at some of the other leaders besides Yoda and Palpatine—more to the point, the ones who actually accomplish good and noble things—and see if the elitist model really holds up:

Padmé Amidala. Despite her title of "queen," she was, in fact, an elected official. Most of her effectiveness was banished to the deleted scenes section of the *Revenge of the Sith* DVD, where it was revealed that she was among the senators trying to put a lid on Palpatine's power grabs.

Bail Organa. He was instrumental in getting Yoda and Obi-Wan, as well as Amidala's children, to safety. He was the one who raised Leia, and obviously did it right, given her history. He's also an elected official.

Princess Leia Organa. She was one of the driving forces of the Rebellion, which was why she was such a valuable captive to Vader in *A New Hope*.

Mon Mothma. She was in charge of the Rebellion in *Return of the Jedi*. Those same *Revenge of the Sith* deleted scenes reveal that she was a senator and also part of the cabal that resisted Palpatine.

Han Solo and Chewbacca. Without them, the Death Star doesn't blow up the first time. If not for the timely arrival of the *Millennium Falcon*, the rebels would've had their heads handed to them in *A New Hope*. And in *Return of the Jedi*, it was Chewbacca, aided by the Ewoks, who got the force shield down on Endor.

The Ewoks. They're a cooperative bunch, in the literal sense, in that they work together as a group, don't seem to have much of a hierarchy, and wind up taking down lots and lots of Empire troops, not to mention helping Chewie bring down the Death Star's force shield.

Lando Calrissian. He was the one flying the *Falcon* in *Return of the Jedi* when it blew up the Death Star the second time.

Tellingly, aside from Leia, none of these people are imbued with the Force, and neither the princess nor the viewers are aware that Leia is chock full of midichlorians until the very end of *Return of the Jedi*.

I think Lucas did this completely on purpose. The ultimate message of Star Wars is *not* that the elites deserve to be in power and that the light side of the Force is the ultimate arbiter of what is good and noble, because all the important stuff is accomplished by folks not burdened with the Force—or, in the case of Leia, living in ignorance of her Force-itude.

Ultimately, light side, dark side, it doesn't matter: power corrupts. Yoda, Mace Windu, Obi-Wan Kenobi and the other Jedi are so arrogantly sure of themselves that they completely miss Palpatine's subterfuge. The entirety of Jedi Knighthood is made out to be a bunch of bumbling idiots in the prequel trilogy. Later, Yoda and Obi-Wan lie to Luke about his parentage and withhold knowledge about his sibling. Yoda insists that Luke is not ready in *The Empire Strikes Back*, yet Luke ignores him, goes off, and actually acquits himself just fine. Obi-Wan is also pretty free with his mind-controlling powers in *A New Hope*, which is entertaining until you actually think about it for a few seconds and realize that they're arguably the actions of a sociopath.

Palpatine isn't much of an improvement, as he plows through hench-Jedi for no compellingly good reason. There was no need for Palpatine to send Darth Maul after Amidala and her escorts in *The Phantom Menace*, because the whole point of the exercise was for Palpatine to heroically save the Republic, and he needed Amidala safe for that. In *Revenge of the Sith*, he lets Anakin kill Count Dooku/Darth Tyranus, sacrificing a hench-Jedi of many years' standing who was kind enough to manufacture a war for him, all in the hopes that it might turn this whiny twerp into a better hench-Jedi. Wouldn't it have been better to have all three Darths, Vader, Maul *and* Tyranus, to help with the whole rule-the-galaxy thing? Plus, of course, there's his dopey handling of Luke in *Return of the Jedi*, referenced above. (I'm told that the rationale behind these moves is well explained by the novels, which doesn't surprise me, as it is often left to the tie-in novels to fill in the back alleys and side roads of the franchise.)

And Luke himself is affected by the Force. His treatment of Jabba's people in *Return of the Jedi* is pretty scary, and his clothes grow progressively darker as the films go on—not the most subtle bit of symbolism, but that doesn't make it illegitimate. Throughout, Luke is repeatedly tempted to go hog-wild with his Jedi powers and barely holds back.

In the end, though, despite the large numbers of people saying, "May the Force be with you," after 1977, the Force isn't what saves the day. Whenever the good guys score any kind of real victory— the two Death Star destructions—it's due primarily to the actions of the regular folks. When the Jedi Knights are slaughtered, it's only through the efforts of another normal person—Bail Organa—that the last four Jedi are kept alive. Yoda and Obi-Wan take no responsibility for actually raising Luke and Leia, leaving that to the non-Force folks as well. Instead they hide, Yoda on Dagobah, Obi-Wan on Tatooine, waiting for someone else to come along and do the job they utterly failed at.

That, actually, is telling. For twenty years, the last two adult Jedi just sat around doing nothing. The Rebellion was instead started by regular ol' folks who were mad as hell and wouldn't take it anymore. Yoda held his own against Dooku and Palpatine; Obi-Wan defeated Darth Maul and all but killed Anakin Skywalker—wouldn't that kind of power have been a little useful to the Rebellion? Talk about shirking your responsibility. . . .

One of the biggest problems with *The Phantom Menace* was that it made it clear that the prequel trilogy was going to be the science fictional equivalent of doing three movies about Joseph Stalin's youth and casting him as the tragic hero/victim. Indeed, that fear was realized in far too many ways, and also served to emasculate a character who had been one of the coolest villains ever. (Hearing Hayden Christensen's whiny dialogue coming from James Earl Jones's voice at the end of *Revenge of the Sith* was quite possibly the most depressing moment of modern cinema.)

But what the prequel trilogy made clear was that the Force was not the be-all and end-all, and it reinforced what underlies the other three films, in particular in the ending of *Return of the Jedi*—that people must make their own destiny, and not let those born to power oppress them. If people fail to do that, you get Palpatine, granted supreme authority over the Republic to tumultuous applause—an authority he gained due to the incompetence of the *other* people with power, the Jedi Knights.

Far from promoting an elitist agenda, George Lucas has shown us that the elitists, the ones who are born to power—like, say, sons of presidents who feel that family connections entitle them to power over anyone actually competent to hold elected office—are the ones who lead us to ruin.

Keith R. A. DeCandido has written for practically every media universe *except* for Star Wars. Look for the following fiction of his in 2006: the World of Warcraft novel *Cycle of Hatred*; the Buffy the Vampire Slayer novel *Blackout*; the Starcraft: Ghost novel *Nova*; and short stories in the anthologies *Furry Fantastic*, *Hear Them Roar*, *Age of War: A Classic BattleTech Anthology*, and *44 Clowns: 11 Stories of the 4 Clowns of the Apocalypse*. His other Smart Pop ramblings have appeared in *Finding Serenity*, *The Unauthorized X-Men*, *The Man From Krypton* and *King Kong Is Back!* His official Web site is at DeCandido.net. He is both a registered Democrat and a proud liberal. Nyah!

THE COURTROOM

DROID JUDGE: Mr. Brin, your witness.

DAVID BRIN: First, while use of the terms "Queen" and "Princess" are obviously meant to evoke a fantasy feeling, and might otherwise be overlooked, isn't the notion of Amidala's "election" accepted just a bit too blithely? In Earth's history, royalty were sometimes "elected," but in nearly all of those cases—for example the Holy Roman Empire—the "voters" were a narrow elite of fellow aristocrats. Otherwise, how to explain the election of a mere teenager to lead a whole planet? A teenager already (obviously) used to putting on airs, with an aloof demeanor? (A narrow planetary aristocracy? That would include Senator Palpatine. The implication that they are cousins is never made explicit, though it is intriguing. By implication, would not Amidala likely also have midichlorians?)

In any event, doesn't the plot itself disprove your assertion of Nabooian democracy? The Trade Federation hunts Amidala down in order to get her to sign away her planet's rights. Her signature alone—even when coerced—can overrule all other planetary institutions! A bizarre situation. But there it is. Can this be democracy?

The crux: democracy is about replacing arbitrary personal rule with accountable institutions. But institutions do not function in this universe. Ever. Would you care to explain how this can be interpreted as anything but elitism?

KEITH R. A. DECANDIDO: One can be an elected official and still have broad powers, as the second presidents to carry the names of Roosevelt and Bush can attest. And given that Star Wars planets seem to be the equivalent of states in the U.S., I don't see this as all that big a deal, necessarily.

Also, that isn't what a democracy is about, either. The word simply means that the people run the government, either directly or through elected representatives. Checks and balances are a particularly American part of the process.

In any case, it comes down to the fact that Lucas went to the trouble of saying she was elected. The title of "Queen" carries with it the connotation of being appointed, whether by fiat, heredity or conquest, to the role of monarch. Lucas wouldn't have bothered pointing out that she was elected unless he wanted to give the government the connotation of democracy of some kind. I think it's best to apply Occam's Razor here—the simplest explanation for why Lucas made the queen an elected official is because he wanted to give the impression that she got her position from the will of the people. If he didn't, there was no point in even mentioning it.

(Side note: the only reason we have the whole "Princess" and "Queen" stuff isn't because he's trying to use fantasy tropes, but rather the plot of *A New Hope* was heavily inspired by the Akira Kurosawa film *The Hidden Fortress*, and that film had a princess, too.)

DAVID BRIN: As for Princess Leia, she is anything but a normal person. She is a midichlorian mutant, like her brother, is she not?

KEITH R. A. DECANDIDO: Yeah, but we didn't know that, and neither did the character, until the chronological end of the story line. While Leia has the Force, the fact that she has it doesn't affect her actions as one of the heads of the Rebellion. While the novels that pick up where *Return of the Jedi* left off were free to deal with that, it's an irrelevancy to the films themselves. She didn't know she was a "midichlorian mutant," and didn't use the concomitant abilities.

A difference that makes no difference is no difference. Leia may as well have been "normal" for all that it affected what she did.

DAVID BRIN: Anyway, I am forced to ask again, if this were the point of the series, would not some character, at some point, have said even a *sentence* to guide the audience to notice? So that more than 1% of viewers would get and grasp this important point? Together, Yoda and Palpatine get almost an hour of screen time to yammer against open civilization. Sure, they both fail. But should not somebody get a minute to say something like—

"Oh yeah? Well, up yours, you two masters. We're free men and women and...furry things! We're small and weak as individuals, but our institutions will be strong. You can't force us to do nut-hin'...."

KEITH R. A. DECANDIDO: Actions speak louder than words. Lots of people speechify in the Star Wars films, and they all come to a bad end. The biggest heroes are the ones who shut up, ante up and kick in. Heck, two of the biggest heroes (Chewbacca and R2-D2) don't get a line of intelligible dialogue between 'em!

CHARGE 2

While Claiming Mythic
Significance, Star Wars Portrays
No Admirable Religious
or Ethical Beliefs

May the Midichlorians Be with You

WITNESS FOR THE PROSECUTION:
John C. Wright

L ADIES AND GENTLEMEN of the jury, do not be deceived. We are all fans of Star Wars, some of us more so than is healthy or wise. Some of us flatter these films by imagining that they have some deep metaphysical, ethical or spiritual meaning. But this is merely flattery.

I cannot truly discuss the ethics and religion in Star Wars, because, honestly, there is nothing to discuss.

A religion has many elements, but a real religion makes some attempt to account for the great mysteries of the universe. A real religion addresses metaphysics, spiritual powers, martyrdom, ethics, fate, salvation, miracles, and life after death.

Star Wars does not address these issues, and does not try to.

Remember what Star Wars is.

In the midst of the murmuring sloughs of the 1970s, *Star Wars* shook the movie world like a trumpet blast: a triumph of sheer youthful energy and imagination at a time when all other movies were wallowing in themes of despair. The moment those letters began to scroll up the screen, everyone in the audience knew what kind of film it was meant to be: a serial, a chapter-play, a Buck Rogers film, a Flash Gordon epic, a tribute and a culmination to all those forgotten matinees of yesteryear when the wonder and grandeur of outer space could be purchased for a nickel. As a Flash Gordon epic, *Star Wars* is perfect, and outshines it predecessors and its many imitators.

Observe what *Stars Wars* is not.

I cannot call it a great film, unless I use the term in the same way I talk about a great wad of cotton candy or a great fireworks display. I have been awed some Fourths of July with the sheer noise and light and color of the pyrotechnics, but I've never seen the secrets of life and death, or good and evil, or any great statements of philosophy written in the rocket's red glare.

Great books of literature wrestle with the deep questions of religion and ethics. Adventure stories written for boys depict sword fights on burning decks beneath the hurling moons of Barsoom, exploding planets and beautiful alien princesses. If you are going into a Flash Gordon serial seeking help for a moral quandary, you will not get your nickel's worth. There is not a nickel's worth of religion or ethics in *Star Wars*.

The religion of the Force is not a religion: it is an atmosphere, a spooky hint of mystic powers and hidden forces meant to lend an air of exotic supernaturalism to the proceedings. The Force is there for the sword fights. The Force is meant to explain why a kendo fencer can perform amazing leaps, parry laser bolts or make a single a one-in-a-million bull's-eye shot into a ray-shielded thermal exhaust port with a proton torpedo and blow up a space station the size of a small moon. An atmosphere is not a religion.

As far as ethics, *Star Wars* is a Boy's Adventure Tale: a combination of *Treasure Island* and *Under the Moons of Mars*, *Robin Hood* and *Zorro*, and *Sea Hawks* and *Three Musketeers*. When the lovable rogue Han Solo belies his solitary name by returning to aid our hero in the fight, we see the sum of the ethical posture of the tale, such as it is: "All for one and one for all." It is the Code of Bravery. Only the comedy relief sidekick is allowed to express any cowardice; and that in words only, not in any serious action.

Star Wars rises head and shoulders above other Boy's Adventure Tales by adding one additional moral theme: forgiveness breeds repentance. Although it is clumsily handled, there is some moral depth to the conceit: Luke's forgiveness saves his father's soul. It is worth noting that this is not an act called for by the Code of the Jedi. The Jedi Code, as depicted in the movies, consists of one slogan: Hate, Fear and Aggression are the Dark Side. This one slogan is both clumsily handled and morally shallow. It is worth noting that passive serenity is the only thing explicitly called for by the Code of the Jedi, and that none of the Jedi act this way, nor could they, not if we wanted to watch them in an adventure story.

That is about all we have by way of ethics. I intend to show in my testimony that every last detail of the religion and ethics in Star Wars is driven by the needs of the plot, or the need to establish atmosphere.

METAPHYSICS: THE MYSTICAL FORCE
IS THE MYSTICAL FORCE

Let us review what little is known about the metaphysical theory, such as it is, of the Force.

We first get the hint that we are in a mystical milieu rather than a scientific universe when Uncle Owen dismisses Ben Kenobi as "that crazy old wizard." The line is there for atmosphere. The Force is wizardry.

Ben Kenobi is next revealed to be Obi-Wan Kenobi, the last of the Jedi Knights, an order of swordsmen with mystic powers. More atmosphere. This time, the atmosphere is distinctly oriental. Kung fu films delight in portraying martial artists who gain superhuman abilities through rigorous study and meditation. The Force sounds charmingly exotic.

The Jedi are sword fighters, of course. The sword is the preferred weapon of the Galactic Empire in every tale from *Flash Gordon* to *Children of Dune*.

Obi-Wan urges Luke to study the Force, as his father did before him. From this we learn that the Force can be studied: mastery of it is a matter of training, not of credo. You do not train by reading the Holy Scripture in Greek; you train by doing one-handed handstands while levitating crates on the Swamp Planet.

Study of the Force it is not for learning how to be stoic in the face of adversity, as is the study of philosophy, or for discovering moral truth, as is the study of ethics, or for the salvation or enlightenment of the soul, as is the study of religion. It is for doing super-ninja-leaps with Way Cool psychokinetic powers.

We are introduced to the other remaining practitioner of "that ancient religion": a figure of Gothic menace and sinister aspect, complete with black cloak, Nazi helmet and Doctor Doom-style skull mask, known as Darth Vader!

A more perfect movie villain there has never been: He cannot step through the flaming airlock of a captured spaceship without hisses and boos spontaneously erupting from the Saturday Matinee audience. He sounds like the Lion King's father selling telephones and can strangle nay-saying imperial bureaucrats with his ominous mind-powers. Way Cool.

Note that there is no doctrinal difference between Obi-Wan and Darth. It is not as if one is a Protestant and the other a Catholic, one Shi'a and the other Sunni. We find out that Darth serves "the dark side" of the Force, and uses his mystic powers for Evil rather than Niceness.

This is to serve the needs of the plot. The idea of "the dark side" is thrown in merely to allow Darth and Obi-Wan both to be mystically powered samurai-knights on opposite sides of the conflict. If the Force were a god like Odin or Zeus, the audience would be puzzled why the Sky Father is supporting both sides of the conflict. Therefore, the Force itself has to be neutral, an inactive and nondemanding sort of god, but with a "dark side" so that the bad guys can make amazing leaps, read minds and strangle people by psychokinesis.

In one short scene, we get the explicit description, such as it is, from Obi-Wan: the Force is an energy aura created by all living things. Life creates it. It sustains all life and "binds the galaxy together"—a phrase that sounds Way Cool and means exactly nothing.

Then does it control our actions? In part, but the Jedi can also command the Force to do amazing leaps and parry laser bolts. Your eyes can deceive you: don't trust them! Reach out with your feelings. Hokey religions and archaic weapons do actually turn out to be a match for a good blaster at your side; and in my experience, there is no such thing as coincidence.

I think that just about covers it.

In terms of atmosphere, the idea that there are no coincidences and that a Jedi relies on his feelings rather than his eyesight is there to buttress and foreshadow the scene where Luke turns off his targeting computer, relies on instinct and makes a final desperate shot with a proton torpedo to blow up the Death Star.

Obi-Wan does not say a single word more about the Force than what is minimally necessary for that one-in-a-million shot to seem mystically inevitable rather than a matter of dumb luck.

SPIRITUALISM: NOW THAT I'M ENLIGHTENED, CAN I BOOT PEOPLE TO THE HEAD?

What one can and cannot do with the spiritual powers of the Force is also determined by plot considerations.

In *Star Wars* we see Obi-Wan use the Force to talk his way past a patrol of stormtroopers. We learn that "the Force can have a powerful effect on the weak-minded." Way Cool. What's it mean?

It means nothing. Like all wizards in every Boy's Adventure Tale since the world was made, the wizard-helper has to have enough mystical power to be able to help the hero in tight scrapes, but not so much as to be able to overwhelm the plot, solve the major problem or render the hero redundant. If Obi-Wan had been able to paralyze masses of stormtroopers with hypnosis, there would have been no gunfights with blaster-weapons. The audience wants to see gunfights, ergo, no mass-hypnosis.

When the planet Alderaan is blasted to smithereens by the Death Star, Obi-Wan reacts like Mr. Spock sensing the USS *Intrepid* being eaten by a giant space-amoeba: his psychic powers tell him something Big and Dreadful has happened. Cue the Big and Dreadful John Williams music.

This is foreshadowing. This is not a prophetic vision like the Apocalypse of St. John. This is not even a riddling utterance of the Oracle at Delphi foreseeing that a great empire will fall if Croesus attacks Persia. It is not even a plot-driving visitation, like the appearance to a horrified Hamlet of the ghost of his tormented father crying foul murder. The power here is not a prophetic power.

It is a comic book superpower. Obi-Wan is worried because his spider-senses are tingling.

Now, of course, it is Way Cool when Obi-Wan can sense things other men cannot sense, or know things lesser mortals do not know. On the other hand, it is also Way Cool when The Shadow can cloud men's minds with a mysterious power he learned in far-off Tibet.

The prophetic vision of Luke seeing his friends tortured on the Cloud Planet is a plot point to get him to break off his training and go save his friends. Will they die? Well, always in motion the future is, so the future-vision thing can't really tell us one way or the other, because prognostication is inevitable only in a Greek tragedy.

In Boy's Adventure stories, the power of prophecy is like seeing the Bat-Signal. You see a mysterious vision that tells you there is a villain in Gotham and you need to go fight him. Way Cool.

MARTYRDOM: LIVE FAST, DIE YOUNG, AND DON'T LEAVE ANY SORT OF CORPSE AT ALL BEHIND

When Obi-Wan dies, he dies because he puts his weapon up. Obi-Wan promises Darth that "If you strike me down, I shall become more powerful than you can possibly imagine." This is setup for the scene when, at the moment all hope is lost, and Luke in his space-ship is making one final desperate run against the target, he hears the ghost of Obi-Wan telling him to Trust the Force.

The formula demands the wizard-helper has to die so the child-hero can grow up. It is atmospherically more noble for Obi-Wan to die because he chooses without fear the hour of his death, than, for example, to be shot to bloody bits by sneering stormtroopers while clawing at the hatch of the *Millennium Falcon* begging to be let in before it takes off.

And his death is eerie: there is no body. There is no reason why there is no body. It is just eerie for the sake of eerie. But neither is there any point to this death. There is no announced theory of martyrdom in this background. There is no evidence that Obi-Ghost is more powerful than Darth can possibly imagine. Freed from the limitations of his physical body, Obi-Ghost does not crush the Death Star like an egg with his mind-powers.

And there is no real reason why Obi-Wan has to be a ghost in order to whisper advice to Luke. He could have used a radio. There is no hint of any belief of life after death anywhere else in the story, but having a friendly ghost show up to help you in your hour of need is kind of spooky, and really rather satisfying.

In any case, it is Way Cool.

ETHICS: THE CODE OF THE JEDI

There are two ways to look at the ethics in Star Wars: First, what do the characters do? Second, what do the Jedi say people should do?

The first is clearly driven by script considerations. Yoda and Obi-Wan are forced by the script into the awkward posture of having to explain, in *Return of the Jedi*, why no one told Luke in the first movie who his dad was. Well, Obi-Wan did not know who his dad was back in the first movie because George Lucas had not made it up yet. Originally, Anakin Skywalker was a Jedi Knight, a cunning warrior and ace pilot killed by the evil Lord Vader during the Clone Wars. Later, in *The Empire Strikes Back*, this past is amended to the much more interesting (and, yes, even brilliant) idea of making Vader Luke's father.

The absurdity of crabby Uncle Owen complaining about his nephew having too much of his brother in him, when that brother is Darth Vader, Dark Lord of the Sith, is not mentioned. As if Sam Gamgee the gardener turned out to be the cousin of Sauron the Great. ("Aye, Mister Frodo, my cousin has a big place down south aways, but he don't tend it right like I do my potater patch here.")

But now Luke demands why Obi-Wan didn't tell him, and Obi-Wan has to make some lame excuse. But it is not Obi-Wan's fault. The Way Cool idea that Luke is Vader's long lost son has to be retrofitted in.

Likewise for the scene when Princess Leia gives Luke a big smooch to make Han Solo jealous. At that time, she was not Luke's sister. The idea that she is, invented later, is backfilled, and so the scene which was originally quite cute is now in hindsight quite gross. Maybe George Lucas will computer-edit future rereleases of the film, so that in this scene Leia has the features of Hayden Christensen, and Han will shoot first before she kisses him.

Let us turn to the ethics of the Jedi Code itself.

What is the Code? In *The Empire Strikes Back*, we find out from the frog Muppet Yoda that the dark side involves anger, fear and aggression. It is faster and easier than the light side, but not necessarily stronger. Don't give in to the dark side or forever will it dominate your destiny!

Still later, in *The Phantom Menace*, the Muppet has been replaced by CGI, and clarifies the previous words of wisdom: Fear leads to anger. Anger leads to hate. Hate leads to suffering. This is all about as profound as saying "Mean people aren't nice."

But the idea that Fear is the only source of Evil is the only theme that runs consistently through all six films.

Even in *The Phantom Menace*, the only reason to doubt that Anakin should be trained is that Yoda "senses much fear in him." Had Yoda sensed that Anakin, as an ex-slave, was burning with the desire to strangle Watto, his ex-owner, with psychokinesis, and kill the Jedi who left his beloved mother in her slave-chains back on the Sand Planet, this would have made sense. (It would also have been interesting.)

But Yoda's misgivings, such as they are, have no support. At no point does young Anakin display even a twinge of fear, neither in a Ben-Hur-style chariot race, nor while blowing up enemy starships during combat. Since I know boys his age afraid of the school bus or the neighbor's dog, kids who have never been under fire in combat, to me it looks like the fatherless moppet suffers from psychotic recklessness, not cowardice.

Had the little boy destroyed the space station while laughing with maniac bloodlust, shooting paratroopers as they bailed out, and picking off women and children in the mess hall, shooting down hospital ships and giggling while the nurses died of lingering radiation burns, this might have served as a hint of the dark side to come, and Yoda could have said he sensed "much aggression" in him. (It would have also been interesting.)

But no. The plot requires that Yoda express misgivings to foreshadow the corruption and downfall of Anakin, and since fear and hate are the emotions condemned in the sketchy Star Wars ethic as bad, fear must be attributed to little Anakin whether this makes sense or not.

If taken literally, the injunction to avoid bad emotion means that even One Moment of Bad Emotion would instantly turn one into a loyal minion of the dark side. This idea is so dumb that no one could take it seriously.

But this is exactly the idea that governs the Star Wars universe. Both the attempted seduction of Luke and the successful seduction of Anakin to the dark side are provoked and culminated by One Moment of Bad Emotion.

The Evil Emperor in *Return of the Jedi* attempts to seduce Luke to the dark side by the simple expedient of taunting him. If Luke kills the Emperor in anger, you see, forever will the dark side dominate his destiny! The fact that countless millions of worlds would be free of tyranny is held to be of no account here. And killing the Emperor in a moment of icy calmness does not, for some reason, seem to be in the cards either.

If the Dark Emperor makes Luke angry, even for one instant, then Luke is immediately transmogrified to the cause of Badness, and presumably loyal to the Emperor. Ergo Luke gets taunted by the Emperor. The Emperor is trying to piss him off. To show he is not getting angry, Luke tosses his weapon aside, so that he can be martyred, or something, I guess. The whole moral calculation involved here is not clear to me.

Darth Vader is overcome by pity for his long-lost son (or maybe noticing that the withered old freak was trying to get the boy to kill him) and so Vader throws the head of the Imperial government down one of those electrified pits Evil Villains leave lying open in their throne rooms, and into an atomic reactor. For some reason, the Emperor cannot save himself with his immense psychokinetic superpowers from a fall down a shaft. The Emperor is short-circuited or something. He dies.

So the moral of the story is that good guys cannot be morally allowed to kill bad guys, except when they can. Or something.

But in any case, a single moment of anger will turn you Evil.

FATE: NO MAN ESCAPES HIS SCRIPT

Now, before you scoff, I must point out that in *Revenge of the Sith*, this is exactly what happens to young Anakin Skywalker. He wants to save his wife, whom he foresees will die in childbirth. The Evil Emperor has promised him the secret of resurrection of the dead (way cool!) if Anakin joins the dark side.

Now, I know what you are thinking, ladies and gentlemen of the jury. Earlier I argued that the prophetic powers in Star Wars serve no plot function, and are merely present for atmosphere. But that is not the case here. Here, the vision of Padmé's death in childbirth is indeed like seeing the ghost of Hamlet's father, and is not here just for atmosphere, or foreshadowing, or like the Bat-Signal: it is the main driver of the plot. The vision produces fear that drives Anakin to his treason and his downfall.

It is a plot point: in fact, it is the main plot point. It honestly has something of the stature of a real Greek tragedy. The husband's attempts to save his wife are what drive him into madness and evil, which in turn drives the wife into such deep despair that she gives up the will to live and perishes on the operating table. His own acts, trying to avoid fate, bring his fate upon him.

The moral of this Greek pessimism is that knowing the future does no one any good: it merely tells you enough to torture you with fear and doubt until your own actions bring about what you most fear. Perfect passivity and renunciation of all emotional attachment would be the only logical response to such a universe. That would and should be the moral point of the story, if the story were making a moral point.

It does appear that the story is making exactly this moral point and no other. When a tormented Anakin comes seeking comfort for his fearful vision, Yoda intones in his Frank Oz voice: "Death is a natural part of life. Rejoice for those around you who transform into the Force. Mourn them do not. Miss them do not. Attachment leads to jealously. The shadow of greed, that is." This is the only explicit statement of the Jedi Code in all six movies: it is a doctrine of utter renunciation and detachment.

But appearances can be deceptive, ladies and gentlemen of the jury. Your eyes can deceive you. Don't trust them. What looks like a moral point is actually one more case of something being forced by plot requirements.

The plot requirements in the Anakin trilogy are different from those in the Luke trilogy. In the second trilogy, Anakin himself is the wizard-helper and the main character. Like in all wizard stories, he has to delve too deep into the Things Man Was Not Meant To Know and get corrupted. In this case, his curiosity drives him to delve into the ultimate mystery of all human life: he wants to know how to turn aside Fate and Death, and save his wife from the Grim Reaper.

The plot requires this ambition to be portrayed as immoral or irreligious. So a moral code utterly irrelevant to anything else in the plot or story has to be cobbled together to condemn this ambition.

Given the thin and sketchy nature of the Force religion, a sort of pseudo-Buddhism is about the best any writer could come up with to say why meddling with What Is Meant To Be is a bad idea. You should not discover the "unnatural" means used by the Sith to resurrect the dead because, well, being in love is too much like jealousy. Attachment to loved ones is bad, for some reason.

Of course, if the Sith had come up with a safe method of performing a cesarean section, the moral conundrum would lack the overtones of Anakin's making a devil's bargain to save his wife's life.

So letting the beautiful young bride die in childbirth has to be "a natural part of life" and wanting one's wife to live (what ordinary people call "love, honor and cherish") has to be cast in terms of "the shadow of greed."

But perfect passivity is not really the moral point of the tale. The point, the one hammered home, is that Fear and Anger and Aggression are Bad Things, and One Moment of Bad Emotion Turns You Bad.

So all this prophecy and angst and Anakin whining is all set up for when, in a moment of fear and anger, Anakin strikes down Mace Windu from behind. (We all know this scene is pure fantasy, because really, Samuel L. Jackson can kick anyone's ass. I mean, really.)

Now, the motives of young Anakin have been established: he is half-maddened by understandable human fears for his lovely young bride, and fears she will die. He is a good guy, a little whiny, but basically good... until the One Moment of Fear and Anger. It is like getting bit by the Werewolf. One bite and you're a monster. No shades of gray here: suddenly Anakin is as evil as evil can be.

Not five minutes after his Moment of Bad Emotion, Anakin, now crazy as a bedbug and his eyes glowing wolf-yellow, is slaughtering groups of waif-eyed little muffins known, for some dumb reason, in the Star Wars universe, as younglings. Then Anakin is strangling and beating his young bride, the one for whom he sacrificed his honor and his position, and blithering on about ruling the universe.

Why does he kill children, strangle his wife and want suddenly to rule the universe? Why does this have nothing, nothing at all, nothing at all in the slightest way remotely related, to do with his previously established motivation? Because he had One Moment of Bad Emotion, and gave in to the dark side, and forever it will dominate his destiny.

Let us pause for a deep breath to appreciate the utter and perfect shallowness of this idea. Out of all the moral complexity of human experience, of bad guys doing good things for bad reasons, good guys doing bad things for good reasons, guys who are partly bad and partly good doing things for mixed reasons, we get this: mad is bad. One second of anger or fear, and you are lost, that's it, game over.

SALVATION: THE BLOOD OF VENGEANCE WASHES SIN AWAY

Ah, but a second murder can utterly wipe out the stain of sin! In *Return of the Jedi*, Darth Vader is redeemed (I guess) when he suffers One Moment of Love and Pity for his son, who is being tortured to death before his eyes by electrical shocks. He kills the Emperor, and then for some reason not clear to me, croaks out a last word of affection and immediately dies. Later shows up as a blue ghost to show that the Force forgave him. Or something.

Because killing the Emperor in a moment of anger is okay, if it is an act of treason, but not if it is an act of war.

I am sure all the murdered folk on the planet Alderaan are happy in the afterlife now because Darth and his boy had a moment of father-son bonding. Or something.

MIRACLES: THOSE PESKY MIDICHLORIANS

I should mention that the only other fact known about the Force is that that midichlorian bodies in the bloodstream give an accurate and scientific reading on how powerful a student will be.

The midichlorians can also create a fertile baby out of nothing when Fate determines the need to restore balance to the Force. This is the account of the mechanism by which miracles occur in the Star Wars universe.

Once again, this is not a religious or ethical idea, or even a science fiction idea. This is driven by the plot.

The plot required that Qui-Gon have a means to confirm that young Anakin was Destined To Be Big Stuff, and so the plot required that Qui-Gon have a Destined To Be Big Stuff detector. The Big Stuff detector needs something to detect, and ergo there needed to be Stuff.

Ergo the destiny-meter, which detects whether you have a significant amount of Force-Flowing-Through-You microbes in your bloodstream. The midichlorians flow through you literally along with your white blood cells. The scene was only a few lines long, and so the explanation had to be short.

The fatherless birth of Anakin was one of the clumsiest bits of Star Wars lore ever. There are other myths where, for example, Juno gives virgin birth to Vulcan, but only one religion in the modern occidental countries in the world where the Virgin Mother makes an appearance. The child she bears is not the Evil Magic Ninja Boy.

But once again, the fact that Anakin was conceived of the Holy Midichlorian, and Born of the Blessed Virgin Shmi, has no plot point and tells us nothing about the religion of the Force. It is here for atmosphere, to make Anakin seem to be Big Stuff.

The prophecy that "The Chosen One Will Bring Balance To The Force" is the same kind of purely pointless atmospheric gesture. The prophecy turns out to be false, as best anyone can tell, but the writer was too lazy to give it that tragic ambiguity like the prophecy about Oedipus killing his father.

What is meant by "balance" is never mentioned, or why we should want it, or who did the choosing, or what it all means. There is no plot point here. If the movies were edited and revised (yet again) by George Lucas at some future point, and all reference to the prophecy removed, no action by any characters would change or would need to change. There is simply no evidence that the Force was "out of balance" at the beginning of *The Phantom Menace*.

Now, if that movie had started with the Jedi Council (perhaps because they involved themselves too much with the compromises and betrayals of politics) finding their control over the Force slipping away, their prognostication going dim, their way-cool psychokinesis powers getting all butterfingery, worrying about how to get their vanishing powers back, it would have made sense. If then the Jedi Council discovered this Anakin creature who had been created without a father in a lab by the Sith, and agreed, despite omens and warnings by Yoda that this would end badly, to train the Sith boy hoping his better nature could be reached, then this talk of the Force being "out of balance" would have made some sense (and it would have been interesting). The decision to train Anakin would have meant something; it would have been a moral decision with consequences: an act of arrogance and ambition on the part of the Jedi Council, which would have led directly to their downfall.

LIFE AFTER DEATH: RETURN OF THE BLUE GHOST

We saw earlier that Anakin's desire to save his wife had to drive him to the study of Things Man Was Not Meant To Know: the black magic of necromancy and of survival after death. We also saw earlier that having the wizard-helper of the child-hero showing up after death to whisper encouragement was Way Cool.

There is a throwaway line in *Revenge of the Sith* where Yoda tells Obi-Wan to study the technique of surviving bodily death. Surviving bodily death is apparently a learned art, like the Flying Unicycle of Death Rotary Kick Technique. It is ninja-magic, not anything that is part of an ethical, mystical, metaphysical or religious structure.

Yoda obviously knows the Technique, too. There is a scene in *Return of the Jedi* where he dies for no reason, lying down because he is tired, and then vanishing. More atmosphere. He had to be dead so he could not answer any follow-up questions, and croaking out a riddle as your dying words is very atmospheric. Now, he shows up as a blue ghost later on because he has other lines to say. But there is no point to his dying and no point to his reappearing as an apparition, except that the script requires it.

Apparently it is okay for Obi-Wan to study the death-surviving technique, so that he can return as a saint after martyrdom and make lame excuses to Luke over that whole fibbing-about-your-dad thing, but Anakin's desire to look into it is horrific and unnatural. This contradiction is never explained.

Of course, Vader, once he redeems himself by killing the Emperor, is granted ghosthood, even though he has not studied this technique. No: the ghost of Anakin Skywalker appears after the death of Darth Vader so that Luke can smile in solemn happiness at his father, and not for any other purpose. It is there for atmosphere. The happy ending must be happy.

And the Evil Emperor obviously does not know the technique, because he dies and stays dead. (Unless someone hits Lucas over the head with a bag of money and holds him at fanpoint until he makes a seventh movie. Palpatine could return as a blue ghost and possess the body of Leia's daughter St. Alia-of-the-Knife. That would be Way Cool.)

Had the Emperor actually known necromancy, we could have seen the final, dramatic confrontation on the Volcano Planet between Anakin and Obi-Wan end in a fashion that made sense: Obi-Wan should have and would have killed Anakin, and stabbed him once or twice or fifty times to make sure he was dead, shouting out through his tears, "Younglings! You killed the younglings!" and leaving the corpse to rot. The Emperor would have arrived to take the burnt corpse and Brought Him Back To Life, with the help of the horrifying Doctor Doom-style mechanical suit to sustain the artificial mockery of unnatural vitality. Anakin's undead brain, swimming with midichlorians, could have been moving his mostly dead limbs through psychokinesis. That would have made the scenes in the first trilogy somewhat eerie and chilling in hindsight. It would have made sense. (And it would have been interesting.)

There is nothing in the Jedi Code, or the religion, morals or ethics of Star Wars, that make any sense of Obi-Wan's action of turning his back on a severely wounded Bad Guy and walking off to go tell Nayland Smith that Fu Manchu must have died in that explosion. No one could live through that!

But Obi-Wan walks away because the script requires it.

And that's all there is to the Force in Star Wars, both in this scene and all the others. The Force is not about religion or ethics or anything. The Force is what the script forces.

John C. Wright is a retired attorney, newspaperman and newspaper editor, who was only once on the lam and forced to hide from the police, who did not admire his newspaper. In 1984 he graduated from St. John's

College in Annapolis, home of the "Great Books" program. In 1987 he graduated from the College and William and Mary's Law School (going from the third oldest to the second oldest school in continuous use in the United States), and was admitted to the practice of law in three jurisdictions (New York, May 1989; Maryland, December 1990; DC, January 1994). His law practice was unsuccessful enough to drive him into bankruptcy soon thereafter. His stint as a newspaperman for the *St. Mary's Today* was more rewarding spiritually, but, alas, also a failure financially. He presently works (successfully) as a writer in Virginia, where he lives in fairy-tale-like happiness with his wife, the authoress L. Jagi Lamplighter, and their three children: Orville, Wilbur and Just Wright.

THE COURTROOM

DROID JUDGE: Mr. Stover, do you wish to cross-examine?

MATTHEW WOODRING STOVER: Absolutely. Mr. Wright, first I suppose I'd have to ask about your definition of a "real religion," which I quote here: "A real religion addresses metaphysics, spiritual powers, martyrdom, ethics, fate, salvation, miracles and life after death." Are you aware that by a strict application of this definition, you've disqualified the bulk of our world's spiritual traditions? Was this Christian/Islamist bias intentional?

JOHN C. WRIGHT: Objection; leading the witness. Mr. Stover is trying to palm off an assumption on the jury by making a logically impermissible statement in the form of a question.

DROID JUDGE: (*apologetically*) Mr. Wright, you cannot object. You are a witness, not counsel.

JOHN C. WRIGHT: I'm not asking that the counsel's question be ruled out of order; I'm merely pointing out a logical flaw in the question. Mr. Stover states that non-Christian religions on Earth do not have metaphysics or views about life after death, or the other qualities listed here. If he means that a non-Christian religion can be found that lacks one the qualities listed, the statement is correct but irrelevant; if he means that all non-Christian religions lack any of the qualities listed, the statement is false.

Certain religions on Earth are more complex or simple, depending on their history. All real religions have at least some of these properties I list: I do not make the statement that all religions have all of them. Some do not revere martyrs, for example, and others do not attribute spiritual powers to their practitioners. For the purpose of my argument, I need but show that the Force in Star Wars does not address any of the items on the list, to show that it is not a religion.

Ladies and gentlemen of the jury, do not be deceived by a crass rhetorical trick of calling my position a "bias." Obviously the honorable counsel for the Defense has nothing else to present to you by way of argument.

MATTHEW WOODRING STOVER: So the short answer is, "I meant 'or' instead of 'and' (maybe 'and/or'),"and no bias was intended. Fine. You could have just said so.

Moving on.

Would your reaction to the "religious" aspect of Star Wars change if the goal of the "religion" involved was not reward in a life after death, but rather a virtuous life in this existence, as in Judaism? Would your reaction change if the issue were not Salvation, but rather Enlightenment, as in Buddhism? If, in fact, the most profound realization of the spirituality involved was the tat tvam asi—thou art that, the great spiritual principle of non-duality, the fundamental unity of All That Is (that "binds the Galaxy together")—which is the goal of religious and spiritual practice from China and Japan through India and the Middle East to nearly all Western mystic traditions?

JOHN C. WRIGHT: The question again contains a logically impermissible inference. Mr. Stover is trying to attribute to an argument a conclusion not in the argument, a rhetorical trick called a "straw man argument"; instead of addressing the questions raised, Mr. Stover rails against an imaginary opponent constructed to be weaker than his real opponent.

If I had made this following argument: "All real religions are about winning afterworldly rewards, and Star Wars lacks this and ergo is not a real religion" then his comment would counter that argument. But that is not the argument I made; ergo his comment is irrelevant.

There is some palaver in the movies about avoiding anger, but no hint that the goal of the Jedi is to become "one" with the Force after death, or to abide by the laws honoring the covenant God made with his ancestors, or to escape from the woes of reincarnation into detachment of Nirvana.

Nowhere in my article do I mention one "goal" for religion as opposed to another. I merely point out that the "goal" of studying the Force is to do way-cool ninja-leaps.

MATTHEW WOODRING STOVER: For the record, the goal of studying the Force is to become a Jedi, which by definition involves oneness with the Force (not in the afterlife), and adherence to a strict code of conduct developed over 25,000 years.

Moving on.

Are you familiar with the Buddhist doctrine of the Eightfold Path, where all daily activities, pursued in the proper spirit, lead toward Enlightenment? Are you familiar with classical Zen, which finds Enlightenment specifically the study of the martial arts—training to do the earthly equivalents of, as you so vividly put it, "super-ninja-leaps with Way Cool psychokinetic powers." If study of the martial arts can be a religious practice on Earth, why not in Star Wars?

JOHN C. WRIGHT: I am quite familiar with authentic Zen Buddhist practice. I once studied at a Zendo under a Roshi.

The question yet again contains a logically impermissible inference. This is the formal logical error of the excluded middle. Merely because some Buddhists can use martial arts as a meditative technique appurtenant to their religion, it does not follow that all martial arts studies constitute a religion.

Certainly the Jedi in Star Wars are meant to have an exotic, oriental flavor to them: they are fencing with nuclear kendo sticks, after all. But the same flavor could be attributed to any movie where ninjas fly around on wires or perform spooky magic tricks. The spooky ninja-magicians in Star Wars are following in the footsteps of Bruce Lee, not following in the footsteps of the Enlightened One.

MATTHEW WOODRING STOVER: I now direct your attention to your observation "If the Force were a god like Odin or Zeus, the audience would be puzzled why the Sky Father is supporting both sides of the conflict. Therefore, the Force itself has to be neutral, an inactive and nondemanding sort of god, etc." Since you are apparently the last person on Earth who hasn't heard that the Force was a direct metaphor for the ancient concept of the Tao, let me direct your attention to Stephen Mitchell's translation of this passage from the Tao Te Ching: "The Tao does not take sides."

Perhaps it would be easier for you to understand if, instead of the Force—instead of calling it a god, which it is not, and is never said to be—we call it Life. After all, Life is what it's about, yes? And Life gives us everything that's good, and a great deal that's bad: Poetry and art, beauty and family, civilization and science...and it also gives us smallpox and Ebola, aggression and greed and jealousy and murder. Without bias or prejudice. Without taking sides. Whether it's good or evil depends on what we do with it. Does using the word Life as the metaphor help clear up your confusion?

JOHN C. WRIGHT: The question yet again contains a logically impermissible inference. It is an informal error of logic to assert that "everyone knows" such-and-such, or to address the person rather than the argument. The former is called *argumentum ad populum*; the latter is called *ad hominem*.

The formal logical error of the undistributed middle is also present. Merely because a misunderstanding of Taoism represents the Tao as ethically neutral does not mean that all ethically neutral phenomena are religious.

Electromagnetic energy, for example, can be used both for the electric toothbrush and the electric chair. It is neutral. By the logic of the honorable counsel for the Defense, a film portraying electricity as neutral would be "religious" because life is neutral.

A vague awe and respect for "the life force" is not a religion. It is not even a philosophy: it is a sentiment. Star Wars does have a sentiment. It does not have a religion.

If "everyone" knows that Star Wars is a metaphor for Taoism, then "everyone" has not read enough Lao Tzu to have a serious discussion on the matter. I suppose that is fine, because those who follow the Tao say that the Tao that can be spoken is not the spoken Tao. Those who truly follow, on the other hand, follow, and do not say.

The Tao might not take sides, but, under heaven, there is a way to follow the Tao and a way not to follow it. Taoism has a definite ethical character and metaphysics which Star Wars does not have, and, as a bit of boy's adventure fiction, is not meant to have.

The question is not whether the Force is neutral, but why it is neutral. It is neutral because the plot requires duels between good and bad psychic swordsmen.

It is not neutral because the movie is Taoist in message or sentiment.

It is Taoist to say: The wise ruler sees that the bellies are full and the minds are empty. The crooked tree is useless to the carpenter, and therefore it flourishes. What is the shape of an uncarved block? What did your face look like before you were born?

It is not Taoist to say, "Do not give in to fear and anger, or forever will it dominate your destiny!" or, "In my experience, there is no such thing as coincidence."

I do not recall, in the scene where Qui-Gon measures the midichlorian blood count in his young apprentice, that what was being measured was Anakin's potential to embrace these questions and paradoxes.

If Star Wars counts as a movie of religion equal in stature to Taoism, why, then, so does *Flying Ninja Guillotines of Death* or *Lightning Swords of the Shogun Executioner*.

MATTHEW WOODRING STOVER: I have no further questions for this witness. Pointing up the numberless confusions and misrepresentations in the balance of his testimony serves no purpose, as many of them proceed from his fundamental misunderstanding of the metaphysical premises of the Saga; I'm simply trying to help him understand, not to embarrass him.

DAVID BRIN: Objection!

MATTHEW WOODRING STOVER: You object to my trying to help him understand?

DROID JUDGE: Sustained. Save your speeches for your closing statement, Mr. Stover.

MATTHEW WOODRING STOVER: Fine. The Defense's witness can handle the ethical end of the argument; I call novelist, critic and all-around swell guy Scott Lynch.

The Son of Skywalker
Must Not Become a Jackass

or Finding the Ethical Core
of the Star Wars Films by Ignoring
the Ghosts and Muppets

WITNESS FOR THE DEFENSE:
Scott Lynch

I HAD TO LIE during my interview with the evaluation board of my first volunteer fire department. Because of Star Wars.

Or perhaps it was more of a calculated omission. In response to the question, "Why do you want to be a volunteer firefighter?" I rattled off a string of boilerplate platitudes—it seemed like it might be fun and interesting, a chance to serve the community, nobody likes to see his neighbors screaming and on fire, et cetera. The members of the board nodded sagely, examined the line on their evaluation form that read *Possible Raving Freak Y/N*, circled *N*, and that was that.

How might they have replied if I'd cleared my throat and said, "I've wrestled with a deep-seated desire to be a Jedi Knight ever since I was old enough to tie my own shoes, and this seems my best chance to act on that desire in some fashion"? Replied? Hell, they would have pinned me the floor and helped the nice men in white coats jab the needle into my arm.

Nonetheless, it's true. I have a Jedi complex dating back to that fateful afternoon in 1983 when my father took the five-year-old version of myself to see *Return of the Jedi*, a film that was to my brain what an industrial electromagnet is to a handful of iron filings. Some days, I might as well be standing on a street corner holding a hand-lettered cardboard sign: *Will deflect blaster bolts with lightsaber for food.*

It could be said that the Jedi represent an ideal I have never been able to forget—an ideal that, in my own bent and silly and imperfect fashion, I still try to cherish.

Dr. Brin, in his generous introduction (and I do mean that—remember, this is a guy who's carried out nothing less than an intellectual serial mugging on the prequel films over the past half-decade), alludes to the emotional impact of *The Empire Strikes Back* and the promise therein, in his words, "that meaning can coexist with adventure."

The Star Wars films, like the first Matrix film (my much-abused brain recoils from acknowledging the existence of the later two), possess what I often refer to as "opt-in philosophical depth." They can be enjoyed, without diminishment, as nothing more than amiable, fast-moving action/adventure pieces overflowing with visual innovation. They can also be divertingly dissected on a deeper level—the level of Campbellian journeys, mythic resonance, political allusion and ethical argument.

It is this last quality, the ethical component of the Star Wars films, that I credit in hindsight with cementing them as the cultural cornerstone of my early years. My childhood was filled with flashy media—transforming robots, laser blasts, gun battles, spaceships and so forth—but only the Star Wars films seemed to provide instruction in something to *aspire* to. I was raised atheist in a home pleasantly free from political, philosophical or theological dogma, and I am unashamed to admit that most of my initial notions of higher virtue were shaped by the actions of fictional rebels—and one fictional knight—in a galaxy far, far away.

LET'S TALK ABOUT WHAT WE'RE NOT GONNA TALK ABOUT

Now, technically, the subject of religion in the Star Wars films comes under my purview along with ethics, but I'm not going to pound many keys on its behalf. I consider the topic too slight to discuss with more than grunts and hand gestures, unless those involved in the discussion want to spin wild exaggerations and extrapolations of the subject to keep the conversation going. Frankly, I'd rather stick a dry spaghetti noodle in my ear and attempt to scratch my hypothalamus.

Simply put, the "religion/spirituality" (quotation marks well deserved) of the Star Wars films, as revealed on-screen, amounts to nothing worth qualitative analysis. The closest any character comes to uttering a religious opinion is Yoda in *The Empire Strikes Back*:

YODA: Size matters not. Look at me. Judge me by my size, do you? Hmm? Hmm. And well you should not. For my ally is the Force, and a powerful ally it is. Life creates it…makes it grow. Its energy surrounds us and binds us. Luminous beings are we, not this crude matter.

However, inasmuch as this has the outward appearance of religiosity, it must be remembered that Yoda has nine centuries of insight into the nature of life, death and the Force—coming from him, this is not an expression of theological opinion but rather a straightforward report on how the universe functions. It's the metaphysical equivalent of a mechanic explaining how your car's alternator works.

There are several references in *A New Hope* to the "religion" of Darth Vader and Obi-Wan Kenobi, but I think we can safely dismiss those as a mere expression of the context in which laymen (Han Solo, the Death Star command staff) frame the mysterious abilities of the Force-sensitive.

Although the Jedi of the prequel trilogy are steeped in the trappings of religion (they have a "temple," they meditate, they have a considerable fetish for robes and platitudes), it seems clear that they do not pray and they do not anthropomorphize the Force. The attitude the Jedi display toward it is akin to that of a nuclear technician to his reactor—respect and veneration, certainly, but not worship. Additionally, their meditation seems mostly to be a form of mental self-maintenance, designed to prevent them from exploding into kill-crazy lightsaber rampages for minor aggravations like, say, Meatless Tuesdays in the Jedi Temple cafeteria.

Other than that, no character in any of the films expresses faith in a higher power (well, nobody who isn't an Ewok), or pleads with one for intercession, or draws open strength from theological beliefs. In my opinion, rumors of genuine religion in the Star Wars films are greatly exaggerated. That which doesn't exist can't really be attacked and, conveniently, requires no further defense. As Watto might say, "I need something more real...." So let's get back to ethics.

WHO ARE YOU GOING TO BELIEVE, ME OR THAT OTHER TRILOGY?

The two Star Wars trilogies were filmed nearly two decades apart, and it's fair to say that there is a significant difference in the ethical substance of each set of films. This raises the question of which trilogy should be considered to have, for lack of a better term, precedence in the presumed articulation of the series' ethical vision. The original trilogy, for being the chronological culmination of the six-episode story? Or the prequel trilogy, for being George Lucas's more recent work, and for the fact that he conceived and directed it from a position of commanding influence, effectively able to do whatever he damn well pleased?

The latter argument might make for intriguing speculation, but for the sake of my argument I'm going to go with the former. After all, we're discussing the ethical content of the films as expressed within their fictional narrative; clearly the chronology of that narrative deserves to win out over the chronology of film production.

With that settled, I can begin to lay out my position that the critical ethical development—the moral articulation which can be considered "victorious" over all others in the Star Wars narrative—is the manner in which Luke Skywalker becomes a Jedi Knight. Lucas has said that the twin trilogies are about the fall and redemption of Darth Vader, but I believe that's only true to a point. Vader is indeed a primary lens through which the events of the films are examined, but if we want to uncover the strongest, most consistent and most admirable thread of virtue in the tapestry, we should pay less attention to the father's journey, and more to the son's.

FIRST WE GOT PUNKED BY THE SITH. THEN THE LITTLE BASTARD FACT-CHECKED US.

To understand Luke's struggle (and his triumph), one might begin by reflecting on the Jedi who instruct him in the birds and the bees of Force sensitivity.

The Star Wars films establish beyond a glimmer of all possible doubt that Obi-Wan Kenobi and Yoda, wise and well-meaning as they are, are not the sort of guys you'd want to trust with the management of your mutual fund. The venerable Jedi Masters are actually quite the pair of shifty-eyed sons-of-bitches, and the web of guilt, lies and manipulation they construct over the course of the two trilogies is epic.

Detractors of the films (and of the personal vision of George Lucas) enthusiastically seize upon this point as though it were a revelation—as though the series' writer/creator and its fans might somehow be surprised to learn that the two older Jedi are frequently evasive, selfish and dishonest. But while some second-guessing of Lucas's judgment in the construction of his films is justifiable, in this instance it seems both uncharitable and easily refuted. Lucas clearly worries a great deal about the ethical image his characters present—in at least one instance, he worried far too much.

In the original version of *A New Hope*, Han Solo is accosted by Greedo in the Mos Eisley cantina. Han keeps the Rodian bounty hunter talking long enough to stealthily unholster his blaster pistol beneath the table and caramelize the poor fellow like a glazed ham. Apparently, Lucas fretted about Han Solo's image enough to design an infamous alteration in the 1997 special edition of *A New Hope*. In the modified film, Greedo actually snaps off a blaster shot a split-second before Solo does and misses, ludicrously, from the distance of two and a half feet.

Not only does the added blaster bolt look silly, it wasn't necessary in the first place. There is absolutely no doubt that Han shoots Greedo in clear self-defense, immediately after Greedo tells him that he doesn't care about bringing him to Jabba the Hutt alive:

HAN SOLO: Even I get boarded sometimes. Do you think I had a choice?

GREEDO: You can tell that to Jabba. He may only take your ship.

HAN SOLO: Over my dead body!

GREEDO: That's the idea… I've been looking forward to this for a long time.

Yet even this supremely justifiable preemptive blasting was deemed unwholesome enough to warrant a jarring change. Now, with that under his belt, does George Lucas strike you as the sort of writer/director who could plow through six films blithely unaware that two of his central characters like to fold, spindle and mutilate the truth?

Sure Obi-Wan and Yoda are a pair of liars (and wouldn't you feel like fudging the facts a bit if the alternative was to admit that the Sith played the Jedi like a cheap trombone, and that your bad judgment helped usher in decades of bloody tyranny?). Obi-Wan and Yoda are liars because their deceptions set them up in direct ethical opposition to Luke, for the sake of the story. Materially, the two elderly Jedi are Luke's allies. Morally, the two of them are villains—yes, villains—that Luke must confront and overcome on several occasions in order to bring about a true and lasting victory over the Sith and their Empire.

Make no mistake: Luke's saga in the original Star Wars trilogy isn't a rediscovery of the ways of the Jedi of the Old Republic. It's the story of how he puts himself on an escape trajectory from almost everything they stood for.

OLD REPUBLIC JEDI: AMBULATORY OUIJA BOARDS WITH SWORDS

Consider the Jedi of the Republic as presented in the prequel trilogy. By and large, they're as decadent (in their own fashion) as the slowly dying government they serve. Insular, ascetic, pompous, detached, overconfident and indecisive—even the better ones display some or all of these traits at various points. Again, critics seem to seize on this as though it were an accident—"How can we completely sympathize with this pack of arrogant space hippies?" The only reasonable response is: What makes you think you're *supposed* to completely sympathize with them?

The list of moral screwups perpetrated by the last generation of Old Republic Jedi is pretty overwhelming. Ponder:

- When presented with the most powerful Force-sensitive being in centuries, they decide not to guide him in any fashion. Apparently, leaving him to run around and discover his powers on his own (or under the tutelage of interested third parties like the Sith) is a much better idea.
- When presented with clear evidence that a Sith is behind the Republic-shaking events on Naboo, they dispatch the same Master/Padawan team that has already failed to beat the Sith once, with no reinforcements. Apparently, the thought of sending three dozen bright young lightsaber duelists to beat Darth Maul like a dirty carpet doesn't occur to anyone—and as a result, Qui-Gon Jinn is slain.
- When presented with the massive ethical quandary of a huge army of sentient beings cloned to serve as blaster fodder, the Jedi shrug their shoulders and put the poor suckers to immediate use without discussion.
- When they become suspicious that someone or something is manipulating Chancellor Palpatine, the Jedi Council continues to place the burden of spying on Anakin—a Jedi known to be insubordinate, proud and volatile, with possibly compromised loyalties. We all know what happens next.

When Obi-Wan Kenobi meets Luke Skywalker in *A New Hope*, he speaks wistfully of the Republic era as "a more civilized age." He neglects to mention, of course, that the tragedy of the Old Republic Jedi was at least partially self-inflicted. He begins his association with Luke not just by lying to him about his father's fate, but by attempting to inveigle him into an undeservedly charitable view of the Order that Obi-Wan accidentally helped destroy. The message is clear in the prequels, and Obi-Wan's behavior only amplifies it in Episodes IV–VI: the path of the Old Republic Jedi is something Luke must shun, not celebrate.

ETHICS 101: A FRIEND IS SOMEONE
WHO'LL STUFF YOU INTO A GUTTED TAUNTAUN

So much, then, for the prequel trilogy, a murky series of events in which few characters, even the survivors, manage to cover themselves in glory. The Jedi display an almost callous disregard for the emotional comfort of the boy who grows up to lead their slaughter—even Anakin's closest friend, Obi-Wan, is capable of turning a remarkably cold and dismissive shoulder toward him. Consistent ethical behavior is nowhere to be found...and the Galaxy suffers for it.

By contrast, the ethical core of Episodes IV–VI is almost ebullient; the unpretentious message enshrined at the heart of the original trilogy's story boils down to "stick with your friends and loved ones even when the whole universe seems to have it in for you." In *A New Hope*, Luke rushes off alone the moment he realizes his aunt and uncle might be in danger—a foolish but highly compassionate decision. He then elects to stay with the Rebellion and participate in a suicide mission rather than escape with Han. In the end, his example inspires Han to return as well, postponing his vital reckoning with Jabba the Hutt for the sake of saving his friends and their cause.

The displays of loyalty in *The Empire Strikes Back* are heartbreaking. Han risks a bitter, lonely death for a slim chance of finding Luke alive. Luke stubbornly ignores Yoda's pleas to finish his training in favor of rushing off to help his endangered friends. Lando Calrissian, in the hope of redeeming himself, gives up his entire Cloud City mining operation while trying to save Han, Leia and Chewbacca. Most strikingly, Luke chooses to fling himself to possible death rather than accept Darth Vader's offer of a partnership to rule the Galaxy—a partnership that would surely destroy his friends and everything they've fought for as members of the Rebel Alliance.

Luke's moral resolve is an inarticulate and even shortsighted thing, but it shows him to be ethically superior to his teachers—he will not allow his friends to suffer while he stands by and does nothing for them, and he won't even consider using them as chess pieces in some far-ranging game of Jedi against Sith in which the lives of the non-Force-sensitive do not count. The Jedi of the Old Republic discouraged the emotional connections of love and friendship; Luke is defined to his very core by those connections. The efforts of Luke's mentors to mold him in the fashion of their generation of Jedi—more ascetic, more detached, more aloof—fail continually, and while they are cranky about this failure, events prove them wrong in every respect.

Luke, driven by compassion, holds out hope for the redemption of his father in *Return of the Jedi* even as a ghostly Obi-Wan grumpily continues to assert that Vader isn't worth redeeming. Kenobi seems to want Luke to atone for *his* mistakes in the quickest, crudest way possible—by killing Vader so Obi-Wan won't have to think about the problem anymore. Of all Obi-Wan's faults, this one seems the most petty and grievous. Even after the full revelation of every lie Obi-Wan and Yoda previously fed to Luke, Obi-Wan continues to begrudge Luke the feelings that define him: steadfast love, undying loyalty and unquenchable hope. Nowhere is the contrast between the Old Republic Jedi and Luke more apparent; never is Luke's commitment to his own ideals more critical.

A more arrogant and detached Luke, an Old Republic-model Jedi such as Yoda and Obi-Wan might have forged out of a more complacent young Skywalker, would surely have met with disaster in his confrontation with Vader and Palpatine aboard the second Death Star. Palpatine's superiority over Luke is readily apparent; the young Jedi has no defense against the Sith Lord's dark lightning.

Killing Vader outright or disdaining him as beyond redemption would have done no good; then Luke would have died or been suborned to the will of the Emperor in Vader's place. Struggling against Palpatine would have been to no avail, with Luke so overmatched. Only Luke's feelings for his father—his decision to spend what might be his last few breaths pleading for Vader's aid—succeed in turning Vader against the Emperor. The Sith Lord dies by his apprentice's hand, but it is Luke's love and loyalty that put that hand in motion.

At the end of the cinematic Star Wars saga, Luke Skywalker inherits the mantle and powers of the Jedi without the hang-ups that brought the Order down at its nadir—the pompous senses of entitlement, superiority and emotional detachment that his mentors failed to truly kindle in him. Luke faces his destiny as the first of a new breed of Jedi, compassionate and sociable, a more faithful friend and a more honorable foe than the Knights of old. The practical moral qualities he articulates by example are immediately applicable in the real world, and worth aspiring to.

With great power must come a certain amount of healthy self-doubt, and a certain amount of trust in the people closest to you. In embracing this, Luke's personal triumph becomes the Saga's ethical vindication.

Scott Lynch was born in St. Paul, Minnesota, in 1978 and currently lives in Wisconsin. His first novel, *The Lies of Locke Lamora*, will be released in June 2006.

THE COURTROOM

DAVID BRIN: Your Honor, the Prosecution is perfectly willing to stipulate that Luke Skywalker is a righteous dude and a swell guy. He may be dim, but at no point is he anything other than a stalwart fellow, ethical, brave and true. He well and truly represents what we have already accepted as the superficial—or childlike—moral lessons of Star Wars. For example, "be loyal to your friends," "be brave" and "mean people suck."

Furthermore, we are further willing to admit, as Scott Lynch ably points out, that Luke winds up defying his Jedi Masters, questioning their authority, overcoming their mistakes and helping to bring about a new Order that might—one can hope—rise above the flaming lunacy that both sides of the old Force represent.

Nevertheless, the question at issue here is not the relative goodness of Luke Skywalker, but the lessons that are taught by this science fiction epic.

Both Jedi and Sith get—across all six films—about an hour of on-screen time to lecture us about their horrific light-and-dark versions of nastiness. Are we supposed to then rely on the public to analyze the situation, in the *very* last five minutes of *Return of the Jedi*, and say to themselves, aloud: "Aha! Luke and his friends rejected all that Force crap in favor of a world of openness and egalitarian democracy!"

Are we, really?

SCOTT LYNCH: The estimable Persecutor (er, Prosecutor) is being chronologically uncharitable; Luke's rebellion against the old-Order Jedi doesn't come in the last five minutes of the last film; it's already a major plot point in the middle of *The Empire Strikes Back*. Luke's journey from wide-eyed acceptance of anything Obi-Wan says to sadder, wiser skepticism covers a film and a half. Throughout that second half of the original trilogy, Luke sets himself firmly and consistently in opposition to the ascetic, emotionally isolationist philosophy of his elders. Furthermore, it is not the Force that Luke rejects (for the Force itself can no more be rejected in Luke's universe than the laws of gravity can in ours), but rather the idea that a Jedi Knight should be willing to sacrifice his friends and loved ones just so he can stay appropriately Zen.

As for the "childishness" of Luke's moral example, well...to paraphrase something our chief counsel for the Defense once wrote, I would suggest that the reflexive need to belittle straightforward heroism is too often a defense mechanism designed to deal with the unpalatable fact that we ourselves tend to fall short of our own highest ideals...that because we have perhaps failed to be the men and women we know we should be, the sight of unvarnished virtue stings as much as it inspires.

DAVID BRIN: Isn't that like asking the public to notice that (in *ROTJ*) none of the throne-room shenanigans matter at all to the fate of the universe? Yes! Only non-Force guys, like Chewbacca and Lando, actually save the day. But can you count on the fingers of one hand the number of people who noticed that?

SCOTT LYNCH: Actually, that's not entirely true. The seeming sideshow in the throne room keeps the attention of the two most powerful Sith Lords in galactic history fixed firmly on their little family squabble while the Rebel junior varsity goes for the Death Star's jugular. One can only imagine what else might have gone wrong for the Rebellion if Vader had been available to lead the battle on the forest moon himself ("I love the smell of blasted Ewok in the afternoon...hooooo-paaaaah...smells like...victory....").

And what if Palpatine had been at leisure to work his own mischief?

Free, for example, to reach out across space and telekinetically set the space-toilets in every Rebel cruiser to "reverse purge" at the same time?

And given that the Prosecutor can no more telepathically analyze the reactions of several hundred million film viewers than I can, might it not be fair to call rhetorical grandstanding on the second question?

CHARGE 3

Star Wars Novels Are Poor
Substitutes for Real Science Fiction
and Are Driving Real SF
off the Shelves

Novels, Novelizations
and Tie-ins, Oh My

WITNESS FOR THE PROSECUTION:
Lou Anders

A LONG TIME AGO, in a decade far, far away (1978 to be exact), Alan Dean Foster wrote the very first Star Wars spin-off novel, *Splinter of the Mind's Eye*, which is pretty much where all the trouble started. Intended originally as the basis of a potential low-budget sequel, the story takes place entirely on a fog-shrouded planet, and stars only Luke, Leia, C-3PO and R2-D2. (Han Solo is noticeably absent, as Harrison Ford had yet to sign to return.) I remember the day my father brought it to the dinner table. I was impressed at the "legitimizing" of the film by seeing it rendered in so distinguished a medium as print. Of course, I lacked the vocabulary to express it in quite those terms then. But it wasn't until a decade later, in 1987, when West End Games began licensing the Star Wars Roleplaying Game, that the "expanded universe" of Star Wars continuity began to be codified and refined. This larger body of Star Wars canon grew through the popular Dark Horse comic book license that soon followed. Then, in the early 1990s, when Bantam published Timothy Zahn's Thrawn Trilogy, interest in the novelizations really took off, catapulting the universe of Star Wars media tie-ins to its current level—*New York Times* best-selling books and a gigantic cash cow for Lucasfilm and all of its subsidiaries.

Now, let's get something straight here at the outset. I'm not a big fan of media tie-ins and novelizations in general. I don't believe that they are a good thing for the genre, per se, and I frequently bemoan the fact that they are bought and consumed in numbers that dwarf the "real" stuff by many orders of magnitude. In short, anyone who equates Elminster with Gandalf or Merlin isn't going to rate too highly in my book. But despite all the above, I come neither to praise Star Wars novels nor to bury them. While I'd rather apply leeches under my tongue than have to read a Forgotten Realms novel, several of my friends have delved into media tie-in territory for love, not money, and I'll concede that not all of them are the utter drek they are so often characterized as being. As a reader, I've even enjoyed that guilty pleasure myself a time or two, though it's been a few years, and it is a *guilty* pleasure.

Still, meat loaf is meat loaf, and filet mignon is filet mignon. It's okay (and probably necessary) to eat both, but it's important that we can all tell the difference, whatever our subjective tastes. So, while we're defining our terms...Star Wars is:

- Three good movies.
- One movie about violent teddy bears that seems much better now in retrospect.
- Two horrendously bad movies with unprecedented special effects.
- Some embarrassingly hackneyed Christmas specials (two with the aforementioned bears).
- A recent and very slick series of animated shorts much cooler than most of the above.

All told, and despite the aforementioned animated shorts, this is not a wonderful batting average when it's all laid out. That rival franchise with the same first word in its name at least had seventeen years of good television and maybe four good films before it started going south. Yet this uneven collection of celluloid tales—little more sophisticated at the outset than a 1930s Flash Gordon serial—is merely the hub of a media empire that spans comics, role-playing games, video games and approximately one hundred novels, many of which are, curiously enough, *much better than their source material*. Indeed, I cannot begin to count how many times a Star Wars fan apologized to me for liking *The Phantom Menace*, agreeing with me that the storytelling was inept, the plot ridiculous, the acting horrendous, the humor flat, the sexual politics dangerous and offensive, but shamefacedly maintaining that they liked it *despite* the fact that it *wasn't any good*. So great was their love of the enormous expanded universe of Star Wars lore that surrounded the franchise that they could love the body while admitting that the spine it hung on was flawed and rotten. It was as if, forgive me, Star Wars was in fact some vast galaxy of ancillary matter surrounding a center comprised of a vast black hole. In fact, it has been noted more than once that this greater body of continuity may be the point these days. As Neal Stephenson wrote in the *New York Times* June 17, 2005 issue, "These newer films don't even pretend to tell the whole story; they are akin to PowerPoint presentations that summarize the main bullet points from a much more comprehensive body of work developed by and for a geek subculture."

Geek subculture indeed. I admit to a certain geek attraction when I note the convenient timeline at the start of a particular novelization, tying all of the previous Star Wars novels together and showing me where they fall in relation to the six films. And the books come with icons on their back covers, identifying into which of the five major eras (Sith, Prequel, Classic, New Republic or New Jedi Order) the story falls. What self-respecting continuity lover wouldn't fall for that? And Star Wars comes complete with a galaxy of extemporaneous material that has built up over almost three decades! But that it ever would have come to this, where the words "Star Wars" or "Star Trek" are practically synonymous with science fiction in the minds of the general populace and both are franchises worth hundreds of millions of dollars (if not billions), no one could have foreseen.

So, more power to Mr. Lucas. Why be a Scrooge and begrudge him his science fiction empire? It's all in good fun anyway, right? Yes, but:

TO BEGIN WITH, IT ISN'T REALLY SCIENCE FICTION

In his introduction to *The Best Military Science Fiction of the 20th Cen-*

tury, Harry Turtledove writes that "Written science fiction is often thought-provoking; filmed sci-fi is more often jaw-dropping. The two usually appeal to different audiences, which aficionados of the written variety sometimes forget to their peril—and frustration." This frustration Turtledove notes is why some on the literary side of the fence have taken to distinguishing between "SF" literature and "sci-fi"—their somewhat derogative term for the flood of brainless action-adventure films and television shows which use science fiction iconography as a setting or backdrop for adventure without appropriating its sophistication or meaning.

James Gunn expands on this notion in his essay "The Tinsel Screen"[1] to say, "Printed science fiction and science fiction film seem to have little to do with each other, and there are virtually no good films that are also good science fiction. Star Wars is a simple and charming fairy tale set in scenes in which science fiction paraphernalia is lying about.... The problem with the science fiction film may be that it adds nothing to science fiction except concreteness of image—and that may be more of a drawback than an asset."

Wait a minute! Star Wars not science fiction, you say? Surely you jest. It's full of robots and spaceship battles, isn't it? What could be more science fiction than that? True enough, but from its opening moments, when the film tells us that it is set "A long time ago, in a galaxy far, far away"—a deliberate invocation of "once upon a time"—we know right where we stand. We are in a tale of knights with sabers fighting in a battle of good versus evil. A story of princesses and dark lords, torn from the pages of *Ivanhoe*, The Lord of the Rings and tales of King Arthur. In fact, early in *Star Wars: A New Hope* there is a scene in which C-3PO, newly acquired by the Owens, calls the young Luke "sir." Our hero responds with "Luke," to which the obsequious droid responds by immediately calling him "Sir Luke." The boy responds, "Just Luke," but the allusion to courtly titles is made. It's a clever bit of business to drive home the point that this is a tale of fantasy, which is what George "I don't have to know what a parsec is" Lucas has always maintained that it is.

---

[1] Gunn, James. "The Tinsel Screen." In *Teaching Science Fiction*, edited by Jack Williamson. King of Prussia, PA: Owlswick Press, 1980.

Okay, so Star Wars isn't true science fiction. Why is this bad? A number of reasons, including:

THE PROBLEM OF WIDER PERCEPTION

Star Wars is seen as being indicative of the science fiction genre by the majority of moviegoers. In the October 14, 2005 issue of the *Times*, mystery writer Ian Rankin complained at the underrated status afforded writers of crime fiction, while noting, "We don't get as raw a deal as science fiction writers. Science fiction is dealing with some of the biggest ideas—where we are going to go as a race—but for some reason it's not taken seriously." Now why do you suppose that is? Stephen Baxter, one of the top talents of the current crop of hard SF writers, sees the gulf as existing at its widest point in its most public face.

> I think Fred Pohl said several times that Star Trek is really good science fiction for about 1920. And I think that's the trouble really. The sophistication that you get in the best literary SF is far in advance of what you get on the average in media SF. There are obviously exceptions, but on the whole, especially the stuff that's in the public's face—Star Trek, Star Wars—what the critics know about—it is just so far behind, the use of ideas and so forth. I think that's the trouble. We're all judged by that label, especially given the preponderance in the bookshops of media tie-in books and epic fantasy, and then science fiction and hard SF especially is just a tiny corner. It's difficult for them to get through the prejudice.

Getting through the prejudice. Which is a shame, because as many doors as Star Wars has opened in terms of special effects and imagination (and it has opened quite a few), it has also ushered in an era in which science fiction is seen as childish escapism and "serious" science fiction films have been extremely hard to produce. Like James Bond movies having to up the ante every time, no science fiction film could be made today on anything approaching a large budget without a prerequisite number of explosions, vehicle (car or spaceship) chases and fights, whether lightsaber duels or Matrix-style kung fu. And while this has made for some wonderful popcorn cinema, I can't help but wonder what we are missing out on. Imagine for just a moment, if you will, the resulting films we might have been given had Stanley Kubrick's *2001* emerged as the benchmark against which Hollywood had set itself these past decades. If that cinematic masterpiece, and not Lucas's space opera, had inspired a sea of films with Oscar-caliber scripts and Oscar-caliber performances in the science fiction genre. What kind of a filmic landscape would we have had then? Like the number of licks it takes to get to the center of a Tootsie Pop, the world will never know.

The problem we face is that the general perception of our genre as overrun with Star Trek and Star Wars fans, and providing material only on a level with their tastes, may be a factor in keeping a larger populace from checking it out. How many of us, working professionals in this business, when asked what we do, inevitably have to endure quips about one or both of these two franchises? Wouldn't it be nice, just once, when explaining, "I work in science fiction," to have someone say, "Ah, yes, science fiction. That Samuel R. Delaney is a modern-day James Joyce, isn't he?" or "Did you know that Kurt Vonnegut's Kilgore Trout was named for Theodore Sturgeon?" Or, "You guys really have a handle on explaining to the rest of it where the whole world is heading. Thanks!" But alas, too often, it's all jokes about Spock ears and lightsabers and why don't you ever try writing a "proper book"!

Now, lest you think this is all just a bunch of sour grapes, there are some very practical, economic reasons why media tie-ins and novelizations are bad for business too.

THE BUSINESS OF WRITING

"They're bad because they've killed the midlist," explains Mike Resnick, a seasoned professional who knows more about the business of writing than just about any other writer I know.

> Essentially the argument is this: writers as different and as idiosyncratic as Harry Turtledove, Gene Wolfe and I were all allowed to build our advances and audiences over a period of more than a decade. But today, with the midlist totally taken over by media books, there seem to be almost no novels in the $12,500 to $45,000 range. Instead of building from $5K to $9K to $14K to $20K and so on, now you go from $6K to $40K—an enormous leap of faith that most publishers

are unwilling to make—or you stay at $6K. Why take a chance that you'll earn a $27K advance when they *know* a Trek book or a Wookiee book will earn out with no effort on the publisher's part?

Why indeed? This has led to our current situation, a shrinking of the midlist where publishers burn through promising new authors faster than Fox turns over new television shows, and scores of deserving talent are being discarded where an earlier age would have allowed their works to grow and take root. Do not believe otherwise. This is a very real problem, resulting in a sea of broken careers, and the genre is the poorer for it.

Nor are the works of which we're being deprived the only way in which the quality of the science fiction genre is being affected. Novelizations and tie-ins have another crime to answer for, as Resnick explains, "They're bad because they teach writers bad habits. Eight hundred years of literary evolution says that the protagonist must grow and change from his experiences—but novelizations of TV series require the same familiar character *not* to change. And they teach writers to be lazy—why describe how a process works when you can simply say, 'They stepped into the Transporter beam,' and ten million kids know what it means?"

Look, you say, I work long hours, life is tough enough, and when I come home, I want something light and fun. What does it matter if I want some turn-your-brain-off entertainment anyhow? Or, in other words...

WHY IS BAD WRITING BAD, ANYWAY?

First of all, let's define what we mean by good writing first, shall we? I don't think we can come up with a better definition of good literature than that supplied by the inestimable Gene Wolfe, who said, "My definition of good literature is that which can be read by an educated reader, and reread with increased pleasure." Or, as Samuel R. Delaney put it in an interview with Adam Roberts (*Argosy* magazine, January/February 2004), his writing is not generally intended for readers "who are not terribly interested in getting any other pleasure from a book except the one they open the first page expecting."

By contrast, when you read a novelization, not only are you getting exactly what you are expecting, you are almost certainly not getting a writer's best work. For starters, who would give away his best ideas, when he won't own the fruits of the labors? Writers save their best material for *their own books*, and put in the tie-ins that which they can bear to give away.

I've said it before and I'll say it again: science fiction is *the* genre that looks at the implications of technology on society, which, in this age of exponential technological growth, makes it the most relevant branch of literature going. We've lived through at least one singularity with the birth of the Internet, and the way this has transformed everyone's life in just a few short decades cannot be overlooked or downplayed. But this is only the start, and the close of the twenty-first century will look absolutely nothing like its inception. This hasn't ever been true in history before. The future has overtaken the present and things are only speeding up. The future exists first in imagination, then in will, then in reality, and the types of dreams we dream today will determine the world we and our children live in tomorrow. Our world is dreaming some dark dreams now. We need to dream better, as if our life depended on it. I suppose that it all comes back to meat loaf and filet mignon. If tie-in properties could be a gateway drug to the real stuff, wonderful. But if they pass in the mind of the majority *for* the real stuff, trouble. Because, my friends, the real stuff is important. The future is a very powerful force, if you just tap into it.

Lou Anders is an editor, author and journalist. He is the editorial director of Prometheus Books' science fiction imprint Pyr, as well as the anthologies *Outside the Box* (Wildside Press, 2001), *Live Without a Net* (Roc, 2003), *Projections* (MonkeyBrain, December 2004) and *FutureShocks* (Roc, July 2005). He served as the senior editor for Argosy Magazine's inaugural issues in 2003–04. In 2000 he served as the executive editor of Bookface.com, and before that he worked as the Los Angeles liaison for Titan Publishing Group. He is the author of *The Making of Star Trek: First Contact* (Titan Books, 1996), and has published over 500 articles in such magazines as *Publishers Weekly, The Believer, Dreamwatch, Star Trek Monthly, Star Wars Monthly, Babylon 5 Magazine, Sci Fi Universe, Doctor Who Magazine,* and *Manga Max*. His articles and stories have been translated into German, French and Greek, and have appeared online at Believermag.com, SFSite.com, RevolutionSF.com and InfinityPlus.co.uk.

THE COURTROOM

MATTHEW WOODRING STOVER: Okay, let's break this down. Your first objection is that (*gasp!*) Star Wars is fantasy. Say it ain't so! Uh, moving on—

Your second objection is that Star Wars is "seen as being indicative of the science fiction genre by the majority of moviegoers." In other words, it's been really, really successful. Uh, okay: guilty as charged.

Your third objection is that it "ushered in an era in which science fiction is seen as childish escapism and 'serious' science fiction films have been extremely hard to produce." Which leads me to my first question: Are you seriously trying to tell this Court that there was an era, previous to Star Wars, in which science fiction was *not* seen, by the wider public, as childish escapism, and "serious" science fiction films were actually *easy* to produce? Are you trying to say that there is not more serious—or at least attempting to be serious—SF cinema now (e.g., *Donnie Darko*, *Primer*, *Solaris*, *The Butterfly Effect*, et al) than at any time in Hollywood history? I remind you that you are under oath.

LOU ANDERS: First of all, commercial success is not a barometer of quality, and you know that, or anyway you should. More power to Dan Brown for coming up with *The Da Vinci Code*, but the hackneyed prose he serves up wouldn't fly in the genre next door. And if the size of your audience is an indication of talent and literary merit, then *Fear Factor* is gripping, psychological drama. You will recall that I never faulted anyone his entertainment, simply bemoaned those who can't tell shit from Shakespeare and insist the one is the other.

Second, (with thanks to James Gunn):

145

1898	*The Astronomer's Dream*
1899	*She*
1902	*A Trip to the Moon*
1906	*The ? Motorist*
1909	*A Trip to Jupiter*
1910	*A Trip to Mars*
1919	*The First Men in the Moon*
1925	*The Lost World*
1926	*Metropolis*
1930	*Just Imagine*
1931	*Frankenstein*
1932	*The Island of Lost Souls*
1933	*King Kong*
1933	*The Invisible Man*
1933	*Deluge*
1935	*Transatlantic Tunnel*
1936	*Things to Come*
1937	*Lost Horizon*
1950	*Destination Moon*
1951	*When Worlds Collide*
1951	*The Thing from Another World!*
1951	*The Day the Earth Stood Still*
1953	*The War of the Worlds*
1954	*1984*
1955	*20,000 Leagues Under the Sea*
1956	*Forbidden Planet*
1956	*Invasion of the Body Snatchers*
1957	*The Incredible Shrinking Man*
1958	*The Wonderful Invention*
1960	*The Time Machine*
1960	*Village of the Damned*
1963	*The Day of the Triffids*
1964	*From the Earth to the Moon*
1964	*Dr. Strangelove*
1965	*Alphaville*
1965	*The 10th Victim*
1966	*Fahrenheit 451*
1966	*Fantastic Voyage*

MATTHEW WOODRING STOVER: What year was that boring piece of crap—sorry, cinematic masterpiece (if you're really, really high)— *2001: A Space Odyssey* released? 1968, wasn't it? So it had almost a decade to inspire filmmakers before Star Wars made its debut…and yet, mostly it inspired clouds of suspiciously scented smoke at midnight showings. Could it be that the real problem has been failure of the "serious" science fiction types you pine for to produce something entertaining enough to capture the popular imagination? Or do you consider the real problem to be that the public's just too stupid to appreciate what you consider the Good Stuff?

LOU ANDERS: Neither. The public has no problem with distinguishing the good stuff, hence the widespread acknowledgement of the first Matrix, and the failure of the third. Or the success of The Lord of the Rings. Furthermore, quite a few critics at the time praised Jackson for providing the first trilogy that didn't disappoint as it played out, with frequent negative comparisons to *The Phantom Menace* and *Attack of the Clones*. Oddly, though, the new Star Wars trilogy reverses the trajectory of the typical trilogy in that Lucas did provide a strong finish after two unwatchable movies. If one were to line up the six Star Wars films in their numeric order, you would get an interesting bell curve. Of course, *The Ewok Adventure* and *The Star Wars Holiday Special* somewhat distort the symmetry.

Also, *2001* was nominated for Academy Awards in the categories of Best Director and Best Writing, Story and Screenplay. How many science fiction films are given that respect these days?

MATTHEW WOODRING STOVER: I see you quote Mike Resnick saying that novelizations teach writers to be lazy; does Mr. Resnick characterize James Blish (author of more than ten volumes of Star Trek episode tie-ins) as a lazy writer? Do you? How about Joe Haldeman, author of the Trek tie-in *World Without End*? How about Greg Bear (author of *Star Wars: Rogue Planet*)? Sean Stewart (author of *Star Wars: Dark Rendezvous*)? How many more top-rate authors would you like to have the opportunity to personally insult?

LOU ANDERS: Just one.

MATTHEW WOODRING STOVER: Let me direct your attention to this statement of yours: "By contrast, when you read a novelization, not only are you getting exactly what you are expecting, you are almost certainly not getting a writer's best work." First, as any self-respecting Star Wars fan will tell you, you're just flat damned wrong on the first point; any reader of the New Jedi Order will have at least *three* novels in that list (one of them, most likely, *Traitor*, by Your Humble Counsel for the Defense) that he will tell you contained elements that shocked, dismayed, surprised and/or stunned him. On the second point, well—you're not a novelist. Let me put it this way: if you were a writer whose books sell, say, thirty-odd thousand copies, and you had a chance to write a novel that you *knew*, from the *start*, would sell a *minimum of half a million copies*, and would introduce you and your writing—and your concern with serious fiction—to millions of fans (because those books get passed from hand to hand as well), would you piss on the chance and hold back your best work?

LOU ANDERS: You are correct; I am not a novelist. What I am is an editor. And speaking in my capacity as an editor, who reads and evaluates hundreds of manuscripts a year, if the Star Wars novelization I read in preparation for this anthology is indicative of the respective author's "best work," I would hate to read his own original material. I gave up on page 188, having endured the shameless padding and horrendous transgressions of the most basic rule of writing—"show, don't tell"—far longer that I would normally tolerate, for the purposes of this essay. Furthermore, I am also a consumer, who has as much right to vote with his dollar as anyone else, and more of my own hard-earned cash won't be going to LucasBooks anytime soon. But that's just me. Have a happy Life Day!

MATTHEW WOODRING STOVER: Shameless padding? "Show, don't tell"? Is that all you've got? No wonder you're an editor instead of a writer. That's the most pathetic excuse for a personal insult I've ever heard. I get better than that from the semi-literate wannabes on the Web.

"Stover makes Dan Brown look like Tolstoy."

"*Heroes Die* is the kind of book a demented third-grader might finger paint in his own vomit."

"The only way *Blade of Tyshalle* could be any worse is if it had been edited by that pseudo-intellectual human pimple from Pyr."

As trash-talk goes, Mr. Hundreds-of-Manuscripts-per-Year, yours barely makes it to the level of a stuck-out tongue.

(Reaction in the courtroom)

DROID JUDGE: Order! Order! Mr. Stover, you are out of line!

MATTHEW WOODRING STOVER: What else is new?

DROID JUDGE: Do you have an actual question?

MATTHEW WOODRING STOVER: No, Your Honor. I'm finished with this son-of-a—ah, witness.

DROID JUDGE: Mr. Stover, you are to treat all witnesses with respect. Please don't make me warn you again. You may now call the Defense witness.

MATTHEW WOODRING STOVER: Actually, I have three witnesses on this charge.

DROID JUDGE: *(severely)* You know only one witness per charge is allowed.

MATTHEW WOODRING STOVER: I ask the Court's indulgence in this case. There are multiple charges here: that Star Wars is unfairly crowding out other books, that Star Wars novels are not as good as original novels, etc. I'd like the freedom to address these charges.

DAVID BRIN: If I may, Your Honor. Each of us needs to give a little. After all, the topic is popular culture. Mr. Stover has permitted me a bit of speechifying, during cross-examination. In return, I've been relaxed about his—colorful language. We can give way on this point, as well.

DROID JUDGE: Very well, Mr. Stover, I'll indulge this. Please call your witnesses.

MATTHEW WOODRING STOVER: My first witness is fantasy writer Laura Resnick, who will discuss the realities of the bookstore shelves. My second witness is novelist and Star Wars writer Karen Traviss, who will discuss the literary merits of Star Wars novels. My third witness is Kristine Kathryn Rusch, a science fiction and fantasy writer who will explain why Star Wars is just what the genre needs.

Are Brain-Dead Chimpanzees
Eating My Shelf Space?

WITNESS FOR THE DEFENSE:
Laura Resnick

SEVERAL YEARS AGO, a heated debate raged in the Science Fiction and Fantasy Writers of America (SFWA), a respected national organization, about whether or not work-for-hire novels should be eligible for the Nebula, the prestigious annual literary award voted on and presented by the SFWA. Some members argued that such books were as well written and worthy of recognition as any other kind of novel; other members argued that the very nature of work-for-hire should exclude it from Nebula consideration. And in a particularly memorable written statement, one prominent SFWA member dismissed work-for-hire novels as something that any brain-dead chimpanzee could write. In other words, work-for-hire books emerged as a controversial issue among science fiction and fantasy writers, one that provoked fiery arguments and open insults in a professional forum.

A work-for-hire novel is a book on which the novelist is a hired hand, so to speak, rather than the original creator and exclusive copyright owner of the work. One very common form of work-for-hire—a form which you may well have read without even realizing it—is the ghostwritten novel; this is a novel written by someone other than the purported author. For example, the well-muscled, golden-haired, Italian-born model Fabio did not write the romance novels that bear his name. Those books were written by a ghostwriter. (I apologize if this revelation comes as a terrible shock and you feel your innocence has been irrevocably destroyed.)

However, a ghostwritten book is merely one type of work-for-hire. Many work-for-hire novels are actually written by the person whose name is on the cover. The distinguishing feature of a work-for-hire novel is not who wrote it or who's taking credit for writing it, but rather, who owns the intellectual property rights to the work.

When a novelist thinks up an idea and writes the book (for example, my next novel, *Doppelgangster*, due out in December 2006), she is the sole creator of the work (unless she turns out to be a plagiarist, in which case we have a moral obligation to dismember her slowly with rusty implements), and she owns the intellectual property rights to that work (unless she signs a really bad contract). Such a novel is referred to as an "original" novel. This doesn't mean the author had a brand-new, never-before-explored idea or has produced a staggering work of breathtaking originality; it means that the author is the exclusive creator and copyright owner of the material.

As copyright owner of the work, she (and, later on, her heirs) has the right to license the novel for publication. This is habitually referred to as "selling" a book; but, in fact, novelists don't actually *sell* books in most instances, despite that common phraseology. We typically license publication rights to a publisher for a specified period of time. For example, my original novel *Fallen from Grace* (a romance novel which I wrote under the pen name Laura Leone) is licensed for exactly three years from the date of publication. (Most licensing arrangements are much more complicated than that, but I can't imagine that you really want the tedious details.) After three years, the publisher of *Fallen from Grace* will no longer be entitled to keep printing copies of the book; and at that point, I will be entitled to "sell" it to another publisher. (Whereas if I try to resell the novel prior to expiration of the licensing agreement, the publisher can sue me for breach of contract.) And if, by some chance, I become internationally famous after death, my heirs will able to sell *Fallen from Grace* again, this time for a blue fortune, and toast my memory with Dom Perignon. (It sounds improbable, I know. But, hey, look at what happened when T. S. Eliot's *Old Possum's Book of Practical Cats* was adapted for the stage, years after the poet died. It became *Cats*, the long-running international hit musical with the prophetic motto, "Now and Forever." And Eliot's estate became one of the richest in publishing history.)

In addition to such vulgar considerations as mere money, copyright ownership also means that, unless I sign a really bad contract, I have artistic control over my material. No editor or publisher can make substantive changes to my text without my permission (which—editors everywhere, please take note—will *never* be forthcoming). For example, no one can legally rewrite one of my characters as a raccoon. I mention this because it actually happened to a friend of mine who signed a really bad contract. (I'm not kidding.)

None of the above, however, applies to a work-for-hire. Instead, a novelist is contracted to write material to which someone else owns the intellectual property rights. She may be treated with deference and her written work scarcely altered by anyone; or she may be dropped from a project 100 pages into the book, and her position— even the material she's written for the project—offered to someone else. I mention this because it happened to me on the only ghostwriting project I ever worked on. (And, as is often the case with ghostwriting, I signed a confidentiality agreement, so I can say nothing about the book or who hired me. However, I was paid fairly, treated courteously, and I agreed with the decision to drop me from the project on the basis that my writing style wasn't right for it.)

As previously mentioned, ghostwriting is just one kind of work-for-hire book. The most common type of work-for-hire in the science fiction/fantasy genre is known as the "media tie-in" novel. This refers to any book whose creative origins are derived from a media entity, such as cinema, TV or gaming. Examples of media tie-in series in SF/F include Star Trek, DragonLance, Highlander, The X-Files, Roswell and Tomb Raider books. And, of course, the single most successful and prominent media tie-in series ever to flood the bookshelves is probably Star Wars.

The specific characters and universes of these various series are the intellectual property of the media conglomerates which own the rights to the films, the games or the TV shows that are the basis of the books. If I tried to publish and profit from a novel about the frankly dysfunctional Skywalker family of the Star Wars universe without getting the written permission and legal cooperation of Lucasfilm, I would almost certainly be ruined by the massive lawsuit they'd bring against me to protect their intellectual property. Del Rey Books, a division of Random House, can publish Star Wars books because it has a licensing deal with Lucasfilm to do so. And the novelists who write and deliver these books to Del Rey are engaged in work-for-hire; they are neither the original creators of the Stars Wars characters and universe, nor do they control the intellectual property rights to these books. Additionally, their artistic control of the Star Wars novels they write is limited by Lucasfilm. A work-for-hire novelist may wish with all her heart to kill off Han Solo permanently in her book, for example; but unless Lucasfilm agrees to this (which seems unlikely), the book will never get published (and the author will never get paid). Han Solo is not the novelist's character, and his destiny is not under her creative control.

Such books are at the heart of the debate that led one SFWA member to publicly describe a number of his colleagues as "brain-dead chimpanzees." Quite a *large* number of his colleagues, in fact: hundreds of media tie-in novels written by dozens of SF/F writers have been published over the past decade or two. And Star Wars alone accounts for a large percentage of that figure, since it has endured as a popular publishing phenomenon longer than any other series (with the possible exception of Star Trek, which began its tie-in publishing venture back in the late 1960s, though there was a definite lull for a decade or two after that brief flourish).

Like most other media tie-in series, Star Wars probably hit its commercial peak in the 1990s, which was when media tie-ins became a notable fiscal force in SF/F publishing, as well as a notable *physical* force, taking up a lot of shelf space in the SF/F section of bookstores. Since that peak period, the phenomenon has receded a bit, but it has by no means faded away, nor does it seem likely to do so in the foreseeable future.

And "shelf space," far more than Nebula Award recognition, is the key issue in the debate about media tie-in novels. A question posed often among SF/F writers (and not always in the most rational, respectful terms, it must be admitted) is whether the shelf space inhabited by media tie-in novels should instead be reserved for original novels. (To reiterate, "original" means that a book—whether brilliant and innovative, or shamelessly clichéd and derivative—is the artistic creation and intellectual property solely of its author.)

It's worth noting that no one ever seems to argue that original fiction should be eliminated entirely from SF/F shelves in favor of media tie-ins. (Writers have expressed *fear* that this will happen, but no one ever proposes it as a jolly good idea.) All debate on this subject seems to be about whether SF/F shelf space should be allotted entirely to original fiction, and media tie-in novels either eliminated completely (in an ideal world); or their shelf space reduced considerably; or the books all moved to some other part of bookstore, opening up their shelf space in the SF/F section for original fiction. And when I say there's "debate" on this subject, I mean there are passionate but probably pointless discussions among writers. Bookstores, after all, have made their decision clear by shelving SF/F-related media tie-in books in SF/F sections nationwide for two decades. So I don't think *they're* debating this a lot.

Bookstores are retail businesses, and they allot so much shelf space to media tie-in books for one good reason: there's a demand for the books. If readers didn't buy media tie-in books, then the books would be given little or no space on bookstore shelves. The shelving of media tie-ins isn't a plot to destroy original fiction and forcibly turn the world into Star Wars-reading zombies; it's just business.

Similarly, if publishers didn't get a lot of orders from distributors and head buyers for media tie-in books, they'd stop publishing them. Publishing is a business with very narrow profit margins, and those margins are made still narrower by the large chunk of the sales profits that media conglomerates typically demand in exchange for licensing their publishing rights. Therefore, the *only* media tie-in series that keep releasing fresh books are those that are selling well. If your favorite media tie-in series has disappeared from the shelves, that's because it ceased to be profitable enough for any publisher to renew the licensing agreement.

This is also why the suggestion, sometimes made in a plaintive wail, that publishers might start acquiring and publishing more original SF/F fiction (or at least invest more in marketing the original fiction they acquire) if they'd just stop acquiring and publishing so much of that damn media tie-in fiction, is naïve. Publishing houses publish media tie-in novels for the same reason that booksellers order them: there is a market for them. If a publishing house closed down a profitable tie-in program, this would not improve the fiscal resources of the house; and it takes fiscal resources to finance the expansion of any publishing program (such as increasing the quantity of original SF/F fiction that the house acquires). If you don't believe me, go buy stock in a publishing house that's restructuring or starting to expand its publishing program. You'll learn quickly.

Therefore, it's more logical to assume that, if anything, the existence of a profitable media tie-in program at a publishing house is a good thing for its original-fiction program, because there are probably some profits flowing into the house; if not, though, the tie-in licenses will not be renewed. Indeed, despite the precarious climate of the current publishing market, Del Rey, which publishes the popular Star Wars tie-ins, is currently expanding its original-fiction program in SF/F.

So, okay, publishers and bookstores are businesses, they're in this for the profits, they publish and shelve media tie-ins because they make money doing so. But what about the writers? Are they braindead chimpanzees churning out this talentless stuff simply in pursuit of a profit? What about readers? Are they the *real* brain-dead chimpanzees, gobbling up formulaic novels about movie characters instead of reading worthy original fiction?

Well, first of all, brace yourself for a shock: although I don't know any writers who got into this business for the money, we all *need* money and *like* money. Some of us sometimes even write something strictly *for* the money. Or, as my father, science fiction writer Mike Resnick, has been known to say on occasion: "It's noble to starve for your principles, but it's chicken shit to make your wife and children starve for your principles." I myself have occasionally written something just because I wanted the money. And I imagine that a few media tie-in writers have written a few books (perhaps even a few Star Wars books) just because they wanted the money.

However, most media tie-in writers enjoy the work and are passionate about doing it. I know, because they're always saying so (firmly, loudly and sometimes belligerently) when original-fiction writers accuse them of doing it just for the money, or because they don't know any better, or because they lack principles, or because they're not as talented as we are, yada yada yada. Many tie-in writers are fans of the TV shows and movies they write about, and they thoroughly enjoy writing novels set in those universes. Many of them are good writers, and most of them also write their own original novels when not busy writing tie-ins.

Despite the fact that writers like and need money just like mere mortals, no one ever got into this business for the money; we write because we *like* to write. (Or we at least have a love-hate relationship with writing.) And we generally write *what* we like to write, too. I write fantasy instead of horror because I like fantasy and I don't like horror. I don't write tie-ins because I'm not interested in tie-ins, but I write essays because I *am* interested in essays. In this respect, I'm not unusual: I am much better—and much more successful—at writing what I like to write than at writing what I do not like to write.

So rather than being unprincipled opportunists in it strictly for the money, or brain-dead chimpanzees who can't write anything else, most Star Wars work-for-hire novelists like writing the books. It's true that in many cases, their original-fiction careers are not as lucrative or busy as their Star Wars careers; but then again, *I* like writing romance, and my romance career is not as lucrative or busy as my fantasy-writing career. That doesn't mean I'm in fantasy for the money or because I can't do anything else; but it does mean that I sensibly invest more of my time in writing fantasy, where my work is in demand, than in writing romance, where it is not. To assume that someone only writes a Star Wars novel because he wants the money or isn't a good enough writer for original fiction is to assume that media tie-in books are necessarily "lesser" novels.

Which is the same assumption that goes along with criticizing someone for *reading* tie-in novels. I am frankly not a fan of Star Wars novels or any other media tie-in novels. I also don't like horror novels, techno-thrillers or sagas, and I am not a fan of the original fiction of Isaac Asimov, Danielle Steel, Stephen King or Ernest Hemingway. Your mileage may vary. All art is subjective, and there are indeed media tie-in writers who I consider better novelists than some prestigious award winners I've read. Readers are entitled to find the SF/F that they want to read, be it a Nebula Award-winning original-fiction novel or a Star Wars book. Whether one is better than the other is strictly in the eye of the beholder. And if anyone ever tries to make me read another Thomas Hardy novel, I will complain to the UN High Commission for Human Rights.

Finally, what makes any discontented original-fiction novelist with sagging sales suppose that media tie-in readers would suddenly flock to his work if only all those damn Star Wars novels weren't crowding the shelves? Doesn't it seem more likely that if media tie-in books disappeared from SF/F shelves, media tie-in readers would venture into the SF/F section of bookstores far less often, spend less money on books and be even less likely to buy an original-fiction SF/F novel on impulse?

Laura Resnick is the author of twenty original-fiction novels, including *Disappearing Nightly* and *Doppelgangster*. You can find her on the Web at www.LauraResnick.com.

Driving GFFA 1

or How Star Wars
Loosened My Corsets

WITNESS FOR THE DEFENSE:
Karen Traviss

SOMEBODY DUMPED A FERRARI in my drive last year.
They were kind enough to leave the keys in it. Now, there are a few things you can do with an unexpected Ferrari. You can leave it standing in the drive and polish it, or you can use it to do the school run, or you can jump in, slam your foot to the floor and see how fast that sucker can fly.

On February 26, 2004, Del Rey and Lucasfilm left a Ferrari in my drive. So I decided to burn rubber.

It's been the most productive ride of my life. I describe it unashamedly as the best thing that ever happened to me, and that's not just because it was good for business in a pragmatic marketing and money kind of way, but because it also liberated me as a writer. It was superficial lust at first sight financially but then the relationship blossomed into true love, and nearly two years later I can look back and see that Star Wars changed my life in ways far more complex and far-reaching than just putting food on my table.

The call came out of the blue. "Would you like to write a book for us?" asked Shelly Shapiro at Del Rey. "It's tied in to a video game called *Republic Commando*."

I knew nothing about Star Wars and even less about media tie-ins—and completely zero about gaming. This was my first year as a novelist: my debut novel, *City of Pearl*, wasn't even on the shelves yet. I did some rapid research, but friends warned me I'd be ruining myself as a serious author, as if I were some pedigree poodle who'd jumped over the wall to be spoiled for breeding by the attentions of the neighborhood mutt.

"It's rubbish," said a friend. "You've got a career as a serious writer ahead of you. Don't touch it."

I never was much good at taking advice.

The game was about a commando squad; I was a military special-ist, both as a former defense correspondent and a military SF author. It sounded right up my street, although I'd have to finish the novel in eight weeks to meet my other book commitments. But I couldn't ignore the fact that grabbing the coattails of the most successful fran-chise in history would give me the kind of exposure and fast-track to my career that I simply couldn't buy.

And they were paying me for the privilege. It was too good to be true.

What brand-new author *wouldn't* want a crack at a readership of hundreds of thousands? Who wouldn't want that kind of publicity and opportunity in her very first year in print? I felt the Force was with me. In fact, I was so determined it was going to *stay* with me that I nailed its bloody feet to the floor.

But it was a single line of a conversation with the LucasArts content manager that really lured me into the GFFA[1] at a much deeper level.

There was the small problem that I knew zip about Star Wars in March 2004, although I'd reviewed the movies as a very young jour-nalist. (No, really. I was tall for my age.) I liked the Vader guy, I re-called: commendable management style, cool outfit. But that was about it. I had to start doing my homework. I don't read novels, not even if I'm paid to, and anyway the Republic Commando world was brand new, so the continuity would largely be created by me, work-ing alongside the game team. I plunged in with all the confidence of the joyously ignorant.

---

[1] Galaxy Far, Far Away—what Star Wars fandom calls the Star Wars universe.

And *joyful* pretty well summed up the whole experience. I had total freedom to create the plot and my own characters, including what
became known as "that crap Jedi," the plain, skinny, not-very-gifted
but very hardworking Etain.

I had a superb continuity minder at LucasArts called Ryan Kaufman,
who was on call 24/7 to answer my queries and clear up points like
how the armor codpieces fitted on the commandos. No detail was too
small, and he never lost patience with my endless questions.

"Let me get this clear," I said. "Somebody creates a secret clone
army. Then they maneuver the Jedi into using them to fight the Separatists."

"That's right," said Ryan.

"So. . . ." My journalist brain was whirring. I had no preconceived
happy notions about Jedi. I was new in town. "This is a *slave* army.
They're bred to age at double the rate and die young. They have *no
choice*. And the Jedi just take them and use them as cannon fodder?
No questions asked? No big moral debate?"

"You got it," said Ryan.

I was outraged. "And these are the *good* guys?"

That was the exact moment at which Star Wars moved from being
a nice little earner into *something I really, really wanted to write*.

Jedi. The elitist bastards! These poor bloody clones, used and discarded...and of course I was told about Order 66 from the start.
Serves the buggers right, I thought. The spoon-bending hippies
would get what they deserved for their complicity in maintaining a
slave army.

I wrote *Republic Commando: Hard Contact* like a maniac for eight
weeks, grabbing every spare second from my job, fueled by abstract
anger, drawing on the energy you derive from seeing the strange and
the new. I loved every second. I knew I'd almost weep when I was
finished. (Yes, I nearly did.)

I slipped into a new way of working right away. I'm a hard SF writer, and the GFFA is not hard science. It's allegory and myth wearing SFnal clothes. But as I can only function as a hard SF type, and
I take the military authenticity seriously for a whole raft of reasons,
I did the most realistic job I could within the confines of continuity. Somehow, without reading a word of Star Wars, I took the British

SAS and SBS and turned them into Omega Squad, a group of four na-ïve but pretty adept clone soldiers who win through by persistence, skill and comradeship. The Jedi Padawan who they team up with is, frankly, pants. She's not exactly the A-Team; they have to help *her* out. There's no Luke or Obi-Wan Force leaping to the rescue in this book, no sirree. This is the triumph of the ordinary man—no, the tri-umph of the most oppressed.

Inevitably, hard SF clashed with SW continuity at a number of points. I knew that was the internal ecology when I took the Lucas shilling, so I had no real problem accepting there was no time di-lation with FTL and all those other pesky unscientific things. Like cloning humans and maturing them at double-time....

Oh. *Oh.*

And this was the point when I became liberated from my hard SF corset and was forced to look at much, much bigger themes than epi-genetics and military economics. I had to go beyond the top dressing of the science and look at the impact these technologies had on in-dividual people. That's what I *thought* I was doing in my own series. But thanks to my epiphanic experiences writing Star Wars, I found I was only doing a lite version of that. I was still too caught up in the science. It stopped me exploring the characters to their limits.

In my own universes, I would never have looked at cloning at all. I felt it was a path too frequently trodden; I didn't think I'd have any-thing new to say. Had I tackled a clone army in my own terms, I'd have become engrossed in the failure rate, the developmental prob-lems and the psychological mess that kids raised by aliens would have become—if they survived gestation in tanks at all. It would have been a very different story.

But all that detail was done and dusted before I arrived on the scene. I had to work with the continuity from the movie *Attack of the Clones*, in which the cloned men are around ten years old but near-ly twenty biologically, and fully trained elite troops. Rather than re-strict me, though, it freed me to look at the ethical and human side of the equation. They're child soldiers. Their lives and rights have been stolen from them in the name of might, right and the Republic. And nobody in the Republic seems to object—least of all the Jedi. It's the kind of moral mire into which you can fling yourself.

By that stage, I was about to storm the barricades. Order 66? I'd have *volunteered*, mate.

One of the themes that most occupies me as a writer is the dividing line between the "us" that we treat with respect and can empathize with, and "them"—the external bin into which we dump those who we can crap on and get away with it. It can be gender, species, race, age—or genome. Wherever it's drawn, and whether we know we're doing it or not, it's the tipping point where people—decent people on the surface, people like you and me—rationalize and justify their exploitation and abuse of those who are different. *They're not like us.* So they don't *feel* like us, do they? They're the enemy, they're just kids, they're savages, they're only animals, they don't feel pain or loss or love. We can do as we like with them; because we *can.*

You can see the pattern now. This one book caught me at the right time and on the right issue. It was the big red Ferrari. All I had to do was abandon a fear of speed and get in.

So what's it like to be a clone? How does it feel to be raised in a sealed environment by aliens, and know nothing but combat from the time you can walk? How do you deal with the outside world? And how do you change when you see what the world is, and what's been done to you, and what you can never have? One of my readers—an academic from MIT, in case you believe a demographic stereotype of fandom—said that everything I write is about the politics of identity. And that acute observation has helped me understand why the GFFA and I seem to be made for each other.

My love affair with the GFFA was cemented. Murky politics; love it, love it, *love* it. Moral ambiguity: bring it on. Big human issues: slavery, war, love, jealousy, poverty, misery, greed, ambition. This is the stuff that a journalist can get stuck into. Lucasfilm let me go as dark as I wanted to. They let me write a real war story about real men faced with difficult moral choices every day. I poured my guts into it because I was suddenly free of the need to get stuff like the FTL physics right, and I was ambushed by the emotional element of the universe. It was like moving from doing technical drawings to creating impressionist paintings with vivid colors. I saw the world in a new light.

I finished *Hard Contact* with a sense of bereavement. I'd created a huge backstory in order to write it because I needed to know what happened to all the characters from birth to death, and part of that was expanding the Mandalorian culture. I even started building the language. When I turned in the manuscript, I wanted to go on with the story. It *mattered* to me. And that passion transmits itself into your writing, and your readers notice.

At that point I had to start my third Wess'har Wars book, *The World Before*. I came to it as a different writer because of the way *Hard Contact* had taken the brakes off me. I'm a journalist by trade: I was trained *not* to feel about the subjects I covered and to keep my distance, an approach I carried over into my *City of Pearl* books.

But as an author, you *have* to feel for each character—and feel *vividly*—for that power and passion to penetrate the filter of cold paper to reach the reader. By breaking that ingrained habit, I wrote a far better book in my own series. I say that because readers noticed the shift in gear, and told me so.

The liberation continued. I went on to write more Republic Commando books and other Star Wars novels. The sequel to *Hard Contact*, *Triple Zero*, was an even more emotional experience for me, and I burned through it in five weeks. That confirmed something else for me: I wrote better when I shut out everything else and took a run at it. Too much time to think, and I lost the fire. Without Star Wars and the punishing schedule that went with it, I might never have discovered that.

I've had sneers from writers who say there's no artistic challenge or merit in writing in someone else's universe. Needless to say, they've never done it. I wish they would: they'd learn a lot. Resisting the urge to mount the curb and mow them down in my Ferrari, I like to point out that it takes a new level of discipline to fit canon and remain true to the shared universe while keeping the original style and approach that the publisher signed you for in the first place. And writing characters who've been known and loved by fans for thirty years—like Luke and Han—is genuinely challenging. I know. I've just done it, and it's hard. When I want a rest, I go back to my own series. It's far easier in skill terms.

Star Wars has taught me a huge amount about the craft of writing in a very short time. The learning curve for me since March

2004 has been the north face of the bloody Eiger: I've worked with composers and artists, I've worked with other authors on a joint series, and I've even created a full working language, Mandalorian. I'm now teaching it to fans. Would I have developed any of those skills—or had that much varied fun—if I'd only been writing my own reality-grounded, hyper-accurate *realpolitik* series? I doubt it very much. Star Wars kicked me hard up the arse, and it was the making of me.

The restrictions of media tie-ins force you to grow. Ironically, the freedom lies in having to think outside your *own* creative box. Canon and continuity make you work harder to find work-rounds: necessity really is the mother of invention. And—to use my favorite analogy—there are no oranges in Star Wars. You have to reexamine the nuts and bolts of your writing because it's a wholly constructed universe, so analogies about surfaces like orange peel are denied you. All your own-brand clichés are out of reach. You redefine your approach. Even the age range of the audience made me stretch my skills: denied my usual palette of salty Anglo-Saxon expletives, I had to learn to write authentic soldiers' dialogue without four-letter words and explicit sexual references.

Yes, it can be done. And I think I'm a better writer for having learned that.

So I grew. And I gained, and so did my non-Star Wars books, which sold better and were better books because of Star Wars and its influence. And I got paid. Lucasfilm and Del Rey liked me and I liked them, so I signed to do more work for them. With my other series, that enabled me to leave the day job and write full time. Does it get any better than that? I don't think so.

I'd be lying if I said the money wasn't a factor. Of course it is. I'm a jobbing writer, and I have been all my working life. But without less tangible benefits, no amount of money stops you getting pissed off with a job you don't like. I know: I've done that too many times in the past. There has to be *more*. Life's too short to have a job that saps your will to live.

In the GFFA, the bonuses for any writer are legion if you want to reach out and grab them. I've reached a whole new audience who might never have picked up my *City of Pearl* books, but who now do just that. I've had very rewarding contact with the fan community, who've been a sheer delight and have made me feel valued and welcome—and even a cynical old hack like me needs to be liked sometimes.

Star Wars fans are also pretty sharp intellectually, and the level of debate is high. I'm not referring to the continuity arguments—and yeah, how big *was* Vader's Super Star Destroyer?—but to the long, sometimes heated and constantly educational debates I have with readers about duty, obedience to authority, the nature of sentience, political expedience and the existence (or not) of evil. Those aren't lightweight issues. They inform our views of the real world. And I don't know any other entertainment franchise that stimulates moral debate quite as well as Star Wars. It's a mythological epic in the fullest sense, providing us with cultural icons and reference points; and what writer doesn't want a piece of that?

So you have choices with media tie-ins, as you have with that Ferrari someone dumped in your drive.

You can park it and look at it: in other words, you can just phone the book in and assume the reader doesn't notice or even care. (Oh, they do, believe me. And how.) Or you can just use the Ferrari for shopping and stick to the speed limit: the book is just a media tie-in and nobody thinks tie-ins have to be good books, do they? Nobody expects you to bust a gut and go for broke on it. Just coast. It's okay.

Or you can look at that shiny Ferrari and say: "Holy shit! I bet this thing can do 150 mph! Let's find out!" You can look at a big, fast, famous car whose keys have been pressed into your sweaty palm and just drive its guts out. You can throw yourself into that tie-in work and see how far and fast you can take it, and how far it can take *you*.

And you can experience the thrill of taking the curves a little faster than you thought you could and still be alive to tell the tale. Everyone needs a bit of adrenaline and stress to push their personal limits.

I'm still on the road in that Ferrari. And not only am I enjoying the drive much more now I know the layout of the dashboard: I'm a better driver because of it.

Karen Traviss is a British author whose Wess'har series has received critical acclaim. Her debut novel *City of Pearl* (2004) was nominated for the Philip K Dick and Campbell Awards. A former defense correspondent and TV and newspaper journalist, she also writes Star Wars novels and short fiction. She lives in Wiltshire.

Barbarian Confessions

WITNESS FOR THE DEFENSE:
Kristine Kathryn Rusch

S INCE THIS BOOK is titled *Star Wars on Trial*, and I am testifying for the Defense, let me proceed as if I were sitting in the witness chair. No, you don't have to swear me in. I'll raise my right hand if someone wishes, but let me simply say that when it comes to the future of science fiction—one of my passions—I feel as if I'm always under oath.

First, my credentials. I am a Hugo Award-winning science fiction writer who has, joyfully and without remorse, written nearly thirty tie-in novels. Since someone writing for the Prosecution will probably mention the words "art" and "literature," let me add that for more than a decade, I edited the two most literary publications in the SF field—*Pulphouse: The Hardback Magazine* and *The Magazine of Fantasy and Science Fiction*, for which I and my authors were nominated for dozens of awards. We even won a few. I have received awards in a number of genres, not just SF. Of my mystery series, written under the name Kris Nelscott, Salon.com said, "Somebody needs to say that Kris Nelscott is engaged in an ongoing fictional study of a thorny era in American political and racial history. If that's not enough to get 'serious' critics and readers to pay attention to her, it's their loss."

"Serious" critics and readers have paid attention: I have received several literary awards—given by people who only think of writing as "literature" and "art"—and I have become a darling of book clubs. Meanwhile, I glam around in my secret identity as a romance writer (Kristine Grayson, for those of you who don't know), and I skulk through life as the SF/fantasy/horror writer Kristine Kathryn Rusch.

All three of us (as well as several of my other pen names which shall go unnamed) read everything we can get our hands on. From classics to mystery novels, from literary short stories to the latest Nora Roberts, from science fiction novels to tie-ins, I read. And read. And read.

My catholic reading tastes (small "c"—look it up) and my catholic writing tastes match my entertainment tastes. I record fifteen hours of television per week (although I only have time to watch six hours per week; I catch up during those endless months of reruns). I watch two to three movies per week, sometimes more during peak seasons like Christmas and summer. Last week alone, I saw *Harry Potter and the Goblet of Fire* and *Good Night, and Good Luck*—one at an art house (guess which) and the other at the cineplex down the street.

I am one of the heretics who believes that art must be enjoyed first and analyzed later.

I am also a member of the Star Wars generation. Sixteen years old when the movie came out, at a first-night screening with a dozen of my high school buddies, I watched the world change right in front of me. Did I know that E. E. "Doc" Smith had done something similar thirty years before? Of course not. My small-town library never had that kind of trash (their words, not mine). Had I memorized the science fiction canon? Hell, I didn't even know there was such a thing as science fiction. Or fantasy. Or genre, for that matter.

And I didn't care.

All I wanted that night was a bit of entertainment. What I got was an addiction that has lasted through my adulthood.

I often say that I came to science fiction because, at thirteen, I fell in love with a classic *Star Trek* episode called "City on the Edge of Forever," written by someone named Harlan Ellison. My best friend, Mindy Wallgren (one year older, two decades smarter), told me that Ellison wrote short stories, and if I liked the episode, I'd love the

short fiction. She gave me a Hugo Award collection edited by Isaac Asimov, and I read every story in it. Then books by every author. And then more books, and more books, and more books.

But you must remember: I had no idea what genre was, so I didn't know where else to find wonderful stories like the ones I had just read.

Now fast-forward three years. I'm sitting in that theater and absorbing *Star Wars* like there's no tomorrow. And I buy not my first but probably my fifteenth tie-in novel (yes, we have to count those Partridge Family books (yes, there were Partridge Family books)). Next to that Star Wars novelization (which I should have kept, dammit!, considering how much the thing's worth now), I find a bunch more of those books like the ones I read in my Star Trek/Harlan Ellison phase. So I buy those too.

One of them is *Dune*, which had a very Star Wars-like cover. I fell in love all over again.

When Glenn Yeffeth asked me to contribute an essay to this volume, he sent me a list of topics, asking me to choose one and take the Defense or Prosecution position. There was no contest; I had to take Defense. I love Star Wars, especially Episodes IV, V and VI. Especially Episode V, known to you non-Star Wars buffs as *The Empire Strikes Back*, screenplay written, by the way, by a classic science fiction writer, a woman named Leigh Brackett.

I'm here to discuss the charge "Star Wars novels are poor substitutes for real science fiction and are driving real SF off the shelves." I will show, among other things, that Star Wars is exactly what science fiction needs right now. One of the questions Glenn posed is this: to what extent is current SF writing influenced by Star Wars? The answer is simple: not enough.

I'll start by looking at the definition of science fiction, otherwise known by the various abbreviations SF, SFF and SF/F. Those abbreviations, used in the SF field only, mean the same thing in his questions. Science fiction—as a marketing category—is called SF. Science Fiction The Marketing Category includes fantasy novels. Later reviewers and critics sometimes called the category SF/F to acknowledge the two different genres labeled as one. Because of that confusion,

the Science Fiction Writers of America wanted to acknowledge their fantasy base, so they started calling themselves SFFWA, which led to SF being labeled, in the SF field, SFF.

Why is all this important to my essay? Because, in the dark days before literary tropes hit sf (which in my essay, lowercased, stands for science fiction only), the sf and fantasy genre had the same goals. Large-scope stories, in which worlds or universes were at stake, created new but oddly familiar settings that were far enough removed from real life so that readers could escape their mundane existences. The lead character was not the protagonist; he (and it was usually a he) was the hero. He often followed the Hero's Journey (see Joseph Campbell, whom Lucas says he gleefully plundered). No matter how dark the journey, the reader will follow the hero because, the reader knows (and is reassured on a deep level) that the hero will triumph at the end.

When literary tropes hit sf in the 1960s, solid characterization, good sentence-by-sentence writing and dystopian endings became commonplace. "Realism" both in character actions and in scientific approach became more important than good storytelling.

Fantasy continued its heroic ways, promising—and usually delivering—those uplifting endings, those fascinating worlds and those excellent (heroic) characters. But science fiction started resembling the literary mainstream. The novels became angst-filled. The protagonists, demoted from their heroic pedestals, lost more than they won. The worlds became as ugly or uglier than our own.

Suddenly, sf became unreliable. Readers had no idea if they would find uplifting stories or dystopian universes. They didn't know whether, if they plunged through 600 pages of nasty, ugly worldbuilding, they would ever emerge into any sort of light. Sometimes, the sf devolved into one long scientific exposition. Or into jargon-filled, hard-to-follow stories that realistically explored situations set up in the bad old days of preliterary science fiction.

Science fiction editors and critics declared that something which had been done before—such as time travel to Hitler's Germany or space opera like E. E. "Doc" Smith's Lensman series—was unacceptable for the new generation of readers. The assumption was *and still is* that if someone in science fiction literature—anywhere or at any

time in science fiction literature—has written a known work on a topic, that topic is off-limits to future generations of sf writers.

That assumption arose when publishing was small, when sf was a community of readers who numbered in the hundreds. Walter Jon Williams calls this community "the science fiction village." In a marvelous essay published in *Asimov's*, he writes:

> Along with the fiction, the [sf] culture grew more sophisticated along the way, but it retained a proudly self-made quality, standards that it considered unique to itself, and a specialized vocabulary to describe both the texts, the contents of the texts, and the special view of life that was considered particularly scientifictional. Fandom may not necessarily be a way of life, but it's definitely a point of view.[1]

A problem arose for sf fandom, which controlled sf publishing, when people like me entered the mix. We received our introduction to sf through the media. Williams explains the dilemma:

> . . . electronic media brings science fiction to its audience free of Science Fiction Culture, the history and view of science fiction laboriously hammered out over the last sixty or seventy years.... Science Fiction Culture places the work in its context, relates it to other work, to traditional themes in science fiction, to contributions of individual editors and magazines. All of this is necessarily absent from visual SF, which—also necessarily looks at SF as a grab-bag full of ideas useful to put Scott Bakula in jeopardy again this week.[2]

But the only way the Science Fiction Village can protect itself against Media Barbarians pounding at the gates is to keep the village small. Such a task was easy in the early years of sf fandom. It's not so easy now.

The world has changed since the Science Fiction Village was created. After World War II, countless people went to college on the G.I. Bill. Those people became readers who bought books and read to their children at night. Readership grew across the board. So did

---

[1] Williams, Walter Jon. "Thought Experiments: The Science Fiction Village." *Asimov's Science Fiction*, July 2005, 22.

[2] Ibid., 25.

the book-buying public. Book sales expand every year from one to 5%, a phenomenal and consistent rate of growth not seen in most other industries.[3]

Fiction markets have expanded. In 2004 alone, 2,550 books "of interest to the SF field" were published as originals or reprints. This total number of books does *not* include gaming novels, movie novelizations or original novels written in a media universe (like the Star Wars novels).[4] The days of being able to read everything published in SF in one given year are long gone.

So the new reader coming in, the one with a voracious appetite for SF, has a wide range of choices. The problem is that most of those choices respond to or build on ideas found in novels so long out of print that libraries and specialty used bookstores no longer carry them. Many of the sf editors still working today live in the Science Fiction Village. They are buying novels that appeal to a few thousand people, forgetting about (or ignoring) the barbarians at the gates.

It is impossible—physically impossible—to catch up on the language of Science Fiction Culture. I have immersed myself in it for thirty years now, ever since I discovered it, and I'm still reading the classics. What I didn't understand in the early sf novels and short stories that I read I researched. I forced myself to pass as a Science Fiction Villager, and lo and behold, they actually took me in.

But I'm a barbarian. Of the 1,417 original SF books published last year,[5] I read ten of them. Six of those books were short story collections. Two of them I wrote. The other two were novels by people whose sf I'd read before and liked. Of the remaining 1,407 books, I probably handled 750 of them and replaced them on the shelf. Honestly, most of the 750 novels I put back looked like work.

I read fiction for entertainment, relaxation and enjoyment. If I want to work, I read the history, literary essays, biography, science and legal books that grace my shelves.

Last week, for the first time in more than a decade, I saw an sf novel on the bookstore shelves that made my barbarian self reach for the

---

[3] *Publishers Weekly* year-end statistics, taken from their Web site, www.publishersweekly.com.

[4] Dozois, Gardner. *The Year's Best Science Fiction: Twenty-second Annual Collection.* New York: St. Martins Press, 2005. Dozois got his numbers from *Locus* magazine.

[5] Ibid.

book with joy. The cover had a picture of a derelict spaceship. The back cover blurb talked about far futures and finding artifacts in outer space. The cover quote said, "In the old tradition of *Astounding*."

Because I had been burned before, I read the opening few pages, and a section out of the middle. And then I bought the book. I haven't read it yet, so I won't say the title here.[6] But I will say that haven't been this eager to read an sf novel in almost twenty years.

Why am I eager to read it? Because the novel promises the very things that Star Wars gives: an escape, a journey into a new yet familiar world, entertainment. *A good read.*

The things you still find in fantasy fiction (there, charge #6: slain like the dragon it is). The things that sf jettisoned in the erroneous cold equations practiced by the New Wave.

The things that bring barbarians into the Science Fiction Village.

Why do I want barbarians in the Science Fiction Village? Forget that they're my kith and kin. Think for a moment about the shelf space argument (good old charge #3). Large genres do not care about how much shelf space goes to tie-in novels. The mystery genre has a plethora of tie-ins, from Murder She Wrote to CSI. The romance genre has fewer, but almost every single romance movie that comes out has a novelization attached to it. In those genres, no one talks about the tie-ins "stealing" shelf space, even though, logically, there should be less shelf space because of the very size of those genres. In 2004, romance novels accounted for 39.3% of all adult fiction sold. Mystery and thrillers came in second with 29.6%. General fiction, which is what most of us would call the "literary mainstream," was 12.9% of all adult fiction sold, followed by "other fiction," a category that includes such things as western and men's adventure, at 11.8%. SF came in dead last at 6.4%.[7]

---

[6] Okay. It's Jack McDevitt's new paperback *Polaris*.

[7] Statistics compiled every year by the Romance Writers of America (www.rwanational.org). These statistics come from two studies commissioned by the organization. One study "is tabulated by mathematician Olivia Hall, who draws data from mass-market book distributors' yearly release information; from figures released by the American Bookseller[s] Association; and from reports by Ipsos-BookTrends reports, an independent market research firm that studies book trends. This study is updated yearly. Another study focuses on reader demographics, book content, and book-buying habits. It is conducted via telephone survey and in-person focus groups by Corona Research, a market research firm in Denver, Colorado." Other studies, conducted by various organizations, have similar figures. Anyone who doubts these numbers can do his own tally using books in print numbers: total fiction books published into the number I used above. I prefer the RWA statistics; they're less dismal for SF publishing.

SF—y'know, the genre that includes fantasy. I have no idea how low the sales would be if we were only talking about science fiction all by its little ole self.

SF is committing the common sin of a dying literary genre. It blames its problems on the outsiders—the tie-in novels, and by extension, the barbarians at the gate—who are crowding the shelves and taking away space for "good" sf.

"Good" sf can retire to the specialty press where the Science Fiction Village can read and discuss it. It's time to return to the gosh-wow, sense-of-wonder stories that sf abandoned when it added literary values to its mix, the kind of stories that Star Wars, and by extension, Star Trek, Stargate and all those other media properties have had all along.[8]

SF's insularity is murdering the genre. Remember that publishing is a business. As a business, it is driven by sales figures, by profit and loss statements. For too long, sf has been in the loss side of the publishing column. As a result, fewer and fewer sf books are being published.

The figures I quoted above for 2004 are down from 2003. In that year, SF counted for 7% of all adult fiction books sold. In 2001, SF counted for 8%. The literary trend spirals downward while the media trend goes up. Half the new television dramas introduced in 2005 were science fiction or fantasy, or had a fantastic element. Most of the movies in the top twenty for the past five years have been SF. Nearly all of the games published have been SF.

If we bring even one-tenth of the people who play the games, watch the movies or read the tie-in novels into the literary side of SF, we'll revive the genre. In a few years, we could overtake mystery or even, God forbid, romance.

Let's put it another way. When Star Wars fans go to the bookstore like I did thirty years ago, they buy the latest novelization. Then they patrol the aisles for something similar—and find nothing. The books that would interest them are hidden between the jargon-filled limited-access novels that fill the shelves, behind the dystopian novels

---

[8] In fact, I believe the Star Trek juggernaut faltered when it lost track of the same values that sf literature forgot: the excellent storytelling, the Hero's Journey, the strange new worlds (familiar and yet unfamiliar) promised in the voice-over for the first and second series.

that present a world uglier than our own, the protagonists who really don't care about their fellow man/alien/whatever. A few attempts at reading that kind of book, and the SW reader returns to the tie-in shelf where the heroes are indeed heroic, the worlds are interesting and the endings are upbeat.

Recently, *Publishers Weekly* interviewed six sf specialty shops across the country, and asked their proprietors which books they consider must-haves. Not a single science fiction book on the lists has been published in the last five years. Fantasy novels include books published recently, but not sf.[9]

Science fiction, small case, is not producing novels that a large group of people want to read. And that spells the death knell for the literary genre at a time when, ironically, interest in SF is expanding.

Fantasy will take care of itself. It has kept the tropes that bring in readers. It is a growing genre. The statistics I list above do not include young adult novels, which means that the Harry Potter phenomenon is missing from the 6.4%. But the gaming novels, movie novelizations or original novels written in a media universe (like the Star Wars novels) are included in that number. Which means that the actual percentage of SF books in relation to other adult fiction titles sold is even lower than 6.4%. Significantly lower.

The literary genre, on whom we modeled this debacle, saw the error of its ways about five years ago. Now, you'll notice, literary fiction has become general fiction (see above) and publishes things sf sneers at—alternate histories set in World War II (Philip Roth, *The Plot Against America*); time travel novels (anything by Jasper Fforde); and scientific adventure fiction (anything by Michael Crichton). The literary genre has also reclaimed plot. Or, as Pulitzer Prize-winner Michael Chabon (author of the first-draft screenplay for *Spiderman 2*) calls it, entertainment.

In his opening to *The Best American Short Stories*, Chabon writes:

> Entertainment has a bad name. Serious people, some of whom write
> short stories, learn to mistrust and even revile it. The word wears

---

[9] Sidebar to "A Hobbit Takeover?" *Publishers Weekly*, April 4, 2005. Retrieved from Web site archives.

spandex, pasties, a leisure-suit studded with blinking lights. It gives off a whiff of Coppertone and dripping Creamsicle, the fake-butter miasma of a moviehouse lobby.... Intelligent people must keep a certain distance from its productions. They must handle things that entertain them with gloves of irony and postmodern tongs. Entertainment, in short, means junk, and too much junk is bad for you....

Chabon goes on to say that those serious and intelligent people are wrong. Because they have strangled entertainment in the literary field, the field has narrowed unpleasantly. He continues:

The brain is an organ of entertainment, sensitive at any depth and over a wide spectrum. But we have learned to mistrust and despise our human aptitude for being entertained, and in that sense we get the entertainment we deserve.[10]

Chabon's argument applies to the sf genre. We have gotten the entertainment we deserve, and it is slowly strangling the publishing arm of our great genre. Is current SF writing influenced by Star Wars? No, not nearly enough. We need more grand adventure, more heroes on journeys, more uplifting (if not downright happy) endings. Yes, we can keep the good sentence-by-sentence writing, the good characters and the lovely descriptions the New Wave steered us to. We can even keep the dystopian fiction and the realistic, if difficult-to-read, sf novels, so long as we do them in moderation. They cannot—and should not—be the dominant subgenre on the shelves.

Are tie-in novels taking shelf space away from SF? Hell, no. The tie-ins, from SW to Trek and beyond, are keeping SF alive. If we, the sf writers and publishers, want more shelf space, we have to earn it. We earn it by telling stories, some of them old faithfuls that the fans like to read, the things that have been published before. We earn it by entertaining. We earn it by creating characters as memorable as Luke and Han and Darth Vader.

We don't earn it by whining that a movie has encroached on our genre. Barbarians are taking over our little village!

Well, let me remind you of the things I said in the beginning of this essay. I am a barbarian in villager's clothing. I snuck into the SF

---

[10] Chabon, Michael. Introduction to *The Best American Short Stories 2005*, edited by Michael Chabon. New York: Houghton Mifflin, 2005.

Village long ago, but I sneak back out every night for a little forbidden entertainment.

Open the gates, people. We barbarians aren't here to trash your genre. We love it too. We love it for different reasons. But the village can become a city.

In fact, it needs to become a city in order to survive. So let us in. We can save the SF genre.

We're the only ones who can.

———

Kristine Kathryn Rusch is a best-selling novelist who has written a Star Wars novel. She's also an award-winning editor and writer, with two Hugos and a World Fantasy Award, as well as many other awards in science fiction, fantasy, romance and mystery. Her most recent science fiction novel is *Buried Deep*. Her next is *Paloma*, which will appear in October. Under the name Kris Nelscott, she has just published the sixth book in her critically acclaimed Smokey Dalton series, *Days of Rage*. Her works have appeared in fourteen countries and thirteen languages.

THE COURTROOM

DROID JUDGE: Mr. Brin, you may call any of the three Defense witnesses to the stand.

DAVID BRIN: I'd like to thank these three witnesses for their thoughtful testimony. I have no need to cross-examine.

Speaking only for myself, I must say that I do not blame Star Wars in any central way for the decline of high-quality literary science fiction. A far bigger culprit would be projects like this one, which, over the last few years, have lured me to spend time that I might otherwise have devoted to my latest novel!

Indeed, I have little complaint over movie-book tie-ins. I know that some of the authors of Star Wars novelizations have striven hard to insert bits of actual plot logic, going to creative—even heroic—lengths to find logical explanations for fundamentally illogical events. If George Lucas had asked any of this coterie of writers to help with the later scripts, well...just note that *one movie had a pro involved*—Leigh Brackett in *TESB*—and that film remains the favorite of nearly everybody, from highbrow to low.

Moreover, tie-in novels do encourage reading! They encourage reading of adventure stories in the right part of the bookstore...though not the right portions of the shelf. For, without any doubt, this is all part of the boom of fantasy and the decline of SF.

I think there are "forces" at work here that are much darker than Star Wars. Something is pulling us back toward the way of life that we had almost escaped. Toward feudalism and king-worship and kowtowing to priests and gurus. Toward a steady decline in confidence. In each other. In our civilization. In democracy. In science. And in ourselves.

No, if Star Wars has damaged the power of science fiction as a genre, it is only a small player in a larger trend. For this reason, the Prosecution accepts the case that these fine witnesses presented today. We move for dismissal of this charge.

MATTHEW WOODRING STOVER: For once I agree with the Prosecution. Dismiss this charge.

DROID JUDGE: No, all the testimony on this charge was compelling, including that of Prosecution witness Lou Anders. I'm going to let the charge stand and let the jury decide.

CHARGE 4

Science Fiction Filmmaking
Has Been Reduced by Star Wars
to Poorly Written Special Effects
Extravaganzas

Millions for Special Effects,
Not One Cent for Writers

WITNESS FOR THE PROSECUTION:
John G. Hemry

IN THE BEGINNING, there was a spaceship.

Then there was another spaceship. A really big one, chasing the first spaceship.

After that came the real fun. Guys in white armor firing blasters! Comic-relief droids! A beautiful princess with an attitude who kicks butt! A menacing figure in black with the voice of James Earl Jones! A colorful rogue! A wise old teacher who was what everybody wanted their grandfather to be like! A big, hairy Wookiee! Best of all, a typical teenager stuck in the middle of a nowhere place who just knows he's special, and turns out to be so special he's going to save the entire galaxy!

And the audience saw that it was good.

Star Wars made a lot of movie viewers happy, made George Lucas a lot of money and made dollar signs pop up in the eyes of movie studio executives everywhere. Perhaps most importantly, the original Star Wars movie (*Episode IV: A New Hope*) raised the bar for what an SF movie should be. Star Wars wasn't just fun, it wasn't just exciting, it was also a great story, well told and well acted.

This shouldn't have been a big deal, but it was. One of the unfair things about science fiction is that the field always seems to be judged by the general public based on the lousiest representatives of the genre. And (let's face it) SF has been cursed with some incredibly poor movies. The movie usually cited as the worst movie of any kind of all time is *Plan 9 from Outer Space*. *Plan 9* has about the same relationship to SF that a Twinkie has to actual pastry, but in the minds of the public, SF is all too often the Twinkie of the movie world.

Star Wars: A New Hope blew that away. Then came *The Empire Strikes Back* with the incomparable Leigh Brackett working the screenplay, and SF movie fans could strut into the local cineplex with their heads held high. *Return of the Jedi* wasn't up to the standards of its predecessor, but it was plenty good enough.

So what's the problem? Isn't it a foregone conclusion that the Star Wars series has been good for SF movies?

No.

Unfortunately, like a fantastic one-night stand without forethought, Star Wars produced some unwanted consequences. All too soon after the success of *A New Hope*, the children of Star Wars started appearing in our movie theaters and television screens. And all too often that, to put it mildly, wasn't good.

In fairness to George Lucas, who did a bang-up job on the first three Star Wars movies, there have been two phases to the saga of SF movies moving to the dark side. The first phase, built around those first three Star Wars movies (which are now the *second* three movies, but we'll get into that later) could be called the It's Not George's Fault period. The second phase (the What Was George Thinking? period) spread the fault around a bit more.

In retrospect, the negative fallout from *Star Wars: A New Hope* could've been predicted. Any movie that generates a good profit also results in a burst of copycat movies seeking to cash in on the first movie's success. Unfortunately (with rare exceptions), the copycats never bother to actually figure out what was really responsible for the first film's triumph. In the strange alternate reality known as Hollywood, spending tens of millions of dollars on a lousy knockoff movie is a lot easier than going to the mental effort of trying to figure out what really made the original so good.

As movie studios began churning out flicks allegedly inspired by the success of Star Wars, it was obvious that what passed for creative talent in Hollywood had actually seen only the first few minutes of the movie. They'd seen the big spaceship. Then they stopped watching, because to Hollywood's collective mind the big spaceship was clearly what had made Star Wars a success.

The ancient among us will recall that when old-timers like Gene Roddenberry started out doing SF, they came up with an idea for a story, then created some spaceships to match. After Star Wars succeeded so well, and Star Trek became a cult favorite with amazing legs, the movie studios decided to try to copy this success by reversing the process. They'd come up with spaceships and then, if the budget permitted, maybe a few ideas and maybe a story.

Then again, maybe not.

Enter: *Star Trek: The Motion Picture*. Enter: *The Black Hole*. Movies featuring endless shots panning across big spaceships, until you found yourself checking your watch and wondering if you could hit the restroom, then the snack bar to pick up some more popcorn, and come back to find the big spaceship shot still continuing. In the bad old days, this sort of thing was the filler a movie would gain to pad out a story that wasn't quite long enough. But after *Star Wars: A New Hope*, too many studios decided that the filler was supposed to take the place of the story. Viewers, dazzled by all of the special effects, weren't supposed to notice that there was a glaring lack of plot, realistic characters and intelligent dialogue in those scenes that didn't feature big spaceships.

In many ways, the epitome of these movies featuring big spaceships filled with a strange lack of substance was *Battlestar Galactica* (the 1978 version). (Yes, it appeared on TV, but the pilot was a movie. A movie appearing in the same period of time as *Rescue from Gilligan's Island*. The bar for high achievement in TV movies was not a lofty one in the late 1970s.)

The pilot episode, in between shots of big spaceships, actually did have a story of sorts for a while (don't sign peace treaties with homicidal robots), but even in that first movie the story sort of wandered off in the second half with a weird casino world interlude (which did, of course, feature spaceships). Worse was to come, though. After the pilot, the series apparently budgeted all of its funds for more big spaceship shots and decided not to worry about a comprehensible story line. The poor cast was left to wander through plots of weekly episodes which had been ripped off from old movies (such as *The Towering Inferno*, *The Guns of Navarone* and even *Shane*) with little regard for whether or not they made sense in the context of the series.

The lack of storytelling sense and dependence on special effects was in some ways epitomized by the apparently random decision to kill off the heroic male lead's love interest during the pilot. But that was okay, because they replaced the woman with a *robot dog*! Who'd want to watch a wife and mother character played by a real woman when they could watch a cute special effect? Because Star Wars had proved that viewers loved special effects, right?

Then there was the late 1970s incarnation of *Buck Rogers*, but the less said of that the better. About the only thing that movie and subsequent TV series did share with *Star Wars: A New Hope* was locking the cast (especially the men) for eternity into the hell of 1970s hair styles. (*"Luke, use the hair clippers."*)

But, as said before, all of this was Not George's Fault. That'd be like blaming the Beatles for "Billy, Don't Be a Hero." Yeah, the Beatles changed the direction of rock and roll music, but the inspiring example of *Abbey Road* couldn't be blamed for whatever other people decided to do with that direction. The first three Star Wars flicks stood as examples of How To Do It Right no matter how many other films Did It Wrong. George Lucas couldn't be blamed for all the schlock-meister productions trying to cash in on the idea that SF movies could be moneymakers. He couldn't be blamed for producers and directors who thought the special effects were the movie and traditional storytelling things like plot were unnecessary.

A good single example of the difference between the original three Star Wars movies and the many knockoffs they inspired lies in the female characters. *Star Wars: A New Hope* had a wonderful female character in the strong, smart and dynamic Princess Leia. What did other movies and TV series do with that? They created lead female characters who were prostitutes (*Battlestar*) or fashion models who looked great in their skintight outfits (*Buck Rogers*). Not so much characters as eye candy, an extension of the special effects concept to the leading women in the shows. Even the Star Trek movies maintained this trend, keeping the female characters very much secondary in terms of plot, action and significance. (Quick, name a female character from a Star Trek movie. Uh...Uhura?)

It's baffling but (at that time) also Not George's Fault that Hollywood keeps forgetting one of the enduring mysteries of the male mind, namely that tough girls with guns are as sexy as it gets. SF has always had a natural ability to exploit this since it can set stories in other places and times where such female characters are plausible. Who can ever forget Han Solo declaring, "I love you," in *Return of the Jedi* when Leia flashed her blaster at him? Yeah, baby. This important social dynamic wasn't lost on everybody. When Ripley showed up to start kicking alien butt she was in the same mold as Leia, a smart and tough lady who might not be a superwoman but wasn't going to give up and wasn't going to be beaten.

Unfortunately, all of that was about to change, in the form of the second Star Wars trilogy, which is now the first Star Wars trilogy even though it's the second. (Right here you see part of the problem. Placing films in proper order shouldn't sound like a time travel paradox.) Little did those awaiting the new trilogy realize that *The Phantom Menace* didn't refer to the Sith, but rather to what the film itself was going to do to Star Wars as a shining example of good SF and good movies.

The ugly truth was that George Lucas had painted himself into a corner with the first/now-second trilogy. An evil galactic empire with scads of star destroyers and hordes of stormtroopers (plus, not one, but two Death Stars) had been defeated by one (count 'em, one) Jedi helped by his oh-my-gawd-I-kissed-my-brother sister, a tribe of cute, merchandisable aliens, one big Wookiee, that lovable rogue, another lovable rogue (this one ethnic), and various other humans and aliens wearing the Star Wars equivalent of red shirts. In a series of films on the downfall of the Republic, how could Lucas possibly explain how the bad guys had triumphed in the first place over a whole *mess* of Jedi with mind-powers and lightsabers (even if one of those Jedi did sound like Grover)?

That was the basic problem posed by *The Phantom Menace*, *Attack of the Clones* and *Revenge of the Sith*. Good writers could've come up with some plausible and exciting explanations for all that in a Fall of Rome-type epic spanning the three films. Instead, Lucas chose to solve it by a story arc that actually had been predicted by none other than Mel Brooks in a single short phrase years before. In Brooks's SF movie parody *Spaceballs*, there's a scene where the villainous Dark Helmet has just tricked the hero, and gleefully declares that evil is certain to triumph because "good is stupid."

For reasons known only to him, George Lucas took "good is stupid" and ran with it. Even worse, Lucas decided to expand the concept to include "good can't act good" and "good has lousy dialogue." Just to make it abundantly clear that stupid was the theme for the new trilogy, Lucas introduced the character of Jar Jar Binks. In a remarkable advance since the days of the original Star Wars trilogy, and thanks to the wonders of the latest digital technology, a filmmaker was finally able to bring to life other worlds, fleets of spaceships, alien creatures and the walking/talking personification of stupidity.

As might be expected, this overall concept had some negative effects on the films. When wooden acting and clichéd dialogue don't hold the audience's interest, and when everybody watching knows the bad guys are going to win, that leaves only two things to hold the audience's interest. One is the age-old game personified by *Mystery Science Theater 3000*: finding so-bad-it's-sort-of-funny things to comment on ("What the hell is a midichlorian?" "Just steal the damned thing like Han Solo would've done!" "Whoa, nice abs on the princess!"). The other is (you guessed it) special effects.

In a throwback to the days of *Captain Video* or *Radar Men from the Moon*, the latest three Star Wars movies became about the special effects. The stories were lame, with characters who often seemed to be wandering through, barely interacting with each other. The Jedi powers were rendered as both awesome and ineffectual so as to prevent those powers from actually influencing events. ("The girl we thought was a handmaiden is actually the princess! I wonder why my mind-reading powers didn't pick that up!" or "Drat, yet another alien species my mind-control powers don't work on!") How did the incredibly wise and powerful Jedi triumph in *The Phantom Menace*? By accident. When the cute little Anakin flew through a special effects spectacular space battle and just happened to sail through a protective shield that keeps out weapons but not enemy spaceships and just happened to pull the trigger that destroyed the robot controls conveniently left in the most exposed possible location. Not exactly "use the Force, Luke."

But, hey, look at those giant underwater creature special effects. Why are the Jedi in a submarine in the first place, anyway, when it doesn't really have anything to do with the story? Oh, yeah, so the film could stick in those giant underwater creature special effects.

I could go on with the next two films but it'd be a depressing litany of similar stupidity and special effects-driven plots. I suppose in one way the *The Phantom Menace*, *Attack of the Clones* and *Revenge of the Sith* trilogy did succeed as a story. When evil is certain to triumph in the third film, one thing that helps keep the viewer looking forward to that ending is constantly demonstrated idiocy by the good guys. If somebody's too dumb to win, watching them lose does generate a certain perverse satisfaction. (It's possible to argue that this represents a triumph of the dark side of the movie viewer.)

Now, it's possible to make perfectly good and even great movies based on the principle that everybody in the movie is stupid. There's been a lot of great horror movies built on that concept ("Something is out there hunting us, so let's all wander off by ourselves so it can kill us one by one"), though a great many more very bad horror movies have also used it. *Alien* used a people-doing-stupid-things plot. So did the even better sequel *Aliens*. (This worked particularly well in *Aliens* because so many of the characters were in the military, and anyone with any experience in the military knows that as sure as the sun rises, you're probably going to get ordered to do something stupid at least once a day.) But *Aliens* generated more tension and drama with a scene containing no special effects ("They're inside the room!" "Where?") than all three of the latest Star Wars films did in their ponderous special effects-laden entirety.

But then the Colonial Marines in *Aliens* wouldn't have been at home in the latest three Star Wars movies. The Marines were great characters, interacting in a very real way with each other. That's what made the movie real, too, not the cool special effects. Kind of like Luke and Han and Leia.

Contrast that to what state-of-the-art digital filmmaking allows. Everyone has read George Lucas's descriptions of how he'd pull one take with one actor and insert another take with another actor into the scene. Two takes, one scene. Assume for the sake of argument that really does allow the insertion of each individual best performance. What's missing is actual human interaction, all the countless visual and verbal cues that one or more humans are really dealing with each other. There's a disconnect when that interaction is broken and two different interactions are stuck together. Our minds, designed to process how people communicate, consciously or subconsciously spot the problem. It makes the whole thing look phony, and makes even good actors look bad.

The negative effects of the godlike powers of digital editing didn't stop there. Creativity remains an undefined and poorly understood aspect of human genius. In movies, it's also all too rare. *A New Hope* and *The Empire Strikes Back* had gobs of creativity; *Return of the Jedi* less so but still an acceptable amount. Where's the creativity in the latest three Star Wars films? Could it be possible that creativity doesn't flourish when a director is focused on making sure every single pixel is doing exactly what the director wants? Watching the latest three Star Wars movies, it's impossible to erase the image of the director using a digital hammer to pound every trace of spontaneity and inspiration out of the film and the actors' performances.

The great distinctive things about the original Star Wars movies also went away. Remember tough girls with guns? By the time *The Phantom Menace* appeared, the girls in Star Wars had lost a lot of their mojo. The princess in that film got in some gun time, but was memorable mostly for incredibly elaborate clothes and for giving the eye to a little boy (the sort of scene that unites the audience by making everyone go "ew" at once). By the time *Revenge of the Sith* showed up, the new princess had regressed to the point of wandering around weepy-eyed and pregnant, powerless to change a tragic course of events (how are you going to be a good mother when you can't even keep your husband from going over to the dark side?). Blame it on the plot, blame it on the actors, blame it on the direction—the sad truth is that at her toughest, the princess in the latest three films couldn't shake a blaster at the princess in the first three films. In contrast to Amidala the overdressed, Leia looks tougher even when she's in a brass bikini. (Or maybe that should read Leia looks tougher *especially* when she's in a brass bikini.)

Thus the What Was George Thinking? period, the time span when great storytelling was digitally erased from the Star Wars saga. Instead of being "A New Hope" for better-quality SF movies, Star Wars became the ultimate example of special effects over story, over acting and over dialogue. Yes, *A New Hope* resulted in lots of rotten SF movies hitting the screens, but it also inspired some good stuff and it taught a generation of moviegoers that SF and good movies are not incompatible things. The success of the original three Star Wars films at least illustrated that good SF movies could make good money.

Now Hollywood knows (or thinks it knows) that lousy SF movies with great special effects can also make good money. The one positive effect of Star Wars, the good example it offered, has vanished. If we got lots of bad movies out of a good example, what will happen in years to come after the financial success of the latest three Star Wars movies? We'll see more and more really bad SF movies, because everybody knows SF movies don't need plot, character, acting, dialogue or any of that other stuff that other movies need. No, they just need big spaceships and explosions.

We're already seeing this today, when we no longer have to shell out ten bucks or more to sit in a movie theater to watch an SF movie with bad acting, bad plot and bad dialogue. Now we can watch the same kind of bad SF movies anytime we want to in the comfort of our homes on the Sci Fi Channel, which is cranking them out at a dizzying pace. It's a Lovecraftian tragedy, really, of good examples spawning bad imitators, and then spawning even worse prequels which will themselves spawn unspeakable imitations.

In the bad old days before *Star Wars: A New Hope*, when people thought of SF movies they thought of *Plan 9 From Outer Space*. Now, after the latest three Star Wars films, when people think of SF movies they think of *Plan 9 From Outer Space* and Jar Jar Binks. Not just bad, but stupid, too. That's the SF movie legacy of Star Wars.

John G. Hemry also writes under the name Jack Campbell and is the author of several novels, including the first and so far only legal thriller military SF series (a.k.a. JAG in space), which includes *A Just Determination*, *Burden of Proof*, *Rule of Evidence* and *Against All Enemies*. His latest space opera is *The Lost Fleet: Dauntless* (August 2006) under the Jack Campbell pen name. John loves the first Star Wars trilogy but wishes George had stopped there. He wanted to marry a woman like Leia and ended up with one who's pretty darn close but even better. He's also the author of the Stark's War series and numerous short fiction stories, as well as nonfiction articles on topics like interstellar navigation. A retired U.S. Navy officer, he lives in Maryland with his wife "S" and three children.

THE COURTROOM

MATTHEW WOODRING STOVER: (*checks his notes; mutters indistinctly*)

DROID JUDGE: Mr. Stover? Your cross-examination?

MATTHEW WOODRING STOVER: Uh, let's see... this is where I'm supposed to come up with some questions to make the case that the prequel trilogy is actually brilliantly written, with sparkling performances all around?

DROID JUDGE: Yes...? And...?

MATTHEW WOODRING STOVER: I'm thinking! I'm thinking! Give a guy a month or two, huh?

DROID JUDGE: Mr. Stover—

MATTHEW WOODRING STOVER: I mean, *Revenge of the Sith* won the People's Choice Award for both Favorite Movie 2005 *and* Favorite Movie Drama 2005—so it's clearly indefensible—

DAVID BRIN: Objection! Defense counsel is trying to argue facts not in evidence!

DROID JUDGE: Sustained. Remarks regarding *Revenge of the Sith* winning the People's Choice Award for both Favorite Movie 2005 and Favorite Movie Drama 2005 will be struck from the record.

MATTHEW WOODRING STOVER: All right. Fine. I'll take one for the team. Mr. Hemry, as I understand your testimony, you don't actually blame Star Wars or Mr. Lucas for the slew of embarrassingly bad big-budget sci-fi disasters that befouled eighties cinema. That you place blame instead on the lemming mentality of the Hollywood shit factory. So the actual crux of your argument—the crux of the Prosecution's *entire case on this charge* (lacking similar big-budget lemming die-offs following the prequels)—is that made-for-Sci Fi-Channel movies pretty much suck. This, the Defense is willing to stipulate. In fact, it seems as though many of them suck on *purpose*, but that's another issue. Mr. Hemry, you write SF legal thrillers, can you explain to the Court the logical (and legal) fallacy known as *post hoc ergo propter hoc*, and explain how this fallacy is the entire basis of your argument? Or would you like me to do it?

JOHN G. HEMRY: Will the judge kindly remind the Defense counsel that this is a court of law, not a basketball court, and trash talk won't score any points for him?

DAVID BRIN: I agree, Your Honor.

DROID JUDGE: Sustained. Let's keep it PG-13, Mr. Stover.

MATTHEW WOODRING STOVER: (*mutters indistinctly*)

JOHN G. HEMRY: The Prosecution is deeply saddened that the Defense has grossly misstated the Prosecution's case in a blatant attempt to mislead the Court. Nor will the Court be fooled by the Defense's attempt to impress the jury by showing that he can recite a Latin phrase which, in fact, has nothing to do with the Prosecution's case. Contrary to the claims of the Defense, the Prosecution did *not* directly link such brilliant films as *The Empire Strikes Back* to the current crop of "Sci Fi" movies. No, such films reek of (and "reek" is an appropriate term in this case) the example created by the unholy union of the once-great *Star Wars* legacy with Jar Jar Binks. The inspiration (if I may use such a word in relation to Sci Fi Channel movies) for those awful creations is to be found in the prequel trilogy. The Defense can't argue with a straight face that the movers and shakers in the movie industry haven't been looking at the financial success of the films in the prequel trilogy and paraphrasing the famous line from *The Treasure of the Sierra Madre*: "We don't need no stinkin' writers."

This is the Wookiee in the room that the Defense is trying to ignore, the Sith behind the curtain, the alien in the egg. As the Prosecution agreed, the original Star Wars trilogy can't be directly faulted for the junk that attempted to cash in on its success. But the prequel trilogy must bear responsibility for what it has done, making bad writing, bad acting and bad stories not only profitable, but also once again the image of SF in the eyes of the general public.

The Prosecution is willing to stipulate that *Revenge of the Sith* won the People's Choice Award for 2005, but challenges the Defense to name the last five films that won that award. This is not a mark of immortality, but of fan enthusiasm. Professional wrestling has many devoted fans as well, but that doesn't make it art.

MATTHEW WOODRING STOVER: The Defense is not willing to stipulate anything about professional wrestling, having no expertise on the subject; it appears to the Defense to be a violent variant of *commedia dell'arte*. And while the Defense admittedly cannot name the last five films that won the People's Choice Award, the Defense is similarly incapable of naming the last five films that won the Golden Globe Award, the Screen Actors Guild Award, the Film Critics Circle Award or the award of the Academy of Motion Picture Arts and Sciences, also known as the Oscar. Defense counsel is notoriously dim on this subject, as he is on so many others.

Post hoc ergo propter hoc means "This followed that, therefore that caused this." A car ran over my foot after George Bush was elected, therefore the Republican victory broke my toes. In other words, simply because a slew of crappy SF flicks showed up on basic cable after the prequel trilogy came out does not in any way show that the prequel trilogy caused that slew of crappy SF flicks; all it shows is that special effects technology has become cheaper, that the Sci Fi Channel has been making money off the Stargate franchise, and that not enough decent screenwriters live in Hollywood.

DAVID BRIN: Objection! Defense is again trying to argue facts not in evidence!

MATTHEW WOODRING STOVER: Oh, fine. Withdrawn. This whole trial thing is too damned complicated, anyway. Can't we just have a couple drinks, stand around and argue?

DROID JUDGE: Mr. Stover—

MATTHEW WOODRING STOVER: Yeah, I know. Call Bruce Bethke.

Good. Bad. I'm the Guy with the Lightsaber.

WITNESS FOR THE DEFENSE:
Bruce Bethke

I. INTRODUCTION

The history of American cinema can be described as a case study in evolution by means of punctuated equilibrium. The "equilibrium" part of this expression is fairly easy to understand: making movies is a hellishly expensive and labor-intensive business, and whenever you have that much money and that many people's careers on the line, the innate conservatism of the group always comes to the fore. There is a film industry truism that nothing succeeds like success, and another that holds that the quickest way to find success is by clinging tightly to the coattails and following closely in the footsteps of someone else who's already found it. The net result of these two ideas is that movie studios quite naturally have an ingrained tendency to become cinematic sausage factories, churning out mile after mile of motion picture by-products while very rarely departing from the established recipes.

It's the "punctuated" part of the expression that makes for an interesting discussion. Every now and then, while the rest of Hollywood is busy making remakes of adaptations of old TV sitcoms, a filmmaker comes along with a movie that is so fresh, so different and so seemingly original that it makes everyone else spill their kiwi frappuccinos in their rush to grab its coattails. More to the point, every now and then a film comes along that upsets the paradigmatic fruit cart and so insinuates itself into the larger zeitgeist that it becomes a cinematic watershed, and in some way the history of movies is forever after defined in terms of those films that came before, versus those that came after.

As you may have guessed, I believe beyond a shadow of a doubt that *Star Wars*[1] is one such film. The original 1977 movie had such an enormous impact, and left its footprints so far and wide across our popular consciousness, that there is simply no ignoring it now. The social phenomenon that is Star Wars is like a granite mountain or a law of physics; any work of fiction that comes afterward must either acknowledge its presence or find a way to work around it. For good or ill, *Star Wars* is a movie that has changed the world.

In being this, it joins a rather elect and somewhat peculiar company. *The Jazz Singer* (1927), *The Maltese Falcon* (1941), *The Ten Commandments* (1956), *Psycho* (1960), *The Graduate* (1967): all of these are films that changed their respective worlds, and all changed them in different ways and for different reasons. Nor is there necessarily a correlation between being a "great" film and being a "good" film: George Romero's original 1968 version of *Night of the Living Dead*, for example, is almost universally regarded as a lousy picture, but ever since, it's been impossible to venture into the same territory without either paying homage to it or working against it. D. W. Griffith's 1915 epic *The Birth of a Nation*, on the other hand, is generally considered a great film that forever changed the way dramatic narratives unfold on screen—but watch it as I have, with a roomful of African American film students, and you might come away with a somewhat different impression. And while Leni Riefenstahl's 1935 masterpiece *Triumph of the Will* is unquestionably a great film, it is equally unquestionably an *evil* film, right down to the blackest depths of its utterly rotten core.

---

[1] I am, of course, referring here to the original 1977 film, which was initially titled simply *Star Wars* and was only later renamed *Star Wars, Episode IV: A New Hope*. Since the latter is a rather unwieldy name, and since STE4ANH looks like something a 14-year-old might text-message, I will refer to the original movie as *Star Wars* throughout the remainder of my testimony.

What, then, makes *Star Wars* both a great film and a *good* film, and one that's been both very good to its creator and a positive influence on the films and other works of fiction that have come after? Well, to assess the impact of something, you must first determine how to establish a baseline, and in this case I believe the proper way to start is by asking one question: what was the state of sci-fi[2] in films in the years immediately preceding the release of the original *Star Wars*?

II. BEFORE STAR WARS: THE CREATION MYTH

George Lucas is on record as saying that his original script for *Star Wars* was heavily influenced by the writings of Joseph Campbell, and that his intention all along was to create a modern mythology that recapitulated the archetypal "monomyth" described in Campbell's book, *The Hero with a Thousand Faces*. Given Lucas's self-conscious myth-making, then, it is entirely fitting that another creation myth has sprung up around *Star Wars*, and it goes something like this:

Before *Star Wars*, sci-fi movies were the redheaded stepchildren of low-budget B-grade drive-in horror films. In those dark days cinematic sci-fi was a wasteland, populated only by mad scientists, giant insects, invading aliens, robots resembling ambulatory jukeboxes and the occasional oversized Japanese reptile.[3] The scripts were universally awful, the acting even worse and the special effects laughably bad. The story always revolved around some sort of homicidal monster and the new and exciting way it killed its victims, and the plot always centered on the two-fisted, square-jawed hero and the clever way that he and his screaming lady love interest found to unmask and defeat said monster. After the 1950s ended, the situation got even worse, and you could count on your fingers all the serious, big-budget sci-fi movies made between 1960 and 1977—and even then, some of them were pretty dicey in their claims to be "major" pictures.

After *Star Wars* sprang fully grown from the brow of Lucas, the field of science fiction experienced a great renaissance, and sci-fi writers and filmmakers alike finally got the attention they deserved.

---

[2] The term "sci-fi" was coined by writer, editor, agent and sometimes actor Forrest J. Ackerman, who is just about the nicest guy you could ever want to meet. It is used here with both permission and the greatest affection and respect. Yo, 4E!

[3] My personal favorite being Gamera, the giant, flying, fire-breathing, saber-toothed turtle.

The Academy of Motion Picture Arts and Sciences at last began to recognize the long-standing creative genius of sci-fi filmmakers and issue Oscars accordingly, major stars at last began to take roles in sci-fi movies, and studios around the world finally began to give their sci-fi filmmakers serious budgets to work with.

In making *Star Wars*, then, George Lucas single-handedly revitalized science fiction, led it out of the tawdry drive-in wilderness, and made it the loved, respected and highly profitable member of the family of creative arts that it is today.[4]

The problem with this creation myth, of course, is that its central assertion is easily proven false. While there certainly were plenty of low-budget films in the 1950s, with titles like *The Crawling Spleen* and *Attack of the 50-Foot Tapeworm*, there were also serious-message pictures such as *The Day The Earth Stood Still* (1951), *This Island Earth* (1955) and *On The Beach* (1959); taut and effective thrillers such as *The Thing from Another World!* (1951), *Invasion of the Body Snatchers* (1953) and *Them!* (1954); and big-budget effects pictures such as *Destination Moon* (1950[5]), *When Worlds Collide* (1951[6]), *War of the Worlds* (1953[7]), *20,000 Leagues Under the Sea* (1954[8]), and *Forbidden Planet* (1956). Nor were the 1960s the doldrums that the creation myth would make them out to be: in those years we saw *The Time Machine* (1960[9]), *Robinson Crusoe on Mars* (1964), *Fahrenheit 451* (1966), *Fantastic Voyage* (1966[10]), *One Million Years B.C.* (1966[11]), *Planet of the Apes* (1968[12]), *2001: A Space Odyssey* (1968[13]), *Charly* (1968[14]) and *Marooned* (1969[15]).

---

[4] In fairness, we must note that Lucas himself has never made this claim. Rather, fans and critics have often made this claim on his behalf.

[5] Winner of the Academy Award for Best Special Effects, 1950.

[6] Winner of the Academy Award for Best Special Effects, 1951.

[7] Winner of the Academy Award for Best Special Effects, 1953.

[8] Winner of the Academy Award for Best Special Effects, 1954.

[9] Winner of the Academy Award for Best Special Effects, 1960.

[10] Winner of the Academy Award for Best Visual Effects, 1966.

[11] Okay, so it was a silly movie that depicted early humans and dinosaurs living side-by-side. But what's not to like about a movie in which Raquel Welch spends the entire film running around in a fur bikini?

[12] Which eventually grew up to become a five-movie pentology and a TV series.

[13] Winner of the Academy Award for Best Visual Effects, 1968.

[14] Winner of the Academy Award for Best Actor in a Leading Role, 1968.

[15] Winner of the Academy Award for Best Visual Effects, 1969.

Wait a minute. *Charly*? *Marooned*?

If those last two titles seem unfamiliar: good. Because this brings up a very important point.

III. THE THREE Rs OF SCIENCE FICTION

One of the problems we encounter when trying seriously to assess the impact of *Star Wars* on science fiction in films is one of definition: just what *is* science fiction?[16] Is *Dr. Strangelove* science fiction? Certainly it was made by the brilliant Stanley Kubrick, whose next two films were the sci-fi masterpieces *2001: A Space Odyssey* and *A Clockwork Orange*, respectively. Without question, nuclear Armageddon and its aftermath has been the subject of a ton of overtly sci-fi movies, from any number of low-budget 1950s atomic mutant horror shows to Mel Gibson's krovvy-splattered Road Warrior series. But is *Dr. Strangelove* **sci-fi**?

And if so, does that mean *Fail-Safe* is as well? For that matter, what about the 1962 version of *The Manchurian Candidate*? The 2004 remake, with its plot switch to mind control via implanted computer chips, clearly was science fiction and was marketed as such. But what of the original, in which unwilling subjects' minds were controlled using drugs and implanted memories, not unlike the methods used in *Total Recall*? How about the 1968 social-upheaval fantasy *Wild in the Streets*? Or the early James Bond films *Dr. No* and *Thunderball*?[17]

You see, the problem we face when discussing anything involving genre fiction is that the membrane between "genre" and "mainstream" is constantly shifting and extraordinarily permeable. If a piece of genre fiction reaches a wide enough audience, then by definition, it *becomes* mainstream. In science fiction, especially, this shifting boundary is a daily problem for practitioners in the field. Things that were once sci-fi—computers, spaceships, lasers, genetic engineering, test-tube babies, cars that know where they're going and talk back to you, killer viruses that erupt from nowhere and threaten millions—can very quickly become tomorrow's news, or worse, yesterday's history.

---

[16] Four-time Hugo Award-winning editor George Scithers has been known to define science fiction as, "Whatever I'm pointing at when I say, 'That's science fiction.'"

[17] Winner of the Academy Award for Best Special Effects, 1965.

In the case of *Marooned*, then, we had a major-studio, major-budget, major-star-powered sci-fi thriller about a disaster in space, that was based on a novel by established SF pro Martin Caidin and had the bad luck to precede the real-world drama of Apollo 13 by a mere six months. In the case of *Charly*, on the other hand, we had a movie based on the Science Fiction Hall of Fame story "Flowers for Algernon" by Daniel Keyes. It's the heartbreaking tale of a retarded man who undergoes an experimental medical procedure to increase his intelligence and becomes a genius, only to realize that the experiment has been a tragic failure and he will just as quickly revert to his original mind. The title role earned Cliff Robertson an Oscar for Best Actor, but today, only obsessive fans and critics recognize *Charly* as being science fiction.

This suggests that the reason why so many people seem to think there was a sci-fi drought in the years before *Star Wars* is not that serious, major-studio SF films were not being made; they were. Rather, it appears that despite all educational efforts to the contrary, the majority of the population still suffers from SAMMS: the Saturday Afternoon Monster Matinee Syndrome. Science fiction in film is equated with *The Brain from Planet Arous*, *Earth vs. the Flying Saucers* and old Flash Gordon serials, not because these are truly representative samples of what was being made, but because these were the only films that were both old enough and *cheap* enough to be shown on the local UHF station during non-prime-time hours.

Thus, we discover another principle: in the world of motion pictures, more so than in any other human activity, *perception always trumps the truth*. In this case, a widespread perception has developed that all other arguments are just pedantic nonsense and pathetic cries for respectability, and that *real* science fiction is defined solely by presence of the Three Rs: *rocket ships*, *robots* and *ray-guns*.

IV. GROKKING THE ZEITGEST OF THE 1970s

To understand the astonishing impact of *Star Wars*, then, it's necessary to cast a wider net. We not only need to survey the other films that were being released at about the same time, both inside the genre and out in the mainstream, we need to develop at least a superficial understanding of what was going on out there in the larger popular culture.[18]

In television, for example, *Star Trek* and *Lost in Space*—both quintessential "Three Rs" shows—had long since been canceled, but they lived on in reruns, and Gene Roddenberry was stumping around the country trying to raise the money to shoot his *Star Trek* movie. New sci-fi TV series were not entirely absent from the major networks—*Planet of the Apes*, *Logan's Run*, *The Questor Tapes*, *Genesis II* and *Man From Atlantis* all had their shot at prime time—but most of these series are, thankfully, forgotten now.

In cinema, major-studio SF films continued to be made, but they were by and large either dystopian and nihilistic things or else barely recognizable as sci-fi, when not both. For example, Michael Crichton's 1971 medical thriller *The Andromeda Strain* seems restrained now in comparison to the Ebola-inspired films that have come since, not to mention the latest CNN headlines about West Nile and Asian bird flu. Crichton's next film, *WestWorld* (1973), sent a remorseless killer robot chasing after Richard Benjamin more than a decade earlier than *The Terminator* (1984), but today it is best known as being the inspiration for a particularly good *Simpsons* episode. In 1973 we learned that *Soylent Green* is people—need we say more?—and Woody Allen released *Sleeper*, but in keeping with the principle that the mainstream always assimilates successful genre films, *Sleeper* is now considered a comedy, not sci-fi, even though the Three Rs are present in abundance.

George Lucas took a crack at depressing dystopias in *THX 1138* (1971), John Boorman had his turn at the same in *Zardoz* (1974), and two young guys named John Carpenter and Dan O'Bannon made an utterly insane little low-budget movie entitled *Dark Star* (1974), after which O'Bannon decided his "alien loose and wreaking havoc inside a spaceship" idea needed a more serious treatment, and the result was *Alien* (1979). A young actor by the name of Don Johnson starred in Harlan Ellison's postapocalyptic nightmare *A Boy and His Dog* (1975), while Roger Zelazny's postapocalyptic nightmare *Damnation Alley* (1977) got turned into a Jan-Michael Vincent starring

---

[18] No problem. It was the 1970s. Superficial was in.

vehicle. In the year 1 BSW (1976) *Logan's Run* won the Academy Award for Best Special Effects,[19] for a story about a dystopian future in which social stability is maintained by the simple expedient of executing everyone who reaches the age of thirty—and this movie was successful and popular enough to be spun off into a TV series!

Perhaps the defining sci-fi film of the pre-Star Wars 1970s, though, was Douglas Trumbull's *Silent Running* (1972). Expensively produced, well acted, beautifully photographed—Trumbull went on to work on *Close Encounters of the Third Kind*, *Star Trek: The Motion Picture* and *Blade Runner*, among others—*Silent Running* features a trio of squat robots who are clearly in R2-D2's direct lineage and a painfully overwrought ecological "message" script that's about as subtle as spending ninety minutes getting clubbed over the head with a five-pound organically grown heirloom zucchini. By the time *Silent Running* grinds down to its final, depressing, hopeless ending, you're left with a very slight feeling of sympathy for the surviving robot, and a profound sense of relief that at least it's over and you won't have to sit through *that* again.

And that, in a nutshell, is the lingering legacy of the years immediately before *Star Wars*: at least they're over, and we won't have to go through that again. In the larger world of mainstream cinema, Hollywood produced a lot of movies that left the audience with that feeling: *Five Easy Pieces* (1970), *Diary of a Mad Housewife* (1970), *The Harrad Experiment* (1973), *Last Tango in Paris* (1973), *One Flew Over the Cuckoo's Nest* (1975), *Barry Lyndon* (1975), *Taxi Driver* (1976), *The Goodbye Girl* (1977)....

America in the mid-1970s, you see, was deep in the throes of what President Carter termed a "national malaise." We were trying to sober up from our post-Vietnam War hangover, but inflation and fuel prices were rising fast, thermostats and friendly governments were dropping like flies, and the country as a whole was fresh out of heroes. Our astronauts were unemployed: the last three Apollo moon missions were canceled due to lack of funding, and the first space shuttle would not lift off until 1981. Our cowboys were discredit-

---

[19] Actually, the Academy has changed the name of the award several times over the years, and *Logan's Run* won a "Special Achievement Award." It shared this honor with the Dino De Laurentiis remake of *King Kong*, but let us not speak of that awful abomination here.

ed: in less than twenty years we'd gone from "winning the West" to "exploiting the Native Americans" and from *Shane* (1953) to *Soldier Blue* and *Little Big Man* (both in 1970).

Our military was even more deeply discredited: in less than a decade John Wayne had gone from the widely praised *The Longest Day* (1962) to the even more widely damned *The Green Berets* (1968). Even the police were now villains: Officer Friendly and Sergeant Friday had been replaced by *Dirty Harry* (1971), a surly, brutal man only slightly better than the criminals he pursued. And when we in desperation finally turned to our political leaders for hope, what we got was President Carter on TV, wearing a sweater he'd borrowed from Mr. Rogers and telling us that we'd better tighten our belts and learn to smile, because things would never be this good again.

There. *That* was the prevailing spirit of the 1970s. That was what was in our hearts and minds when we plunked down our five bucks and walked into the movie theater. And then some pale blue letters appeared on the screen: *A long time ago, in a galaxy far, far away. . . .*

And the first brassy fanfares of John Williams's unabashedly triumphal score erupted from the speakers. . . .

And 121 minutes later, the first waves of baby-boomer teenagers came marching out of those theaters, giddy from a megadose of the Three Rs, humming the *Star Wars* theme[20] and ready to enlist in the Rebellion and join the fight against the evil Empire, if only someone would tell us just where exactly the evil Empire was.[21]

V. LIFE IN THE YEAR 28 ASW

Twenty-eight years later, it remains almost impossible to overstate the impact of the original *Star Wars*. No, George Lucas did not single-handedly rescue and revitalize cinematic science fiction. As I've shown, Hollywood never stopped making big-budget sci-fi films, and many of the films that appeared in the years immediately after *Star Wars*—*Close Encounters of the Third Kind* (1977), *Capricorn One* (1978), *Battlestar Galactica* (1978), *Buck Rogers in the 25th Century* (1979), *Alien* (1979), *Star Trek: The Motion Picture* (1979), *Flash*

---

[20] Well, at least it wasn't the Horst Wessel song.

[21] Did *Star Wars* help elect Ronald Reagan? It's at least worth considering.

Gordon (1980)—were in development long before *Star Wars* ever opened. It takes quite a while to make and distribute a major motion picture, or even a cheap one: Roger Corman, the King of the Low-Budget Quickies, was not able to get his *Star Wars* coattail-grabber, *Battle Beyond the Stars*, into release before 1980.

But once again, we're straying into the no-man's-land between perception and truth, and the point is not worth arguing over. There *was* an enormous boom in both film and print science fiction in the decade after *Star Wars*, and while some of us might think that the writing just possibly had something to do with it, if others want to credit the *Star Wars* coattail-effect, so be it. To dispute this point now is to overlook Lucas's one great, single and hopefully lasting accomplishment. In making *Star Wars*, George Lucas did just what he claims he set out to do:

He reintroduced the hero.

Consider that for a moment. In an industry dominated by a follow-the-leader mentality, at a time when scripts were full of cynical, violent and foulmouthed antiheroes and Linda Lovelace movies were playing in first-run theaters, George Lucas gave us Luke Skywalker: a pure, honest, good-natured and unalloyed hero. He gave us a stout-hearted lad who was loyal to his friends and uncompromising to his enemies; who, when faced with the choice between good and evil, chose *good*; and who, in the final scene, did not utter a pithy epigram as he finished off his greatest enemy, but actually tried to *save* him.

That is Lucas's great contribution. Luke Skywalker's cinematic progeny live on, not in the big-budget splat-'em-ups or the later Star Wars episodes,[22] but in the movies like Harry Potter and The Lord of the Rings. Movies with kindly hearts. Movies with *heroes*. And for that one accomplishment alone—even if that were his *only* accomplishment—I am willing to forgive George Lucas for everything he's done ever since, including *Howard the Duck*.

P.S. But all the same, Han *did* shoot first.

---

[22] Or are they earlier? I can never keep this straight.

Bruce Bethke works, writes, and when time permits, lives, in the frozen northern reaches of Minnesota. In some circles he is best known for his 1980 short story, "Cyberpunk." In others, he is better known for his Philip K. Dick Award-winning novel, *Headcrash*. What very few people in either circle have known until recently is that he actually works in super-computer software development, and all of his best science fiction gets turned into design specifications for future products.

Bethke can be contacted via his Web site, http://www.BruceBethke.com.

THE COURTROOM

DROID JUDGE: Mr. Brin, your witness.

DAVID BRIN: The Prosecution will gladly stipulate the honorable Mr. Bethke's central point, that the original *Star Wars* movie, later called *Episode IV: A New Hope*, was revolutionary in that it stimulated ebullience, wonder and joy, where SF filmmaking had been obsessed with the dark and depressing.

So? We are not here to look at Episode IV all by itself. Indeed, a key Prosecution contention has been that the joyful, can-do spirit of Episodes IV and V was gradually eroded and betrayed, as time went on, until a dreary sense of utter fatalism took over. One that eats away at us, even now.

Consider *The Phantom Menace*. Can you point to a single heroic act, by any Jedi or those poor, slaughtered Gungans that even remotely makes a difference or makes anything better? Palpatine's plan was to use the crisis to get appointed Chancellor, and then be seen coming to the rescue. This plan was accomplished, and he grins while the surviving heroes foolishly celebrate a totally unvictory. Bummer!

The Prosecution accepts Mr. Bethke's point about Episode IV. But isn't it only half a point. What about today? What has Star Wars done for us lately?

BRUCE BETHKE: An excellent question. This is why I believe it's essential to talk about Star Wars as *two* series, set in the same universe, but separated by sixteen years. In the original 1977–1983 series we were plunging into an *unknown* universe, with each new scene revealing a new wonder or a new thrill, and at the end of the series the future of every character still living was still wide open. In the later 1999–2005 series we were returning to a *known* universe, and to the stories of characters whose fates were already long since

decided, so of course these episodes are saturated with dreary fatalism. *We know how it all ends.* There is little room for surprise or
unexpected character development, as the characters' futures are
closed. The story of Anakin's rise and fall unfolds with exactly the
same sense of slow and awful inexorability as a slow-motion car
crash on an icy road. All that's left to do is to marvel at the scen-
ery while it happens and try to enjoy the ride. (Er, I just remembered that you live in California. Does this metaphor make sense
to you?)

In a peculiar way, I believe Lucas was a victim of his own early
success, and the later trilogy is in some strange sense a 1980s period piece. I think he felt trapped by the story lines he'd already
ended, the situations he'd already explained and the wonders he'd
already put on-screen, and this sense of being trapped shows up,
however subconsciously, in the story he wrote. I'm sure there were
things he didn't think of when he made those early films, that he
thought of and would have found really cool to use in the later films, but he *couldn't*, because they would have contradicted
his own established orthodoxy. For example, in a universe where
clones are apparently cheaper and have fewer rights than droids,
and the man-to-machine interface is seamless—witness the Skywalker boys' repeated resurrections from the spare parts bin—it's
surprising that clones aren't routinely vivisected and turned into
integrated weapons systems or truly mechanized warriors, *a la*
General Grievous.

There must have been a *lot* of ideas like this that occurred to
Lucas while he was making the later series, and he must have
found it enormously frustrating to be unable to use them.

So, to answer the question of what Star Wars has done for us
lately:

1. As I said in the main body of my testimony, it restored the
cinematic fortunes of the unalloyed hero. To give us Luke Skywalker in an age of rampant antiheroes, and to give us a film in
the 1970s that lacked the seemingly obligatory profanity and nude
scenes, was a move of great courage. I do believe that the success
of Star Wars is what made films like the Lord of the Rings movies,
The Chronicles of Narnia and the Harry Potter series possible.

(To truly appreciate what a departure the original three movies were, just imagine what they would have been like if they'd been made by Sam Peckinpah or Martin Scorsese.)

2. It made it much easier for subsequent SF films to get the green light for production and the budget needed to do the special effects right. One need only compare the Academy Award-winning special effects in *Logan's Run* (1976) to anything made after 1980 to appreciate the difference. So for example, while the success of Star Wars did not make *Star Trek: The Motion Picture* possible, it quite likely had a strong effect on the amount of time and money that Paramount was willing to put into effects in postproduction, and it probably had a *very* profound effect on *Star Trek II: The Wrath of Khan*, which is the movie that really launched the rebirth of the Star Trek franchise. In fact, in my mind's ear I can almost *hear* some Paramount studio executive saying to Roddenberry, "Gene, baby, loved the first movie, but for the next one, you really need to blow up some spaceships. And are you *sure* you can't have Kirk and Khan get into a big laser sword fight at the end?"

3. It raised the bar and provided the impetus for major and continuing advances in special effects technology, especially in the areas of CGI and SPMD programming models. I realize this is a two-edged sword and that in my other testimony I criticize the later movies for overuse of CGI, but speaking now on a purely personal level, as someone who has a circuit board from S/N 108 hanging on the wall above my desk, I think that this was a truly great thing.

S/N 108, I should point out, was the Cray X-MP supercomputer used to generate the CGI footage used in *The Last Starfighter* (1984), *2010* (1984), *Dune* (1984), *Labyrinth* (1986) and the pilot for *Star Trek: The Next Generation* (1987). This machine was returned to Cray in 1987 and kept running as a test bed and as the backup for a meteorology system in India, until we finally decommissioned and scrapped it in 2001. Not a bad track record for a twenty-year-old pile of hardware, eh?

4. It gave us the film career of Harrison Ford. Without *Star Wars* there would have been no *Raiders of the Lost Ark*, and Ford would probably have spent the rest of his career playing supporting roles

in clunkers like *Force 10 from Navarone*. The fact that Lucas later changed the cantina scene would seem to indicate that he really didn't understand what he'd created in Han Solo, and the fact that there is no comparable character in the later series seems to indicate that he really didn't understand that it was Harrison Ford who was the star of the original series.

Look: *Han shot first*. It's a defining moment for his character, easily equal to when Rick Blaine plugs Major Strasser in *Casablanca*, and I could write a lengthy essay on this topic alone. But I'm trying to reach a conclusion here, so we'll move along.

5. Finally, from a writer's point of view, the Star Wars series taken in toto has taught us all a very important lesson, and this is: *prequels are bad*. Science fiction writers should always strive to go forward, into the unknown, and to tell the story that has not been told yet. Speculation is more interesting than history: the story whose ending is not known in advance is *always* more interesting to more people than the story that goes back and explains how things got to be the way they are now. From the very first frame of *The Phantom Menace* we know that the Jedi will be destroyed, the Republic will fall, and the Empire will rise. In retrospect, then, Lucas's single biggest mistake was to go back and tell the story of the rise and fall of Anakin, rather than to go forward and tell the stories of the further adventures of Luke, Han and Leia.

Once Lucas committed to making a prequel, though, there was no way that the second series could be anything but depressing, futile and fatalistic.

DAVID BRIN: If the ebullience of Episodes IV and V helped engender other fun SF films in their day, is it possible that the dour, simmering pessimism of Episodes I–III has been just as influential, helping bring us to the point where it's hard to name more than a few optimistic sci-fi films in the last ten years?

Make your own list. Find more than one or two exceptions to the tone of defeatism, failure and predestined doom that pervades everything from *The Matrix* to the new *Battlestar Galactica*.

BRUCE BETHKE: I'll admit my list is pretty short: *Men in Black, Men in Black II, The Hitchhiker's Guide to the Galaxy, Independence Day, Stargate*—and now that I think about it, I'm pretty sure *Stargate* is more than ten years old. Maybe *Red Planet*, if you count a "survival against impossible odds" story as being optimistic; maybe the comic books movies such as *Hellboy*, *Spider-Man* and *X-Men*, if you want to stretch the definition of sci-fi far enough to include them.

But I don't think we can lay the blame for this on Episodes I through III. As I think the list of precursor films described in the main body of this testimony shows, sci-fi has *always* had a profoundly pessimistic streak. Even in print, optimistic SF stories are rare; by and large, sci-fi is the literature of disaster, human extinction, inhuman invasions and the end of the world as we know it. Even the Hitchhiker's Guide series *starts* with the complete destruction of the Earth and the near-total annihilation of humanity, and even the genre's most optimistic stories usually require the viewpoint characters to experience some difficult dislocations, terrifying transformations and painful sacrifices before the ostensibly happy ending is reached.

I believe the reason for this is far older than and goes beyond the influence of a few recent movies. I might even go so far as to claim that it's a fundamental principle: *science fiction is the literature of people who are deeply discontented with the way things really are right now*.

I mean, when you're telling the optimistic story of contented people, you're peddling a utopia, right? And what's more boring than utopia? The readers, writers and fans of science fiction have always shown a pronounced preference for dystopia. If you present them with a utopia, they immediately start looking for the blue pill, the seamy underside, the dirty little secret that underlies everything, the Morlocks munching away in the dark, or at least the incinerator that everyone goes into when they turn thirty.

The people who *are* content with the way things are now are not reading or watching sci-fi, they're not imagining themselves living other lives in other places and times, and they are most definitely not following this trial. They're off somewhere else, reading and watching stories about the sex lives of doctors and lawyers.

So who cares what they think? Clearly, *they* are not going to be part of the next stage of human evolution!

CHARGE 5

Star Wars Has Dumbed Down the Perception of Science Fiction in the Popular Imagination

It's All in the Numbers

WITNESS FOR THE PROSECUTION:
Tanya Huff

WAY BACK IN LATE AUGUST of 1980, five of us were driving from Toronto down to the World Science Fiction Convention in Boston. For reasons I can no longer remember but I'm sure made sense at the time, we left home at one A.M. and arrived at the Canada/U.S. Thousand Island border crossing at five A.M. Our ages ranged from eighteen to twenty-three, and we were not, at that hour, looking our best.

Now, we'd all been across the border to science fiction conventions before and we were all expecting trouble trying to explain to a civil servant working the end of the night shift—an armed civil servant at that—where we were going and why. Neither the hour, nor our youth, nor the fact we were a mixed group (three men, two women) was working in our favor. Lying never occurred to us. It might have been a Canadian thing. It might have been because we figured we were too damned tired to lie convincingly.

So we paid our toll and crossed the bridge and rolled up to the only station open at U.S. customs and immigration. A beefy, middle-aged man peered into the car.

"Where you going?"

"Boston."

"Why?"

"We're attending the World Science Fiction Convention."

"Science fiction?" he demanded suspiciously.

And before any of us had time to imagine the inevitable strip searches and start panicking, my ex smiled brightly and said, "You know, like *Star Wars*."

The guard's suspicion morphed instantly to delight. "*Star Wars?*" he repeated, smiling broadly. "I loved that movie! Saw it three times." And he waved us through.

In the summer of 1980, George Lucas was already changing the public perception of science fiction. Only three years after *Star Wars*'s debut on May 25, 1977, with *The Empire Strikes Back* only four months into its first run, three years before the Ewoks, nineteen years before Jar Jar Binks, it was already well on its way to becoming an accepted definition.

Twenty-five years later, Star Wars continues to control the public perception of science fiction—not by sustaining that early mass hysteria but by having changed the production and marketing of an entire genre.

Before 1977, the public's perception of science fiction wobbled about between the old Buck Rogers serials, the rumor that Charles Manson was a huge fan of Robert Heinlein's *Stranger in a Strange Land*, a somewhat skewed perception of the way the genre dealt with social commentary, and a remarkable string of less-than-stellar television shows. Science fiction was considered to be both kid's stuff and weirdly dangerous, probably having, given the times, something to do with drugs.

If you read it, you were considered weird at best and very likely a social outcast. Pocket protectors and psychotropics figured prominently, albeit dissonantly, in the nonreader's visualization of an SF fan.

On the bright side, thanks to writers who had emerged out of literature or the social sciences rather than an engineering background, there had begun to be a slow acceptance of science fiction among academics and reviewers. According to Magic Dragon Multimedia, which offers chronologies of science fiction literature and authors:

> The 1970s was not a decade of stylistic revolution such as the "New Wave" of the late 1960s, but perhaps a decade of consolidation, where

the lessons learned from mainstream literature, "New Wave" exper-
imentalism, and the classics of science fiction were melded into a
healthy hybrid. For example, leading author of the literature of para-
noia Thomas Pynchon published a mainstream bestseller which used
experimental techniques and was unquestionably science fiction:
Gravity's Rainbow.[1]

It was still possible to read every major work in the field. This is not
to say that everyone did, or even that I did, only that I could have
and that there were many who made it a point of honor. Those of us
who haunted the dark corners of specialty bookstores—where the
staff definitely *had* read every major work in the field, most of the
minor works and more than likely a couple of manuscripts provided
by regular customers—were expected to be able to talk as animated-
ly about Gene Wolfe as we did about Andre Norton or Larry Niven
or Anne McCaffrey.

That changed with *Star Wars*.

But wait, what about *Star Trek*, you ask. Wasn't the original *Trek*
(1967–69) hugely popular?

Yes. And no.

The original *Trek* was hugely popular among those who have always made up the science fiction audience, but I don't remember it
being exactly must-see TV among the general population. We read
the James Blish novelizations (I have the fifteenth printing of book
one—July 1972), we watched the appalling cartoon, and, suddenly
more visible than we'd ever been before, we accepted slings and ar-
rows of those who just didn't get it.

Some people came into science fiction through Trek, some people
remained exclusively Trekkie (or Trekker), but there weren't enough
of them to affect the genre as a whole.

The Trek phenomenon is more about staying power than size.

Don't ever let anyone tell you size doesn't matter.

To paraphrase the late, great Douglas Adams, *Star Wars* was big. If
you think space is big, well, take a look at what George Lucas did to
it. According to IBM.com, *Star Wars* (now known as *Star Wars IV: A
New Hope* but not by those of us who saw it first in 1977) is number

---

[1] http://www.magicdragon.com/UltimateSF/timeline1980.html#70sDates.

two in the top-grossing films of all time with U.S. box office earnings of $460,935,665. That's almost $461 million in the United States alone. On May 25, 1977, *Star Wars*'s opening day totaled $254,309 from just thirty-two theaters. That was Wednesday, there were forty-three theaters by Memorial Day Weekend, and the box office gross had risen to $2.1 million.

According to ABC News online, *Star Wars* had over the course of its first run 178,119,595 admissions. That doesn't mean 178,119,595 individuals. I personally saw it once a week for the seven remaining weeks I was posted in Victoria, B.C., five times once I got transferred to the East Coast and once in Mann's Chinese Theatre that winter when I was staying in L.A. Even the decidedly non-fannish border guard had seen it three times by 1980.

If we assume, just to get us a little closer to a number we can work with, that I was fairly typical of the non-obsessed fan and divide those 178,119,595 admissions by thirteen—recognizing that for every person who saw it once there was someone who saw it twenty-five times—we still have 13,701,507. Let me spell that out for you: thirteen million, seven hundred one thousand, five hundred seven people.

Thirteen million, seven hundred one thousand, five hundred seven people all, if not obsessed, at least fascinated, with the same thing.

And they wanted more. Science fiction was no longer weird; it had become trendy.

Movies—even the fascinatingly bad movies like *Battle Beyond the Stars*, which immediately jumped on the Star Wars bandwagon—take time to produce, so a large part of that nearly fourteen million headed for bookstores. Some of them very probably for the first time ever.

Those of us who were already readers had a couple of reactions. Some of us welcomed these new numbers, the thrill of being suddenly popular going to our heads. Some of us sneered at the Johnny-come-latelys with so much to learn about what it meant to be an SF fan. Some of us ran for cover. Many of us managed all three reactions simultaneously.

But what we missed, what hadn't actually occurred to most of us, with our noses buried in books and our conversations peppered with phrases like, "If it can't be expressed in figures, it is not science; it is opinion,"[2] was that these new people in our playground weren't science fiction fans; they were *Star Wars* fans. They wanted more *Star Wars*, and there were a lot of them, and they'd already proven themselves willing to pay for what they wanted.

Publishing companies are not in business to promote whatever specific branch of literature they produce. They do not exist to nurture talent or to enrich the lives of their readers. They are in business to make money. If they can also promote, nurture and enrich, even better, but if they don't make money, they disappear. Before 1977 science fiction publishers made enough to stay in business but not much more; there just weren't enough of us buying their books. What profits there were got funneled back into the companies.

Then all of a sudden a cry of "We want more Star Wars!" went up across the land and the novelization which had been released by Ballantine/Del Rey a year earlier to typical science fiction numbers was suddenly in great demand. By 1980, and the twenty-fourth printing of the paperback, there were five million copies in print. (I'm looking at my copy of the paperback, and that's the number splashed across the cover.) Five million copies at $2.50 translates to $12,500,000, and that's more than enough to be noticed.

According to Sarah Brouillette in "Corporate Publishing and Canonization: Neuromancer and Science-Fiction Publishing in the 1970s and Early 1980s," (Penn State University Press) "From 1977 alone, production was up 21%."

Thanks to *Star Wars* the audience for science fiction had expanded enormously. Unfortunately, the weight of those numbers insisted that *Star Wars*-type stories be produced. Spin-offs appeared. In 1978 there was *The Doomfarers of Coramonde* and *The Starfollowers of Coramonde*. In 1979 there was *Han Solo at Stars' End* and *Han Solo's Revenge*. In 1980 there was *Han Solo and the Lost Legacy*. All of these published by Ballantine/Del Rey, which had (and still has) a contract with the Star Wars Corporation.

Other publishers, understandably, wanted in on the action. How hard could it be? After all, *Star Wars* was nothing more than old-fashioned space opera mixed with some New Age "living force," vaguely

---

[2] Heinlein, Robert A. *Time Enough for Love*. New York: Putnam, 1973.

spiritual flavoring. It was heroes and villains and very little science. It exploited the most basic of all fairy tales—the hidden prince who would discover his destiny and become something larger than life. Most of all, it was fun—George Lucas's gee sparkly method of story-telling could be enjoyed with critical and analytical thought turned off for the duration. Best of all, a book purchased by those nearly fourteen million *Star Wars* fans would allow a lot of promoting, nurturing and enriching of the rest of the genre.

So here we are, entering the 1980s. Star Wars is a worldwide cultural phenomenon and a useful shorthand for getting carloads of science fiction fans across international borders. Science fiction publishers are actually making money. What's the problem?

Strangely enough, the problem is that, because of Star Wars, science fiction publishers are actually making money.

One of the tenets of capitalism is growth. Corporations, the backbone of the capitalist system, must continue to grow or they die. One of the ways they do this is by acquiring profitable businesses and adding them to their bottom line. The moment small specialty publishers began to make money, they suddenly became attractive to corporate publishing.

Back in the early 1980s when I started working at Bakka Books in Toronto (now Bakka-Phoenix and still North America's oldest science fiction bookstore), there were dozens of small imprints handling science fiction. Even Playboy had a science fiction imprint. The power to buy manuscripts rested in a lot of individual editorial hands. There was room for the weird and the wonderful. For hard science and engineering. For social commentary. For literary merit. Very few of these imprints made much money when looked at one by one, but the genre as a whole, supported by those nearly fourteen million *Star Wars* fans, was actually running comfortably in the black.

And then, one by one, over the years the smaller imprints began to disappear.

Right now, Holtzbrinck Group, a transnational German-based media corporation, controls (among many, many others) these familiar North American publishers: Macmillan, St. Martin's Press and Tor—all of whom have imprints of their own. Bertelsmann AG, another transnational German-based media corporation, controls Random House, Inc., which is responsible for Ballantine, Del Rey, Del Rey/ Lucas Books, Fawcett and the entire Bantam Dell Publishing Group. Pearson, PLC, an international media corporation based in the U.K., controls Penguin Putnam, which is responsible for Ace, Berkley, Penguin, Jove, NAL, Putnam and Viking. This didn't happen all at once, of course; it took years of larger companies devouring smaller imprints who were then devoured in turn. At Bakka we called it "Pac-Man Publishing" because imprint after imprint got munched.

Three international media corporations control most of the genre publishing in North America. Genre publishing made profitable and therefore acquirable by the massive influx of Star Wars fans.

And again, what's the problem? It's already been established that publishing companies must make money or they don't last. Isn't this just a difference of scale?

Yes. And no.

Back before Star Wars, the people in charge of the publishing companies were, if not also the people who chose the books, not very far removed. Now, the people in charge answer to the shareholders and the shareholders could care less about promoting, nurturing and enriching. Marketing has more power than editorial, and marketing is all about numbers.

Remember those 13,701,507 *Star Wars* fans?

That was a rhetorical question, by the way, since I doubt at this point you're able to forget them.

And lo, as corporations began to take over genre publishing, Marketing looked at what was selling and said, "Damn, this Star Wars stuff is selling like crazy. Let's give the readers more of what they will pay us money for." And Editorial said, "Wouldn't it be better if we gave the readers books that would challenge them and make them think? Books that explore new ideas and delve deep into the human psyche trying to find out just what it is that makes us human?" And Marketing said, "Are you nuts?"

I'm paraphrasing a bit, obviously.

Now, trends come and trends go, and we might, as a genre, have been able to get through this and eventually make up lost ground, except *Star Wars* was not a one-hit wonder—unlike *Gone with the*

Wind, which is the only movie ever to rake in more at the box office. *The Empire Strikes Back* was the highest-grossing film of 1980,
and any hysteria that may have begun to die down in the intervening
three years was ramped right back up again. In 1983 *Return of the Jedi*
did the same thing. It seemed Star Wars hysteria was self-sustaining
for three years and then needed a hit. Unfortunately, in 1986 there
was no new Star Wars, as Lucas had walked away from the series.

"What will we do?" cried Marketing. Unfortunately, before Editorial could make its voice heard, they answered their own question.
Movie tie-ins were clearly hot properties. And if movies, why not
television?

In 1997 John Kessel, referring to the Star Wars phenomenon, said,
"Ask yourself why 60% of SF today arises out of the media."[3]

60% in 1997.

In 1999, Star Wars came back. It has been said that *The Phantom
Menace* was the most eagerly anticipated sequel in the history of motion pictures. All right, technically it was a prequel, and people quoted were usually fans or in marketing, but that doesn't change the fact
that most of the 13,701,507 million of us went back to Luscasland,
all of us trained by over twenty years media tie-ins to expect a new
surge of Star Wars books.

Nor were we disappointed.

May 2002, and *Attack of the Clones* goosed the marketing hysteria by earning $110 million in its first four days of North American
release. May 19, 2005, and *Revenge of the Sith* opens at theaters all
around the world to record box-office grosses. It was déjà vu all over
again, except this time, the marketing forces were already in place.

Amazon.com, the largest online book retailer, has a Star Wars store.
The day I wrote this, a simple Star Wars search gave me 203,459 hits.
At Barnes and Noble online, 1,412 hits under books alone. Even up
here in Canada, with roughly one-tenth of the U.S. population, a search
in books on chapters.indigo.ca came up with 1,014 responses.

In large chain bookstores, the books that sell are given the prime
positions. They're given the displays with brilliant eye-catching head-

---

[3] Kessel, John. "Twenty-Nine Years, Twenty-Nine Books: The Works that Most Influenced Science
Fiction, 1963–1992." http://www4.ncsu.edu/~tenshi/index2.html. Originally published in *Science
Fiction Age*, 1997.

ers. They're given the shelves that are the most visible from the common areas of the store. What science fiction books have the highest numbers in chain bookstores? Go on. Take a look. I'll wait here. The evidence certainly suggests that those books are media tie-ins. Movies. Television shows. Computer games.

Yes, computer games. Which would not be as advanced as they are without the CGI developed by George Lucas's Industrial Light and Magic, a company made possible by the success of Star Wars.

Of course there are other books in the stores. The year I was on the jury for the Philip K. Dick Award, I was amazed by how many smart, exciting, convention-breaking books are still being written. Mind you, many of them are coming from independent presses, most of their marketing done by word of mouth, a large percentage of their distribution done over the Internet one sale at a time, and most of them never see the inside of a large chain store where books are treated as product.

However, large chain stores are exactly what the general public wants in a bookstore. They can get a coffee and a paper and pick up the latest celebrity offering and maybe wander around a bit to see what's happening in the rest of the store. An SF fan might indulge a craving for trendy bit of fluff and then move on to find something a little more substantial, but the general public, wandering past Mysteries and into Science Fiction while sipping their pumpkin latte, takes one look at shelf after shelf after shelf of media-tie ins and thinks, understandably I'm afraid, that this is all that Science Fiction is.

Why do we care? We care because that author writing the smart, exciting, convention-breaking book is barely making a living, and, eventually, the knowledge that multinational corporations are making millions from books that say little more than "good is better than evil because good has snappier dialogue" will have one of two effects—that author will realize he or she doesn't want to be associated with that kind of thing or that author will sign on to do the next blockbuster novelization.

Oops. Lost another one.

And we could have never devolved to this point without Star Wars.

Star Wars was the grandpappy of media tie-ins and has become a shorthand definition of science fiction for an entire generation. It isn't just that Star Wars—simple, sparkly and not exactly cohesive under critical analysis—has wiped out any literary merit science fiction had gained in the minds of the general public; it's worse: there are adults, with children of their own, who have never lived in world where science fiction wasn't reeling under the weight of Star Wars. There are adults who have never known the science fiction section of bookstores when they weren't dominated by media tie-ins.

We, science fiction writers and fans, were used to being considered weird, but now we, as a genre, are being dismissed as shallow, sparkly and not, let's face it, particularly smart if Star Wars is the best we can do.

In 1980, a U.S. border guard waved five fans across the border by accepting a definition of science fiction as *Star Wars* and saying, "I loved that movie."

In 2005 one of those same fans went to her travel agent for plane tickets to the World Science Fiction Convention in Scotland, and her travel agent said dismissively, "I'm not into that Star Wars stuff...."

Tanya Huff lives and writes in rural Ontario, Canada, with her partner Fiona Patton, six and a half cats and an unintentional Chihuahua. Her latest book and the third of the Tony Foster novels, *Smoke and Ashes*, will be out in hardcover in June 2006.

THE COURTROOM

DROID JUDGE: Mr. Stover?

MATTHEW WOODRING STOVER: Yes. Thank you, Ms. Huff, for sharing your experiences with the Court. Tell the Court, if you will: in the days when science fiction was not "that Star Wars stuff" but was instead "that Flash Gordon stuff" or "that Buck Rogers stuff," do you seriously think that the reputation of the genre was substantially better in the popular imagination? What evidence do you have for this?

TANYA HUFF: Back in the days when science fiction was, as you call it, "that Flash Gordon stuff," its reputation was much as it is now. And that's the problem. I'd like to think that after all those years of good writing as well as social and scientific considerations that we, as a genre, might have progressed beyond "gee sparkly" and "gosh wow" or even "good Lord..." in the popular imagination. We were, in point of fact, garnering some serious attention in the years immediately pre-Star Wars—as you yourself said in your 2001 SF Site interview:

"That's what the New Wave did for SF: injected real literary quality—a concern with character, relevance and plain old-fashioned good writing—that helped rescue SF from the scrap heap of spacecraft, robots and ray-guns."

Then the bright lights and the witty repartee and the overwhelming weight of the Star Wars phenomenon knocked us back a few decades as marketing took over from content. Also, I would argue that in the days when science fiction was, as you call it, "that Buck Rogers stuff," the genre had no actual reputation in the popular imagination, if you define popular as "prevalent among the general public," as the general public spent no time thinking of science fiction at all. These days, post-Star Wars, the general public has no choice but to notice us and form an opinion—it would be as difficult to ignore an elephant in the living room.

MATTHEW WOODRING STOVER: Have you ever taken the time to correspond with SF fans who have become SF fans precisely because of Star Wars? That for whom this "simple, sparkly, not exactly cohesive" saga was a "gateway drug" to a profound and serious lifelong commitment to the wider genre we all love (at least one of whom has become a spectacularly talented novelist who is a witness for the Defense in this very trial)? Do you have any idea how many of them are out there?

TANYA HUFF: As a matter of fact, I'm married to an SF fan who came into the genre with Star Wars. She's now working on her fifth novel for DAW Books. Star Wars was indeed her "gateway drug to a profound and serious lifelong commitment to the wider genre we all love," but she kicked the drug and moved on to become a talented novelist who writes books of brilliant complexity. I would argue that in order to become the writer my wife is or the writer the witness for the Defense is, you must move past simple, sparkly and not exactly cohesive—you must move on. And there's the sticking point.

I was the mass market buyer at Bakka Books in Toronto for eight years. Throughout the eighties and early nineties I worked the Bakka table at Toronto conventions. During that time, I watched the genre change from the front lines, and I spoke to hundreds of SF fans weekly. For every one of them looking for a book that could expand their universe, at book that could raise questions, a book that would make them think, there were easily a couple dozen looking for the same thing they read the week before. And the week before that. Yes, we have always had lazy readers—every genre has lazy readers—but I would argue that the weight of the Star Wars phenomenon expanded our cadre of lazy readers far beyond where it would have been otherwise. We're looking at a generation who have been told cradle to grave what to think. Media informs all of their choices—what cereal to buy, what car to drive, what music to listen to, what books to read. Star Wars has told them that this is what science fiction is, and given the amount of space media tie-ins take up in our bookstores—virtual and physical—a depressingly large number of them have never questioned that.

There are many people who came into the genre with Star Wars; there are many more people who define the genre by Star Wars.

MATTHEW WOODRING STOVER: Speaking as an author who was indeed barely making a living writing convention-breaking books, and who did indeed sign on to write a blockbuster novelization, are you entirely certain it's appropriate to describe me, personally, as lost? Are you willing to concede even the possibility that some writers might write as seriously for Mr. Lucas as they do for themselves, and then take their borrowed celebrity back to their own careers, to support their nasty habit of writing convention-breaking books—and in the process, lead some not-inconsiderable numbers of Star Wars ex-geeks with them, giving them a taste for SF Beyond the GFFA—so in fact helping to support the rest of the genre?

TANYA HUFF: Am I willing to concede the possibility that some writers might write as seriously for Mr. Lucas as they do for themselves? Sure. But I'm a big believer in anything being possible. Actually, let's turn that around: Am I willing to concede the possibility that some writers might write as seriously for themselves as they do for Mr. Lucas? God, I hope not. Unless things have changed a great deal since I last looked at the work-for-hire market, the work has to be completed within a very curtailed time frame. Good books can be written in three months, sure, but under a deadline so tight there's little room to explore possibilities—significant wordage must be cranked out daily because falling behind isn't an option. This is not a situation where you can get an extension for the demands of either art or craft—these books are marketing driven and marketing doesn't work that way. Timing is everything. Again, unless things have changed in the last few years, writers produce work-for-hire work under very strict parameters—you may not, for example, cause the characters to act in ways that haven't already been predetermined by the source production. You may not allow the novel to develop organically under the demands of story. I'm not saying these are badly written books—although some of them undeniably are—nor am I saying that books written without these constraints are all well-written books—because some of them undeniably aren't. What I am saying is that I sincerely hope that when writing for themselves, these authors take the opportunity of time and freedom of artistic expression a lot more seriously than they take a three-month deadline and characters they cannot change.

As for borrowed celebrity... well, I've seen a lot of people buy media tie-ins over the years, and I can pretty much guarantee you that nine out ten of them don't care about the author. There is no borrowed celebrity because there is no celebrity. There's only three months of your life you got very well paid for—and hey, that's nothing to sneeze at, but career-wise, to the book-buying public, it means little.

Is there a chance that a Star Wars fan will see your name on a non-Star Wars book, recognize it and buy it, moving away from shallow and sparkly and into the genre as a whole? There's a chance. If nine out of ten fans don't care then there's obviously one who does, and for you, personally, that 10% may well lead to a significant sales bump of your other work. Unfortunately, though, for the genre as a whole, when we're talking Star Wars numbers, it's those nine who don't care who count, because when you're talking about 90% of Star Wars-sized numbers, you're talking about a lot of people. Enough people to skew the genre. To paraphrase from an earlier fandom: "Marketing to the many outweighs the needs of the one."

Do I think it's appropriate to describe you as lost? Ask me again in five years.

MATTHEW WOODRING STOVER: Thank you, Ms. Huff. I certainly hope to. If I live that long; there's a rumor that the Sith are out to get me. I'm not sure I believe it. Does this look like a Kaminoan sabre-dart to you?

DROID JUDGE: Mr. Stover—

MATTHEW WOODRING STOVER: Yes, yes. Call Richard Garfinkle.

On Not Flying Solo in Hyperspace

WITNESS FOR THE DEFENSE:
Richard Garfinkle

W E ALL KNOW THE SCENE. The *Millennium Falcon* flee-ing pursuit jumps into hyperspace. For a moment the stars become lines and the audience cheers. At least that's what happened the far too many times I saw the original *Star Wars* at the age of fifteen (this was before it was *A New Hope*). I'm putting in the biographical information because it should be held against me in making this strangely slanted defense. I was at the right age to have my head blown off by the visuals of *Star Wars*.

Don't get me wrong, this was not by any stretch of the imagina-tion my first exposure to SF. I was a science fiction fan long before I saw the movie. I had read my way through most of the major writers of the time and several from before that time, and had watched *Star Trek* and *2001* and all the other required viewing for a fan of that era. Everything that showed up on the screen in that initial viewing of *Star Wars* I had already read from one author or another: hyperspace from Niven, robots from Asimov, an order of psychic good guys from E. E. "Doc" Smith. Even at the overly impressionable age I then was, I knew that I was watching fun sci-fi, not original science fiction.

At the time I had no ambitions to be a science fiction writer, nor were my friends proto-writers. We did not discuss the movie in terms of its place in the canon of science fiction; we just sat back and enjoyed the view, the dialogue (particularly Leia's dialogue) and the events as they unfolded before our eyes. We had no concerns about the movie's relation to the broader context of science fiction.

Now, far too many years later, I am called to look back upon it from the seat of the writer and ask whether or not the source of the experience I had as a fifteen-year-old has created a general perception of SF that is good for the field overall.

In two critical respects the Star Wars movies have been good for SF, although the ways they have been good are backhanded.

I do not defend the movies as good SF; they are not. However, I do maintain that they did a great favor for all of us who write SF and those who read that writing, because they took away the need for post-Star Wars SF writers to waste space explaining certain things. I also maintain that in the long run the Star Wars movies will have done us a very strange favor by drawing the audience for cinematic writing to the cinema. These two favors are not strictly connected, so I won't bother to try. I will start with the case that is easier to make.

STAR WARS HAS GIVEN US USEFUL SHORTHAND

One of the most common problems facing a writer, particularly an SF/F writer, is having to explain what his or her characters are undergoing and what they are seeing and what the implications of those experiences are without losing the audience's interest. In some genres this is not a real problem. Romance writers and their edgier counterparts can spend page after page going on about the minutiae of certain commonplace events without worrying about boring their readers. But in SF/F the writer has to explain the less racy aspects of the world the characters are in and sometimes has to clarify such oddities as doors, windows, foods, means of transportation, religions, architectural styles, etc., etc., etc. All books, classes and workshops on writing SF help student writers deal with these problems using a variety of strategies and tricks which I won't detail here. But behind all the sophisticated methods lies the simplest trick, a writing tool that is employed every day by everybody: familiarity.

This tool is based on the principle that it is easy to write what is familiar to the audience. An example: for just about the last century a writer could pen the following sentence without risk of confusing the reader:

Norma answered the ringing phone.

However, if an author in 1850 had tried to write a story with telephones in it, that author could not have written the above, because no one would know what a telephone was, why it rang or what it meant to answer it. This hypothetical author would have had to explain how a telephone worked or how people used them in their daily lives. Depending on the author's skill this would have taken anywhere from a paragraph to several pages. As a real instance of this, L. Frank Baum in the book *Tik-Tok of Oz* (1914) has a magical wireless telephone. He needs a paragraph to explain it to an audience used to wired telephones. Nowadays one could use the phrase "magic cell phone" and need nothing more.

A basic truth of writing is that what is familiar is easy to write and easy to communicate. Speechwriters for politicians use easy short phrases (such as "I love my country," "Support our troops," "Enemies Bad!") that are familiar to their hearers and will quickly connect to their audiences' thoughts. A person trying to write something subtle, unfamiliar or nuanced to counter one of these slogans has to take a lot of time, effort and well-chosen words to create as strong a mental connection as familiar phrases can bring across in just a few words.

The point is that the single sentence above about the telephone communicates the same information as a multipage explanation of the prevalence and usage of the telephone in our society.

Herein lies the help Star Wars has given us. It has placed a number of science fiction concepts into the realm of the familiar for the broad mainstream audience. In so doing it allows present-day writers to say things like:

The ship jumped into hyperspace.
The hologram showed their battle tactics.
The evil overlord killed his third subordinate of the morning.

Star Wars was by no means the first popular sci-fi to do this favor for the field in general. It is thanks to Buck Rogers and Flash Gordon that we can casually use ray-guns in stories, and thanks to Star Trek that people can teleport all over the place (as long as you call it beaming). Post-Star Wars movies like *Back to the Future* have done the same thing with time travel, drawing it down into a commonplace.

So what's the benefit to writers?

We are relieved of the need to explain those concepts Star Wars placed in front of the audience. This gives us more space in our writing to talk about other things we want to talk about. Everything that need not be explained is a savings to writers, giving us more room to work. This is also of benefit to readers, who don't have to slog through explanations to get to the meat of the story and are not forced to waste mindspace taking in basic ideas when the author would rather explore beyond those ideas.

One can think of Star Wars and other popular sci-fi as labor-saving devices like electric mixers or power drills. They reduce the work of some tasks, leaving us time, space and energy to concentrate on our stories, characters and those aspects of our worlds that are interesting and unique.

It might be argued that the above only works if we make our worlds like the worlds of sci-fi, but even if our worlds are radically different, we can take advantage of the familiarity they have created.

Consider the following possible line from a piece of hard SF:

> *"No, we can't get around the speed of light. Listen to me! There is no hyperspace, no warp drive, none of those damn cheats. Einstein found the limit and we're stuck with it. Now shut up and drive; it's a long haul to Alpha Centauri."*

The above example uses our readers' awareness of these sci-fi tropes to say they don't exist in the story being written. We don't have to explain the speed of light limit or talk about the ways it can't be broken; we only have to reference the canonical cheats and say they don't work.

This is by no means the limit of the ways to use the familiar. We can draw upon these tropes to put in twisted variations:

"You want to fly in hyperspace, girl, you try it. It ain't like the vids have it. Hyperspace isn't some flat safe place. It's like a river. It's got currents and eddies and falls and it's got, well, let's call them fish for want of a better word."

This paragraph creates a kind of hyperspace wholly unlike the Star Wars concept, but it still exploits the conception portrayed in the movies. Since the idea of space travel through an alternate space is already in the reader's mind, we can change it.

Consider the panoply of things presented by the six Star Wars movies, good, bad and indifferent: space battles, robots, aliens of many shapes, clones, tepid systems of spirituality and magic powers, cyborgs and so on. None of these are original, but that's not important. They have become familiar, and that is all we need to exploit them for our own ends.

Uh, and the interests and amusements of our readers. Yeah.

STAR WARS SPELLS DOOM FOR CINEMATIC BOOKS

Having been canonical, I'm now going to become all heretical and stuff (insert obvious dark side joke here). Star Wars was and is astoundingly visual. The first movie was, if not the marker point, certainly one of the points at which special effects came of age and emerged as a strong, vital part of moviemaking.

Many writers' reaction to Star Wars—in particular the reaction of the generation of writers who grew up on it—was to create strongly cinematic writing, books and stories that were heavily visual because the strongest impressions made on the authors were visual. This tendency has grown even stronger in recent years with the increase in quality of movie, TV and video game special effects. It is becoming canon in the teaching of writing, particularly SF/F writing, that one must be visual and concrete.

I would like to venture the opinion that this is fighting a losing battle. Visually, books cannot compete with movies anymore. The special effects have become good enough that, in terms of pure, in-your-eyes imagery, imagination fails in comparison to the best work that comes out of Henson's Creature Shop, the various animation studios and the specialty CGI workshops. Furthermore, since these effects are continually improving, I think that the movie creators have not only edged out the book authors on this one point, but that the gap is only growing to grow. In the field of visuals, we who write books will be left behind.

Writers therefore have three courses of action: try to outdo the movies in SFX (this is no longer possible), treat books as farm teams for movie scripts (that is, write books for the purpose of having them adapted as movies), or (and this is the one I favor) concentrate on the non-cinematic strengths of writing. In other words, write not for the superficial sensory imagination but to the deeper aspects of imagination.

I favor the third option for several reasons. First, it's the kind of writing I like to do and to read (which is why you should distrust everything I say on this point). Second, it plays to the strengths of writing as an art form. Third, in the long run I think it's the only thing that will help writing to survive as an independent art form (as opposed to being an adjunct to moviemaking). And fourth, writing was never the best visual art; it never succeeded well when it directly competed with painting, dance and sculpture—let alone with movies and TV.

What are the strengths of writing that I'm talking about?

That this question can even be asked shows how far we in the field have become dominated by the visual. If you consider what writing does best, you can quickly see that it is the art that has the easiest time dealing with and playing with the meaning of things. Words are the strongest conveyers of meaning; they are weak at conveying image, appearance and even sound. Meanings are what words were created to convey, and words are our raw materials as paint is for painters and stone for sculptors. Wordsmith is a synonym for writer, and we work words the way a blacksmith works iron.

Writing is also the best medium for conveying the processes of thinking. In every other art form, giving the audience the thoughts of the beings involved is hideously hard. It is considered a great tribute to a painter if you can look at an image in one of his or her works and figure out what is supposed to be on the mind of the person depicted. The same difficulty applies to acting; it is the epitome of an actor's art to let the viewer into the character's mind.

But in writing, this is so easy that we don't even notice that we're doing it:

Fred hated Wilma. The fire truck's sirens brought back the air raid fears
of Charlie's youth during the Blitz. Agnes wished Walter wouldn't talk to
their children in that squeaky voice; it was creepy, not funny.

Writing is strongest at getting inside of things, of seeing below the
surface into the depths, into the associations of things and thoughts,
because that's how words work. Words are themselves associative,
drawing out memories and ideas in multiple ways.

Consider these two words combined to create another word:

Death
Star
Death Star

The thought that is elicited by the third word is not the combination of the thoughts from the first two; it is a distinct remembrance.
The same of course applies to Millennium and Falcon.

Even if one is not playing around with names, one can see how association changes meaning.

Red means a particular color.

Red light means stop.

Red light district means a place you shouldn't go but are tempted
to.

The absolute best writing uses these connections and associations,
as well as burrows into the minds of characters to create a scene that
exists mostly below the visible surface. But so does mediocre, ade-
quate and bad writing. There is no need to be a genius writer in order
to write about the connections of people's thoughts, the associations,
the emotions, the feelings, the ways people think, the paths they follow that lead to their salvation, damnation and day-to-day living. To
bring these out does not require great writing as it does great acting,
great painting or great dancing.

This is a good test for what is easiest in a particular art: is genius
required to do it?

Let us return to Star Wars and consider the character of Anakin
Skywalker. The most recent three movies have been about Anakin's
fall into darkness and his taking of the Jedi with him. I do not pro-
pose to do more than hint subliminally, using the subtle arts of writ-

ing, as to how well I think this was portrayed (badly). The portrayal of such a fall on the screen would take a combination of great actor, director and screenwriter. But in a purely written story, it's not much work. The conflicts and confusions of such a character could be easily put down on paper. I don't think there's a need to give examples since the number of literary characters who fall believably into darkness is enormous (particularly in Russian literature).

It may sound like I am advocating the removal of all visual elements from writing, which I am not. Rather, I think that writing has never been strongest at the purely visual. I think we are better off putting our efforts into those parts of writing that writing does best and that are hard for other arts.

Here's another such strength: movies take great effort to create a mood from their visual environments, using lighting and atmosphere to make things feel a certain way to their audiences. But a writer can do so in a single line.

Consider rain:

Bone-bit, coat-soaked, Harry ducked into the archway to shiver away from the winter's-coming-and-you-can't-stop-it rainfall.

And rain:

Slipping down and rolling over together in the no-longer-mist, May and Oliver reveled in the spring rainfall.

Not great prose, of course, but it doesn't have to be; that's the point. Mood is easy for writing, hard for movies.

What does all this have to do with the effect of Star Wars on the consciousness of our audience? Here we enter the realm of prediction...and I must confess that my track record on predictions is not a good one, so take everything to follow with a decent-sized ocean's worth of salt.

It seems to me that Star Wars and the movies and TV shows that were created because of its success have molded an audience that will soon no longer find special effects special. They will come to expect impressive effects as a matter of course. Indications are that they probably already do. The special effects-heavy moviemakers have been handling this rising expectation by targeting their movies at a particular demographic, mostly teenaged boys. This gives us a growing audience beyond this age that will be slaked on visual effects.

Several different desires are likely to rise up in the minds of such an audience. Some will want to get a new fix of SFX, but they are bound to disappointment as the next dose will seem duller than the last. Others will find themselves dissatisfied with the simple presence of SFX and want something more in their entertainment. Those are the ones that writers should go after.

This segment of the audience will be amenable to books that will feed the parts of their minds that the movies have neglected. The moviemakers will not notice this audience since they have set their sights on a demographic, not a group of individuals. They are catering only to an age group, not asking what those same people will be doing for entertainment when they are beyond that age group. I think that written science fiction and fantasy can bring them in if it does not try to be second-rate moviemaking. If the books this audience is given are too cinematic, they will only disappoint, whereas if the books show what the movies cannot and do not, they can bring in, hold and nurture the orphans of Star Wars who will grow up as SF readers.

CLOSING ARGUMENTS FOR THE DEFENSE

Star Wars has placed a set of tropes and visual expectations into the minds of a vast audience and has disseminated those tropes and expectations into the ambient culture.

This has given SF/F writers a base of materials from which to more easily work and which we can more easily transcend if we choose to do so.

Thus it can be argued that although Star Wars creates an overly uniform view of SF, we can use that uniformity in order to spring forth into a greater diversity of science fiction. In this way the influence of Star Wars on public consciousness has been a good one.

The Defense rests without any obligatory Using the Force, Fandom Menace or New Hope jokes. Thank you.

Richard Garfinkle is the author of two science fiction novels: *Celestial Matters* (which won the 1996 Compton Crook Award for best first novel in science fiction) and *All of an Instant*. At present he is engaged in the more dubious practice of writing non-fiction science popularization. He lives in Chicago with his wife and children.

THE COURTROOM

DAVID BRIN: Let me see if I get this line of defense. Are you saying that special effects extravaganzas like Star Wars will help literary science fiction, because they will eventually tire people out, making them want something more than special effects?

RICHARD GARFINKLE: Not quite. I am saying that SFX movies have two effects: First they make it impractical for written SF to rely on mindless action sequences since it is no longer possible for imagined SFX to be better than shown SFX. Thus writers are confronted with either giving up on writing books and only writing scripts, or moving away from SFX and toward what writing does best: delving into thought and meaning.

Second, because SFX are the mental equivalent of empty calories, they do not in the long run satisfy their audiences. It is true that the adolescent demographic (from, say, age ten to eighteen) will likely always want SFX, but what happens to those same people when they grow older and are no longer satisfied with things going boom? If writers concentrate on audience, not demographic, they can catch those people as they age out.

DAVID BRIN: Yes, films can familiarize concepts. But a good film, like *Dr. Strangelove*, can do that as easily as a bad one can (e.g., doomsday weapons and callback codes).

Are we to be glad, then, that space fighters bank and slip, as if using airfoils in an atmosphere, simply because this hearkens to the earlier romance of World War I fighter aces? The cool retro-rocket maneuvers of the fighters in *Babylon 5* were as fun to watch, but also offered something to the mature mind.

Must we be grateful that Star Wars familiarized us with terms like hyperspace, when a show like *Stargate* actually explored it a little, too? After so many years, and billions of dollars, might one ask that the biggest sci-fi epic of all time at least give a nod toward our prefrontal lobes?

RICHARD GARFINKLE: Of course, a good film can give more than a bad film, and if there were good films with the same popularity as Star Wars (for example, the Lord of the Rings films, which of course have a literary connection), more could be brought out from them than from the more superficial qualities of Star Wars. But the question was not were there better possibilities than Star Wars; the question was, is there a legitimate defense for the Star Wars films? I never claimed that Star Wars was the best vehicle for disseminating this understanding, only that it did so disseminate.

DAVID BRIN: You suggest that, as the audience ages, they will move from SFX movies to more thoughtful forms of science fiction. Can you support this hope with any evidence? In the gaming industry, thoughtful, adventure-scenario games like *Myst* and *Legacy of Time* have been almost entirely replaced by action and effects-heavy offerings, like *Halo*, with no apparent end to the upward ratchet of effects-craving. Isn't this similar to what we contend has happened via sci-fi films and books?

RICHARD GARFINKLE: Your own examples above serve as evidence. *Stargate* and *Babylon 5* do not just introduce new concepts; they draw on older ones. *Babylon 5* relied on hyperspace without having to explain it. *Stargate* also did so. Both of these expanded on the audience's familiarity with hyperspace. As for gaming, computer gaming is not yet a mature entertainment form, but even so, look at the socialization that is forming in the MMRPGs. Indeed, the makers of *Star Wars Galaxies* were annoyed to discover that people playing in their universe didn't just want a hackfest; they wanted to live in the world. To be moisture farmers and traders, not just Jedi Knights and Sith Lords. In short, even Star Wars fans want more than the superficial.

CHARGE 6

Star Wars Pretends to Be
Science Fiction,
but Is Really Fantasy

Star Wars: Fantasy, Not Science Fiction

WITNESS FOR THE PROSECUTION:

Ken Wharton

L ADIES AND GENTLEMEN of the jury:
Most people would agree that there's a difference between fantasy and science fiction—except, of course, for people who shelve books in chain bookstores—but what exactly is that difference? Unless we can agree on this basic distinction, there would be no point in arguing that Star Wars was one and not the other.

At first glance it might seem like the key difference between the two is whether the story uses science or magic to explain any speculative story elements. But one problem with this approach, as Arthur C. Clarke famously pointed out, is that "any sufficiently advanced technology is indistinguishable from magic." There's some truth to this, which means that simply using science or technology is not enough to make a story science fiction. And, to take the other extreme, any system of "magic" that follows universal, well-understood rules would effectively make the study of this magic a science.

But surely we can agree that there's a real difference between magic and science, between rules made up for a story and the rules that actually might govern our universe. Here's a thought experiment: Pick some speculative element from a science fiction or fantasy story, and imagine asking the author *why* that element works the way that it does. Then ask *why* about the answer, and then *why* again, like an over-curious nine-year-old. If the trail of "whys" eventually leads to something we know about the real world, shouldn't we call that science fiction? If it leads to a snappy "Just because!" well, wouldn't that make it a fantasy?

In this way of thinking, the important point is not whether the story is about dragons or rocket ships, but rather the attitude of the story toward those speculative elements. If the story treats those elements as a natural extension of the real world, if the story implies that the string of "whys" would intersect with known reality, then it's science fiction. But if those elements are just some big "what-if" exercise, then that part of the story is fantasy.

This explains why typical science fiction is set the future, something that might result from present-day reality. Fantasies, on the other hand, are often set in some alternate world with no clear connection to our own. There's no need to explain the location of that alternate world, or how exactly to get there from here. In a fantasy those answers will come down to magic, or at least a "Just because."

This distinction between science fiction and fantasy is the only one that really draws a meaningful line between two fundamentally different ways of telling a speculative story. And while it's still possible to find examples that blur the distinction between the two, those borderline cases are forced to treat the story inconsistently. For although fantastic premises must be simply accepted, science fiction premises not only *can* be questioned, but *will* be questioned by the audience. You can't ask an audience to both take something as a given and also question it, which means that attempts to blur my suggested distinction between fantasy and science fiction will simply lead to bad storytelling.

And so, with these thoughts in mind, let us turn our attention to Star Wars. Specifically, I will now introduce Exhibit A:

"A long time ago, in a galaxy far, far away...."

The very first line in each movie screams out that we're on the fantasy side of the divide. Sure, we sort of know where and when this is taking place with respect to present-day Earth, but there's no connection between anything in this story and known reality. These events are not some future history. They're not even some secret past history. By placing the setting in the distant past, in a faraway galaxy, George Lucas was effectively introducing an alternate fantasy universe. You can't get there from here.

Lucas puts this text at the beginning of his movies for a reason. Not only to create a sense of epic myth, but also to make sure the audience wouldn't question some of his premises. Indeed, in the commentary on the special edition of the original *Star Wars*, Lucas himself gives us Exhibit B:

> Since it's based on a very, kind of, old story, and not a high-tech story, it's more of a fantasy film than a science fiction film.

If Lucas had a better understanding of the difference between fantasy and science fiction I could rest my case right here. (And we also wouldn't have had to suffer through the midichlorian debacle in Episode I, but we'll come back to that subject later.)

Unfortunately, while Lucas is admitting it's a fantasy, this confession seems to be based on the misimpression that it is technology that makes science fiction. But as Clarke tells us, technology and magic can be indistinguishable—you can use both in a fantasy, so long as they're just "what-ifs" without a well-thought-out connection to known science. Similarly, the issue of whether a story is "old" or not—a retelling of old myths—doesn't necessarily make it fall in one category or the other. Still, Exhibit B is useful, because it tells us a bit about Lucas's motives. He's not striving to make this science fiction, which means he's not striving to connect his premises to reality. This is reinforced elsewhere in the same commentary, when Lucas says:

> And in terms of fantasy films and everything, I can't stand it when you sit around and try to explain why a teleporter works....

Clearly the technology in these movies does not make them science fiction; they're treated as what-ifs, so they might as well be magic. But the heart and soul of Star Wars, the speculative element that arguably made the movie so incredibly successful, is the idea of the Force. Enter Exhibit C, spoken by Obi-Wan Kenobi in Episode IV:

> [The Force is] an energy field created by all living things. It surrounds us, it penetrates us, it binds the galaxy together.

I trust that I don't have to bring in any physicists as expert witnesses to tell you that there is no such thing. This is a fantasy premise, through and through; a what-if that the audience fully accepts because by this point in the movie it's clear that we're watching fantasy, not science fiction. Three different characters in Episode IV, including Han Solo, refer to the force as a "religion." A startlingly effective religion, for sure, but the repetition of that word throughout the movie is no accident. A religion is something that you take on faith, not something that you test with science. The line between faith and science is very similar to the line between fantasy and science fiction, and Lucas is clearly putting faith and the Force on the same side of the line.

The issue here is not whether the Force is real or not in the movies. Han himself is converted from his original view that "There's no mystical energy field that controls *my* destiny," and few would argue that Luke's success at destroying the Death Star resulted from his skill at bull's-eyeing womp rats. The issue here is that the audience has faith that the Force exists in the Star Wars universe, despite the fact that there is no connection between the Force and anything we know about the real world.

And what holds it all together is that the audience doesn't want answers, the audience is willing to just accept the premise. Lucas himself goes to considerable effort to make sure this remains the case, by *not* asking "why." Consider Exhibit D, Lucas's commentary on Episode I:

> Every time these rather larger concepts come into play—how does the galaxy work, what is the Force, all this kind of stuff—you have to be very sort of cryptic and deal in almost fortune-cookie descriptions of things.

Here, Lucas describes the perfect strategy for creating a fantasy world that the audience will accept. By keeping the explanations fuzzy, he avoids any temptation to make a connection between his premises and the real world. However, the irony of Exhibit D is that this very sentence of commentary overlays the precise part of Episode I where Lucas most deviates from his own successful formula—the part where we learn that the Force is related to something called "midichlorians."

And here, I must admit, the line between fantasy and science fiction gets a bit blurry. First let's look at the hard evidence in Exhibit E, a quote from Qui-Gon Jinn in Episode I:

> Midichlorians are microscopic life-forms that reside inside all living cells....We are symbionts with them....Without the midichlorians life cannot exist and we would have no knowledge of the Force. They continually speak to us, telling us the will of the Force.

Suddenly the Force is starting to look a lot less like fantasy, and a lot more like science fiction. After all, cells and microscopic life-forms are real, so by making these statements Lucas is connecting the Force with known science. Lucas confirmed this connection in a later interview, stating that—in his mind, at least—there is a direct parallel between midichlorians and real-world mitochondria.

> It means that between the Force, which is sort of a life force, and reality, the connectors between these two things are what we call midichlorians. They're kind of based on mitochondria, which are a completely different animal, that live inside every single cell and allow it to live, allow it to reproduce, allow life to exist. They also, in their own way, communicate with the Force itself.[1]

By tying one aspect of the Force into mitochondria—an aspect of our reality—Lucas has now dipped a toe into science fiction territory. Using my own definition of science fiction, I cannot help but concede that the midichlorians are, in fact, a science fiction element. But

---

[1] George Lucas, interview by Jim Windolf, *Vanity Fair*, February 2005.

I will argue that this is the exception that proves the rule: Star Wars is inherently a fantasy, and this new science fiction element simply doesn't fit. First, though, we need to be very clear that this new development does not change the status of the Force itself. The Force, as we can see from Exhibit E, is clearly distinct from midichlorians. One is an "energy field," and the other is a "life-form" that allows humans to interact with the Force. Because there is no description of the mechanism by which these microscopic life-forms can communicate with the Force, this means that the Force is still safely in fantasy territory; it's still a what-if, not a technology. Lucas says this explicitly on the DVD commentary:

> The midichlorians are sort of a side issue, not the spiritual, metaphysical part of the Force....

Fair enough. But we still have to decide whether the "explanation" of midichlorians is enough to pull all of Star Wars into science fiction territory. If this were the case, then this knowledge of how the Force expresses itself through certain individuals would suddenly enlighten all of the previous movies. We could then go back and see how the original Star Wars trilogy wasn't really fantasy, but could now be reinterpreted as science fiction. Episode I would be the key turning point in all of this, and presumably *The Phantom Menace*—and in particular the exciting news concerning midichlorians—would be wildly hailed by Star Wars fans as pure genius.

(Pause for laughter to die down.)

Yes, this idea seems rather amusing, because as we know just the opposite is true. With the possible exception of Jar Jar, the midichlorian scenes were some of the most reviled in the entire six-movie epic. In one notable fan-edited version of Episode I, these particular scenes were removed entirely.

But why? Why did the fans not like learning a little bit about how this universe worked? A surfing expedition through Star Wars Internet sites reveals that the fans care deeply about the various intricacies of the Star Wars universe. Why then would a little exposition cause so much discontent?

If you turn to the fans themselves for an answer to this question, you will hear a thousand different explanations. Many of the complaints would have to do with new questions that arise as a result of this new information. If innate ability to use the Force is based on microscopic life-forms, couldn't this technological fact be used to enhance Jedi abilities? The biotech in this universe is advanced enough to clone people—why not use it to manipulate the midichlorian count? For that matter, if you're going to clone someone, why not pick someone whose cells can harbor a whole bunch of midichlorians in the first place? And how do these life-forms interact with the Force anyway? For that matter, how do people interact with *them*? The new questions go on, and on and on.

Some of these questions may have answers; others clearly do not. But what I think even many of the upset fans do not realize is that what upsets them is not the lack of answers—what upsets them is that they have been led to ask these questions in the first place! By hinting that this is a science fiction story, Lucas switched the audience's mental gears into a trail of "whys" that they had never asked of the original trilogy. For science fiction premises not only *can* be questioned, but they *must* be—or else it isn't science fiction. And once the questions start, once the audience has switched over into science fiction mode, no question can remain off-limits. Trying to walk the line between fantasy and science fiction, trying to have some premises be what-ifs and other premises tie into reality, is only going to annoy the audience.

For example, when we learn in Episode I that Anakin might have been conceived by the midichlorians, we hardly know how to take this piece of information. From a science fiction perspective, this is ludicrous to the extreme; midichlorians are not only a completely different life-form, they apparently play such a critical role that they have presumably been around from the very beginning of life itself. So where did Anakin's Y chromosome come from? This is clearly a case of Lucas throwing out another "Just because," and hoping the audience just accepts it. But the audience can't accept it, because these microscopic life-forms aren't a "fortune-cookie description"; they're a concrete, science fiction premise. By forgoing the fantasy framework in one way, we are no longer able to suspend our disbelief in this other way. You can start to see why the midichlorians dismayed so many fans.

An analogy that comes to mind is that of the curious American movement in which some fundamentalist Christians are trying to have "intelligent design" (ID) taught as an alternative to evolution in science classes. ID is basically an assertion that evolution alone is not sufficient to explain the complexity of biological life, and some "designer" (a.k.a. God) must have done something, somewhere, somehow. Supporters such as the Discovery Institute claim that ID is a "theory" (using the colloquial sense of the word) that rivals the "scientific theory of evolution," careful not to mention the fact that a "scientific theory" is the highest level a scientific hypothesis can ever attain; only ten to twenty hypotheses have ever been so accepted and so widely applicable as to attain "theory" status. Given that ID does not even put forward a single testable hypothesis, it does not connect with known reality, and, using our earlier definitions, this makes it a fantasy.

Now, imagine how the ID community would react if the Discovery Institute started to fund actual scientific research on testable hypotheses. Suppose they wanted to see whether human beings are indeed special to the hypothesized "designer." They could fund an effort to study DNA sequences of many different species to determine where and when in the past half-billion years the "designer" had chosen to induce complex mutations, and from this determine which lines of organisms the designer had spent more effort "designing." If humans were indeed special, that should show up in the analysis; if, instead, the "designer" was more interested in pygmy octopi, that might show up as well.

I think it's pretty obvious that, faced with such an honest attempt to connect their assertions to verifiable reality, most ID supporters would throw a fit. They don't want to question how their "designer" made everything happen any more than I wanted to question the Force. More than that, they would soon realize that to pursue this line of scientific thinking would be to subject God to scientific analysis. And once the trail of "whys" began, applying the well-honed tools of scientific discovery to topics ordinarily reserved for divine revelation, they wouldn't be able to keep *any* questions of religious knowledge off-limits to science. Even the Kansas School Board might quickly backtrack, revoking their new definition of "science" and returning to the days to where science only dealt with natural, not supernatural, phenomena.

The point here is that you can't go halfway, explaining some of your premises with actual science, while saving "Just because" for other fantasy premises. The inconsistency is just too much to bear, even for those who favor teaching intelligent design.

So the issue of the midichlorians boils down to introducing a science fiction element into a well-established fantasy story. And the response from the fans was clear; this new element simply didn't belong. Lucas heard the complaints, and sure enough, we didn't have to listen to much other midichlorian business in the last two movies. Instead, Lucas went back to his own advice from Exhibit D and returned to the fantasy framework that worked so well in the original movies. Midichlorians is the science fiction exception that proves the rule: Star Wars is a straight fantasy.

And so, ladies and gentlemen, apart from this minor exception of midichlorians, what we have in the Star Wars films is a detailed alternate universe, with no direct connection to our own except on a mythological level. The message from Exhibit A is uncontested; unlike standard science fiction, these stories take place in the distant past. This is not a tale of the future of humanity—it resonates for mythological reasons, not because of any direct connection to our world.

The magic in this fantasy tale is called the Force. It is magic because it needs, and has, no explanation; it's just taken as a given. Were this a science fiction story, the Force would have to have some mechanism that ties in with what we know about the real world. Subatomic particles, dark matter, something. But Lucas wisely chooses not to go this route, and when he does slip up, at least he only does it on what he calls a "side issue," and not the key magical element of the story.

I hope it's clear that fantasy and science fiction, while both perfectly valid approaches to telling a speculative story, are fundamentally incompatible. You can't both ask "why" and not ask "why" about the same premise, any more than you can try to seek the same piece of knowledge through both divine revelation and the scientific method, any more than you can answer "Just because" and "Because" to the same question. And in nearly every way, Star Wars falls on the fantasy side of the divide.

And with that, I rest my case. Now, if you'll excuse me, I need to get down to the clinic for my weekly midichlorian transfusion.

Ken Wharton is a physics professor at San Jose State University. He is also the author of the science fiction novel *Divine Intervention*, along with a handful of short stories. For his fiction, Ken has been a finalist for the John W. Campbell Award for best new writer, the Philip K. Dick Award and the Nebula Award.

THE COURTROOM

DAVID BRIN: If Your Honor will allow? I would add a few remarks in support of my esteemed colleague, Dr. Wharton.

MATTHEW WOODRING STOVER: Oh, come on!

DROID JUDGE: We've given you a lot of leeway, Mr. Stover. I'll allow this.

DAVID BRIN: In my opinion, the distinction between science fiction and fantasy has very little to do with technology. As Dr. Wharton points out, Star Wars cares little about science, but a great deal about sword fights. In comparison, Anne McCaffrey's Dragons of Pern series is true SF.

No, this distinction is not about hardware. It is first and foremost about how the author feels about society and the concept of human improvability and change.

For forty centuries, most of humanity lived under one form or another of elitist feudalism. Wherever people discovered both metallurgy and agriculture, some big men picked up metal implements and used them to take away other men's women and wheat. And—just as predictably—some nerdy guys in cloaks would follow those warlords, waving their arms and chanting about how *good* this was. The alliance of aristocrats and cleric-magicians was so pervasive, only a few societies could claim to have escaped the almost universal pattern.

We carry echoes of that long era, deep inside. Generation after generation, when most of our ancestors bowed low to the king and shaman, partly in fear and partly in sincere devotion...because that sincerity was a survival trait. Indeed, we are all descended from those kings, who got lots of extra breeding privileges. Is it any wonder we have a weakness for stories about anointed ones, princes or heroes who are destined, by blood, for greatness?

And yet, despite that pull, a couple of hundred years ago something happened. Our greatest minds started imagining a new way of doing things. One that emphasized both fair competition and open cooperation among people who are mostly equal and free. One in which you would be judged according to your deeds and character, and not who your father was. Where nobody could predict your destiny from blood or heritage, leaving it at least partly in your hands to shape, as your talents and courage and hard work might allow.

Is it any accident that true science fiction emerged at the same time as the Enlightenment? As democracy and industrialism and education and science—for all their flaws—started changing all the old rules? Science fiction is the literature of this revolution. It considers the possibility of change—both good change and horrific mistakes—but, either way, it looks change in the eye, and keeps asking, "Where do I fit in all this?"

Many people find this frightening. Their motives may be religious or economic or artistic...but the reactionary sentiment always boils down to the same thing. "We've gone too far. We need to go back. To old ways. Better ways. When people were in touch with their...."

Well, fill in the blank. Souls? Feelings? Proper place in the cosmos? Call it certainty, the one thing that science fiction abhors...but fantasy revels in. Certainty that good is pretty and evil ugly. That leaders are born and common folk should follow. That elites do not have to explain themselves, or answer to institutions, or face accountability.

Why are Anne McCaffrey's novels true science fiction, instead of fantasy, for all their dragons and bards and swords and such? Because, over the course of her series, her characters learn that once, long ago, there were things called "flush toilets," and printing presses, and factories, and computers, and universities...and what is their reaction?

They want all those things back! They demand them back. And you know they will succeed. Feudalism will fade, because it must. It must, no matter how frantically it tugs at our racial memory.

And that's why Star Wars is fantasy. Because, as George Lucas has publicly avowed, it takes the older path prescribed by Joseph Campbell. The path of kings.

DROID JUDGE: Mr. Stover?

MATTHEW WOODRING STOVER: What?

DROID JUDGE: Don't you wish to cross-examine Mr. Wharton? Or Mr. Brin?

MATTHEW WOODRING STOVER: Why would I?

DAVID BRIN: So the Defense concedes this charge?

MATTHEW WOODRING STOVER: What charge? I thought the accusation was that Star Wars pretends to be science fiction, but is really fantasy. Mr. Wharton has eloquently made the case that Star Wars, in clear fact, makes no such pretense. The Defense has already stipulated it's fantasy. What are we arguing about? If you can't prove that Star Wars is faking SF credentials, there's no point in mounting a defense.

As for Opposing Counsel's impassioned speech—which he really should have saved for his closing argument—I believe the point has already been made that the Prequel Trilogy can be read as a cautionary parable, warning against precisely the "certainty that good is pretty and evil ugly. That leaders are born and common folk should follow. That elites do not have to explain themselves, or answer to institutions, or face accountability." After all, every instance of following those dictates in the Prequel Trilogy leads inexorably to galaxy-wide destruction, as Opposing Counsel has pointed out; in Star Wars, certainty breeds arrogance, and arrogance breeds disaster.

Some folk of a moralistic bent might choose to find a lesson for our time in that, as well.

Seeing as how Opposing Counsel seems to be so passionately engaged in defending the essential virtue inherent in the Saga, it would be impertinent to question him.

DROID JUDGE: Then you have no questions for Mr. Wharton, either?

MATTHEW WOODRING STOVER: Oh, what the hell. If you insist.

Dr. Wharton, you claim that fantasy and science fiction are fundamentally incompatible—that, and I quote, "You can't both ask 'why' and not ask 'why' about the same premise, any more than you can try to seek the same piece of knowledge through both divine revelation and the scientific method, any more than you can answer 'Just because' and 'Because' to the same question." Do you have any actual evidence to support this preposterous assertion?

KEN WHARTON: Evidence? You mean... hard evidence? (*Looks around desk*) Well, I have here a Magic 8-Ball. Let's say that'll double for divine revelation in a pinch. And here I have a pencil, with which I can do a scientific experiment. (*Holds pencil in air*) Based on my experience, and the universal law of gravitation, I hypothesize that when I release the pencil it will fall to my desk. (*Drops pencil*) Yup, chalk up another confirmation for Newton. But if I had asked the Magic 8-Ball instead... (*Shakes 8-Ball*)... it says "No." Whatever that means.

MATTHEW WOODRING STOVER: Let me put it another way. A thought experiment, as Einstein would say. If, say, Magellan had prayed to God to tell him whether the world was round, and then (on God's assurance, real or imagined) Magellan went out and experimentally verified his world-is-round hypothesis by sailing around it (well, his ships did, anyway), wouldn't that qualify as "seeking the same knowledge through divine revelation and the scientific method"?

KEN WHARTON: Ah, you mean what if I had a Magic 8-Ball that happened to say "the pencil will fall to the desk"? The point is that, much more often than not, those two methods give you different answers. In that case you have to choose one method or the other. The best you can do, as you suggest in your example, is to use divine revelation to form a hypothesis, but then use the scientific method to test it. But even then, you're asking two different questions: "What hypothesis should I test?" and "Is this particular hypothesis correct?" I have no problem with assigning some questions to one method and other questions to another—so long as you don't use both methods to answer the same question.

MATTHEW WOODRING STOVER: Are you familiar with Schrödinger's Cat? According to the best representations of quantum mechanics, the cat is both alive and dead simultaneously until the observer collapses the wave function by opening the box. Do you understand that quantum mechanics requires us to accept paradox as an inescapable feature of reality? That either/or logic just doesn't work in the real world? Which is another way of saying that it can often be scientifically legitimate, even necessary, to answer "Just because" and "Because" to the same question!

DROID JUDGE: Is there a question in this, Mr. Stover?

MATTHEW WOODRING STOVER: Not so much. What there is, in fact, is an introduction to an alternate interpretation of Star Wars as science fiction of the highest order. Please allow me to introduce my next witness, scientist and hard-as-nails SF writer Robert A. Metzger.

The Kessel Run

WITNESS FOR THE DEFENSE:
Robert A. Metzger

S TAR WARS IS NOT REAL.

But that does not make it any less a scientific marvel, or its visionary creator, George Lucas, anything less than a scientific genius to rival Newton and Einstein. You see, the simple fact of the matter is that you, too, are not real—just a simulation residing in some advanced alien civilization's computer.

And that is the whole point of Star Wars.

While a few cutting-edge philosophers and scientists are just now realizing that you, your dog, your car, the Atlantic Ocean, Mars, the Andromeda Galaxy and anything else you care to name is in all likelihood nothing more than part of a universal spanning simulation, George Lucas realized this thirty years ago. He used his Star Wars films to clue in those few of us who were savvy enough to realize that what on the surface appeared to be a series of films overflowing with scientific inaccuracies and engineering gaffes were actually carefully crafted scientific clues intended to reveal the true nature of our very universe.

Don't believe me?

Perhaps you think that I watched the Matrix trilogy a few too many times? Well, I'm not talking about *The Matrix* and its ridiculous premise that humanity has been rendered into a vast sea of D-cell batteries needed to power up computer overlords.

I'm talking about something else altogether—a simulation of everything. Philosopher Nick Bostrom, director of the Future of Humanity Institute at Oxford, has spelled out the details of this ultimate simulation in a paper that appeared in 2003 in the *Philosophical Quarterly*.[1] Consider his three simple propositions:

> *The chances that a species at our current level of development can avoid going extinct before becoming technologically mature is negligibly small.*
>
> *Almost no technologically mature civilizations are interested in running computer simulations of minds like ours.*
>
> *You are almost certainly in a computer simulation.*

Now of course we have only our own civilization as a reference point to consider those first two propositions. Humans are more than just interested in creating computer simulations of a human mind—we are attempting to do so right now, not only in the quest of a better understanding of what goes on (or, in many cases, goes wrong) in our own skulls, but hoping to create something beyond us. So using humanity as an example, proposition two is certainly false. As to proposition one, Bostrom crunches a few numbers and shows that if we can hold on for just a few more generations, we will have the sort of computing power and hardware necessary to simulate a mind and place it in a virtual reality sufficiently complex so that the simulated mind would consider it "real." If we can make it through the next fifty years we stand a pretty good chance of proving the first proposition false. And if the first two propositions are false (which in all likelihood they appear to be), then there is only one inescapable conclusion—the third proposition must be true.

Yes—you are a simulation living in a simulated universe.

Don't see it?

---

[1] Bostrom, Nick. "Are You Living in a Computer Simulation?" *Philosophical Quarterly* 53, no. 211 (2003): 243–255.

If you crunch the numbers, you find that it requires an insignificant amount of energy to simulate a person as compared to maintaining one in flesh and blood. Just think about how movies are made today: no longer is it necessary to hire tens of thousands of extras for the big battle scenes (think of the Clone Wars battle scenes)—just build them in a computer. The trick is building the first clone warrior—after that, all you need to do is press the copy button. And in the same way, once you can simulate one mind, to do ten, a million or even a trillion is simply a matter of computer storage and number-crunching capacity. Once the threshold of simulating a single mind is reached, the leap to simulating a universe, with nearly countless planets populated by minds, is relatively easy.

Think about it. If a single advanced alien entity could simulate an entire universe, one containing a trillion-trillion-trillion-trillion simulated minds, what do you think the odds would be that you are actually of flesh and blood, living on some mudball in some corner of that alien's universe?

Damn near zero.

For every entity of flesh of goo, there would be trillions of simulated beings.

But the odds that you are real are even slimmer than that.

If we are a simulation, we find ourselves at a critical point in that simulation: we are at the threshold of creating our own simulated minds, and quickly from that point other simulated universes—our simulation now creating its own simulations.

Geometrical progression is a powerful thing.

If we are a simulation, creating our own simulations, then in all likelihood our creators are also simulations. The original creatures of flesh and goo, our primordial creators that started the whole thing rolling, might be hundreds, millions or even trillions of levels away from us.

The conclusion is inescapable. If Bostrom's first two propositions are false, then you, and everything you know or dream, are a simulation.

And so what?

Well, decades before Bostrom and *The Matrix*, George Lucas had realized this—the first on Earth to understand the true nature of our simulated reality. Had he announced this to the world in the mid-1970s he would have simply been written off as a drug-damaged 1960s refugee. So he took another path, creating his own little universe. At that time, he knew he had no hope of creating a simulated mind or universe, the technology not available, so he did the next-best thing—he created a simulated world on film, and filled it with hints as to the nature of our universe, using his scientific prowess to create the sort of scientific errors in his films that the sharpest of minds would recognize as clues that would lead to a true understanding of the nature of our universe, while hopefully not alerting the entities who created us that someone had uncovered the true nature of our universe.

Don't believe me?

Well, let's examine just what Lucas created. The many supposed scientific errors, engineering gaffes and failures to follow through on technical premises that are littered throughout the Star Wars films can be divided into three main categories: the generic sci-fi blunders, Lucasisms that represent head-scratching components unique to his films and lastly, what I like to think of as brain-dead concepts, those that only a dead brain would not find questionable (as you can see, rather aptly named). Let's take a look.

SCI-FI BLUNDERS

If one is to tell the tale of a galactic empire, by definition this implies that there must be a mode of traveling far in excess of the speed of light—that is the only possible way such an empire could be held together. If not, things simply don't work. How can the Emperor expect to keep a tight leash over the citizens of Slop-12, which is 1000 light-years distant, if a round-trip communication takes 2,000 years, and his armada, traveling at even half the speed of light, takes the same 2,000 years to arrive at Slop-12 and put down the rebellion?

Won't work.

So you need the means of pushing people and information faster than the speed of light. Wormholes are a theoretical possibility (by jumping into "hyperspace"), connecting distant points through higher spatial dimensions, but theoretical physicists have now shown that such pathways require what is called negative energy density material (which possesses negative gravity characteristics—masses are not attracted, but repelled). While it is not clear how such material might be generated, it appears that the smallest quantities of it would require the total energy output of entire galaxies—something that Han Solo's *Millennium Falcon* certainly couldn't muster.

So spacecraft, TIE fighters and Death Stars jumping from star system to star system is just not in the cards—this being what many might consider one of the most basic science flaws of the Star Wars universe.

But they'd be wrong.

This is not a Star Wars science error—this is a sci-fi blunder. If you are going to do a space epic then you have faster-than-light capabilities. That is just a given, in the same way that in a western, the good guy's gun never runs out of bullets. This is a sci-fi blunder of the first magnitude, but has nothing to do with George Lucas—this sort of blunder is needed to bring the people into the theater, and keep them glued to their seats.

Sci-fi blunders are those science errors common to sci-fi movies:

Things can travel faster than the speed of light.

When spacecraft explode you can hear it in the vacuum of space, despite the fact that there is no atmosphere in space to carry the compression waves needed for the sound of the explosion.

We can see laser beams, despite the fact that there is nothing to scatter the light in the beam—this being the only way that we could actually see it, not to mention the fact that a laser pulse, moving at the speed of light, would travel the distance between two nearby fighters in millionths of a second, rather than the several seconds shown in the film.

And you certainly don't need a Death Star to shatter a planet. Get a small fighter craft moving at nearly the speed of light and crash it into a planet—the kinetic energy of a craft moving at such a speed is equivalent to the output of several million-megaton hydrogen bombs. No more planet.

None of this means that Lucas is a scientific dolt—merely that he is making a space-based sci-fi film, utilizing the standard infrastructure that the public expects to see in such films. So forget these sci-fi blunders—they have nothing to do with Lucas. We need to look deeper in order to understand what Lucas is trying to show us and to truly appreciate his scientific genius.

LUCASISIMS

Now this is where things start getting interesting, as we examine the scientific absurdities that are unique to Lucas, those that he deliberately chose to put in Star Wars and was under no obligation to include in order to satisfy the sci-fi moviegoing public.

Almost all Lucasisms center around a single concept—the Jedi.

Except for the fact that members of this ancient sect appear to breathe and eat food, little else that they are involved in seems to make much sense from a scientific perspective. When it comes to Jedi, the two primary things that characterize them are lightsabers and the Force—both of which, under the most cursory inspection, can be seen to be complete and utter scientific hogwash.

Lightsabers are such fun, brightly colored gizmos—weapons suitable for close combat, and a sort of emblem that says, "I'm a Jedi, and I can muck around with the Force."

Fine.

The problem is that a lightsaber just isn't going to work. The first big problem is that, just like a flashlight, the stream of laser light goes on and on and on and on, spreading out and diffusing until no longer visible. Besides the fact that you can only see a laser beam if it is scattering from something like chalk dust or fog, you can't just stop it in three or four feet. Light won't stop. The other problem is that when two lightsabers crossed paths, they would simply pass through each other. An intense enough laser beam can melt through the toughest chunk of metal, but it has no heft to it, no mass, nothing that would resemble the clashing and clanging of metal blades, and emit a shower of sparks, when crossed with another laser beam. There could be no such thing as a lightsaber battle. The technically savvy of you know this, and have probably already explained this mistake away by telling your less technically hip friends that the lightsaber is a actually a plasma saber (where plasma is typically a chunk of ionized gas, in which the electrons from a gas atom's or gas molecule's outer orbitals have been stripped away). The big advantage of using plasma, unlike a laser beam, is that it can be bent, folded and even mutilated by magnetic and electric fields. With a plasma saber it would be theoretically possible to get it to terminate a few feet away, and by manipulating their electric and magnetic fields, two plasma swords could clank against each other. The downside is that since the extremely hot plasma is in contact with air, energy will be constantly carried away from the beam and into the air by way of conduction, convection and radiation. The air around such a beam would literally boil (conventional plasmas are confined in a vacuum, which acts as a thermal isolator so power is not continually being drained away). The hand holding the base of the plasma saber, just a few scant inches away from the plasma, would quickly become a charred stump. And what will power the thing as it continually is dumping its energy into the surrounding air? A couple of D batteries in the handle will not cut the mustard—you'd need a small nuclear reactor.

Lightsabers, or their plasma variants, simply won't work.

Does this mean that Lucas is a science lightweight for having created the lightsaber? Of course not. Lucas is using the lightsabers as a device, a type of clue, pointing out to you that what you should be focusing on are not the obviously impossible lightsabers, but the Jedi. The Jedi are more than hooded guys who whisper mumbo jumbo—they have the power to do something impossible, to actually break the laws of physics.

But how can you break the laws of the universe?

Of course you can't—not in a real universe.

But it would be possible to break the laws of physics in a simulated universe if you could access the program creating that universe. This is what these lightsabers are really all about—cluing us in about not only the nature of the Star Wars universe, but by extension, our universe. So we need to focus on the Jedi—they are the device that Lucas is using to reveal the true nature of our simulated reality. What is the other key ingredient of the Jedi? It is, of course, the Force. In the first few episodes of the Star Wars saga, the Force is presented to us as just some sort of mystical thing, little more than a fantasy element. We eventually learn in *The Phantom Menace* that there is more to it than that.

Midichlorians.

These are a form of microscopic life that pervades everything, is collectively conscious and can interact with the Force. The more midichlorians one has within him, the greater is his ability to manipulate the Force. Jedi training essentially comes down to honing one's skill in interfacing with these bugs. What the midichlorians imply is that the universe as a whole is conscious, every part of it in contact with every other part.

Now, of course, any real universe, obeying the laws of physics, would not work this way. When the Death Star obliterated Alderaan, Obi-Wan swooned as he felt all those little midichlorians getting fried light-years away.

Yes, light-years away—and he felt it instantly.

Information cannot travel faster than the speed of light. Obi-Wan could have never sensed the obliteration of Alderaan when he did. Again, this is not another scientific blunder, but shows us in no uncertain terms that the Jedi operate outside the physical constraints of their universe, or perhaps I should say, simulation.

Good.

Now we're getting somewhere.

These bugs are a critical clue. We see them in action within the first few minutes of our first Star Wars experience, when Darth Vader stomps aboard Princess Leia's ship, gets a bit tweaked at the incompetence of one of his toadies, and is able to choke him without actually touching him—his will translated into action with the help of the midichlorians.

This raises an important question.

If Vader, Obi-Wan, Yoda and eventually Luke can access these bugs, convincing them to talk to all the other bugs, which in turn allows them to levitate robots and starfighters, and flip and fly about during lightsaber battles, why don't they really take advantage of these abilities?

Forget the lightsabers. If you can lift a fighter out of a swamp by accessing your midichlorians, it would be a lot easier to simply instruct the little bugs to stop an enemy's heart from beating. Job done. The Rebels had the schematics of the Death Star. Why go to all the trouble of using the Force to drop a bomb down the Death Star's one vulnerable opening, when a Jedi could just take control of the Death Star's central power reactor engineer, have him flip a few switches, overloading the whole thing, and cause the Death Star to explode?

Why can midichlorians be accessed to do only some things?

Because that is just how a simulation works when you are exploiting its bugs (and this is no pun—bugs in a program and the bugs that are midichlorians are intimately related). Just because you can access the subroutine that keeps your feet planted on the floor, exploit a bug in it and then fly about during a lightsaber battle in no way implies that you can will someone's heart to stop.

Program bugs are a hit-and-miss thing—seemingly random and unconnected.

And this is exactly what Lucas is trying to show us. These Jedi are hackers, exploiting bugs in the universe-generating program. It is the only logical reason for the scientific blunders and inconsistent abilities demonstrated by the Jedi.

This should now be obvious to all of you. But if not, I'll offer up one final Star Wars item that will conclusively demonstrate the nature of the hidden reality of the Star Wars universe and ours.

BRAIN-DEAD

What if I told you that I could walk one mile in only half a mile?

You'd probably politely smile and try to quickly get away from me, wondering if I was simply very slow on the uptake, or possibly deranged. You cannot walk one mile in half a mile, any more than you can compress one hour into thirty minutes.

The universe simply isn't built that way.

Or is it?

Consider the Kessel Run. When Luke and Obi-Wan are trying to make a quick escape from Tatooine, they meet with Han Solo, who boastfully informs them that he made the Kessel Run in the *Millennium Falcon* in less than twelve parsecs. Now he does not tell us how many parsecs it would take a standard ship, but his boast implies that twelve parsecs is pretty impressive, and we might assume that other ships require fifteen or even twenty parsecs.

Of course this makes absolutely no sense. A parsec is a unit of distance (3.26 light-years to be precise). Han's boast is equivalent to my boast of being able to walk one mile in only half a mile.

But Luke and Obi-Wan don't question this.

And obviously George Lucas didn't question this—after all, he put it in his film. Now some claim that this Kessel Run business shows beyond any doubt that Lucas is a scientific dim bulb. But giving this just a bit of thought, it soon becomes obvious that the exact opposite is true—this is George Lucas screaming at the audience that not only is Star Wars operating in a simulated universe, but that the audience is also living in a simulated universe.

Obi-Wan and Luke are not surprised by Han's boast, because they know that in the universe in which they live, such things are possible, that there are bugs in the program that can be exploited for just such effects. But it goes way beyond that.

Consider how movies are made.

The production of Star Wars was not a one-man operation in which Lucas did everything from writing and directing to acting to catering to stage design to electrical work to costumes to keeping the porta-potties stocked with toilet paper. It literally takes thousands of people to make such a movie, and before it is released to the public, thousands more will see it, picking it apart, searching for any sorts of errors. Do you think it is possible that of the thousands involved in the production, or the thousands that saw it before its release, not a single one of them knew that a parsec was a unit of distance, and that Han's claim of making the Kessel Run in less than twelve parsecs was total nonsense?

Of course not. I'm sure that Lucas was told hundreds of times about this error. But he didn't change it.

Why?

Because he'd figured out that it wouldn't be an error in a simulated universe, and was leaving it as the biggest clue of all for his audience. He was telling the audience in no uncertain terms that things are not what they seem, not only in his films, but in the "real" world. An error that massive, one that only a dead brain would not balk at, had made its way into this film. But such an error would be impossible—hundreds of people involved with the production would have caught it.

It's not an error, but the truth. You can make the Kessel Run in less than twelve parsecs, and if you understand the true nature of our universe, you can walk one mile in only half a mile.

Find the bugs in the simulation—exploit them, start to subvert the programming to create the type of reality you want. But you've got to be careful, need to be sly, since you don't want to alarm the creators of our simulation that you have figured this out.

So if you're George Lucas, what do you do?

You make millions—no billions—of dollars on these films, loading them with clues that will lead the careful viewer to the inescapable conclusion that our universe is only simulated, and then you use your billions to assemble the best programming minds in a top-secret research facility, where security is tighter than anything found in a top-secret government lab, and turn them loose. That place is real and is called Industrial Light and Magic—the secret research facility of George Lucas, supposedly a facility that generates state-of-the-art movie special effects.

But now you know the truth.

Industrial Light and Magic is searching for the bugs in the code that runs our simulated universe. My argument is foolproof, and is the only logical explanation for the nearly endless scientific errors found in the Star Wars films.

I suspect that with the publication of this essay, one of four things is possible:

I will be labeled a kook.

Industrial Light and Magic will kidnap me and bring me into the inner workings of their bug-searching secret research program.

The aliens running the simulation for our universe will know that the jig is up and will announce their existence by transforming the entire mass of Jupiter into an extra-large version of Jabba the Hutt.

The aliens running the program for our universe will know that the jig is up and turn off the simulation.

Good luck to all of us (and I'm not a kook).

Robert A. Metzger is a research scientist and a science fiction and science writer. His research focuses on the technique of molecular beam epitaxy, used to grow epitaxial films for high-speed electronics applications. His short fiction has appeared in most major SF magazines including: *Asimov's*, *Fantasy & Science Fiction*, and *SF Age*, while his 2002 novel *Picoverse* was a Nebula finalist and his most recent novel, *CUSP*, was released by Ace in 2005. His science writing has appeared in *Wired* and *Analog*, and he is a contributing editor to the Science Fiction Writers of American Bulletin.

THE COURTROOM

DAVID BRIN: This argument was most clever and entertaining. Indeed, I have toyed with the "we are living in a simulation" concept in numerous stories, for example "Stones of Significance," which people can download by visiting my Web—

DROID JUDGE: This is immaterial—

DAVID BRIN: Exactly, Your Honor! If we exist in a simulation, then the distinction between material, living humans, like me, and immaterial, imaginary creatures, such as yourself—

DROID JUDGE: No, no. I put up with your asides earlier, when they were relevant. But not this time. Do you have any actual cross-examination questions for this witness?

DAVID BRIN: Well, yes, Your Honor. Will Mr. Metzger please answer this?

Again and again, Defense witnesses have posed clever excuses for Star Wars, pointing out that (for example) none of the "Force guys" matter in the end, and this must have been George Lucas's point, all along. Now Mr. Metzger claims that Lucas's real purpose is to engage in a vital experiment, allowing simulated beings to explore the limits and parameters of their software prison!

Well, well. But if any of these excuses were true, would not there have been at least a hint about it in character dialogue in some of the Star Wars movies?

Something to help out viewers who are less brainy (or obsessed) than Mr. Metzger, maybe offering a hint?

ROBERT A. METZGER: Mr. Brin's question is most clever—not the actual question, of course, which will be trivial to answer, but the way he posses the question. He asks if there might be a "hint" to the message in George Lucas's Star Wars about the simulated universe we live in, something for those who are less "brainy" than

Mr. Brin claims I am. The not-so-subtle form of his question implies that only an elitist genius could uncover the true meaning of Star Wars, picking up on clues that he wishes you to believe are so subtle that they might not even exist.

Nonsense!

If Your Honor wishes, I can produce any number of witnesses who will attest to my lack of brainpower, even producing technical experts who will state that in actuality I am a total dullard barely able to tie my shoes, or wipe away the drool that continually drips from my chin.

DROID JUDGE: Not necessary, Mr. Metzger. This Court is more than willing to accept as fact your quite obvious mental deficits.

ROBERT A. METZGER: Most gracious of Your Honor. It is a pleasure to be in a Court of a droid of such brilliant intellect, one who—

DROID JUDGE: Enough! You've done more than enough to establish the basis of your intellectual inferiority, so please get on with answering Mr. Brin's question.

ROBERT A. METZGER: Of course, Your Honor. The words of the most well-respected Jedi Knight to have ever graced a galaxy from far, far away will leave absolutely no doubt to the *fact* that George Lucas has presented the viewers of Star Wars not only a tale representative of a simulated reality, but also the revelation that the viewers' own world is a simulation....

DROID JUDGE: On with it, Mr. Metzger! Answer the question!

ROBERT A. METZGER: Certainly, sir. Please consider the revealing scene during which Luke first tests his abilities with his lightsaber against a small training seeker, as he and Master Kenobi escape on the *Millennium Falcon* from Tatooine. Luke is unable to deflect the seeker's laser beams, continually being stung. Master Kenobi tells him, "Your eyes can deceive you. Don't trust them. Stretch out your feelings."

That is no "hint," but a blatant statement about the nature of reality. Kenobi (through whom Lucas is speaking) is clearly saying that your very senses cannot be used to sense the world, and that true reality lies beyond this world, to another place, obviously referring to the true reality outside the simulation. In response, Luke stops trying to "see" the world as presented, but seeks the world beyond the simulation, just like any good programmer, reaching into the code that defines the universe, and he is able to deflect the laser blasts from the seeker. Master Kenobi then offers more wise words, assuring Luke that what he just accomplished was not based on luck. "In my experience, there's no such thing as luck," says Kenobi.

Well, Your Honor, there can be no denying the power of Kenobi's final words. As even Mr. Brin will have to admit, the very essence of luck is based on the chaotic, random nature of reality—which is quite possibly the most fundamental aspect of what we call reality—its very randomness and unpredictability. But to a master Jedi like Kenobi, who has learned to access the programming that defines the simulation he is in, there is no longer any such thing as luck—every aspect of the simulated reality is defined by the program. Kenobi is stating in stark, all-too-apparent words that the world must be a simulation—that being the only possible consequence of a world without luck—and of course using this so-elegant metaphor to let us, the viewers, know that our own world is exactly such a place. Any further examples would be redundant, and I don't wish to take any more of the Court's time on Mr. Brin's ridiculous stance. In fact, if I might add—

DROID JUDGE: You may not!

DAVID BRIN: That was very clever, but does not disprove the charge.

MATTHEW WOODRING STOVER: What charge? You never *made* a charge—

DROID JUDGE: Order! Gentlebeings, restrain yourselves. Whether charges have been made or disproved must be left to the jury. Moving on—

DAVID BRIN: Your Honor, I'd like to call another witness.

MATTHEW WOODRING STOVER: Objection! One witness per charge!

DROID JUDGE: Mr. Stover, you were allowed *three* witnesses on charge #3—!

MATTHEW WOODRING STOVER: Is it *my* fault you bent the rules?

DROID JUDGE: I will grant the Prosecution another witness on this charge.

DAVID BRIN: Thank you, Your Honor. My next witness will demonstrate that Star Wars is more like almost anything else than it is like science fiction. I call science fiction writer Bruce Bethke.

MATTHEW WOODRING STOVER: Objection!

DROID JUDGE: On what grounds?

MATTHEW WOODRING STOVER: Bethke's *my* witness. He can't testify for *both* of us. What, is the Prosecution gonna' stick a crappy goatee on him and pretend this is Bruce Bethke from the Mirror Universe? Or that a "transporter-beam accident" split him into his "light half" and "dark half"? Because—excuse the rivulets of sarcasm streaming from my chin—we all know that's what would happen in *real* science fiction....

DAVID BRIN: Your Honor, we are trying each charge separately. Therefore, it is perfectly possible for a person of Mr. Bethke's caliber to serve as a Defense witness on one charge and as a witness for the Prosecution on another!

DROID JUDGE: Agreed. In the interests of justice, Mr. Bethke can retake the stand.

Star Wars as Anime

WITNESS FOR THE PROSECUTION:

Bruce Bethke

THERE IS A DEFINING MOMENT in *Star Wars, Episode III: Revenge of the Sith*, and it takes place quite early in the film. No, it's not the moment when Anakin Skywalker gives in to his anger, his pain and his desire to emulate Russell Crowe in *Gladiator* by using two lightsabers to slice off Count Dooku's head, only to then spend almost an entire thirty seconds afterward agonizing over the morality of beheading helpless prisoners. Rather, the scene I'm thinking of begins about another minute after that, when General Grievous's flagship takes a solid hit in the vitals and begins to plunge toward the surface of Coruscant, and R2-D2, the Jedi starfighters and pretty much everything else that isn't lashed down begins to fall toward the bow of the ship. During this scene, Anakin, Obi-Wan and Palpatine get to take some pratfalls and do some light heroics in an elevator shaft, as the direction of "down" undergoes several rapid changes—

But think this through with me. They are onboard a spacecraft. In *orbit*. Meaning, in free-fall in a vacuum, as will become evident three minutes later, when General Grievous is blown out the window by explosive decompression and does not immediately plummet to his doom. And yet, for the sake of the action sequence in the elevator, R2-D2 and everything else within the ship briefly behaves

279

as if they have looked down, suddenly noticed the presence of gravity and gone rushing headlong toward that great big round planet-thingy down there, in hopes that it will be their friend.

As I said, this is a defining moment. And what, precisely, does it define?

Well, if you still haven't guessed after watching Episodes I and II, what this scene is telling you to do is to take your mind off the hook. Don't just suspend your disbelief, pay it off and send it home for the day. Buy yourself a jumbo bucket of popcorn, kick back and enjoy the ride, and don't even bother trying to make sense of anything else that you might see or hear in the next 120 minutes. You have entered a world where style and spectacle trump physics and sense; where it's perfectly logical for space battleships to have keels and superstructures and trade broadsides at point-blank range; where *of course* the great starships float serenely through the void, accompanied by the throaty purring sound of dirigible engines. You have entered a place in the universe of fiction where combat spacecraft have wings and engage in swirling space dogfights like swarms of Hellcats and Zeros, where flak bursts and missiles leave smoky black trails through the vacuum and damaged pieces of ships fly away in nonexistent slipstreams, and where gravity works, *but only when it's funny*.

That's right, Jake. You're in Toontown now. And to be specific, you're in the charming little ethnic 'hood commonly called *anime*.

The original three Star Wars movies have often been described as a fantasy trilogy that borrows heavily from Japanese samurai movies. By now, this idea should not come as a surprise to anyone: even George Lucas admits the story line for the original *Star Wars* was strongly influenced by Akira Kurosawa's 1958 historical adventure, *The Hidden Fortress*. Live-action samurai-film themes and tropes abound in Lucas's original three movies, along with an abundance of simple visual styling cues such as the oversized helmets of the Death Star's crew in *A New Hope*, Lando Calrissian's boar's-tusk mask in *Return of the Jedi*, the grotesque face masks on the elaborate but apparently worthless body armor of the Imperial stormtroopers (hey, even an *Ewok* can take one of these guys out), and Darth Vader's gravity-defying and wire-assisted sword fighting moves throughout the entire series. For that matter the basic setup of the original movie should seem completely familiar to anyone who's watched enough oriental action movies, or at least a few episodes of *Tenchi Muyo* or *InuYasha*. To wit: a restless young boy comes into possession of a magical sword, learns that he is actually the son of a great warrior and goes off with his aged sensei to confront an ancient evil and fulfill his terrible destiny.

Then again: from the critic's point of view, one of the truly wonderful things about the Star Wars universe is that the territory is so sprawling and borrows from so many sources that it's possible to find just about anything here, if you look hard enough. For example, the story of the original movie can also be summarized as, "A restless young boy chafes at life on the dusty old family farm, until he meets a wizard and is swept away to a wondrous land where he meets some munchkins, a tin man, a cowardly lion and Harrison Ford as the scarecrow."

When considering the latest three installments in the series, though, the comparison breaks down. Episodes I through III are undeniably big, bold and beautiful. They look and sound incredible and are like watching a century's worth of fantastic art suddenly spring to life. But while *The Phantom Menace* borrows plot devices from Kurosawa again, Anakin Skywalker is no Taketori Washizu, and *Revenge of the Sith* is no *Throne of Blood*. There is something missing in these later movies, and it's something important: a soul, a heart, a human factor, a *je ne sais quoi*.

I first began to suspect what the answer was while watching *Attack of the Clones*. Specifically, I was watching the arena scene on Geonosis and thinking of Ray Harryhausen. In the midst of admiring the intricate and fantastic architecture of the arena, and mentally comparing the set, the rampaging beasts and the army of skeletal droids to similar scenes in earlier movies, it suddenly stuck me: *none of this is real*.

Not Real real, of course; that would be ridiculous. But not even "real" in the sense of being a miniature set with animated models. The entire thing—the arena, the Geonosians, the monsters, the droids and even most of the "human" characters—were all just CGI creations, perhaps adapted from scans of physical models, but with no objective existence anywhere except inside the memory of Industrial Light and Magic's animation rendering system. I was not watching a movie. I was watching the biggest, best, most expensive and most beautiful *cartoon* ever made.

Once you consider the premise that Episodes I through III are not live-action movies with extensive special effects, but rather animated features with a few living actors rotoscoped in, many of the more common critical objections to the movies simply wither away. Yes, of course space warships in the ancient future will resemble World War II surface vessels, right down to the turrets and superstructures, and will maneuver as if they're floating on the plane of the ecliptic: didn't you ever watch Yoshinobu Nishizaki's *Space Cruiser Yamato*? Yes, of course space fighters will routinely sprout folding wings and maneuver as if they're in an atmosphere, and any missiles they launch will follow gracefully looping trajectories: didn't you ever watch *Super Dimension Fortress Macross*? Yes, what better way is there to defend your flagship against attack than with four-legged vulture droids that leap into the sky and morph into sleek and deadly combat craft: haven't you at least watched *Transformers*?

Yes, of course the human[1] characters are dwarfed by their surroundings, and their voices are nearly drowned out by the background noise, and Mace Windu will strike a dramatic pose and deliver a speech instead of the one sword stroke that would settle the whole mess right here and now. Because, when you get down to it, in the universe of the new Star Wars movies, the human characters are *not important.*

What is important in Episodes I through III? While it's tempting to identify raging mechaphilia as the key trait, and a strong case can be made that it's actually ornate costumes and ludicrous hairstyles—the Queen of Naboo may be called in witness—the critical distinguishing trait seems to be the same one that is at work behind the scenes in most anime, and it is this: that fully realized characters are hard to do, and full-motion character animation in the style of the classic Disney cartoons is *expensive.* Ergo, the best way to deliver

---

[1] I use the word "human" very loosely here. In the universe of Star Wars, Gungans, Wookiees and little green Jedi Masters are human, too. But clones aren't.

a commercially successful product without driving yourself nuts or breaking the budget is by making the background paintings as absolutely gorgeous as possible, then restricting your human characters to a few dramatic poses and some long-winded speeches, in between the full-motion battle scenes, which are what the paying customers are really coming to see, anyway.

And make no mistake: Star Wars, Episodes I, II and III are three of the most eye-poppingly beautiful and enthralling movies you could ever want to watch. The water world of Kamino, the lush pastoral landscapes of Naboo and Kashyyyk, and the massive palaces that seem to crop up everywhere look like sorts of things Hayao Miyazaki could do if he had an infinite amount of time and money. The sterile, endless cityscape of Coruscant would fit right into Katsuhiro Ôtomo's *Akira*, while Coruscant's grubby and cluttered underworld echoes Ôtomo's Old Tokyo or Mamoru Oshii's *Ghost in the Shell*. The hellish worlds of Geonosis and Mustafar, with their incomprehensible foundries and rivers of fire, evoke *Now and Then, Here and There*, while the massive battle scenes that slaughter clones, Gungans and robots alike with cheerful abandon pay homage to generations of mecha-based manga, movies and TV series.

But as for expecting to find a fully realized and engaging *human* story in the center of all this noise, beauty and excitement?

Forget it, Jake. It's Toontown.

Bruce Bethke works, writes, and when time permits, lives, in the frozen northern reaches of Minnesota. In some circles he is best known for his 1980 short story, "Cyberpunk." In others, he is better known for his Philip K. Dick Award-winning novel, *Headcrash*. What very few people in either circle have known until recently is that he actually works in supercomputer software development, and all of his best science fiction gets turned into design specifications for future products.

Bethke can be contacted via his Web site, http://www.BruceBethke.com.

THE COURTROOM

MATTHEW WOODRING STOVER: Damn, he's good.

DROID JUDGE: Mr. Stover? Your cross-examination?

MATTHEW WOODRING STOVER: Uh. Okay. Um—all right, Mr. Bethke. When, exactly, did you sell out to the Sith?

DAVID BRIN: (*tiredly*) Objection....

DROID JUDGE: Mr. Stover, behave yourself.

MATTHEW WOODRING STOVER: Do I have to?

DROID JUDGE: Mr. Stover—

MATTHEW WOODRING STOVER: Your Honor, I've got nothing. *Nothing.* This man, by his own testimony, couldn't see the human element in Star Wars; should I question a blind man on the colors in somebody else's garden?

DAVID BRIN: Objection.

MATTHEW WOODRING STOVER: Withdrawn. Your Honor, I must beg the Court's indulgence: I need another witness on this charge.

DROID JUDGE: Oh, please....

MATTHEW WOODRING STOVER: The Defense *must* be allowed a rebuttal witness. Someone who *understands* humanity. Someone who sees the truth of all of us...and laughs at it.

DROID JUDGE: (*resignedly*) Whom do you have in mind?

MATTHEW WOODRING STOVER: The Defense calls science fiction writer, philosopher and humorist Adam Roberts, who will demonstrate that Star Wars falls plainly in the grand tradition of comic science fiction.

DROID JUDGE: Oh, very well. The witness may be seated.

The Joy of Star Wars

WITNESS FOR THE DEFENSE:
Adam Roberts

THE CHARGE IS THAT Star Wars is *fantasy masquerading as SF*?

Have the Prosecution even *seen* these films?

Let me try to understand here. Why would somebody think such a thing?

Well, perhaps because they have an unusually narrow sense of what SF is. Sure:

If we are looking for a rigidly and technically exact transfer of "science" into "fiction," then Star Wars doesn't fit the bill terribly well. If we want an example of a "literature of ideas," then we'll find slim pickings. If our fetishes are *seriousness of purpose* or *emotional maturity* then we'd better look elsewhere. But who says that these are the true benchmarks of SF?

There are other forms of SF than the dull and the weighty, the serious and profound; Star Wars belongs to one of those other forms—a specific, joyous and enduring sort. But that doesn't make it fantasy. (Uh—excuse me—spaceships? robots? a whole planet converted into a giant hi-tech city? *Fantasy?* Puh-lease!)

Actually I'd better rein in my outrage. Now that I come to think of it, there is something interesting in the charge that Star Wars is fantasy: it reveals something important both about the Prosecution's preconceptions about the genre, and their shortsightedness about Lucas's six-piece masterwork. They're missing the point, and I hope to explain how.

Put it this way: Here are two sorts of work from, roughly, the same period as Star Wars, both types being irreducibly SF. On the one hand there are films like Kubrick's *2001: A Space Odyssey* (1968), or books like Arthur Clarke's *Rendezvous with Rama* (1973). On the other are John Carpenter's *Dark Star* (1974) or the first appearance of *The Hitchhiker's Guide to the Galaxy* (1978). Which of these two sorts of SF is the one with which our film has the most in common? Let me give you a hint.

I'm going to make an argument that Star Wars belongs to the second kind of SF. I'll come clean up front and admit that it's not an argument often advanced, and that it may take a bit of getting used to; but once you see where I'm coming from I think you'll not only see how misapplied it is to call Star Wars fantasy, you'll also see why it's plain wrong to point out so-called "plot holes," "inconsistencies," "lack of worthy ethical content" and all the other straw men and straw women the Prosecution have been propping up in this volume in order to knock them down. The point, here, is being missed.

And what *is* the point? Read on and I'll tell you.

PARODY

Star Wars must be the most parodied work of modern times.

I know whereof I speak, for I have parodied it myself. On the back of a couple of (only modestly successful) Tolkien parodies, my publisher approached me with an idea to cash in on—did I say *cash in*? I meant *pay sly, comedic tribute to*—the release of the third Star Wars film. He and I sat in a London bar and hammered out a deal. By "hammered out a deal" I mean that we *got* hammered, and then struck a deal: I would write a parody book six chapters long, each of the 10,000-word chapters parodying a different Star Wars film. I needed to be hammered to agree to this, because the third film had not at that point been released, so the last of my six parodic chapters was going to be a parody of my idea of what the film would be about;

or to apply a technical phrase, "pulling stuff rather frantically out of my hat." We then spent the best part of an hour trying to brainstorm a title for the parody. You know the sort of thing: a cod-title for *The Da Vinci Code* might be *The Da Vinci Cod*. By the same logic, a cod-title for Star Wars might be...?

In your own time. There's no rush.

Actually, when we began go through the options, we realized that most of the titles had already been taken. Why? Because Star Wars is easily the most parodied work of modern times. We couldn't call our parody *Star Bores*, or *Spaceballs*, or *Czar Wars*, or *Fart Wars*—in, fact, pretty much all the likely parodyesque titles, because they had all been taken. We ended up really scraping the barrel. In fact we went further: we threw the barrel away and started scraping the floor *underneath* the barrel. I remember, dimly, banging my shoe on the restaurant table and booming drunkenly, "I insist upon *Sitar Wars*; I want to write in lots of instrumentation from classical Indian music," and my editor going red in the face as he shouted back, "No! No! It must be *Star Warts* or nothing, and you'd better put in *all manner of* pimples, moles and facial disfigurement...."

Of course, as title, neither *Sitar Wars* nor *Star Warts* made the cut. At the end of this little essay I'll tell you the title we eventually decided upon. But before I get to that endpoint I want to reiterate my first sentence for the third time in as many pages, by way of making clear my argument: Star Wars is the most parodied work of modern times *for a reason*, and the reason has to do with the extraordinary and enduring excellence of the original. It is parodied *because* it has such cultural currency, because it is so well-known; it is parodied because so many people, parodists included, love it so much.

Indeed, I want to argue something more. I want to argue that the proliferation of Star Wars parodies in fact uncovers something unique and wonderful about the original, something denigrators of the six films often overlook. A superficial explanation would go something like this: "The fact that there are scores of parodies of Star Wars is a reflection of the fact that Star Wars is inherently ridiculous, absurd, deplorable and derided. Star Wars gets parodied again and again because it is bad. You don't see parodies, after all, of *great* cinema."

But this is not only wrong, it is Wrong and indeed *wrong*. Parody is a barometer of cultural *weight*, not of cultural insignificance. Why would anybody parody something that is very bad? What on Earth, or out of it, would be the point in parodying L. Ron Hubbard's *Battlefield Earth*, say, or Ed Wood's *Plan 9 from Outer Space*? These works are beneath parody. But the greatest cinema gets parodied again and again.

Nobody could accuse Ingmar Bergman of being ridiculous, absurd, deplorable or derided; but his great film *The Seventh Seal* has been parodied almost as often as Star Wars. His black-cloaked white-faced Death crops up in films as diverse as Woody Allen's *Love and Death* to McTiernan's *Last Action Hero*. *The Wizard of Oz*, Kubrick's *2001*, *The Godfather*—these films crop up in parody form in everything from movies to multiple episodes of *The Simpsons* to TV ads. Parody is the homage ordinariness pays to genius. Believe me, I'm a parodist and I know.

The first Star Wars parodies came out pretty much as soon as the first film was released. Michael Wiese's film *Hardware Wars* (1977), a thirteen-minute spoof of the original featuring gloriously wooden actors and props drawn (as the title suggests) from the kitchen and the tool shed, appeared only a couple of months after *Star Wars* itself. Apparently it is Lucas's favorite parody. Mel Brook's feature-length spoof *Spaceballs* (1987) parodies the original at greater length, and with more variable comic effect; although it also takes the opportunity to fit in some *2001* and *Star Trek* parody as well. And you would not *believe* how much parodic Star Wars-themed porn there is out there.

No, really.[1] There is even a prose parody of Star Wars that is also a parody of the conventions of porn writing, as if those two things naturally go together.[2]

Star Wars parody quickly became a staple on TV as well as cinema. The mighty *Muppet Show* persuaded Mark Hamill himself to guest-star in their 1980 parody special episode. Plenty of other TV

---

[1] Even the production companies have got in on the act. At least, I've no reason to believe that Lick-Us Films is named after an actual filmmaker called George Lick-Us.

[2] This is Sean Miller's *The Empire MenaceD: The Unauthorized Autobiography of Dearth Nadir* (Imperial Beach, CA: Aventine Press, 2004). I guess the point is that male adolescence and Star Wars often go together; and that obsessive fascination with sex and *male adolescence* often go together, so there's a sort of association by implication.

shows have followed suit, from *Friends* to *Family Guy*. And above all there is *The Simpsons*. *The Simpsons* is simply stuffed to its yellow gullet with Star Wars parody. There are far, far too many moments to mention here.[3] My two favorites are probably "Mayored to the Mob" (1998), which features a wrestling match called "The Mighty Robots of Battlestar Galactica Versus the Gay Robots of Star Wars!" and "Worst Episode Ever" (2001) in which the Comic Book Store Guy chances upon a box of little-known Star Wars goodies, including "Princess Leia's anti-jiggle breast tape" and a film reel titled "Alternate Ending: Luke's father is Chewbacca."

But Star Wars parodies have not been limited to film and TV. They crop up in every genre and mode. "Weird Al" Yankovic has written parodies of the Star Wars that utilize the idiom of song, and a "Star Wars Gangsta Rap" (2000), available for Flash download from www. atomfilms.com, has even won awards from Star Wars fans themselves. And, in fact, that's an important point: whatever brickbats you may want to hurl at Star Wars fans, you can't accuse them of being uptight or lacking a sense of humor. And that's no coincidence. If they were po-facedly defensive of their favorite films, they would hardly have purchased (in such large quantities) the dozens of comics that have parodied the original, not least amongst them the sensitively titled *Fart Wars* (from Entity Comics, 1997).

And the same is true across the board. *Star Bores*, a book by British humorists Steve Barlow and Steve Skidmore, appeared in 1997, and was reissued with new parody material in 2004. And of course the Web contains hundreds of Star Wars parody sites. Among the best is the Wikipedia parody site Uncyclopedia, which is threaded through with Star Wars parody, not least in its lengthy and often hilarious entry on the film series itself (www.uncyclopedia.org/wiki/Star_wars). The LEGO parody of Star Wars Episode III ("Revenge of the Brick") can be downloaded from the LEGO site (www.lego.com/starwars/default.aspx). Dylan Jones's fan film "Stick Wars" animates crucial scenes from the film using stick men (www.stickpage.com/stickwars.shtml) and is surprisingly funny. And there's the "Official Site Gag"

---

[3] There is in fact an entire Web site devoted to listing the myriad Star Wars parody moments in *The Simpsons*, as you can see for yourself if you direct your browser to www.snpp.com/guides/star-wars.html.

(www.geocities.com/SunsetStrip/Alley/7028/swosg.htm), a nice parody of the official site. It goes on and on.

Here's the obvious question: *why?*

Why are there *so many* parodies of these particular films?

The short answer to the question must be that Star Wars suits parody, in some way. The logic of those films connects in some way with the logic of Lucas's six films.

The purpose of a parody is to make people laugh. To examine why there are so many Star Wars parodies is to examine that weird and as yet unexplained human phenomenon called laughter.

LAUGHTER

Let's get back to my theory. In order to make my case, allow me to call back to the witness bar those two aforementioned SF films: *Battlefield Earth* (directed by Roger Christian in 2000) and *Plan 9 from Outer Space* (1959). Which of these two films is the greater? (I say "greater" because it seems to miss the point, somehow, to ask which of two films is *better* when both films are famous for being very, very bad.)

But when I put the question the answer is obvious. *Battlefield Earth* is strenuously, earnestly, *seriously* bad where *Plan 9* is gloriously, hilariously, *delightfully* bad.

The phrase "so bad it's good" really doesn't apply to the former film, which aims to combine the satisfactions of blockbuster entertainment with a buried, seriously meant Scientological message—aims, and misses. It's so bad it's bad, and that's all there is to it. When we watch it, the pleasure we feel is one of superiority. We watch *Battlefield Earth* to mock.

But *Plan 9* is a completely different matter. It is so unpretentiously and spontaneously bad it goes *beyond* bad, in a strange way, and enters its own bizarrely magical territory. We don't watch *Plan 9* in order to mock it. The laughter it provokes in us is a warm and communal sort. It spills out from the film itself to encompass the story of the making of the film, and the hilarious life of its director. The one star attached to the project, Bela Lugosi, died before shooting. In his place Wood hired Dr. Tom Mason (not so much an *actor*; more the producer's wife's chiropractor) to stand in for Lugosi's parts. Lugosi was small and dark. Mason was tall and blond and bore no facial re-semblance to the horror star. In a stroke of inadvertent comic genius Wood thought he could elide these differences by getting Mason to *hold his cloak in front of his face in every single shot in which he appears*. It is hard to express how singularly delightful and life-affirming it is to watch a film as unpretentiously catastrophically *bad* as this one.

This is a roundabout way of making a crucial point about human laughter. Laughter comes in two flavors: there is nasty laughter and there is nice laughter. There is *laughing at* and *laughing with*. Sigmund Freud, one of the greatest minds to consider this complicated business of laughter, realized this early on. He named the former kind of laughter "witz" (sometimes translated as "jokes") and illustrated it by quoting a great many rather unpleasant jokes, many of them anti-Semitic, or anti-women. The other, "good" sort of laughter he called "humor" (it's the same word in German and English; though we Brits put an elegant second "u" in there after the "o")—and he argued that this served a completely different psychological purpose altogether: this is a positive, social, bonding sort of laughter.

It's easy to think of examples of both sorts of laughter. There is a tiresome and depressing wasteland of offensive humor that mocks minorities (black, Jewish, Irish, homosexual) or which reaffirms misogynist stereotype, or which takes a selfish pleasure in watching the affliction and suffering of others. Such jokes are no more than pointing at a person and braying like a donkey. These sort of jokes are straightforwardly racist, cruel and despicable. They reflect discredit upon the person laughing, and suggest that human nature is a mean, spiteful and bitter thing.

But, thankfully, most laughter is not like this. Most laughter is the good sort. I don't mean that most laughter is *safe*—in fact, it's very obvious that the *reverse* is true. The things that make us laugh often are exactly the subjects about which we are most anxious: death, sex, embarrassment, failure. There's nothing safe about any of this. But the laughter that liberates from these alarming subjects is *inclusive*, not exclusive. Laughter binds us all together; it is our solace in the face of the intractable facts of a heartless cosmos. The greatest humor breaks taboos precisely in order to trick us into facing up to the human condition. It says: Don't bury your head in the sand—we all must die, we all must deal with pain; we're all embarrassed, nerdy and awkward. In a single phrase: We're all in this together.

The best laughter is the sort that we experience in company with our friends and the people we love, that infectious and wonderful laughter that as often as not comes out of nowhere at all when the mood is right, and that leaves everybody feeling stronger and happier. Nasty laughter is a solitary and ultimately, alienating thing. Good laughter is the cement of community.

So where does Star Wars fit into this?

The enormous proliferation of Star Wars parodies taps into something *laughable* about the original six films; but this humor is not of the nasty sort. I want to call it *joy*, a word meant to evoke a special kind of forceful, unifying, positive sense of *rightness*, a bubbling emotional pleasure that can manifest as laughter, but equally well might simply create that glowing sensation of pleasure in the solar plexus, or goosebump stippling, or just a big grin. This is the effect Star Wars has on its enormous fan base.

Perhaps you disagree? Perhaps you feel that, insofar as you can bring yourself to sit through the film, you watch with snooty and condescending disdain? Well then, you are indeed to be pitied. There are some people (poor souls) who really have no sense of humor, who don't get the jokes everybody else is enjoying, who live their lives in chilly isolation from the currents of warm, breathing, joyous human community. May I offer a suggestion? If that's you, it may be that you are trying to analyze the films in a way incompatible with their appeal. Everybody knows that a joke explained isn't funny anymore. What would you say to somebody who reported, sour-faced, that he had just watched a couple of Marx Brothers films and that he disapproved? "All that running around and chattering wisecracking... terrible! What's the *political* and *ideological* implication here? Why don't they show society as being supportive of the little guy? Why do they deal in stereotypes like this? Are they really saying that the police should be mocked and lampooned? In one scene a Marx brother made fun of legal contracts by repeating the phrase 'party of the first part'—don't they see how important and serious legal contracts, and by implication the edifice of the law, *is*?" What could you say to such a person? Nothing, except: I'm afraid you're missing the point.

What's that? You don't think the Marx Brothers can be compared with Star Wars? You think the one was intended as comedy, and the other wasn't?

This is (you're right) the crux of my argument. Because by suggesting that Star Wars is *comedy* I'm suggesting a wider definition of comedy than is usually the case. This is not *Jackass*: it is not laughing at other people. It is joy: it is laughing, or grinning, with others. Those others are the global community of Star Wars fans, the people behind the films' continuing success (each film grossing nearly a billion dollars globally), the authors of the thousands of specialist Web sites and fan forums, the same people who parody and re-parody the whole. And one thing that not even the most mean-spirited Star Wars hater can deny is that these films have created a vast human community of admirers and fans. If you hate the films then you're put in the position of having to look down your nose upon millions upon millions of your fellow human beings. Which, to say the least, isn't very nice of you.

Comedy is more than just moments designed to make people laugh aloud. It is a whole genre of literature, a whole mode of art. We call one-third of Shakespeare's plays comedies, not because they make us laugh (we can be honest: they don't), but because they reaffirm human positivity; because they end happily; because they light a candle of love and communality in the darkness of cosmic indifference. This is where Star Wars belongs.

In a way the films' moments of deliberate comedy are the weakest part of the broader effect. Sometimes the brittle banter of the droids *is* amusing. More often the slubberly pantomime of Jar Jar Binks tries for laughs and misses. I think this is because it is impossible to laugh *with* Jar Jar, that most irritating of screen creations, and so we are thrown back upon laughing *at* him. (This in turn, because of the character's patent relationship with blackface minstrelsy, implicates us uncomfortably as racists.) But Jar Jar is the exception in these films, not the rule. Generally the currency of Star Wars is exhilaration, excitement, glory and hilarity: joy.

The final assault on the Death Star in *A New Hope* is not played for laughs in the sense that a Farrelly Brothers (*shudder*) film is played for laughs.[4] But the exhilaration we experience as the rebels soar away from the detonating space fortress is precisely the currency of joy. It is because the films are expressions of this joy that really small comic triggers—say, Han Solo running chasing a platoon of stormtroopers up a corridor and immediately coming running down again chased *by* the stormtroopers—generate such excessive gales of laughter in the theater when they're played. This is the joy that makes you bounce up and down with excitement at the prospect of another film in the series, that makes you hug yourself or grin. That's the sense in which the films are comedies.

There's one more point to make about these films. One of the chief motors of comedy is precisely incongruity. It is putting the fear-inspiring Spanish Inquisition (our anxieties about torture, pain and death) together with comfy chairs and soft pillows. It is thin stupid Laurel and fat complacent Hardy. Incongruity means the expert coordination of radically differing elements. The Star Wars universe is based on a brilliantly sustained process of creative incongruity: all manner of strange aliens and human beings coexist, elements from a hundred famous SF novels and films are thrown into the mix, and finally—in the prequel trilogy—live action and CGI are incongruously mixed together in every scene. This incongruity is the backbone of the Star Wars universe. Lucas's instinct for the *right* incongruity prevents it becoming merely a mess. But it acts as more than saving grace; it is the fundamental point of the whole. Of course these films have weaknesses: inconsistencies, shifts in tone and color, a plodding apperception of romantic love and a somewhat simplistic understanding of the working of international politics. But these elements do not cancel out the glorious action sequences, the frequently stunning visual aesthetic, the thrills and imaginative stimulation that the films also manifest. The incongruity between the best and the worst of the films—in every individual movie—is precisely the point. The mélange of the Star Wars films are their strength. Because life does not hermetically seal away "high seriousness" and "tragedy" from "comic bathos" and "general grinning hilarity." They are all mixed in together.

---

[4] Ever since seeing that small-minded, nasty-spirited excuse for a comedy *Dumb and Dumber* I have resolved to write to the directors every year exhorting them to change their name by deed poll to "The Farrelly Brothers (*shudder*)." I shall persevere until they agree.

I mentioned *Hitchhiker's Guide* earlier; and in a way I am arguing that Star Wars belongs to the same family as that sublime SF work (and who would call *Hitchhiker's* fantasy?). One difference, of course, is that Douglas Adams could write gags like nobody else could write gags; he was the god of gags; he carried about, as mental luggage, bags of gags, and was surrounded by gaggles of good gags. Lucas isn't in the same continent as far as gag writing goes. But think again; would you really want to argue that *Hitchhiker's Guide* can be reduced to *nothing more than its gags*? Of course not. The reason that show has won so many hearts is more than the jokes and the punch lines; it is because there is a joy at the heart of it—a warmth, a diversity and beautiful incongruity, an exhilaration, all things that are comic in the fullest sense. It's in this way that Star Wars is close kin. This is where Lucas's broadest appeal is located.

The title of this essay itself gestures toward parody. Ever since Alex Comfort's *The Joy of Sex* (another glorious, joyous work that combined the very good—lots of sex—with the very bad—detailed line drawings of an *ugly bearded man* having lots of sex), writers have reverted to that title. But I don't mean it in a throwaway sense. The success of Star Wars is no fluke; it is a function of the film's perfect expression of human joy. This is what makes it a comedy; this is what excuses its weaknesses and reinforces its strengths. This is both what makes it so very parodyable, and what makes those parodies— all of the ones I listed—not snide potshots at the movie, but genuinely affectionate extrapolations of its underlying logic.

What title was my own parody eventually published under? Well, the point of this essay hasn't been to try and flog copies of my own book, but to defend Star Wars from those po-faced, *Hitchhiker's Guide* humorless, overly literal types who cannot embrace the whole glorious messy splendor of the films. But I suppose I promised to tell you the title, and a promise is a promise.

The title we went for was *Star Warped*. I know what you're thinking. It's not, as titles go, one half as funny as *Revenge of the Sith*.[5] But

---

[5] This is what the *Oxford English Dictionary* gives us under *sith*: an archaic and largely dialect word...used especially as an interjection to draw attention or as a conversational filler. Are you telling me that *Revenge of the Interjection to Draw Attention or Conversational Filler* wouldn't make a good parody title?

that's as it should be. Star Wars is the source of the joy, and the humor, into which any parody hopes to tap. To accuse it of incongruity, of stereotypes, of lacking seriousness and depth—all this is spectacularly to miss the point of what the films have to offer. When they're right, they're very, very right; and when they're wrong, they're funny. And not funny in a bitter or unpleasant way; funny in a way that captures the life-affirming, sprawling joy of humor.

So: Star Wars a fantasy? No, no, no. Fantasy, and especially High Fantasy in its Tolkienian form, is all about dignity, weight, seriousness and a hidden message of religious profundity. It is monolithic, often ponderous and arthritic, refusing to accept that society and culture has changed and clinging tenaciously to an outdated past. But SF—the best SF—the sort of SF that *Hitchhiker's Guide* and Star Wars exemplified—is the very opposite of this: it is synthetic and diverse in itself; it delights in sprawl and incongruity; it embraces change and traffics in polymorphous joy.

You know it's true. You've been sitting, very politely, reading all these essays by furrowed-brow writers ponderously pointing out *plot holes* and *failures of moral seriousness* in the universe of Star Wars; and you know that they're all fundamentally missing the point. You feel it in your gut, in your heart, which is where humor lives. Intellectually the Prosecution are marshaling some ingenious arguments; but all they are doing, in a strugglingly circumlocutory manner, is showing that they *don't get it.*

You get it. Enough said.

My advice? Don't fret it. Why try and explain to these anti-Star Wars-ists what they're missing? Has there ever been a case, in the history of the world, when an individual without a sense of humor has been persuaded to *laugh* at comedy—to open his heart to its joy—by force of intellectual argumentation? Haranguing won't convert them. Let them be.

Adam Roberts was born in 1965. He has a day job, as professor of nineteenth-century literature at the University of London, and has published a variety of academic criticism; he also writes science fiction novels and parodies. He lives with his wife and daughter about a third of an inch (on a map, that is) to the left of London, UK. Unlike Star Wars, he has never been on trial. Not so far, at any rate, although he believes that "it doesn't do to tempt fate" and has touched wood.

THE COURTROOM

DAVID BRIN: Your Honor, the Prosecution would like to stipulate that Adam Roberts is a funny guy. And this is a very interesting insight...

...And it has very little to do with the topic at hand. Seriously, if this were crafted to be a scholarly tome about general Star Wars criticism, I would suggest inviting some wonderfully insightful critics of science fiction, such as—

DROID JUDGE: Your point is taken under advisement. Shall we proceed to the next charge?

DAVID BRIN: By all means. The Prosecution now calls Jeanne Cavelos to address the issue of whether *women* ought to have a beef with Star Wars.

CHARGE 7

Women in Star Wars Are Portrayed as Fundamentally Weak

Stop Her, She's Got a Gun!

How the Rebel Princess and the Virgin Queen Became Marginalized and Powerless in George Lucas's Fairy Tale

WITNESS FOR THE PROSECUTION:
Jeanne Cavelos

AGAINST A BACKGROUND of stars and X-wing fighters, Luke holds his lightsaber aloft while Leia crouches below him, brandishing a gun: two tough heroes ready to fight the evil Empire. In my love of *Star Wars*, I spent endless hours longing for "a galaxy far, far away," replaying the movie in my head, studying every detail of the poster on my wall. It seemed to embody the excitement of the movie and its strong heroes, Luke and Leia. But as the Star Wars saga unfolded, I became troubled. While George Lucas brilliantly combined diverse ideas and influences to create something startling and inspiring, one aspect of the movies didn't live up to the rest. I began to notice something new about the poster on my wall. Luke above, superior; Leia below, inferior. It seemed to reflect the treatment of the characters in the movies. The problem is not that the women are supporting characters, though they are. Even a supporting character can be striking and compelling. Han Solo is such a powerful, heroic figure, he nearly eclipses Luke. But the women in Star Wars are not the memorable figures they could be. Compared to their male counterparts, they are inconsistent and underdeveloped. There is a clear lack of focus on these characters on the part of George Lucas and the other writers, a tendency to sacrifice the female characters to make the males look better, and a decided inclination to reduce initially powerful women to inaction and irrelevance. Leia and Amidala, as the two most prominent female figures in the films, exemplify these weaknesses.

Both Leia and Amidala first appear to be strong, heroic women and striking characters. In Episode IV, Leia is a leader in the struggle against powerful, evil forces, a shrewd woman as fast with a gun as she is with a sharp retort. Leia's commitment is unmatched. When we first see her, she is risking her life for the Rebellion. Even when her entire planet is threatened, she refuses to betray the cause. Leia appears to be a key figure in the Rebellion. She is carrying the plans to the Death Star, the most important intelligence the Rebels could hope to have. Darth Vader, one of the top figures in the Empire, is pursuing her and seems to know her well. Leia is also a strong and intelligent leader. Her goal is to get the plans to her father and the Rebels. To do that, she cleverly hides the data in Artoo, directing him where to go, fights the stormtroopers, defies Vader, lies to Tarkin and resists torture. When Luke and Han rescue her from the Death Star, Leia saves them all by instantly coming up with a plan and leading them into the garbage chute. For Leia is not only a leader but a woman of action. She can shoot a blaster, and she's not hesitant to do so. But perhaps the most striking aspect of Leia's personality is her smart mouth: "When you came in here, didn't you have a plan for getting out?" When it comes to insults, Leia can give as good as she gets. She's an energetic and impressive presence, bold, brash, powerful and driven.

As we look more closely at the trilogy, though, we see hints of weaknesses in the character, weaknesses that increase until eventually they drain all strength, coherence and believability out of her. While a well-developed character can withstand some inconsistencies—it's human nature to be inconsistent, after all—the inconsistencies within Leia are so great, they destroy any sense of character cohesion.

———

Throughout Episode IV, Leia appears to be a committed freedom fighter with a clear goal: overthrowing the Empire. Yet in Episode V, Leia's personal determination to fight this fight is undermined at Cloud City. She should be desperately trying to re-join the Rebellion, help them reconstitute their crippled forces and find a new base. Yet she makes no attempt to contact the Rebels or to expedite work on the *Falcon*. She could have ordered Threepio, Chewie or Han to stay with the ship and oversee the repairs. Or she could have made an ally among the mechanics of Cloud City, offering triple pay for overtime. Instead, she leaves it to the men to work things out, while she changes clothes, fixes her hair, frets about the missing Threepio and paces back and forth in her room in the clouds, like an ill-tempered Rapunzel. She seems less interested in rejoining the Rebellion than in nitpicking and proving that Han's decision to bring them to Cloud City was a bad one.

We again see a lack of commitment to her goals when she encounters the Ewoks. When she wakes up in the forest and finds Wicket, she instantly gives up any hope of rejoining her team. Why doesn't she try to figure out the right direction and start walking? That's what Luke does. A dedicated fighter, in the critical moments before battle, should do anything to get where she needs to be. Instead, she follows Wicket, making no attempt to question him about the location of the Imperial shield generator. When Luke and Han at last find her, she appears to have been hanging out in comfort at the Ewok village, changing her clothes and combing her hair. What soldier lets down her hair before the big battle? What happened to the can-do, determined woman who yelled, "Into the garbage chute, flyboy"? Her actions and attitude are completely at odds with what they ought to be. It would have been simple enough for the writers to change these things, to keep Leia's commitment to her cause strong and consistent, but this clearly was not a priority.

In addition to her commitment, Leia's importance is also undermined. Leia initially appears to be a powerful figure, a princess and senator and the bearer of key Rebel intelligence. Over the course of the trilogy, though, her importance dwindles and her power evaporates before our eyes.

Before Episode IV is half over, the Senate is dissolved, making Leia's position as senator irrelevant, and Alderaan is destroyed, making her title of princess meaningless. The power and resources she once commanded are now dramatically reduced.

She should still have power as a key figure in the Rebellion, but that, too, slips away. She remains on the sidelines during Episode IV's big battle. She is a mere onlooker as males pilot the fighters and males direct the battle. She's the cheerleader, there to witness the glory of the males and pay tribute to it. At the awards ceremony, she is in the position of a commander, but she does not wield the power of one. In addition, though she delivered the plans that led to the victory, she receives no medal herself. She is neither a leader nor a valued participant.

In Episode V, the crawl informs us that freedom fighters have been "led by Luke Skywalker." Luke is a commander now and Han a general; both have gained in status while Leia has lost hers.

When it comes time for the Rebellion's evacuation, the order is given by General Rieekan, not Leia. Briefing a small group of pilots, Leia is perhaps the equivalent of a low-level officer.

By the time the Rebels prepare for their ultimate battle against the Empire's new Death Star, Lando is a general too. He's leading the fighters. Han is in charge of attacking the shield generator. Leia has been given no mission, title or job, and it appears that she's played no part in the planning of this major action. The Rebellion doesn't seem to believe she has any useful skills. Since no one needs her, she volunteers to be part of Han's crew. Her status can't get much lower.

Leia could have had a compelling subplot in which she found a new role for herself within the Rebellion after the destruction of Alderaan. Luke, Han and Lando all undergo such a process and grow as characters. Leia, on the other hand, after starting out as a key figure in the Rebellion, becomes marginalized and ends up an unneeded hanger-on, present to witness the heroism of the men.

At least Leia still has her wits and her leadership abilities. Or does she? These, too, are undercut. A shrewd leader must know how to turn any situation to her advantage. After her escape from the Death Star, Leia realizes the *Millennium Falcon* is being tracked by the Empire. This is a brilliant insight. Yet what does she do with this huge advantage? Does she search for the tracking beacon and deactivate it? Does she direct Han to land on a decoy planet, transfer Artoo to another ship and send the plans to the Rebellion? No. Although she has no idea whether the plans will reveal a weakness in the Death Star, she heads directly to the hidden Rebel base she has spent the entire movie protecting.

A strong leader must inspire others to fight for the cause. When it comes time to attack the Death Star, when every ship counts, Leia makes no attempt to convince Han to join the Rebellion. Luke does make an attempt, and Han's change of heart seems to arise out of Luke's comments and Han's affection for Luke. George Lucas chooses to emphasize the bond between the two males and leave Leia on the sidelines.

During the evacuation of Hoth, Leia again appears a weak leader. Han drags her toward her transport, and when their route is cut off by a cave-in, Han informs the transport that he will take Leia on the *Falcon*. She is not making the decisions or even influencing them. She is simply a problem to be handled.

Han continues to make the decisions for the rest of Episode V, with Leia functioning as extra baggage. She has served her story purposes: drawing Luke into the Rebellion, providing the plans that allowed for his heroic victory and falling in love with Han, thus assuring the continuation of the Skywalker line. The vibrant, shrewd, confident woman is no longer necessary, so the story turns her from leader into follower.

While Leia's power, leadership and intelligence fade, Leia's skills as a woman of action are presented inconsistently, jerking her character schizophrenically between action hero and passive victim. After Leia sends Artoo away with the Death Star plans, she hides while Vader kills her crew. Why hide? If her plan is to claim she is innocent of all wrongdoing, why not march up to Vader and try to save some of her Rebel friends? When she's spotted, she fires one shot at a group of stormtroopers and runs into the open, assuring that she'll be captured. These actions undermine Leia's coherence as a character, because the strengths we see in her elsewhere are MIA here. The story requires Leia to send the plans to Tatooine, then to be captured. But the writers could easily have found a way to fulfill the needs of the story while maintaining the integrity of the character. If only they had taken the time to do so.

Within minutes of the movie's opening, Leia is captured, transforming from Rebel fighter to damsel in distress. She spends the next hour as a victim waiting to be saved.

While Leia has some great moments during her escape from the Death Star, most of Episode V is spent building Han up as an action hero by tearing Leia down. When Luke is missing in the subzero temperatures of Hoth, Han goes out to search for him. Leia, who by her own account loves them both, stands around like a helpless wife whose husband has gone off to war. What woman of action, what person who feels loyalty and love would do nothing when she could look for a dying friend? Don't her feelings tell her that Luke is in trouble? If the writers had been concerned with developing Leia's ability with the Force, and the connection between Leia and Luke, this could have turned into an intriguing step in that story line. But instead the friendship between the males and the heroism of Han are stressed, and Leia's character is undermined.

While on Cloud City, Leia seems unable to act. All she can do is complain and worry. When Leia expresses her concern, Han treats her like a child. He kisses her on the forehead, pats her on the cheek and tells her to "relax," he'll handle it. This is not how a person treats his leader. This is not how a person treats his equal. This is how a person treats a misguided inferior. Han has been built up as a great and admirable hero through this episode. If this is what he thinks of Leia, then it is what we think of Leia. She has plummeted from shrewd leader/action hero to damsel in distress to pouting child.

In Episode VI, Leia achieves a perfect three-for-three record, getting captured and awaiting rescue by Luke in all three movies. After failing to free Han, Leia is relegated to the role of a minor foot soldier in Luke's elaborate plan, so Luke's heroism can take center stage. Defenders of Leia's character point to her strangling of Jabba as proof that she's a strong action hero. While she does, at last, take some effective action, how heroic is it to kill a defenseless slug? Luke agonizes over the morality of killing a defenseless Palpatine, and when he finally tries, he discovers the Emperor isn't defenseless at all. If George Lucas had cared as much for Leia's character, he would have given Jabba a gun or toxic slime so he could pose more of an immediate threat. Or had Leia feel some internal conflict over her action. Or made Leia more ruthless and vengeful in her love of Han, qualities that could have had dire and fascinating consequences. As is, Leia performs a brutal act, yet we are not supposed to think her brutal, and she shows no further sign of brutality. Ultimately, the act does not even help their cause, because the entire sail barge is blown up by Luke moments later.

Leia's heroics in Episode VI continue to be second-rate. When they make the assault on the shield generator, Leia is the first to retreat to the bunker door. She stands there with a drooping blaster as Han kills stormtroopers. When she finally does shoot a stormtrooper, the action is so overplayed it's humiliating—Han praises her for doing something he's done a thousand times. Ultimately, Leia is convincing neither as an action hero nor as a passive victim. The coherence of her character has been sacrificed to the story and the male characters.

Another factor undermining Leia's status as an action hero is George Lucas's tendency to put the "girl" on a pedestal. This is most obvious when it comes to pain. Enduring pain and paying a price for one's actions are a major part of being a hero. Yet Leia's suffering is minimized and kept largely offstage. Leia is tortured by Vader on the Death Star, which must be a harrowing experience. We are shown a needle and are told her resistance is "considerable," but we don't see her resistance. Heaven forbid we see a woman in pain! But "sparing" us from that removes the heroism from Leia's captivity and makes her simply an object to be rescued.

When Han, Leia and Chewie are tortured in Cloud City, we see both Han and Chewie suffering, but not Leia. Han's pain is further stressed when Leia, Chewie and the whole cast are marched into the carbon-freezing chamber on Cloud City, so they can witness the price Han pays as he is frozen. It elevates him to great hero status.

Even Leia's psychological pain is minimized. She seems momentarily upset at the destruction of Alderaan, but we never have a sense of the deep, abiding pain she ought to feel at the death of all her people. In contrast, when Luke loses his aunt and uncle, and when Luke loses Obi-Wan, his pain and grieving are given at least a few moments, and both losses have an enduring effect on his goals and feelings. Pain heightens the heroism of the males while undercutting the heroism of the female.

Perhaps the most striking, defining trait of Leia's character is her smart mouth. Yet Leia's insults, which in Episode IV seem smart, funny and assertive, later turn nagging and pessimistic. As most of us—except Threepio—know, nagging others and telling them that all is lost are not good ways to inspire and motivate. When the *Millennium Falcon* is struggling to escape the Imperial forces surrounding Hoth, Leia says, "This bucket of bolts is never going to get us past that blockade." This is not only unhelpful, it exemplifies poor leadership. If only one course of action is available, it is better to offer constructive suggestions than to snipe from the sidelines.

As the struggle to evade the Imperial forces continues, Leia shoots down Han's ideas while offering none of her own. In between her pessimistic pronouncements, Leia questions Han, clearly not understanding his intentions. The writers choose to jettison Leia's intelligence and instead portray her as confused and astonished, to emphasize Han's brilliance and derring-do. The number of questions she asks increases steadily, literally taking her from "smart mouth" to "stupid mouth." She can't keep up with Han's thought process. Further, Han doesn't see fit to answer her questions, treating her with the same respect he gives Threepio.

After the *Falcon* has hidden by attaching itself to an Imperial Star Destroyer, Leia asks Han, "What's your next move?" Even when Han asks her where they should go, she offers no ideas. She apparently has no knowledge of the systems neighboring Hoth, even though they would be critical to choosing the location of a Rebel base. Conveniently, Han's old buddy lives nearby, making Han look competent and heroic. When they arrive on Cloud City, Leia again expresses her displeasure. Han replies, "Well, what would you like?" Leia, of course, has no answer.

———

The most serious blow to the coherence of Leia's character comes with the revelation that she is Darth Vader's daughter. From the beginning of the trilogy, we have seen Leia's loyalty to the man she believes is her father, Bail Organa. She goes to Tatooine at her father's bidding, and she shares with her father a love of their home planet and their people, and a hatred of the Empire. Thus the news that Bail Organa is not her father and that Vader is should be a huge blow to her. Yet Leia reacts as if she's on Prozac, saying she's "always known." This is not convincing on any level. The feisty Leia would fight this claim whether she sensed it was true or not, just as she fought her attraction to Han. Being told that Vader—the archenemy who has pursued her through the trilogy, tortured her twice, killed countless Rebels, frozen her love, tormented and cut off the hand of her other love, and repressed countless planets—is her father ought to trigger the biggest outburst from Leia we've ever seen. It ought to be the climax of an internal conflict that's been building in her throughout. But the character hasn't been given the development and care she deserves. There has been no building internal conflict, except for her minor reluctance to admit her affection for Han, which has no real impact on the plot. If we look at the other major characters, we see that Luke's internal conflict between light and dark is strongly developed, and its resolution determines his success against Palpatine. The resolution of Han's internal conflict—help the Rebels or leave with the money—leads to the destruction of the first Death Star and carries the heavy consequence of his being frozen and delivered to Jabba. Leia is again given short shrift.

Leia's character was clearly not a priority in the original trilogy, where she was shunted aside, undermined and neglected. By the time the last Ewok sang his last "Yub yub," I had accepted this unhappy truth. As I stared at my Star Wars poster and waited the long years for another trilogy, I hoped that the promise Leia had initially shown might be realized in a new character, her mother.

Like Leia, Queen Amidala appears at first to be a heroic woman and a strong, compelling character. Amidala is a committed fighter in the struggle against powerful, evil forces, a strong leader and brilliant prodigy as skilled with politics and diplomacy as with a gun. At the beginning of Episode I, Amidala seems a heroic figure determined to protect her planet and the Republic. She defies the Viceroy of the Trade Federation, telling him that he must reach a settlement. In her makeup and with her mature "queen" voice, she seems an imposing force. While Palpatine says she'll be easy to control, he is later surprised by her determination and resourcefulness. She comes up with a plan to defeat the Trade Federation and capture the Viceroy, a plan that reveals her abilities as a leader, strategist and diplomat. She speaks convincingly to Boss Nass and secures the Gungans' help. But Amidala is not all talk. She is a brave, assertive woman of action. She takes on a key role in the execution of the plan, pulls hidden blasters from her throne and retakes the planet. What a woman! If only George Lucas had let her be that woman.

Amidala's status as a heroic figure committed to fight evil and protect Naboo is quickly undercut. She decides to plead with the Senate for help, but her efforts on Coruscant seem either halfhearted or incompetent or both. Amidala confides to Palpatine that she believes Chancellor Valorum is her biggest supporter. Yet when Valorum greets her warmly and says he has scheduled a special session for her, all she says, in her imperious "queen" voice, is that she's grateful for his concern. She ought to be working to gain every advantage from her alliance with this powerful man. Why not ask to meet privately to discuss her situation? Her people are being slaughtered, and she seems to be giving the cold shoulder to her greatest ally. Whether the "queen" at this point is actually Amidala or her decoy is irrelevant. If it is Amidala, she should say something more effective. If it is her stand-in, then Amidala is showing horrifically poor judgment in allowing her stand-in to function during an interaction with Valorum. Either way, she doesn't seem to care about achieving her goal. The writers could easily have shown her making a heroic effort, but they were not focused on showing her heroism or her struggles.

In Episode II, Amidala is committed to a new goal, the defeat of the Military Creation Act. This undercuts the character in several ways. First, it's difficult to understand why she would be opposed to an army, considering Naboo's lack of an army left it vulnerable to invasion and mass slaughter. If the Gungans had not conveniently maintained a secret, unused army, Amidala's people would have been wiped out. Hasn't she learned anything from that? Or if she is such a devout peacenik, then why has she learned to use a blaster? If she believes that the use of force is a failure and diplomacy is the only right path, why does she have blasters hidden in her throne?

Another problem with this subplot is that her commitment to the cause is only told, not shown, so we never really believe it. This is the case with many traits of both Leia and Amidala. The writers didn't take the time to incorporate into the story events that would have shown the character through action, because these characters were not a priority and most of their actions were believed unimportant to the larger plot. We never see Amidala's devotion to this cause. She only tells Jar Jar about it, at the same time that her actions show us she is abandoning the cause, leaving on the eve of a vote because Palpatine told her she should, for her safety. What we see is not commitment, but cowardice.

Further, once she gets safely to Naboo, she makes no attempt to supervise Jar Jar, lobby the other senators to vote her way or even monitor what happens with the vote. All she seems to care about is flirting with Anakin, making out and then saying no, as if the entirety of Star Wars were taking place in the backseat of a 1956 Chevy.

At the end of Episode II, Amidala is saved by an army whose formation she has crusaded against. Is she troubled that an army was created before the authorization for it existed? Does she rush to the Senate to argue that the army be disbanded and its origins investigated? Or does she acknowledge she was wrong and an army is necessary? No, she goes home and secretly marries Anakin. Her commitment to fighting the evil forces that threaten the Republic has vanished.

The final goal to which Amidala appears committed is staying alive long enough to name her babies. Her commitment to this goal is not undercut, yet the fact that she has it seems completely random and out of character. If these names resonated with her personality or revealed something important about her, this could be a very powerful moment and a triumph for Amidala. But the names mean nothing to us (except that they set up the other trilogy). We sit there, befuddled, wondering where Amidala came up with these names.

Does Amidala, initially a heroic figure committed to the fight against evil, die a hero's death? Is she ultimately a tragic hero, a patriot doomed to fail in the attempt to defeat forces far more powerful? No. She has no hero's death. She makes no great attempt to defeat Palpatine. She stands on the sidelines and cries as Palpatine destroys the Republic. Her death is an accident of health, imposed by the author. Once she fulfills the needs of the saga—falling in love with Anakin and having his children—the sooner she dies, the more convenient it is for a story that has no interest in her.

Amidala appears to be a powerful figure, a queen and a senator, yet her power, like Leia's, slips away. Both women rule planets that are defenseless, so they have no recourse when threatened. Amidala spends the first movie pleading for help. By the beginning of Episode II, she has lost her title of queen. Not long into the movie, in fear for her life, she hands her senatorial powers over to Jar Jar. Amidala's demotion from queen to senator reaches its logical conclusion at the beginning of Episode III. After "saving" Palpatine from General Grievous, Anakin escorts the Chancellor back to the seat of government, where they are met by a group of dignitaries. Amidala stands off to one side by a pillar, and no one seems to notice or acknowledge her. She has become completely irrelevant. Her only act as senator is to attend a meeting at which Palpatine declares himself Emperor. A once-imposing woman, Amidala is disempowered and marginalized until she becomes completely ineffectual.

While Amidala's commitment and power are undercut, her leadership, intelligence and political skill decline over the course of the trilogy. Our initial impression of Amidala as a strong leader quickly fades. A strong leader would not allow her planet to be so defenseless. If her people don't want to have an army or weapons, then she ought to establish a treaty with another planet to defend them. If her only recourse is to "plead" her case to the Senate and the fate of her people depends on that, then she should have arranged for her own escape from Naboo, which she did not. Within minutes of the opening of Episode I, she is captured, like Leia.

A strong leader must know the resources she commands and the options she has. Amidala appears to have no idea that the Gungans have an army and significant weaponry. If she had, she could have used them to repel the original invasion. Instead, she stakes everything on an appeal to the Senate. But when she arrives at Coruscant, she asks Palpatine her options. Apparently she has no clear course of action in mind and has no sense of the alternatives.

A strong leader must command the respect of others. While Amidala is respected by many, including the Viceroy, who considers her a major opponent, she is not respected by two key figures: Qui-Gon and Obi-Wan. Qui-Gon dictates their actions and tells Amidala she "must trust him." When Amidala receives a call from home begging her to surrender to avoid further slaughter, Obi-Wan orders her not to reply. He doesn't even wait to see if she will obey; he is sure she will. As in the Han/Leia relationship, the male characters are built up as strong, assured leaders by their disdain and disrespect for the female.

A strong leader must choose the best course of action and motivate others to follow. Amidala disguises herself so that she can accompany Qui-Gon on Tatooine, gain information and have some input into the situation. Yet she offers no plan and takes no significant action. Like a milder version of Leia, her only input is criticism, and her criticisms are dismissed. Anakin, a child, is the one to come up with the plan to get the money necessary to repair the ship. Anakin is the one to execute the plan by competing in the podrace. Amidala watches the hero anxiously from the sidelines and, when he wins, becomes a cheerleader.

Along with her skills as a leader and politician, Amidala's intelligence also deteriorates. The intelligence of the woman who knew enough to have a decoy is inconsistent with the intelligence of a woman who "sneaks" off of Coruscant wearing a flashy gold headdress and gown that clearly mark her identity. The assassins would have to be blind to miss that outfit! Never has a character been so undermined simply by wardrobe.

Amidala's intelligence and judgment receive another blow when she reveals she's pregnant. She asks Anakin, an unstable, homicidal egomaniac eight years her junior, "What are we gonna do?" If she wants a useful answer, she'd do better to ask Jar Jar.

While Amidala doesn't have Leia's smart mouth, she definitely gains the stupid mouth. When Anakin returns from the burning temple and claims the Jedi are trying to overthrow the Republic, what wisdom and direction does Amidala, a senator, have to offer? "Oh, Anakin, what are you going to do?" George Lucas's focus clearly is on Anakin and what he's going to do. But Amidala should have more on her mind.

Her follow-up? "Anakin, I'm afraid."

As Anakin, a mass murderer, tells her that he's going to end the war, she looks up at him trustingly, like a child, and nods. Then she cries.

Ultimately, her failure of judgment is complete. Obi-Wan tells her Anakin has turned to the dark side and killed children. Though she knows he killed children in his massacre of the Tusken Raiders, she denies it here. How many children does Anakin have to kill before Amidala will help to stop him? Apparently, he hasn't hit the magic number yet.

Amidala could easily have been shown growing and learning over the course of the trilogy, becoming a wiser, more effective leader and cannier politician, a greater adversary to Palpatine. Having a character who might actually be able to uncover Palpatine's plans would have dramatically increased suspense. Yet instead, Amidala becomes weaker and more stupid, so she can be pushed aside in favor of the males.

Like Leia, Amidala alternates haphazardly between action hero and passive victim. In the second half of Episode I, Amidala runs, fights and shoots to liberate her planet. While she is a second-rate action hero at best—she still needs to be saved by Anakin—at least she is taking action, and the attempt to liberate Naboo is successful.

Amidala's image as a decisive, clever woman of action, though, is undermined by the conflicting image of damsel in distress. This comes to the fore in Episode II, as Amidala's decoy is killed. Amidala becomes an object to be protected rather than a compelling character. The danger to her highlights the heroism and derring-do of Obi-Wan and Anakin as they chase down the assassin, rather than revealing her own heroism or, indeed, any aspects of Amidala's personality.

Near the end of Episode II, Amidala makes the jarring transformation from damsel back to action hero. In the arena, she suddenly becomes an expert lock pick. Not only does this make no sense with what we know of Amidala, it's plain old bad storytelling to establish that a character has a particular skill at a climactic moment where that skill is critical. This could easily have been established earlier, so her character would have some continuity.

Her decisions as an action hero also aren't consistent with her character. She claims to love Anakin, yet when they are being attacked in the arena, she frees herself and makes no attempt to help him. This is neither heroic nor loving.

While her performance in the arena is clearly meant to be heroic, her abilities are also clearly meant to be inferior to the men's. Amidala shoots a lot, but we don't see her hit much of anything. Anakin again has to save her by offering her a ride on his beast. Later, as they pursue Dooku, she falls out of the ship. This safely excludes her from the climactic battle, keeping her from true action-hero status. She shows up at Dooku's hangar too late to do anything but shoot ineffectively.

In Episode III, Amidala is back in passive mode. Except for the beginning and the end, she spends the entire movie in her penthouse apartment, changing clothes and gazing out the window. This Rapunzel, though, is more even-tempered than Leia. In fact, for much of the movie, she has that Prozac glow. As the war escalates and the Republic threatens to crumble, she brushes her hair, musing about how to decorate the baby's room. After Obi-Wan has told her his concerns about Anakin, Amidala relates them to Anakin without seeming concerned herself. Anakin confesses he's not the Jedi he should be and claims he's found a way to save her. When your husband claims he's found a way to save you from death in childbirth, wouldn't you ask him what he's talking about? Is he suggesting abortion? Has he learned about a hot new obstetrician on *Oprah*? Has he, by chance, turned to the dark side? Amidala asks none of these things.

Her passivity reaches a character-crushing extreme as the Jedi temple burns. She knows Anakin, her one true love, is there. She knows the temple is on fire. Yet she just stands there—in a new dress—and cries. Can you imagine Han Solo standing there when Leia could be burning? Amidala should be rushing to Anakin's rescue. Or at least calling the fire department. How can this possibly be the same woman who picked locks, rode monsters and shot droids? It can't be. This is not a coherent character; it's a paper doll with too many outfits.

The biggest blow to the coherence of Amidala's character comes in her relationship with Anakin. Though Amidala professes her hidden love for Anakin near the end of Episode II, it's hard to believe she actually loves him or finds anything appealing in the pouting, self-centered Anakin. He argues for a dictatorship, something she would not find funny or charming; he reveals himself to have a stalker-level obsession with her, saying he has thought of her every day since they met and she "torments" him; he proclaims his goal to become all-powerful and end death; and he confesses to the mass murder of Tusken Raiders. At this point, any woman with Amidala's knowledge and commitment to good would be dialing 911 or checking the Yellow Pages for the nearest psychiatric hospital. Anakin is clearly a nutball, and a dangerous one at that. But after his slaughter of innocents, she strokes his head and forgives his action. Apparently mass murder is only a misdemeanor in her universe, and a bit of a turn-on. For shortly after, she agrees to marry him.

Amidala's integrity as a character could easily have been preserved, simply by having Anakin keep his killing spree to himself. For the woman who excuses mass murder is none of the things Amidala is supposed to be. She is not fighting evil forces but excusing them. She is not taking decisive action but sitting idly by. She's not preserving the Republic but enabling its destruction.

The tragedy is that it did not have to be this way. Amidala and Leia could have been coherent, compelling, powerful characters. Their integrity need not have been compromised to meet the needs of the story; in fact, the story would have been more exciting and suspenseful with their full participation. Their competence need not have been undermined to glorify the males; heroes can each have their own strengths, admirable in their own ways. If as much attention had been spent on the women's personalities as was spent on their clothes, makeup and hair, their actions might have been tied together in fascinating character arcs. Amidala might have been the naïve peace-lover who learned the hard way that a world without defenses is a world open to slaughter, might have crusaded for an army of the Republic and triumphed only to find herself duped, might have investigated the suspicious army to uncover its preprogrammed secret orders, might have warned the Jedi only to find she was too late, might have shot herself so Anakin could not turn her children to darkness, might have died a tragic hero's death. Leia might have been the lost leader of an obliterated planet who found a new identity among the Rebels as their head of intelligence, might have been painfully conditioned as a child to repress her Force abilities, might have sensed something breaking free inside her during her torture on the Death Star, might have fought these new instincts and sensations, which carried with them an awakened anger toward Bail, might have electrocuted herself on Cloud City to avoid a second round of torture by Vader, might have recruited Lando's aide into her intelligence network, might have discovered through him the new Death Star, might have faced her own crisis with anger when Luke told her the truth. The characters carry many exciting, unrealized possibilities, unfortunately, because the focus of George Lucas and the other writers was not on the female characters, who were undervalued, underdeveloped and undercut.

The greater tragedy is that these weaknesses are not limited to Star Wars. They surround us. They are more prominent and painful in Star Wars because these movies excel in so many other ways, and because George Lucas's fairy tale means so much to us. As I look at the poster on my wall, at the figure of the heroic woman crouched below the man, I dream about what might have been, "a long time ago, in a galaxy far, far away..."

Jeanne Cavelos began her professional life as an astrophysicist, working in the Astronaut Training Division at NASA's Johnson Space Center. After earning her MFA in creative writing, she moved into a career in publishing, becoming a senior editor at Bantam Doubleday Dell, where she created and launched the Abyss imprint of psychological horror, for which she won the World Fantasy Award, and ran the science fiction/fantasy publishing program. Jeanne left New York to pursue her own writing career. Her books include the best-selling The Passing of the Techno-Mages trilogy (set in the Babylon 5 universe), the highly praised science books *The Science of Star Wars* and *The Science of The X-Files* and the anthology *The Many Faces of Van Helsing*. Her work has twice been nominated for the Bram Stoker Award. Jeanne is currently at work on a thriller about genetic manipulation, titled *Fatal Spiral*. Since she loves working with developing writers, Jeanne created and serves as director of Odyssey, an annual six-week summer workshop for writers of science fiction, fantasy and horror held at Saint Anselm College in Manchester, New Hampshire. Guest lecturers have included George R. R. Martin, Harlan Ellison, Terry Brooks, Jane Yolen and Dan Simmons. More information about Jeanne is on her Web site, www.jeannecavelos.com.

DROID JUDGE: Mr. Stover?

MATTHEW WOODRING STOVER: I'm on it, Your Honor. Ms. Cavelos, con-
gratulations on an eloquent argument. Now. You are aware, are you
not, that Princess Leia is—your argument notwithstanding—both
popularly and critically regarded as the prototype of the female SF
cinematic action hero, the direct ancestor of Ripley from the Alien
films, and Sarah Connor from the Terminator movies, to name only
two. A number of subsequent filmmakers found Princess Leia an
inspiration for their female heroes; I'm wondering where, in cinematic SF, you think Mr. Lucas should have looked for inspiration
for his own. For example, how does Princess Leia stack up—forgive
the pun—next to Dale Arden, for example? Or Captain Kirk's mini-
skirted secretary—er, that is, *communications officer* (yeah, right)—
Lieutenant Uhura? How many people do you think can even name
the character (without looking it up, or having seen the film in the
past month or so—no fair cheating, now) that Patricia Neal played
in *The Day the Earth Stood Still*? How about the girl in *Forbidden
Planet*? The title character's name in *Attack of the 50 Ft. Woman*? The
doctor's girlfriend in *Invasion of the Body Snatchers*? The innumerable adoring secretaries, lab assistants, wives, helpless love interests
and assorted victims who are the only women to even have names
at all in 98% of previous cinematic SF?

JEANNE CAVELOS: It's interesting that, except for Uhura, every example you give is from the 1950s or earlier. You're not really playing
fair. Obviously the images of women in film changed a lot between the fifties and the seventies. *Barbarella*, nine years before
Star Wars, reflected the independent, sexually liberated woman
of the 1960s, while in the 1970s, *Carrie* revealed the dangers of
oppressing female power. Before *Star Wars*, TV shows like *Won-*

der Woman, The Bionic Woman, Electra Woman and Dyna Girl, and *Isis* featured strong women heroes who weren't sidekicks, wives or secretaries. The times were changing, and women in SF/F were changing with them. Leia was not created in a vacuum.

While I agree that Leia has inspired both viewers and filmmakers, to call her the "ancestor" of Ripley is not accurate. While I'm not an expert on the origins of *Alien*, I know that the original script treated all characters as "unisex," not establishing whether they were male or female. The writers generally imagined them all as males. So to say that the writers were inspired by Leia is not true. They weren't thinking about creating a gutsy female character at all. The decision to make Ripley female came late in the process, when the head of 20th Century Fox suggested the switch to create a stronger emotional effect. *Alien* is basically a horror movie, and women often serve as main characters in horror movies—for many reasons, including the fact that women may seem more vulnerable and may evoke stronger emotions in the viewer. I believe both Ripley and Sarah Connor arose out of this horror movie tradition, and embody a mix of the endangered/terrified horror heroine (like Laurie Strode in *Halloween*) with the tough/resourceful SF hero.

Those caveats aside, I agree that Leia marked a major breakthrough for women heroes in film. George Lucas's creation was amazing and groundbreaking. Before 1977, few women in film fired a gun—the symbol of male power—and those few who did generally fired once, missed, dropped the gun and started sobbing. Superheroes like Wonder Woman and Isis didn't use guns; they operated in a rarefied, "separate but equal" universe where a woman could triumph without using such crude weapons. Leia, on the other hand, played by the same rules as the boys and used the same weapons (though she never got a lightsaber—talk about symbols of male power . . .). Even more striking, she stood up to the men. While Colonel Wilma Deering—a precursor to Leia in the 1930s serials George Lucas so loved—outranked Captain Buck Rogers, she didn't insult and belittle him. There was a sort of tacit admission that he was superior, being a male hero, despite his inferior rank. Yet in the original *Star Wars*, Leia clearly believes she knows best and isn't afraid to let everyone know it. And the kicker is—in that first movie—she's almost always right. The damsel-in-distress stereotype is given a quick, no-frills burial when Leia says, "This is some rescue," grabs a gun and takes over the escape. As a seventeen-year-old girl, I was thrilled to see a female hero talking tough, shooting a gun and actually hitting something. George Lucas blazed a trail with Leia that many writers have followed, and all viewers who like seeing independent, self-reliant female characters owe him a debt of gratitude.

It's in large part because he was initially so successful at creating this compelling image of a strong female hero that my disappointment is so great. If she had never been strong, then she would have simply been one of the crowd. But she showed something more, something amazing. Unfortunately, it was short-lived. George Lucas weakened Leia as the series continued, taking away her power, her good judgment, her skills and her gun, and turning her into just another one of the weak women we've seen countless times in SF. While movies like *Alien* and *The Terminator* were making the next quantum leap for the female hero (and then another quantum leap after that with their sequels), Star Wars was moving backward, reinforcing old stereotypes that it had at first eschewed. While we now have characters like Trinity in *The Matrix* and the Bride in *Kill Bill*, Star Wars has moved even further backward, with Amidala the woman dying of a broken heart, a cliché that was old sixty years ago.

MATTHEW WOODRING STOVER: In nitpicking Leia's decision making style, I wonder if you might stop to consider that her intuition is backed by the Skywalker touch with the Force—which has been specifically shown, in her father's case, to involve prophecy. Thus, her actions on Cloud City are perfectly reasonable—nothing else she would have done could change the outcome, and telling Han it's a bad decision is nothing more nor less than the truth, yes? In fact, her power explains nearly every cavil you've made. For example: given that her intuition is backed by the Force, it's a reasonable interpretation to say that in making contact with the Ewoks, she realizes instinctively that they will be the key to the Rebel victory, and that attempting to establish friendly relations with them—by befriending Wicket—is, strategically, the best move she has available at the time, isn't it?

JEANNE CAVELOS: Whether Anakin has powers of prophecy is arguable. Many Star Wars viewers believe Palpatine planted Anakin's dreams of Amidala's death to manipulate him. But to focus on the subject of Leia's decision making, you have my condolences. In the attempt to make her seem wise and helpful, you've contorted yourself into more knots than a Twister champion. If Leia has a "bad feeling" about Cloud City, then she should investigate, not change her clothes and braid her hair. The Force doesn't offer up neat pronouncements like "Nothing you can do will prevent the bad thing that's about to happen, so you might as well give yourself a makeover." Anakin certainly does not accept the idea that his dream will come true no matter what he does; he tries to change it. Leia's character, as established in most of Episode IV, is not the kind to sit back and give up, no matter how bad her intuition might tell her things are.

If the Force provides her with some prophetic hotline to the future, then one thing it absolutely should tell her is that Alderaan will be destroyed. Yet I don't see her shrugging her shoulders and telling Tarkin to fire away. She does everything in her power to stop the destruction of her home.

Thus at Cloud City, she should do the same. If she has a feeling they are going to end up guests of honor at Darth Vader's Torture Party, then she should do everything in her power to get them away from Cloud City. How about booking passage on another ship? She could sell Han's services to the lonely female miners to raise money. Any intuition would only increase her motivation to act. (And while we're on the subject, if Leia has strong intuition, why does she kiss her brother? And why doesn't she sense Vader is her father?)

On the Ewok moon, a strong intuition would again provide more motivation for Leia to act. If she has a sense that the Ewoks are key to the Rebel victory, then she should be much more proactive in gathering intelligence on their abilities and gaining their help. Standing around saying you're lost and eating a granola bar aren't really effective ways of cementing an alliance on a short schedule. Similarly, she fails to work toward an alliance once she gets to the Ewok village, instead giving herself another makeover.

C-3PO does more to gain their help—and that's about the biggest insult I can give to any character, so I'll stop there.

As a friend, I think you really need to break off your unhealthy codependent relationship with George Lucas. His achievements—including the creation of Princess Leia's character in the original film—are amazing, inspiring, groundbreaking. But he's not perfect. The Star Wars films went on to undermine her, neglect her and sap her strength, and the sooner you stop making excuses for that, the sooner you can get out of that uncomfortable-looking pretzel position. I know a good chiropractor.

MATTHEW WOODRING STOVER: Hey, thanks. Can he do anything for this cold chill I get whenever Opposing Counsel looks this way? Or how my mind goes blank whenever he twitches his fingers like that?

DROID JUDGE: Mr. Stover, the Court suspects that the blankness of your mind has nothing to do with Force-based powers.

MATTHEW WOODRING STOVER Probably true, Your Honor. Well, thanks anyway, Ms. Cavelos, and on behalf of Lucas Enterprises and the entire Star Wars franchise, I would like to take this moment to apologize to you personally for not putting some brutal torture of Princess Leia on-screen. It was a mistake. I'm sure we'd all feel better about her character if we could have watched her screaming in agony.

DAVID BRIN: Objection! That's not a question—he's just abusing the witness.

DROID JUDGE: Sustained.

MATTHEW WOODRING STOVER: Don't want to see her in pain, huh?

DAVID BRIN: (*tiredly*) Objection....

MATTHEW WOODRING STOVER: Withdrawn. No further questions.

DROID JUDGE: Mr. Stover, you have not addressed the portrayal of the other female character, Padmé Amidala.

MATTHEW WOODRING STOVER: Your Honor, I most certainly have. I spent nearly a hundred pages addressing exactly that in my novelization of *Revenge of the Sith*, and members of the jury still troubled by this issue can find my arguments in better bookstores everywhere (another shameless self-promoting plug). Next witness!

Fighting Princesses
and Other Distressing Damsels

WITNESS FOR THE DEFENSE:
Bill Spangler

THINGS WERE NOT GOING well for the good guys.

Luke Skywalker, Han Solo and Chewbacca the Wookiee had just infiltrated the detention level of the first Death Star. They had located the missing Princess Leia, but the only way out of the cell block was through a squadron of Imperial stormtroopers.

"This is some rescue," Leia says. "When you came in here, didn't you have a plan for getting out?"

"He's the brains, sweetheart," Han snaps, referring to Luke.

The princess's response is almost as quick. She grabs Luke's blaster and fires at a panel on the opposite side of the corridor. "What the hell are you doing?" Han demands.

"Someone has to save our skins!" Leia crosses the corridor, while laying down covering fire. "Into the garbage chute, flyboy!" she orders.

Star Wars, Episode IV: A New Hope changed the face of movies in many ways. One change that is sometimes overlooked is the role of women in action-adventure films. The Star Wars films gave us women who didn't wait passively to be rescued, women who could match the male characters in independence and resourcefulness.

The above scene captured this new attitude for a lot of people. And that approach received a warm welcome. Like many first-generation Star Wars fans, I made regular trips to the theater in 1977 to explore that galaxy far, far away. On those trips, I often heard cheering and applause when Leia took charge on the detention level.

Although there have been some definite missteps along the way, strong female characters like Princess Leia have appeared in the SW prequel trilogy and in the licensed fiction of the Expanded Universe. In addition, she has made an impact on pop fiction as a whole. Ripley, Sarah Connor, Buffy Summers and Xena can all trace their ancestry back to Leia Organa. Leia even paved the way for another character that Lucas had a hand in creating: Marion Ravenwood, the hard-drinking, tough-talking female lead of *Raiders of the Lost Ark*.

Now, almost thirty years after *A New Hope*, seeing a strong woman in an action-adventure film doesn't produce the same surprise that it used to. So, I think a good way to explain what George Lucas, Carrie Fisher and the other SW creators accomplished would be to compare Leia against other women in pop culture in the 1970s.

Hollywood was willing to cast women as stars in serious dramas during that time. In 1974, Ellen Burstyn starred in *Alice Doesn't Live Here Anymore*. In 1977, the year *A New Hope* was released, Vanessa Redgrave starred in *Julia*, while Anne Bancroft and Shirley MacLaine shared the lead in *The Turning Point*.

Action-adventure films, however, were another matter entirely. The testosterone-laden *Dirty Harry* and *The French Connection* premiered in the early 1970s. They were followed by *The Exorcist*, which featured the young Linda Blair as a damsel in demonic distress.

As far as genre films were concerned, I think the character that came closest to Leia during that time was Zira, the chimpanzee scientist portrayed by Kim Hunter in the first three Planet of the Apes films. Zira didn't have any combat skills—chimpanzee pacifism was a significant plot point in the series—but she was intelligent, strong-willed and unwilling to be treated like a second-class citizen.

The situation on television was a little better. Both Wonder Woman and the Bionic Woman were fighting crime during the mid-70s. People who wanted to watch TV late Friday night—or who had that technological innovation, the VCR—could watch Joanna Lumley invoke the spirit of Diana Rigg on *The New Avengers*.

At the same time, this was the era of *Charlie's Angels* and *Police*

Woman. For those unfamiliar with the latter show, here's how *The Complete Directory to Prime Time Network and Cable TV Shows* describes *Police Woman*: "Sexy Sgt. Pepper Anderson (Angie Dickinson) was an undercover agent for the criminal conspiracy department of the Los Angeles Police Department...she was called on to portray everything from a prostitute to a gangster's girlfriend."

There's a reason why the phrase "jiggle TV" originated in the seventies.

"THE BOYS JUST KIND OF TAG ALONG"

George Lucas has said more than once that the Flash Gordon movie serials were a significant influence in the creation of Star Wars. However, he probably never wanted Leia Organa to be mistaken for Dale Arden, Flash's perpetual girlfriend.

In "The Characters of Star Wars," a mini-documentary on the original trilogy DVD set, Lucas says, "It was always about these twins, and their father....At some point I took the female lead and made her the hero and then, eventually, I shifted it around to the male character."

On the audio commentary for *A New Hope*, Lucas says he considers Episode IV to be Leia's story. "The boys just kind of tag along on her adventure."

Princess Leia is young, Lucas says, but "instead of being kind of an idealistic young farm boy from the nether lands of the galaxy [she's] very sophisticated, an urbanized ruler, a senator....She rules people and she's in charge."

Elsewhere in the audio commentary, he says Leia is "very, very strong even though she's very young....She's pretty much in control of things."

Carrie Fisher told another interviewer that Lucas "wanted me to be proud and frightening....I was not a damsel in distress. I was a distressing damsel."

This approach did cause some problems for Fisher, as a performer and as a writer. In her part of the audio commentary, Fisher says she wanted a chance to ad-lib some of her lines in *A New Hope*. However, she said, it wasn't easy to change Leia's dialogue. "When I would change it, I would make it funny, and really, she's not that funny."

Given that Fisher has gone on to write novels and screenplays rich in humor, it's really not a surprise to hear that her ad-libs were funny.

I think Leia maintains her strength and independence in *The Empire Strikes Back* and *Return of the Jedi*. In the former, she leads the evacuation of Hoth and spars verbally with Han Solo during the long trip to Cloud City. In the latter, Leia takes part in a clever reworking of the Orpheus myth. She enters the metaphorical underworld of Jabba the Hutt, in a daring attempt to rescue Han.

Of course *Jedi* also contains the sequence where Leia is enslaved by Jabba, and dressed in a skimpy outfit reminiscent of the women in metal bras who decorated the covers of science fiction magazines in the 1950s. Now this certainly detracted from her image as a liberated woman, but it should be remembered that, at that point, she wasn't liberated. She was a slave. Jabba had her dressed in those clothes; she didn't choose them for herself.

It's been suggested that Jabba wouldn't have chosen those clothes for Leia, since he probably wouldn't have found her physically attractive. It's not difficult, though, to come up with other reasons why Jabba might've made this choice. That outfit would've kept most women feeling vulnerable and off-guard. It's also an effective way for the gangster to display his new prize to the other members of his entourage.

In any case, if Leia ever felt vulnerable and off-guard, it didn't last for long. She was soon wrapping a chain around Jabba's neck and strangling him to death. It's an impressive feat, given the Hutt's size and the difficulty anybody would have finding his neck.

A more pressing question might be Leia's Jedi training. Specifically, the question is: "What training?" Leia exhibits her Jedi potential more than once during the original trilogy. The best-known time is probably when she receives Luke's telepathic cry for help in *Empire*. However, it has also been suggested that she drew on the Force to survive Darth Vader's torture in *New Hope*. In addition, the superhuman strength she displayed when strangling Jabba may have come from more than adrenaline and rage.

Leia never receives any real Jedi training, though, either in the movies or in many of the Expanded Universe novels set after *ROTJ*. In these stories, her primary power seems to be an empathic link with Luke and her children. Leia's profile in *The New Essential Guide* to *Characters* says that she was always interested in developing her powers, but "politics kept her much busier than either she or her brother would want." This has never been an entirely satisfactory answer to me, although it seems likely that training is going to require a significant commitment of time, even if you factor in Leia's natural abilities and the fact that the Jedi no longer seem to require a lifetime of training, as they did in the days before the Empire.

Author Troy Denning offers an interesting alternative to the "Leia is just too busy" explanation in his novel *Tatooine Ghost*. During the course of the story, she admits to herself that "many of the diplomatic gifts she attributed to intuition were really the glimmering of untrained Force potential." On the other hand, she thinks, "developing her potential would have meant facing the dark side of her heritage and...that thought frightened her as much as having children."

Not having Leia develop her Jedi abilities may have been a decision made by Lucasfilm. If it was, though, it's recently been reversed. Leia is fighting with a lightsaber in *The Unifying Force* by James Luceno, the concluding novel in the New Jedi Order cycle. In that same book, Luke describes his sister as "a knight in her own right, who had for her own reasons resisted taking up the path of the Jedi."

Leia's resistance finally melts in *The Joiner King* by Denning, the next novel in the Expanded Universe chronology. In this story, she decides that she wants to learn the ways of the Force under the tutelage of a nonhuman (but female) Jedi Master named Saba Sebatyne. "After all I've seen and done," Leia says, "...it always comes down to this. To one Jedi, to one blade, standing against the darkness....I'm beginning to understand the Jedi's place in the galaxy—and to see my place in the Jedi."

The following novel, *The Unseen Queen* (also by Denning), takes the believable approach that Leia doesn't immediately adjust to her new status as a Jedi apprentice. Denning notes: "After a lifetime of leadership in both politics and the military, Leia sometimes found it difficult to remember that in the Jedi Order she was just another Jedi Knight—and, as far as Saba was concerned, a fairly junior one at that."

Leia displays some remarkable talents in these books, though. In *The Joiner King*, she shifts a cloud bank to provide cover for the *Millennium Falcon* and in *The Unseen Queen*, she's able to enter a mind meld with other Jedi during a battle (both of which seem to be fairly advanced techniques). Leia's training has been a long time coming—the official chronology places *The Joiner King* a full thirty-five years after *A New Hope*—but it finally seems to be here.

Alderaan's last princess isn't the only strong woman who appears in the original trilogy. *Return of the Jedi* introduces Mon Mothma, one of the leaders of the Rebel Alliance, while in *A New Hope*, Beru Lars demonstrates a different sort of strength as she and her husband carve out a life for themselves on Tatooine.

LIKE DAUGHTER, LIKE MOTHER?

Leia may have inherited her Jedi potential from her father, but many of her talents and character traits apparently came from her mother, Padmé Amidala (played by Natalie Portman). Padmé has been received by the fans with considerably less enthusiasm than her daughter was. However, I think this reaction comes from changes in the real world as much as it comes from differences between the two women. Padmé may never be the icon that Leia is, but I think she may be a more complex, deeper character.

For better or for worse, Padmé is not a trailblazer. When Leia grabs Luke's blaster in the Death Star, it's an unexpected twist. When her mother displays her marksmanship in *The Phantom Menace*, she's establishing herself as part of a clearly defined tradition. Characters like Padmé simply aren't as rare as they were in 1977. And that's a good thing.

This fact may have influenced how George Lucas introduced Padmé. There's no scene in *The Phantom Menace* where she actively takes over a situation, as Leia does in *A New Hope*. She simply moves from negotiating an alliance with the Gungans to planning the liberation of the capital city, as if it were natural and expected. During the strategy session before the climactic battle, neither Qui-Gon Jinn nor Obi-Wan Kenobi question her right to give orders. They do what advisors are expected to do. They advise, leaving the decision making to Padmé. Again, this can be seen as a positive sign.

There is a scene in *Attack of the Clones*, though, that can be interpreted as Padmé actively taking control. When Anakin Skywalker expresses reluctance to go after Obi-Wan, after he may have been captured by the Geonosians, she responds, "He (Mace Windu) gave you strict orders to protect me. And I'm going after Obi-Wan. If you plan to protect me, you'll just have to come along."

Padmé takes the lead in the escape from the arena on Geonosis. She breaks out of her restraints first, then helps to free Obi-Wan and Anakin. Neither of the Jedi seem to have any problems with being rescued by a girl.

Despite her many strengths, Padmé does make mistakes during the prequel trilogy. And they are serious mistakes, with long-lasting consequences.

In *The Phantom Menace*, she moves for a vote of no confidence against Chancellor Valorum, which leads to Palpatine taking power. This decision, though, illustrates an important difference between Padmé and her daughter. Padmé is younger than Leia when we first meet her, and doesn't know as much about other worlds. (For example, she expresses surprise that slavery is permitted on Tatooine). Darth Sidious describes her as "young and naïve" in *Phantom*, and, at that point, the description is accurate.

However, she does understand the peril that her homeworld faces, and the fact that it will only get worse over time. "Our people are dying, Senator," she tells Palpatine. "We must do something quickly in order to stop the Federation." Later she says, "By the time you have control of the bureaucrats, there will be nothing left of our people, our way of life."

Padmé does not support Palpatine because she's going to personally profit from it. She does it because it's the first option she sees that has a chance of success. (Whatever its other problems might be—and I think they're numerous—I think there's a definite theme to *The Phantom Menace*. I think it's about people making bad decisions for good reasons.)

The other major mistake Padmé makes is getting involved with Anakin Skywalker. While watching the prequel films, it's easy to wonder just what she sees in him. For a while, at least, it looks like she just wants to act as his surrogate mother. When little Anakin says "I'll always care for you" in *Phantom*, she replies, "You miss your mother." She calls him a "funny little boy." And she insists on using the diminutive "Annie."

Anakin, though, sees the relationship very differently. She's an angel—his angel, to be exact. When Padmé finally admits to herself that she knows what Little Annie wants, she discovers that she wants it too. Even if the feeling will last for only the few minutes before their execution.

(Interestingly, both Padmé and Leia seem to be attracted to bad boys. Also, both mother and daughter express their love at times when that love appears to be a hopeless cause. It's interesting to consider what might have happened if Leia had known who her real mother was when she started to draw closer to Han Solo.)

Both of these mistakes came from a genuine desire to help on Padmé's part. I think that fallibility adds depth to her character.

Another woman who has a strong presence in the prequel trilogy—although she appears in relatively few scenes—is Anakin's mother, Shmi (Pernilla August). She's not a strong character in the sense that she's a leader, or has active control of her own life. However, she's strong enough to survive life as a slave and to let her son go when he appears to be heading for a better life. (Shmi does play a more active part in *Tatooine Ghost*, as she, Cliegg and Owen Lars execute an elaborate plan to free her from Watto, the junk dealer.)

ACROSS THE (EXPANDED) UNIVERSE

In addition to Padmé and Shmi, the prequel movies introduce several women Jedi, including ones who sit on the Jedi Council. Not a lot of time is spent on them in the movies, but I don't think they receive any less attention than the newly introduced male Jedi, with the obvious exception of Samuel Jackson as Mace Windu. Also, many of these characters are developed in the Expanded Universe stories.

For instance, a Jedi Master named Luminara Unduli and her Padawan, Barriss Offee, have appeared in novels, comic book stories and the *Clone Wars* animated series. In *The Approaching Storm* by Alan Dean Foster, Luminara, Barriss, Obi-Wan and Anakin are sent to the planet Ansion, in order to make sure that the world does not join the Separatist movement. (This is the mission to Ansion mentioned near the beginning of *Attack of the Clones*.)

In this novel, Luminara displays mastery in everything from fighting techniques to dance. At one point, the Jedi quartet takes shelter with a nomadic tribe that welcomes visitors—as long as they are entertaining. For her contribution, Luminara performs an intricate dance that includes very delicate manipulations with the Force. Barriss goes on a solo mission in the Medstar books by Steve Perry and Michael Reaves. During this assignment, she makes a discovery that could lead her directly to the dark side of the Force.

Yaddle, a member of the Jedi Council, is featured in *The Shadow Trap*, a middle-reader book by Jude Watson. A female from Yoda's homeworld, Yaddle can be seen in *The Phantom Menace*—if you don't blink. But she plays a major role in this story. Here's how Watson describes Yaddle in combat:

> She was all grace and flowing movement, her lightsaber a blur... Yaddle took out ten attack droids in what seemed like no time and then buried her lightsaber in the two grenade mortar controls. Within minutes, all of the droids were sizzling in the puddles of water.

And here's how Obi-Wan remembers her:

> She had taken a special delight in the young Jedi students. She had turned a blind eye to their pranks. She had hidden sweets in their pockets.... There were hard lessons to learn. Yaddle had been there in a different way. There had been so many times when he had knocked respectfully on her door with a problem he didn't want to bother Yoda with. Obi-Wan realized how exceptional it was that a member of the Jedi Council had made herself to be so available to every student.

One of the newest female Jedi is Olee Starstone, who is introduced in James Luceno's novel *Dark Lord: The Rise of Darth Vader*. Olee is a Padawan, and Luceno allows her to be young. Roan Shryne, a full Knight, teases her for talking too much. At the same time, though, Luceno gives her the strength and the skills to allow her to survive the chaotic days after Order 66. Even Shryne admits—to himself, anyway—that Olee "demonstrated remarkable courage and was as deft at handling a lightsaber as many full-fledged Jedi Knights. (Shryne) suspected that she had a stronger connection to the Force than he had had even during his most stalwart years as an eager learner."

As a rule, the women Jedi dress basically the same way as the men, although there have been exceptions. I don't want to suggest that George Lucas and his associates have been infallible when it comes to creating women characters. A Strong Woman Character can become a Hot Babe With A Gun if not in exactly the right hands. (Aurra Sing, a character spun off from *Phantom*, comes to mind.) But the treatment of women in the Star Wars universe is one of the things I like about the series and something that I hope can be acknowledged as the accomplishment it is.

Bill Spangler has written both fiction and nonfiction based on TV science fiction series. In addition to contributing to BenBella's *Farscape Forever!*, he has had articles in *Xposé* and *Wizard's Sci-Fi Invasion*, and has written original comic book stories based on *Alien Nation*, *Quantum Leap* and other shows. Bill and his wife Joyce live in Bucks County, Pennsylvania, with two ferrets and a dog.

THE COURTROOM

DROID JUDGE: Mr. Brin, your witness.

DAVID BRIN: I thank Bill Spangler for citing references to some of the Star Wars books. I expected other Defense witnesses to mention these, since I do know that many skilled authors have poured their hearts into the tie-in novels. In some of them, strenuous efforts have been made to compensate for plot flaws in the movies themselves. Certainly there are strong female characters in several.

Still, as long as we are on the topic of Princess Leia, exactly what are we to make of one of the biggest of the Big Five broken promises of the entire series?

In *The Empire Strikes Back*, Yoda and Obi-Wan look woefully at the departing Luke, both of them certain that his rebellious action will result in disaster. (It doesn't.)

"There goes our last hope," says the ghost of Obi-Wan.

"No," answers the oven mitt. "There is another."

That statement—so filled with dramatic portent—promised a big payoff. When we learned that the "other" was Leia, that was just fine! Our appetites were whetted for her to do something marvelous! Only then...

...Do *you* feel that there was a payoff worthy of this clue?

BILL SPANGLER: Leia definitely displays her Jedi powers in *Return of the Jedi*. Did you see the hairdo she was wearing at the Ewok camp?

DROID JUDGE: (*noisily clears throat*) Mr. Spangler....

BILL SPANGLER: Oh. You want a serious answer. Okay....I don't think that Leia could've suddenly manifested powers in *Return* equal to or greater than Luke's. That would've been a *deus ex machina*. And I don't think she could've confronted Vader directly. As Luke says in the film, the Rebels couldn't risk giving Vader the chance to kill the two remaining Jedi directly. (He doesn't say that bluntly, but I think I'm paraphrasing him accurately.) Leia does do things, however, that I think can be considered signs of her Jedi skills. Three immediately come to mind: her strangling Jabba; her receiving Luke's call for help in *The Empire Strikes Back* and her saying in *Return* that she has memories of her real mother.

Also, as I understand it, one of the subplots in *Dark Nest*—the newest SW trilogy from Del Rey—is Leia receiving some formal Jedi training. It's long overdue, but it hasn't been forgotten.

CHARGE 8

The Plot Holes and Logical Gaps
in Star Wars Make It Ill-Suited
for an Intelligent Viewer

Laziness Leads to Sloth, Sloth to Incompetence, Incompetence to Stupidity, and Stupidity to the Dark Side of the Force

WITNESS FOR THE PROSECUTION:
Nick Mamatas

T HE ARE TWO MAIN PROBLEMS with the Star Wars films, which in turn lead to a more general problem with movies. The two problems specific to the films are as follows:

1. Each episode subsequent to Episode IV renders the previous films increasingly nonsensical.
2. Episodes I through III make episodes IV through VI entirely incoherent.

Since the six films and the endless ancillary products have made billions of dollars, this has led to the third, more general problem:

3. Science fiction and fantasy films are unbearably stupid. Indeed, going to see a science fiction or fantasy movie these days is not dissimilar to attending an extended performance art piece which involves several gorgeous people, all in wonderful if somewhat tasteless costume, wheeling a wheelbarrow full of raw, rancid bacon onto a stage. Handed pitchforks by sequined-spangled assistants, the costumed beauties grab hold tighlty of

the handles, stick the spears of the forks into the wheelbar-row, and then *fling* the rancid bacon at the audience, all while screaming, "Eat it! Eat it, you stupid pigs! You morons love it!" The audience leaps to action, scrambling along the aisles and trying to grab up and shove as much of the foul bacon into their fat mouths as they can, stopping only to look up at the performers, point to their stuffed cheeks and mumble through tangles and blobs of rancid meat, "Yuth yuth ah fuff ith!" The stars sneer and howl, "That's right, you jowly bastards, gobble it up, and crap yourselves in glee!" When the meat runs out, the show is over.

Note that I am not talking about the obvious problems with the films—the seagoing physics in an interstellar environment; the act-ing generally so wooden that IMAX viewers can see the termites run-ning out the actors' ears; an economy that contains faster-than-light travel, strong AI *and* chattel slaves but, apparently, no news media—or even how the lightsaber amputations pile up so awkwardly that they go from high drama to creepy fetish to the implied goal of the saber martial art and then back into creepy fetish again. I don't even mean dialogue like "I've been waiting for this moment a loooong tiiiiime, my leeeeetle greeeeeen frrriiiiiend." I'm just talking plot.

Standing alone, Episode IV is a fairly mediocre movie. Young guy makes friends, makes good and doesn't quite get the girl, but that's okay, because there's a sequel in the offing. In Episode V, things get wonky. Why didn't Obi-Wan Kenobi tell Luke that Darth Vader was Luke's father? Clearly, Vader could have told Luke at any time—the guy's pretty much the Vice President of the Empire, isn't he?—so Obi-Wan has no reason to believe that Luke could be kept from the truth. If Vader wanted to blow Luke's mind, he could have had the words "Luke, I am your father, xoxo, DV" burnt into the side of some nearby mountains with the laser cannons of his Star Destroyer at any time. Or how about when Vader confronts Leia? No mention of pa-ternity, or the Force, which is supposed to be strong in her as well. Finally, why couldn't Obi-Wan tell Luke that Leia is his sister for that matter—again, there's no reason to hide any of this.

Of course, in Episode V, Vader declares that he wants to use Luke as a weapon against the Emperor. Given that, it almost makes sense that Vader would wait for some dramatic moment to tell Luke the truth—he had to keep his secret son/secret weapon quiet so that the Emperor would not find out. Except of course that Emperor Palpatine knows that Anakin impregnated Amidala, as we see in Episode III. Thus, a potentially intriguing plot point, one that would also explain why Kenobi never even bothered to alter Luke's surname or place him somewhere other than Anakin's home planet (and the same damn neighborhood!), can be flushed down the toilet.

But wait! we hear millions of fanboys cry, *Anakin thought he killed Amidala, so how would they know about Luke and Leia?* That's almost a good point, except that, between their having Sith powers and political pull on the one hand, and the fact that Luke Skywalker is staying with mutual relatives in the old 'hood and living under his true surname on the other, it should be trivially easy for Vader, or the Emperor for that matter, to find out about young Luke and kill him in his cradle. Or whenever they felt like it. Didn't Luke sense Vader's power and Han Solo's plight from across interstellar space after a few days of hanging out with Yoda and getting Force training in Episode V? How hard could it be?

The problem, simply, is that George Lucas and crew can't handle prequels. For example: In Episode IV, Luke destroys the Death Star by piloting a fighter into the heart of the giant construct. But back in Episode I, young Anakin Skywalker disables the Trade Federation Droid Control Ship in virtually the same way. Why then, wouldn't Vader or, you know, *somebody* fix the rather obvious design flaw in the Death Star? No reason at all; it's simply that Episode IV came first and the scene in Episode I serves no purpose but to evoke the climax of Episode IV.

Anakin, as a child, builds C-3PO and meets R2-D2. Obi-Wan meets both droids. At the end of Episode III, the droids have their memories wiped. But Obi-Wan doesn't (nor, presumably, could he). In Episode IV, he still fails to recognize the droids, and has no reason to simply be pretending not to recognize them. Again, all that happened is that IV came out first, then Episodes I through III premiered decades later.

For that matter, how come Owen doesn't remember C-3PO and

R2-D2 after meeting the droids in Episode II? If he did remember and didn't want to blow any cover he might have, why purchase C-3PO?

Leia, through Episodes IV–VI, is ignorant of her heritage. This, despite the fact that she is a public figure. Did nobody in the Empire ask the Organas from where they adopted this girl? Biochemical technology is such that in Episode I Qui-Gon can analyze a blood sample and send it over Magic Radio Waves to Obi-Wan on the Queen's ship, where Obi-Wan can check the blood for midichlorians. Leia is certainly awash in those sparkly little Force germs, germs that apparently can be e-mailed to people. That she's down with the Force should be the third or fourth most obvious thing in the universe. R2-D2's butt-rocket came in handy in Episodes II and III and could have also come in handy any number of times in Episodes IV through VI. If only someone had thought of the butt-rocket twenty years ago! Uh, I mean twenty years from now! No, wait....

Even acknowledging that a shift from Republic to Empire could have retarded technological progress, or even caused a reversion, why no mention of midichlorians, no glimpses of all the goofy robots and vehicles exclusive to Episodes I–III, no discussion of how the Empire came to be? They also went from tri-wings in Episode III to X-wings in Episode IV. That's the rough equivalent of waking up tomorrow and discovering that every four-tined fork in the United States has been replaced with a three-tined fork.

This was discussed above, but needs to be brought up again to examine from another angle. Why did Obi-Wan take Luke to Tatooine and send him to live with the Skywalkers? It makes no sense at all. As explained above, it couldn't have been part of a masterstroke to give Vader a weapon against the Emperor, which would have had the useful side effect of rehabilitating Vader and righting the error Obi-Wan made years ago. At the same time, Luke on Tatooine and the "Ben" Kenobi "disguise" makes no sense as a trap for Vader. Tatooine is *too* obvious a duck blind for Obi-Wan to snipe at Vader with Luke as a lure. Unfortunately for viewers interested in stories that make sense, there is no third alternative.

Admiral Motti, the scrub Force-choked to death in Episode IV just to show the audience what a baddy Vader is, taunts Vader with the lines "Don't try and frighten us with your sorcerer's ways, Lord Vader. Your sad devotion to that ancient religion has not helped you conjure up the stolen data tapes, or given you clairvoyance enough to find the Rebel's hidden fort—*guk blak duuuh*." Too bad Motti looks a bit older than an adolescent in that scene. Clearly, the fellow had to be alive during the time of Episodes I–III, when the galaxy was lousy with Jedi (and their childlings!) doing magic tricks at every Senate session. It's hard to be an atheist when the Force was a near-ubiquitous part of life in the Republic.

A Short Sampling of Additional Plot Holes in the Star Wars Universe, Provided by Fans during Online Discussions, Since 1997...

Submitted to the Court by David Brin

From *Episode I: The Phantom Menace*

- Palpatine is concerned about being hunted down by the Jedi, right? Yet he has the Trade Federation persecute Naboo, drawing attention to his home planet! Anyway, why does he send Darth Maul to kill Amidala, when Qui-Gon's bringing her to the Senate to do exactly what he wants her to do? (Wouldn't he send a yacht to fetch her, keeping Maul secret a while longer?)
- If the Queen is so influential that she can give one speech and topple the Chancellor of the galaxy, why was she unable to get help from these political allies earlier? Not even a news crew, to broadcast atrocities on Naboo? No big planets who are sick of the Trade Federation, hankering to pounce on its mistake? Everybody's a wimp except for two Jedi and some funky amphibian rastafarians? Boy, that sure was a peaceful Republic!
- What's to keep the shamed, defeated Trade Federation guys from later screaming "It was Palpatine! He made us doo eet!" The fact that the Sith Lord's eyes were in shadow? They really know nothing about a guy they've sworn fealty to and staked everything on? Some savvy traders!

From *Episode II: Attack of the Clones*

- Is there anyone in this universe who could explain the politics of the Republic, what the Separatists are about, or why everybody acts like they have an IQ of maybe four?
- Is anyone else amazed that the Jedi are sent into a death trap at the very moment that Yoda happens to collect a new clone army?

From *Episode III: Revenge of the Sith*

- How did Obi-Wan get Anakin's lightsaber to give to Luke in A *New Hope*? You can plainly see, when they were fighting on the volcano, both lightsabers were blue. But when Obi-Wan gives Luke "your father's old light saber"— it's green! (This may seem a nitpick, but it's one that shows how little they care about "Campbellian" myth-telling. Dig it. Like in The Lord of the Rings, the ancestral sword is an important "talisman" carrying anointed power between hero generations!) In Revenge of the Sith, I expected a tear-jerking scene when the dying Anakin tells his former master, "Please ... give this ... to my son...." But instead? The green sword turns out to be just another of Obi-Wan's many lies.

From *Episode IV: A New Hope*—a biggie

- Okay, Vader questions Leia by hand, with truth drugs, yet never detects her Force and that she's his daughter. Or maybe he pretends not to? Nor to recognize his droids? It all seems so suspicious ... almost as if something's going on that we're never told. Like his role in letting the droids with the plans escape the Senate ship, then helping the kids escape the Death Star, then the contrived theater of his "fight" with Obi-Wan, then doing everything possible to help Luke get his shot at the Death Star's reactor.... All of these could have been foreshadowers to something clever. But instead, they were left as simply glaring holes.

These examples are just the tip of the veritable iceberg. I'm sure there are a zillion fan sites out there with many more examples of failures of continuity, storytelling logic and narrative drive. Despite the endless novels and action figures and cartoons and comic books and role-playing games and kiddie books and all the other ancillary stuff, the Star Wars movies are ultimately fairly easy to avoid if you put your mind to it. However, while the movies themselves can be avoided, they cannot be ignored, because Star Wars ruined American cinema.

The first real modern blockbuster was *Jaws*, but *Jaws* was a self-limiting blockbuster. There was a limited amount of ancillary licensing that could be done with a great white shark, as sharks are natural creatures and in the public domain. Spielberg doesn't make any money from the Discovery Channel's endless Shark Weeks, and no eight-year-old wants a Roy Scheider action figure. Star Wars, on the other hand, created endless intellectual properties, all ripe for the licensing, and it made its billions without a lick of narrative sense.

Prior to *Star Wars*, the 1970s were shaping up to be a golden age for American cinematic storytelling. Think of *The Godfather*, *Five Easy Pieces*, *Taxi Driver*, *Nashville*, *One Flew Over the Cukoo's Nest*, *Dog Day Afternoon*, *Don't Look Now* ... the list goes on. Even post-Episode IV, the 1970s squeezed out *Midnight Express*, *Tess* and *Kramer vs. Kramer*, but the good, character-and-narrative-driven movie was fading fast. By the time Episode V was rolled out, Hollywood had forgotten about storytelling. The age of the blockbuster was here, and more than twenty years later, discerning viewers are still suffering for it. The serious flicks are all but gone; they're indie movies destined for the art house circuit, or foreign fare. And sci-fi? Ugh, sci-fi....

There have been sci-fi movies since the Edison version of *Frankenstein*, of course, and most of them contained B-level actors, B-level story lines and B-level effects. George Lucas, who is little more than Roger Corman with a billion-dollar bank account and no passion for the cinema form, turned the B-movie into every studio's A-list. Since the new prized demographic was the teenager, there was hardly any need to spend any effort on scripts. Money? Sure. Effort? Forget about it.

So today, virtually any science fiction or fantasy film you see will make no sense. Occasionally they'll be funny, like *Ghostbusters*, and sometimes just so gonzo that they have to be appreciated on their own terms, like *Big Trouble in Little China*, but for the most part, the genre movie is nothing more than special effects pornography, with dialogue and characters there only to give the (formerly) optical effects and (currently) CGI a workout. Thus, nonsense like *Sky Captain and the World of Tomorrow*, a movie that couldn't be more insulting to the viewer's intelligence if "Insult the viewer's intelligence at every turn" had been some kind of corporate mission statement.

How about the Batman films, the Matrix movies, or *Spider-Man*? All of those films are essentially empty experiences, the rough equivalent of watching someone else play a video game. And even the energy and ideas that fuel video games can't be generated for long. *Batman Returns* was essentially plotless—quick, tell me what the point of any of the actions of Christopher Walken's character was—and *Batman Forever* and *Batman and Robin* were utterly unwatchable. *Batman Begins* was slightly more intelligent than the kiddie flicks of the 1990s, but made up for it by being simply boring.

The Matrix, like Star Wars before it, attempted to go middlebrow via an appeal to fortune-cookie mysticism, but *Reloaded* and *Revolutions* boiled all that gunk away to make room for more clichéd kung-fu fights, war-movie blocking and CGI explosions. The Spider-Man films, buoyed by Tobey Maguire's charm, are bearable, but already cookie-cutter. Nerd doubts himself, fights man in green, collects a smooch, goes home.

And these are the truly blockbuster sci-fi flicks. What about the second tier? The Blade franchise, *Van Helsing*, *The Brothers Grimm*, *Daredevil*, *Minority Report*—if any of these films were written up as a short story and submitted to your five-cent-a-word "professional" science fiction magazine, they'd get a form rejection letter, guaranteed, and regardless of their provenances as well-regarded Marvel Comics, Philip K. Dick stories or whatever. Good sci-fi films, like *Dark City* and *Donnie Darko* (or maybe I just have a "dark" fetish?) are essentially accidental creations. Mistakes.

The sad thing is that movies do not have to be this way. Yes, film is a visual medium, so films can be primarily visual experiences, but that doesn't mean that films *can't* make sense as a basic narrative. *2001: A Space Odyssey* is primarily a visual experience, but it doesn't use its visuals the way a drunk uses a lamppost, like the post-Star Wars movies do. Star Wars and many of the post-Star Wars blockbusters claim to be carrying on "the spirit of the pulps," but what they forget is that the pulps were often better than the hundred-million-dollar crap Hollywood hands us. The pulps gave us Asimov, Bester, Heinlein, Silverberg and Ellison. The pulps benefited from editors like John W. Campbell, Jr., who knew that his beanie-wearing readers wanted stories that delivered on the action *and* made sense.

Even today, any issue of *Asimov's Science Fiction* or the *Magazine of Fantasy and Science Fiction* has stories superior to any Hollywood blockbuster of the past twenty-nine years, and these dying digest magazines manage to score these stories for less than a dime a word. Compare that to the tens of thousands of dollars spent on scripts, and layers of script doctors, that lead to far inferior products. There is no reason that a primarily visual experience has to be full of gaffes, plot holes, nonsensical motivations and dialogue as crappy as these gems from Episode III:

"My powers have doubled since we last met."

"Your move."

"I think you're mistaken."

"There are too many of them; what should we do?"

"You're alive."

"Surprised?"

"From my point of view, the Jedi are evil."

"So this is how—*choke*—liberty dies. To thunderous applause." (And this out of the mouth of a woman who writes *queen* next to "Occupation" on her tax forms.)

And how could we forget Vader's first line, "Noooooo!" which instantly reminded me of an episode of *Futurama* in which Calculon, the soap opera-acting robot, has a similar line and then explains, "In the first take, the line was 'Yeeeeeeees!'" That is how indefensible Star Wars is: the parodic TV knockoff actually predated the actual filmic event by several years.

When I turned to my friend Jody at the end of Episode III and said to her, "So this is how—*choke*—storytelling dies," all she could do was shrug. There's nothing else out there anymore, except for bad blockbusters. 2005 was an absolute nadir for filmgoing, and yet, from that nadir may emerge—dare I say it?—a new hope. In 2005, America was given a choice: watch *The Island* or stay home, and we chose to stay home. As *Variety* noted in October, "[S]o far this year, grosses of $6.84 billion are 7% lower than at the same point in 2004. Given price increases, total admissions are down even more steeply."[1] It was *March of the Penguins*, a charming French documentary about birds walking across Antarctic ice, that was the year's big hit, while the blockbusters Hollywood rolled out for those of us with more spending money than sense suffered and died like a snotty Jedi childling.

Take the bacon out of your mouths, boys and girls, and let's show Hollywood that we're not going to be fooled by well-cut trailers and nostalgia for our eight-year-old selves anymore. When you see a movie you think might be okay, but that is probably going to suck as much as Star Wars, just stay home.

Repeat after me!

"Just stay home!"

"Just stay *home!*"

"Just stay home!"

Nick Mamatas is the author of the Lovecraftian Beat road novel *Move Under Ground* (Night Shade Books, 2004) and the Marxist Civil War ghost story *Northern Gothic* (Soft Skull Press, 2001), both of which were nominated for the Bram Stoker Award for dark fiction. He's published over 200 articles and essays in the *Village Voice*, the men's magazine *Razor*, *In These Times*, *Clamor*, *Poets & Writers*, *Silicon Alley Reporter*, *Artbytes*, the UK *Guardian*, five Disinformation Books anthologies, and many other venues, and over forty short stories and comic strips in magazines including *Razor*, *Strange Horizons*, *ChiZine*, *Polyphony* and others. *Under My Roof: A Novel of Neighborhood Nuclear Superiority* (Soft Skull Press) will be released in late 2006.

---

[1] Snyder, Gabriel. "NATO, MPAA pass B. O. ball." *Variety*, October 25, 2005. http://www.variety.com/article/VR1117931602?categoryid=18&cs=1.

THE COURTROOM

MATTHEW WOODRING STOVER: (*checking his notes*) Hmm ... "wheelbarrows of rancid bacon" ... "Eat it, you pigs" ... "gobble it up and crap yourselves in glee" ... "When the meat runs out, the show is over." ... Hmm. That's some, er, vivid imagery, Mr. Mamatas. Tell me, do you do a lot of drugs?

DAVID BRIN: Objection!

DROID JUDGE: Mr. Stover, you've been warned about abusing the witnesses.

MATTHEW WOODRING STOVER: Come on, Your Honor—this man has testified that he thinks *Midnight Express* is character-driven drama. And anybody who thought *Dark City* was a good SF film needs to watch it again while sober.

DROID JUDGE: (*severely*) The objection is sustained. Mr. Stover, confine your questions to the witness's testimony.

MATTHEW WOODRING STOVER: Oh, fine. Let's look at a few of your supposed plot holes, then. You claim that Anakin Skywalker piloting an entire starfighter into the main hangar flight deck—the (let me repeat this for the Court) main hangar flight deck—in the center of a Trade Federation droid carrier is "virtually the same" as Luke Skywalker dropping a single torpedo down one tiny unshielded thermal exhaust port on the surface of the Death Star. I'm sorry? Could you repeat that for the Court? Or would you like to simply admit that you weren't really paying attention?

NICK MAMATAS: Oh, of course they were virtually the same. You see Mr. Stover, the Star Wars movies are just that, movies. They are not a memoir of real events. The climactic scene in Episode I is clearly designed to be reminiscent of the climactic scene in Episode IV—despite that Episode I "happened first." They are essen-

353

tially the same. It is very unrealistic that two circumstances that are depicted as incredibly unusual would be so incredibly similar to one another.

And let's not forget the climax of Return of the Jedi, when Lando pilots the *Millennium Falcon* into the core of Death Star II and blows it up from the inside! Amazing, isn't it? Why even bother with fleets of ships and laser battles; clearly all tactical methodology in the Star Wars universe should be oriented toward getting one ship to fly into a entry port of some sort and and zap the enemy with one shot. You'd think someone would move the super-explodey stuff farther away from the entrances after three giant-ass explosions. Or maybe they'd station a Stormtrooper with a bazooka nearby. A Sith University freshman intern with a baseball bat. Something!

Geez, if this were the Narnia book you might be asking me, "How can you say that the fate of Aslan is similar to that of Christ? Aslan is a lion!"

MATTHEW WOODRING STOVER: As for "recognizing the droids," let me ask you this: If a friend of yours had owned, say, a Ford Escort (feel free to pick the anonymously popular vehicle of your choice) that you'd seen for a couple of weeks in, say, 1987, are you seriously telling me you'd instantly recognize the same car if you saw it again today in 2006—because a nineteen-year span is exactly what we're talking about—and wonder why your buddy's underwear wasn't still in the backseat? Bear in mind, here, that both C-3PO and R2-D2 are standard-model droids, of which billlions had been produced by their respective manufacturers and were in service throughout the Galaxy; even their designations are not individual, but rather model numbers, and they have no external modifications whatsoever. Not even paint jobs. Feel free to twist in the wind here; make up whatever justifications you might feel are appropriate.

NICK MAMATAS: If the Ford Escort talked to me and saved my life, sure I'd remember it.

FORD ESCORT: *Honk. Honk.*

ME: What's that, Fordie? Star Wars sucks! My God, you're the smartest car ever. I'll remember this moment for the rest of my life.

MATTHEW WOODRING STOVER: As any self-respecting EU[1] fan knows…

NICK MAMATAS: There are self-respecting EU fans?

MATTHEW WOODRING STOVER: …R2-D2's internal rockets are after-market modifications, not standard equipment on R2-series astromech droids. Are you saying it's clearly impossible that other, further aftermarket modifications could, under any conceivable circumstances, have necessitated the removal of these rockets? What evidence do you have for this?

NICK MAMATAS: No, I'm saying the movies stink. If you have to appeal to non-movie sources like the EU to explain and patch up the events of the movies, you prove my point. Welcome to the smart side of the Force!

MATTHEW WOODRING STOVER: What evidence do you have for the preposterous claim that the starfighters of Episode III are technologically superior to the starfighters of Episode IV? For example, Luke's X-wing has an internal hyperdrive (that takes him to Dagobah, and then to Cloud City, as you might recall), whereas Obi-Wan's and Anakin's require external hyperdrive rings. Is this counting wings thing just a biplane fetish?

NICK MAMATAS: You realize that you're arguing about a form of technology that uses wings in space, right? Wings. In. Space.

MATTHEW WOODRING STOVER: As for putting Luke with Owen and Beru Lars—are you familiar with "The Purloined Letter"? With the concept of hiding in plain sight? Are you saying that Edgar Allan Poe is not for readers "interested in stories that make sense"?

NICK MAMATAS: "The Purloined Letter" is also a fiction; Poe's artistry is that he made us believe it, and it is worth noting that Poe himself felt his ratiocinations were ultimately rather contrived. Are you saying that that short story is some incredible insight into human psychology, and that, say, the best place for Osama bin Laden to hide would be in a giant castle with a neon sign reading "Osama's Place"? At least the titular letter was on a desk with a bunch of other papers; it wasn't in a special envelope marked "Stolen letters—check me out."

I'm sure the petty criminals (in real life) who escape from the cops

---

[1] EU, of course, stands for Expanded Universe, which includes all of the Star Wars books as well as the movies.

only to run home and get caught three hours later cite Poe when they explain to the cops that they aren't really incredibly stupid.

MATTHEW WOODRING STOVER: And where is the evidence that Admiral Motti is an "atheist"? His comment is on Vader's failure, not on the nonexistence of the Force. Would you again like to admit that you weren't really paying attention?

NICK MAMATAS: I'll cite the witness Vader: "I find your lack of faith disturbing."

MATTHEW WOODRING STOVER: Is the entire Court getting as tired of this garbage as I am?

(Reaction in the courtroom)

DROID JUDGE: Mr. Stover—

MATTHEW WOODRING STOVER: What I mean to say, Your Honor, is that we can go back and forth all week with this childish "Is *not!*" "Is *too!*" crap. Let me put a stop to the whole business by calling my final witness, Don DeBrandt.

DROID JUDGE: If the Prosecution has no objection? Very well. Let Mr. DeBrandt take the stand.

Star Wars Versus Science

WITNESS FOR THE DEFENSE:

Don DeBrandt

YOUR HONOR, LADIES AND GENTLEBEINGS of the jury, my esteemed colleagues; thank you for your kind attention. We are here today to try a most complex case, one which on the surface appears simple, but most assuredly is not. The defendant stands accused of multiple plot holes, inconsistency and contradictions of internal logic; in his defense, I intend to take a somewhat controversial approach to the subject, one whose direction will not immediately be made clear. Please bear with me.

First of all, let us define our parameters. While I will cite evidence from the initial three films—hereby known as Episodes IV, V and VI—most of my arguments will focus on the most recent trilogy, hereby known as Episodes I, II and III. It is these three films which have borne the brunt of these accusations, and thus these three films which I will address.

Let us examine the evidence.

In Episode I—a.k.a. *The Phantom Menace*—an important element of the plot concerns a podrace, the outcome of which will determine whether or not the protagonists will be able to leave the planet. Our heroes are able to manipulate those with weak minds—but the mechanic who can fix their ship, unfortunately, is from a race immune to such "Jedi mind tricks."

Certain questions immediately spring to mind. Do they:

A)   seek another mechanic?
B)   find someone with a weaker mind and a working ship?
C)   find someone willing to accept Republic currency, to which they have access to a whole bunch of?

Sadly, the answer is D) none of the above. They gamble their fate on the racing skills of a small boy, whom they just met.

Who has never won a race.

And his Podracer—which he built himself.

Still, it all works out in the end, so they must have known what they were doing. The boy turns out to have a strong connection to the Force, and seems to be subject of an ancient prophecy. Obviously he's an extremely important figure, one who must be rescued and trained and kept from harm. Qui-Gon Jinn, the Jedi Master, clearly understands this.

Then why does he decide to take the boy along on a highly dangerous military mission?

Perhaps he means to use the boy as a secret weapon of some sort? No. He abandons him in a hangar halfway through, telling him to stay put and stay out of trouble—something the boy most impressively fails to do. Jedi Knights may be able to wield lightsabers, manipulate the Force and do impressive backflips, but they have a lot to learn about baby-sitting.

Perhaps this was merely a slip. Qui-Gon is portrayed as a rebel who doesn't always do as he's told, and those types rarely excel at domestic duties. Tell them to blow up a star cruiser, they'll do fine—ask them to change a baby and you'll probably wind up with an upset infant, an unspeakable mess on the ceiling and the charred remains of a diaper pail.

Certainly they would never make the same mistake twice. For instance, having witnessed the consequences of Jar Jar Binks getting involved in anything more complicated than preparing a light snack, they would never give him any serious responsibilities.

Like, say, an important government position. Why, that could lead to a disaster of unmitigated proportions....

Which, of course, it does. In fact, it more or less plunges the Galaxy into an immense civil war which destroys the fabric of democratic civilization as they know it.

Hey, everybody makes mistakes. Unmitigated stupidity on the part of an individual character is not on trial here; we're taking a larger view. Sentient beings are unpredictable and tricky—one can never say with any certainty what they will or will not do. For instance, Anakin Skywalker claims to be tormented by nightmares of his mother. He was taken away from her, the only parent he has ever known, at a tender age—such separation anxiety is understandable. Why, I'm sure he visited her as often as he could the entire time he was in training. . . .

What? He didn't? I guess the Jedi wouldn't let him travel off-planet—what's that? He was gallivanting all over the galaxy with Obi-Wan, on dozens of different missions? Surely he must have at least tried to contact her . . . no? Not even once? I guess communication between planets isn't that easy . . . oh, wait. They send instantaneous holograms to talk with each other all the time, don't they. . . .

I guess he just couldn't afford the long-distance charges.

Anyway, Anakin turns out to be a pretty nasty guy, so not phoning home for a decade isn't that implausible. This is Kid Vader we're talking about, not E.T.

And like I said before, sentient beings are unpredictable. Why, sometimes even the question of sentience itself is murky; look at how droids are treated in the Star Wars universe. On one hand, they're simply objects, to be used as cannon fodder in battle scenes without any messy blood—or, for that matter, consequences—to worry about; you can even have them dismembered or mind-wiped for comic effect. It doesn't matter, because they're not *people*.

Well, except that they have personalities, of course. They bicker, they worry, they make jokes. They strive, they take risks, they even simulate heroism. I suppose a clever machine can fool almost anyone . . . but not a Jedi, of course. Obi-Wan states quite clearly in Episode III that droids can't think for themselves. Which means that treating them like they can actually make decisions is obviously absurd; anything that might appear to be a personality quirk—bravery, fussiness, fear—is either faulty programming or a trick of our perceptions. If we're searching for truly sentient beings, these droids aren't the ones we're looking for.

That's enough consideration of such unquantifiable areas as intelligence and motivation. Before we become mired down in concepts like "good" and "evil," let's examine something a great deal more solid: weapons.

I don't mean the neon swizzle-stick hedge trimmers the Jedi like to play around with; I'm talking about hardcore, continent-busting, spacefleet *munitions* here. I'm talking about armor, I'm talking about ships, I'm talking about lots and lots of *guns*.

We all know where the clone army came from. But where in the name of Jabba's left armpit did all their *stuff* come from? I mean, did the Republic just happen to have a huge honkin' space navy in *mothballs* somewhere?

What?

I apologize, Your Honor. Yes, I was getting carried away. It won't happen again.

Let's move on to an even more specific use—or rather, misuse—of weaponry. General Grievous, the leader of the droid army, unveils a rather unsettling surprise when confronted by Obi-Wan Kenobi; not only does he know how to use a lightsaber, he has *four* of them—and four cybernetic arms to wield them with. Since these arms are mechanical, they can do things human arms can't; spinning like windmills, for instance.

This should enable the General to cut Obi-Wan to pieces. Obi-Wan only has one blade, and can thus only parry strikes from one side at any given time. Even if the General is using two blades for defense, he can still simply attack from both sides at the same time.

Which he never does.

Maybe this is just a Jedi mind trick. Grievous isn't actually a robot; he's some kind of little beastie in a cybernetic suit, so presumably that sort of thing would work on him. Of course, you couldn't pull that sort of stunt on another Jedi; not only are Jedi well-versed in the ways of the Force, they're also the ultimate lightsaber fighters. In the thick of a deadly serious hand-to-hand battle, they routinely pull the kind of midair acrobatics that would get an Olympic gymnast an eleven from a Russian judge, so there is *absolutely no way* one could be fooled into misunderstanding what is or isn't a viable combat strategy.

Like whether or not standing a few feet up an embankment from your opponent—an opponent that you, yourself, *personally trained* to jump at least twenty feet in the air while doing a somersault—is going to give you any sort of practical advantage in a lightsaber duel.

Obviously, it isn't. He's just going to bound into the air like a big, angry kangaroo, flip around at the zenith—possibly getting in a few swings while he's up there—then land on his feet and continue to attack. Right?

It was a rhetorical question, Your Honor. Yes, I know that under those self-same conditions Obi-Wan managed to lop off both Anakin's legs and one of his arms in a single strike. Your model isn't programmed for irony, is it? . . .

Up until now, all I've done is ask questions. I've made a few suggestions as to the answers, but nothing definitive—if anything, I've taken the position that the answers to certain questions aren't really important, or at least not as important as a good punch line. This is more than a cheesy ploy on my part; it is, in fact, my entire cheesy strategy.

I may have given some of you the impression that I believe Star Wars is full of gaping plot holes—holes, one might say, big enough to drive a starship through. While this is technically correct, it is not the thrust of my argument.

My argument is that *it doesn't matter*.

Ah, the collective gasp. Thank you; an attorney can go his entire career without ever hearing that magnificent sound. I can die happy now . . . hmmm? No, Your Honor, that is not my immediate intention. Yes, I'll get back to my point.

I don't mean to imply that the flawed structure of Star Wars is irrelevant because the films themselves are of no importance. Far from it—far, far away, and long ago from it. Because I do think these films are important. They are woven into the fabric of our pop culture; they're part of our modern mythos. Many children grew up watching these films, and the images and ideas that flow through them have made permanent impressions.

Not on their intellect. On their *imaginations*.

And now I would like to call on Dr. Albert Einstein.

Thank you for coming, Dr. Einstein. The Court appreciates your cooperation, both in appearing in a pop-culture essay and in conveniently ignoring the fact of your own death. You've chosen to do this, I understand, for one simple reason. Would you please state that reason for the Court?

For those of you on the jury who found it hard to hear Dr. Einstein, I'll repeat what he just said: "Imagination is more important than intelligence."

I'd like to point out that Dr. Einstein is something of an expert witness on the subject of intelligence, being one of the acknowledged great minds of twentieth-century Earth. No, he never did crack that whole unified field theory thing we all take for granted, but there is no doubt he was—sorry, Dr. Einstein, *is*—a genius. One who believes that the ability to make things up is more important than the cognitive powers of the weightiest intellect.

Because when we are children, the world is magic.

Anything is possible, because we haven't learned what is *impossible* yet. Our ignorance is our bliss. We believe in Santa Claus and fairy princesses and disgruntled Wookiees, and we don't ask for detailed technical explanations. What we want is heroes and monsters and robots, aliens and spaceships and battles against impossible odds. We want to be thrilled; we want to be amazed. We don't want to see the universe as it is; we want to see it as it *should* be. We want energy cannons in outer space that make cool sounds; we want wise old men to train us in the ways of the Force. We want the good guys to win.

And it's good that children want these things—not for any simplistic moralistic reason, but because all these things stimulate the imagination. Facts stimulate the intellect, and that's a good thing too, but—as Dr. Einstein knows—creativity is a far more rare and precious jewel than intelligence.

Thank you Dr. Einstein. You may step down.

For my next testimony, I would like to call the renowned artist—also from twentieth-century Earth—Pablo Picasso.

Mr. Picasso, can you please give me your opinion on computers?

Thank you. For those of you who don't speak Spanish, he said, "Computers are useless. They can only give you answers." I'd like to point out that Mr. Picasso was widely—sorry, Pablo, *is* widely—considered to be one of the most influential painters of his era. Even though he worked in an entirely different arena, the label "genius" is just as applicable to him as to Dr. Einstein.

Answers are an important and necessary thing. I don't think anyone here—well, possibly that Vogon in the corner—would argue with that. But an answer, any answer, is an ending. Asking a question is a beginning. One is the culmination of a process; the other is the process itself. Which is more important? The destination, or the journey?

One might as well ask whether a parsec is a unit of space or time. The answer, of course, is space . . . but when Han Solo famously claims to have made the Kessel Spice Run in "less than twelve parsecs," the children in the audience didn't care that he got it wrong. They were all too busy wishing *they* had done it, too.

And sometimes, when children grow up, they take their dreams with them. *Star Trek*, which predates the original *Star Wars* by a decade or so, is often cited by professionals in the scientific field as the inspiration for their later work. One of the inventors of the cell phone claims he was simply trying to make a communicator—perhaps a member of this generation will wind up creating a lightsaber or a landspeeder.

And if they do, it won't be because as children, they were fascinated by the well-documented, scientifically accurate processes they saw at the movies or on TV. It'll be because something touched them, took them away to a place they loved so much they will spend the rest of their lives trying to find a way back.

Yes, Your Honor, I agree. There is something very sad about that—but there is something noble, too. Chasing the impossible is a heartbreaking task, but it is precisely those people that propel the human race forward. Engineers get behind people and push; dreamers run to the front and pull. And if the path they choose leads off the edge of a cliff, they're always the first ones to hit the bottom.

Thank you, Pablo. You may step down.

Imagination relies on inspiration. Inspiration is when a previously unseen connection between two or more facts suddenly becomes clear. That connection is not a linear process; it is not something that can be accomplished by rational thought or straightforward logic. It is intuitive, organic, unpredictable. It requires a great deal of input, an open mind to receive it, and the proper environment to let that information percolate and interact and grow.

Children's minds are open. The games of childhood are just such an environment. And films—and books, and comics, and video games, and TV shows—like Star Wars provide plenty of input.

Some people—yes, I'm looking at you, Counselor—would respond with the GIGO argument: garbage in, garbage out. Fill a kid's head with junk science, and junk science will be all he ever learns. This is absurd. Do we still believe in Santa Claus as adults? Do we still leave teeth under our pillows, hoping to make a quick buck? By the time we reach adulthood we are quite able to distinguish between reality and fantasy, because we have learned the rules.

Science is, by definition, a process of exclusion; it is the method by which we figure out what can't be done. As a useful tool for intelligent beings, it's terrific. As a philosophy, it's not so good.

Please, please, put down your weapons. All I'm saying is that no matter how vital or useful science is, it needs an emotional counterweight; it needs compassion, curiosity, inspiration. It needs imagination. It needs *balance*.

Perhaps this is the most contradictory yet profound message in the entire trilogy. Anakin Skywalker is the Chosen One, the one who will bring balance to the Force. At the time of his birth, there are many Jedi Knights and only two Sith Lords; thus, it would seem that bringing balance to the Force would consist of slaughtering a whole bunch of Jedi. This is exactly what happens.

Was this a good thing?

Yes.

Because, no matter how nice the Jedi seem, no matter how evil the Sith are, they both represent natural forces. The Jedi are selfless and the Sith selfish; the Jedi champion freedom, the Sith believe in control.

Neither system can be allowed too much power. A free, democratic society can be corrupted by manipulative individuals like the

Emperor; a tyrannical dictatorship with all of its power concentrated in an ultimate weapon or despotic ruler can be destroyed by a single skilled pilot or champion. Impose order and you destroy free will; give people unchecked freedom and the system will tear itself apart in bickering and civil war.

The Jedi do not represent science. They represent chaos...and chaos is necessary for freedom. Chaos is all those things we don't understand but are driven to try. Chaos is imagination; chaos is the new, the unknown, the mystery. Chaos is childhood. No, we don't want to live in world run by children—but we don't want to live in a world without them, either.

The Star Wars universe is like a Zen *koan*, an inherently contradictory saying that is not meant to make sense, but rather to stimulate thinking. In closing, I would like to leave you with my favorite *koan* from Episode III, spoken by the Jedi Knight Obi-Wan Kenobi during his climactic battle with his apprentice:

"Only the Sith think in absolutes."

Nothing further, Your Honor....

Don DeBrandt has been accused of authoring *The Quicksilver Screen*, *Steeldriver*, *Timberjak*, *V.I.* and the Angel novel *Shakedown*, as well as writing several books under the pseudonym Donn Cortez: *The Closer*, a thriller, *The Man Burns Tonight*, a mystery set at Burning Man, and the CSI:Miami novels *Cult Following*, *Riptide*, and the upcoming two-part *Harm For the Holidays*. He does not deny these charges.

DAVID BRIN: Lovely. What fun. And, of course, as you point out, *fun* is the *main* point of entertainments such as Star Wars.

And yet...

...and yet, Mr. DeBrandt, are you telling us that a story must *either* be fun *or* intelligent?

Let me put it to you that there are counterexamples. Books and tales and movies that *both* entertain *and* give a nod or two in the direction of craftsmanship, plotting, consistency and something for the adult in us to chew upon.

Wasn't *Raiders of the Lost Ark* just such a marvel? Combining rollicking lowbrow fun with remarkable internal consistency and some thrilling glimpses at a few really big ideas? Don't many of us feel that way about *The Empire Strikes Back*? George Lucas took part in those works. He saw that they were good and beloved. So, could it have hurt to incorporate a little consistency and brains and heart—and maybe a smidgen of maturity—into the other films, as well? What resources were lacking? Money? Time?

Certainly none of those things, which George Lucas had, and plenty. So I submit to you, Mr. DeBrandt, wasn't the missing ingredient something called *respect*?

DON DEBRANDT: My esteemed colleague misconstrues my point. A story can be fun, or intelligent, or both. Certainly, those stories that manage to incorporate both are of a much higher quality than a story that ignores one in favor of the other.

While there is a single, defining element lacking in the Star Wars movies, it isn't respect. It's a composite of those things you've already mentioned: consistency, brains, heart and maturity.

It's sense.

In order to fully enjoy the spectacle of Star Wars, you must suspend your disbelief. Every mistake, every contradiction, every single piece of information that just doesn't compute interferes with that process. But the universe Lucas has created is so fascinating, so fun, we want to believe; and so, rather than simply ignoring that which doesn't make sense, we put our imaginations and minds in gear, and try to fix it.

In your own words, Mr. Brin: "I care because I passionately believe that important stories ought to make sense." As well you should—and when a story does not, you apply that passion to finding a way to make it make sense. It is precisely that process that is responsible for this very book, and whatever pearls of wisdom are contained within.

When a rational and inquisitive mind is confronted by the engaging yet irrational it often responds in this manner. This process is not usually appreciated by those undergoing it; the most common reaction is a deep irritation.

But isn't that always how pearls are formed?

DROID JUDGE: Mr. Brin, do you have any further witness testimony?

DAVID BRIN: No, Your Honor. Though I want to thank Mr. DeBrandt for a cogent and courteous argument. It's the kind that makes all of this wrangling fun.

DROID JUDGE: Mr. Stover?

MATTHEW WOODRING STOVER: No, Your Honor.

DROID JUDGE: Then you may each give your closing statements. Please address your comments to the jury. Mr. Brin, you first.

CLOSING STATEMENTS

CLOSING STATEMENT FOR THE PROSECUTION

David Brin

WELL NOW, WASN'T THAT FUN? If only most "trials" could be as extravagant, harmlessly entertaining and so worth the price of admission!

Of course, a bit of humility is called for. Especially since all of this wrangling amounts to very little more than poking at the edges of a truly substantial mythos. Indeed, as a social phenomenon, Star Wars has grown huge—the six-hundred-pound gorilla of movie sci-fi.[1] And yet, isn't that enough reason to take a closer look? Should we leave to "experts"—like movie critics and academic literary mavens—the task of examining such an important piece of popular culture? Shouldn't *anything* that gets big and powerful—from presidents to epics—merit skeptical examination from the people, as well?

Or is that just my way of pleading that I shouldn't be kneecapped for taking up this quixotic bit of windmill-tilting! After all, there must be an expression for fools who go out of their way to challenge kings, emperors or eccentric billionaires. In other times, such people were used for kindling! Nowadays? Well, if you never see another movie made from one of my books, draw your own conclusions.[2] Just kidding!

Okay, let's get serious. It's time to sum up, and then hand this

---

[1] Speaking of big gorillas, run out and get *King Kong Is Back* (David Brin, editor, BenBella Books, 2005).

[2] Frivolity aside, my real punishment is all the *time* that went into this critical appraisal of a successful series that can easily afford to shrug off a few ankle-bites by the likes of me. Heck, the angriest letters I've received have been from my own fans! (*Come on, Brin, drop this silliness and write your own stuff!*)

matter over to the jury. An *informal* jury of public opinion that will gather at a Web debate site organized by Benbella Books, to argue, deliberate and finally cast their judgment on the indictments discussed here.

Would I have done anything differently, now that this brash and rambunctious book is drawing to a close?

Well... I do wonder if we should have tried harder to recruit someone to *praise* old Yoda, perhaps from among his fiercest partisans, during a decade of online controversy since that first *Salon* article came out. I wonder about this because the Defense team, chosen by BenBella and Mr. Stover, seemed reluctant to stand up for a grumpy green goblin-guru who is the central preachifying figure in the Star Wars universe—who sermonizes for the better part of an hour (in total) about life and how it ought to be lived. Their chosen tactic—casting Yoda overboard, into the category of big-time movie villain—may not sit well with some hardcore Star Wars fans out there...

...and those fans are welcome to step forward during the coming jury deliberations! By all means, get your own arguments organized. Then put your hands out, like Frank Oz, and give Yoda some backbone! Make the elusive emerald elf-illusionist come alive! Choose between Brin and Stover you do *not* have to do! Justify how the lime-colored asbestos oven mitt's secrecy, lies, bullying, bad manners and relentlessly awful decision making all add up to *wisdom*...you can do! Well, try.[3]

If the approaching debate is anything like those earlier wild online discussions, there should be a lot of freewheeling excitement and some wondrously creative back-forth bluster. Oh boy, there's nothing more fun.

Just remember this, members of the jury. It's only about a bunch of silly sci-fi flicks. So let's *keep* it fun.

What would I like best? I figure at least a few of you out there will mull over the clues that have been gathered together, for the first

---

[3] Of course, Yoda says, "There is no try." I always wondered why more SW fans didn't balk at this statement, all by itself. In real life, effort and practice, failure and gradual improvement are the paths to skill and success. Yes, "there is no try" sounds very cryptic and guru-like. But isn't it also just plain...offensive?

time, in this volume. Hints that have always been right there in front of us. Not in the movies themselves, but in the *holes*, the glaring gaps that lie between those scenes that made it to the screen. The flagrant plot inconsistencies, many of which seem to *point* in the same weird direction, toward the same hidden plot twist. Is it possible to imagine just five minutes here, five minutes there, that would combine *just so*, in such a way as to bind together and make sense out of a mortally wounded story arc? Clues to a hidden *plot behind the plot*, turning chaos into sense?

Imagine *Episode III 1/2: The Darth Design....*

Only, now I'm getting a sharp look from the Droid Judge, telling me to settle down and stop dreaming. Because it'll never happen. We are stuck with what we've got. Something far different than we seemed to be promised, in the ebullient aftermath to *The Empire Strikes Back*.

A tale not of confidence, but *fatalism*, in which a majority of brave deeds accomplish less than nothing.

A mishmash, in which light shows and earsplitting sound matter far more than plot.

In which costumes and computer graphics count far more than character or dialogue.

Where science, history and credible philosophy *might* have been given at least a modest place at the table, but instead wound up insulted at every turn.

Where even the rigid story arc prescribed by Joseph Campbell would have been a huge improvement, if only it had been followed at all![4]

An epic where civilization is relentlessly portrayed as a hopelessly futile endeavor, subject to the whim of all-knowing elites who may use any means—from lies to mass murder—while citizens stare in dull confusion, their institutions impotent, their wishes ignored, their immense potential brushed aside. A potential that might have been shown for what it really is, something more powerful, by far, than any "Force."

---

[4] Tell me, who is the "hero" in *The Phantom Menace*? There is a mentor archetype, a precocious kid, a princess, mystic helpers, comic relief, a sidekick...but no hero! Oh, it *should* have been young Obi-Wan's "journey"—but he was left on the ship through the whole middle, with nothing to do!

To our surprise, the Defense did not put up much of a fight over any of this. Indeed, a few of their witnesses sounded even harsher toward the films than I have been! They tell us that the whole melodrama is about the *betrayal* of civilization, by *both* groups of Force-users. Light and dark. Jedi and Sith. Elites who must both be overcome, amid torrents of blood, in order for renewal to be achieved!

Wow.

Still, it makes me wonder. Did the Defense take this tack because—at last—it has become impossible to keep making excuses for Yoda after all? Or because they sincerely believe this new line of argument, that the Star Wars series is an epic tragedy about Darth Vader coming into his ordained role as a righteous Scourge of God, cleansing the universe of both evil Jedi and evil Sith... and the Old Republic must go, too... like baby with the bath water?

I can't help but shiver at such dedication and ruthlessness. At best, if we accept this, then we have all been watching something very, very, very dark. There's a lot more here than just waving your flashlight and making *zhvoom* sounds, or saying *Luuuuuuke* into a two-liter Coke bottle!

Oh, by the way, in answer to Don DeBrandt, let me assure you that I am perfectly capable of liking silly fluff! I am a big fan of both *Galaxy Quest* and *The Fifth Element,* and I never asked either film to make a scintilla of sense. If Star Wars had not been so ponderously lecturey, it might have been filed under the same category. But with more than an hour of preachy lectures and a relentless series of bummer scenes in which brave heroes die for nothing, I think we can admit that this epic *wants* to be held to a higher standard. And we have a right to do exactly that.

In order to keep my summation within bounds, let us put aside some of the charges for debate online. Those concerning Star Wars and *women*, for example, or whether the series has *harmed science fiction.* Witnesses who felt strongly about those issues have had their say, and I have little to add.

No, I want to stay focused on the subject that I think we all find most fascinating. The core Defense excuse for Star Wars—that it really is about common folk rising up, in the end, shrugging off mystical elites and taking charge! This Defense argument offers a couple of advantages, right from the start. For one thing, it lets them escape one of the most glaring plot holes of all, *the fact that none of the Force-people actually make any difference in the final battle between good and evil.*

After all, in *Return of the Jedi*, it is the Wookiee who captures an Imperial walker, brings it back to the power station, thus enabling the commando team to blow it up...allowing Billy Dee Williams to dive the *Millennium Falcon* into the Death Star II, blowing it up (yes, that old stunt), which ultimately empowers the Rebellion's final victory. Was George Lucas aware that no "Force" at all was involved in this final triumph? The simplest hypothesis, in a series story arc already full of holes, might suggest that it's yet another oversight, because no one was at the plot-tiller.

But maybe not. One Defense witness claims that the throne room confrontation scene—between Luke, Vader and the Emperor—was meant to *distract* Palpatine, so he could not intervene, thus allowing common folk to succeed....

While another Defense witness claims that the throne room fight isn't about galactic power at all! It is about Luke rising above the use of "Force," while sinner Dad helps out—and achieves redemption—by dealing with grouchy-retro Grampa....

While another witness makes the most interesting case of all. *That George Lucas knew exactly what he was doing all along. That it was intentional for the Force not to matter in the Rebels' final victory. Because the New Republic should stand on its own, made up of a trillion proud citizens who won this victory themselves, and plan never again to let themselves be dominated by mystic bullies!*

Isn't this what Matthew Woodring Stover—privy to secret briefings from the Very Source—tells us? That Star Wars isn't elitist at all, because every snooty Jedi and Sith proves impotent in the very end, and civilization emerges to be the "hero" in this journey, after all?

Whoosh. I admit it. I really am fascinated. It's the best excuse so far. I'm open. Convince me!

Though—as I have asked repeatedly—*if this is the core lesson, shouldn't even 1% of the millions of Star Wars fans have actually perceived and grasped it, by now?*

Moreover, I am forced to reiterate that this defense was never raised during any of the *past* arguments over Star Wars, when Yoda's wisdom used to be a matter of faith among Star Wars aficionados. It arose only after more than two decades and under duress.

Are we to believe this lesson will be absorbed and understood in the last five minutes of the entire series, while fireworks explode and a trio of Force-monsters beam at us out of Jedi Heaven... without a single character ever *mentioning* it in words? Saying, in even a single sentence, that *this time, we the people will do it all without gurus!*

Yes, I do believe that good Luke will start a new Jedi Order that's more akin to what good Qui-Gon envisioned. More egalitarian, like the karate studios that any kid can attend nowadays, adding a little skill and discipline to his or her eclectic lifestyle. (Heck, without Yoda, anything is possible.)

But still, must I point out that the *title* of the movie is *Return of the Jedi*? As if that event is the important thing. It is not *Return of the Republic*. Nor is it *Citizens Triumphant*.

The title—all by itself—seems to belie the Defense argument. In fact, it seems to say... *they're ba-a-a-ack*.[5]

Sorry. But I can't look at this the way my kids do—fantasizing I am a Jedi Knight with a nuclear light stick to wave around. Sure, as Matthew Woodring Stover will discover sometime, I'm an above-average saber-wielder. Despite that—or maybe because of it—I could never identify with all those prancing mystics. Rather, I can't help imagining that I am a *dad* on Coruscant, or Alderaan, watching my entire civilization collapse all around me, just because a bunch of arrogant demigods can't own up to their faults and behave like grown-ups.

I don't see the Old Republic as a symbol of foolish haplessness. It is, in fact, the only thing in the series that a decent person could deem worth dying for!

Across more than a dozen hours of screen time, the character I most identified with was a guy who got throttled to death in the *first minutes* of the very first film. Captain Antilles, a brave rebel com-

---

[5] Maybe I am too harsh on *Return of the Jedi*. Perhaps the whole first (second?) trilogy of Episodes IV–VI is in keeping with the spirit of *The Empire Strikes Back*. Still, can anybody doubt that the *other* trilogy, the more recent one, is just a long, unalloyed, fatalistic bummer? In which not a single good or brave deed goes unpunished?

mander who led a courageous, outnumbered crew on a desperate mission, fighting to save a civilization that was betrayed. A civilization that's too gallant to give up, even when its so-called "protectors" have all vanished or gone into hiding. Captain Antilles never gets to utter a sentence. But he stood in there for me. For every other dad. For each citizen who leaves the theater wondering—

Well, that sure was vivid! But is this "art" doing anything more than just diverting people with eye candy? Is it teaching us anything at all that might help us save our own Republic out here in the real world? Does it stoke our confidence? In our ability to know and understand? To negotiate, to solve problems, to stand up for each other, to hold tyrants accountable, and ultimately prevail?

I kept hoping for brief scenes showing Leia following the tradition of her *real* father—the one who raised her. Wearing glasses and poring over paperwork. Soothing allies and brokering agreements. Using her adult version of "force" in the mature way, knitting together an alliance of free peoples. Even a *glimpse* of this—between lavish explosions—would have spoken volumes. But alas.

All right. It's time to close this down and give the Defense their final say. (I await the inevitable insults, confident that sincere readers will know better. I like to poke, provoke, ask questions and stir debate. *CITOKATE!*[6] And never let anyone tell you that I say "obey!")

What I do ask of you jurors is *not* so much to convict Star Wars of any particular fault, but rather, to come away from all of this determined to *ask more from the next set of myths that you are offered.* To at least *notice* when yet another tediously clichéd "chosen one" or preordained demigod inevitably strides onto the silver screen...or your favorite video game. When feudal inheritance and vague mystical claptrap are put forward as reasonable substitutes for an open, confident and scientific society, built upon *both* individualism *and* accountable institutions that we get to criticize and control.

Believe me, there are those in this society—in *any* society—who want us to lose faith in that new way of doing things. They would have us return to simpler, more regal and "heroic" modes.

---

[6] Criticism Is The Only Known Antidote To Error.

Sure, it's much easier to write a violent adventure story with demigods and flaming swords. It was *always* easy to tell fables that way. The cheap, lazy way. It's why stories like that are so numerous. So predictable and banal. And I say this only 10% as a writer. The other 90% is pure consumer. I want to be taken on adventures that rock, *while* expressing something other than complete contempt.

Hey, it can be done. Directors like Spielberg and Zemeckis, like Meyer, Kershner, Cameron, Scott, Howard and the Coens...all have managed to evade these hoary clichés, from time to time. They blaze harder but richer paths. In part, they do it by telling stirring stories about characters who are *only a bit above average*, and thus far more courageous when they stand up against evil. More realistic and far *better* heroes than you'll find in ancient myths. Because they are people we could aspire to be.

Yes, I am asking a lot of you. But there's a payoff.

If you demand better myths, they *will* make them. Stories with rambunctious fun, like Tom and Huck... but also offering some of Huck's wit and fantastic sense of honor. Tales that beckon forth the little boy, without snubbing the brave little girl. Adventures that take us rollicking on pirate ships *without* making all heroism ultimately futile, all spear carriers foolish victims and all civilization useless.

Epics that don't yammer and preach at us for hours, and then say, "hey, lighten up, you're taking us too seriously!"

There are more than enough examples—I have cited plenty—of storytellers who can take you further.

It all starts by saying, enough.

We want more.

CLOSING STATEMENT FOR THE DEFENSE

The Spirit of Play

Matthew Woodring Stover

LADIES, GENTLEMEN AND OTHERWISE, and Artificial Beings of the jury—

I've been having a tough time throughout this trial. You've probably noticed.

I've been having a tough time keeping a straight face.

Probably because I haven't really been trying.

Before I explain *why* I haven't been trying—before I paste that cheerfully mocking grin back on my face—I want to 'fess up to something, in absolute honesty, without any mockery at all.

Sometimes, in the course of these proceedings, I've gotten the sneaking suspicion that the fundamental question actually under consideration is whether *the Star Wars films might have been better movies if David Brin had written them.*

Now, I know that sounds like a cheap dig. It isn't. Because David Brin is a *fantastic* writer; I've enjoyed his novels for years, and if we had come right out and debated that point, I not only would have lost, I may well have surrendered without firing a shot.

So let's imagine, for a moment, a world in which Learned Opposing Counsel and his Sith dupes—dammit, I was being serious—in which Mr. Brin and the Prosecution witnesses had their way. A world in which Luke Skywalker was not a Secret Prince, but just a farm boy with dreams of being a star pilot; in which starfighters were merely clouds of gnats wiped from existence by capital ships bombarding each other from distances so vast they're visible only to each other's instruments; in which spaceships spew reaction gases in absolute silence—

Ahh, you get the picture.

All the political ramifications resolved. All the science holes plugged. The plot smooth and seamless.

Where would we be?

It sure as hell wouldn't be here.

I mean, how many kids run around pretending to be Captain Nemo? Or, really, James T. Kirk? Even Indiana Jones—you don't see toy stores full of plastic whip and hat sets. Compared to the number of little Skywalkers out there...?

Do you think that if it had all been sewn up in the neat package the Prosecution demands, we would have had books about *secondary characters* making bestseller lists? Do you think we would have had the Clone Wars micro-series cartoons, or the superb Clone Wars graphic series from Dark Horse? Would we have had *Knights of the Old Republic* and *Republic Commando* and *Star Wars: Battlefront*?

We would have lost the late Brian Daley's marvelous Han Solo trilogy. We would have lost the X-wing novels—Rogue Squadron would have been only a passing mention in the films, and Wraith Squadron would have never flown. We would have lost the New Jedi Order, and the Dark Nest and Thrawn and Mara Jade and Anakin Solo and Talon Karrde and I don't have room for the whole list.

We would have lost the book you're reading right now.

My final witness, Mr. DeBrandt, was on the right track when he said that the plot holes don't matter. He just didn't go far enough.

The plot holes are *essential*.

Because inside every single hole in the entire Star Wars saga—in every flaw in the franchise—you can find a Cheshire grin floating above a flannel shirt, and a fading echo of...

"Ha-ha—made you look!"

When I was at Skywalker Ranch to meet with George Lucas, I brought up the sliding-around-the-turboshaft business in *Revenge of the Sith*. I said, "They're in *orbit*—gravity just doesn't *work* like that—"

The answer I got, verbatim, was: "That's the *point*."

Each of you on this jury—each of you reading this book—is here because you have one of two fundamental reactions to this.

One is to frown. "Quit it! Quit or I'm *telling*! And I won't be your *friend* anymore!"

The other is to grin right back. "Okay, you got me. What's next? Let's *go*!"

Because your reaction is a choice: You can take that *made you look* as an insult. Or you can take it in the spirit it is intended.

As an *invitation to play*.

George says: "Let's pretend!"

What do *you* say?

Me? I grin. I always have, ever since a hot summer afternoon in 1977, when I was fifteen years old and a kid knocked on my door and told me about this goofy movie he wanted to see.

You saw that grin on my face during my opening statement. You saw that grin every time I got up to question a witness for the Prosecution. Maybe you noticed I wasn't taking this too seriously. Maybe you noticed I was trying more for a smile than to play *gotcha*.

Because they are a real pack of frowners, aren't they? Every one of them, except Mamatas—I couldn't be sure, through the foam on his mouth—and Bethke, who doesn't count, because he was a Defense witness before he fell to the dark side. . . .

Quit it or I'm telling!

What I'm doing here is that nasty rhetorical trick you've all heard of: the *ad hominem* argument, which is to imply that the Other Side is wrong because of who they are, rather than addressing the issues they raise. But this is only half the *ad hominem*, because I'm not saying they're wrong.

What I promised, in my own opening statement, was that the witnesses for the Defense would offer alternate, equally valid interpretations, and that I would leave you, the jury, free to make up your own minds. That's done.

Now I want you to flip back through the testimony. On both sides.

Who's smiling? Who's relaxed, and playful, making jokes and generally having *fun*?

Who's gritting their teeth and citing statistics and oh-so-serious about How Awful Things Are?

Which side, in general, would you rather hang around with?

Which kind of person would you rather be?

I'm not passing any judgments. The world needs frowners. I'm even one of them, more often than not.

But right now, I've got Sith Lords on my tail and a starship to catch.

The late, great Fritz Leiber liked to say that the best way to teach someone something was to make him laugh so hard he didn't notice he was learning. Nietzsche wrote about the masks that truth must wear. The most insightful social psychologist of the classic world, Aristophanes, was also the funniest playwright.

So cast your vote. For either side. Grin with us, or frown with them.

Because who wins this trial really doesn't matter. It's a show trial, y'know—a Sith put-up job from the start. Go ahead and convict.

They'll never catch us.

Listen.

Hear that? Softly, softly, someone is knocking at your door—a long time ago, on a summer afternoon far, far away....

If you let your younger self pull back the curtain... if you let yourself squint out into that brilliant golden light....

It's me and George.

Come *on*—Han's got the *Falcon* in the park behind the basketball court, but there isn't much time—!

Here's your lightsaber....

Come out and play.

THE VERDICT

DROID JUDGE: Thank you, distinguished counselors. It is now time for you, the readers of this volume, to cast your votes based on the testimony you have heard. Your votes are on the following nine charges; for each of these you must cast a vote of innocent or guilty:

CHARGE #1: THE POLITICS OF STAR WARS ARE ANTI-DEMOCRATIC AND ELITIST
  Guilty or innocent?

CHARGE #2: WHILE CLAIMING MYTHIC SIGNIFICANCE, STAR WARS PORTRAYS NO ADMIRABLE RELIGIOUS OR ETHICAL BELIEFS
  Guilty or innocent?

CHARGE #3: STAR WARS NOVELS ARE POOR SUBSTITUTES FOR REAL SCIENCE FICTION AND ARE DRIVING REAL SF OFF THE SHELVES
  Guilty or innocent?

CHARGE #4: SCIENCE FICTION FILMMAKING HAS BEEN REDUCED BY STAR WARS TO POORLY WRITTEN SPECIAL EFFECTS EXTRAVAGANZAS
  Guilty or innocent?

CHARGE #5: STAR WARS HAS DUMBED DOWN THE PERCEPTION OF SCIENCE FICTION IN THE POPULAR IMAGINATION
  Guilty or innocent?

CHARGE #6: STAR WARS PRETENDS TO BE SCIENCE FICTION, BUT IS REALLY FANTASY
  Guilty or innocent?

CHARGE #7: WOMEN IN STAR WARS ARE PORTRAYED AS FUNDAMENTALLY WEAK
  Guilty or innocent?

CHARGE #8: THE PLOT HOLES AND LOGICAL GAPS IN STAR WARS MAKE IT ILL-SUITED FOR AN INTELLIGENT VIEWER

Guilty or innocent?

CHARGE #9: CONSIDERING ALL THE FACTORS ABOVE, OVERALL, STAR WARS HAS BEEN DAMAGING TO SCIENCE FICTION READERS, WRITERS AND MOVIEGOERS

Guilty or innocent?

You may register your votes at www.smartpopbooks.com/star-wars-verdict, where you may also add your witness testimony to the arguments you have read above.

May the Force be with you!

DAVID BRIN: I object!

DROID JUDGE: Withdrawn.

Visit www.smartpopbooks.com/star-wars-verdict to cast your vote.